Beach Management

Beach Management

Principles and Practice

Allan Williams
and Anton Micallef

with invited case study contributions

publishing for a sustainable future
London • Sterling, VA

First published by Earthscan in the UK and USA in 2009

All royalties from sales of this book will be donated to:
The Prostate Cancer Charity
First Floor, Cambridge House
100 Cambridge Grove
London W6 0LE

ISBN: 978-1-84407-435-8

Typeset by JS Typesetting Ltd, Porthcawl, Mid Glamorgan
Cover design by Yvonne Booth

For a full list of publications please contact:

Earthscan
Dunstan House
14a St Cross St
London, EC1N 8XA, UK
Tel: +44 (0)20 7841 1930
Fax: +44 (0)20 7242 1474
Email: earthinfo@earthscan.co.uk
Web: **www.earthscan.co.uk**

22883 Quicksilver Drive, Sterling, VA 20166-2012, USA

Earthscan publishes in association with the International Institute for Environment and
Development

A catalogue record for this book is available from the British Library

Library of Congress Cataloging-in-Publication Data

Williams, A. T. (Allan Thomas), 1937-
  Beach management : principles and practice / Allan Williams and Anton Micallef
with contributors.
      p. cm.
  Includes bibliographical references and index.
  ISBN 978-1-84407-435-8 (hardback)
  1. Coastal zone management. 2. Beaches--Management. I. Micallef, Anton. II. Title.
  HT391.W526 2009
  333.91'7--dc22

                                                2008052632

At Earthscan we strive to minimize our environmental impacts and carbon footprint
through reducing waste, recycling and offsetting our CO_2 emissions, including those
created through publication of this book. For more details of our environmental
policy, see www.earthscan.co.uk.

This book was printed in the UK by CPI Antony Rowe.
The paper used is FSC certified and the inks are
vegetable based.

to Jasper, Henry, Coco
and the late O. A. C. Williams –
true beach lovers

'the lonely beach divided by groynes in an isolation
imposed on the landscape.'

MERCER SIMPSON, 1926–2007

Contents

CASE STUDIES

List of Boxes, Figures and Tables

BOXES

FIGURES

TABLES

Foreword

B each management, a subset of coastal zone management, is the subject of this book, which is divided into two parts: introductory theories, strategies and policy, followed by case studies. The exemplars describe the work of practitioners who implement policy and apply strategies to the best advantage. Perhaps interesting in this regard is the fusing of *content* within *context*, a necessary adjunct to successful beach management. The content of this book eschews coastal engineering because it is adequately dealt with elsewhere in great detail. Focus is thus not especially on engineering but on soundly amalgamated biophysical science and social science, to achieve an advantageous perspective whereby beach management becomes integrated with coastal zone management.

Implicit in this book is consideration of sustainable management practices, as conditioned by anthropogenic parameters and societal demands that hazards and risks be included in beach management plans to protect beach users and infrastructure. Although the term 'infrastructure' is most commonly applied to public and private works on or landward of beaches, it is emphasized here that beaches themselves are infrastructure, and as such they require the same sort of protective consideration given to coastal homes and businesses, roads, electrical power transmission lines, ports and harbours, military installations, and so on. Preservation and conservation of beaches requires special consideration because of the unique geographic and ecological position that beaches occupy between land and water. Attractive as they are to humans for re-creation (created anew) and recuperation of the soul, beaches function as critical infrastructure for shore protection and habitat. Even though beaches function as protectors of dune systems, beaches themselves require tender loving care as these fragile ribbons of sand are vulnerable to a wide range of insults that result in their degradation or death.

This book is thus somewhat unusual, because it contains eclectic points of view that favour understanding of complex spatiotemporal interrelationships, including not only natural processes that are associated with evolution of the environment but also human impacts that affect the health of beach ecosystems. Interestingly, beach management is required because of human interventions that may be wanton or well intentioned. To put it bluntly, beaches the world over are being loved to death by increasing human use and burgeoning demands for competing uses, many of which are antithetical. As such, beaches are battlegrounds where wars are fought between environmentalists, special interest groups, governments, NGOs, private sectors, and even the military (for bases, securitization of buffer zones, landing sites).

With such diverse demands, it is impossible for beaches to fulfil the needs of all interested parties. Beaches, like many other threatened environments (such as coastal wetlands), require an adaptive management approach that can be adjusted to changing human and environmental needs. This book highlights present insight into beach care as seen by specialists who study diverse approaches to integration of scientific principles, standard engineering practices, socioeconomics, politics and legislation within the human dimension as conditioned by cultural mores. Sounds complicated? Well, it is. But, this book manages, under the expert guidance of Allan Williams and Anton Micallef, to merge often-competing points of view into management protocols that actually work, as evidenced by the case studies in the second half of the book.

An undertone carried throughout the book is that beach management is required for many different reasons, salient among which are examples of human disregard for this fragile and valuable natural resource that results in despoliation to the point where managers have to step in and attempt to take control. Management is thus required because, when left to their own devices, humans tend to destroy that which they love. Destruction often comes veiled in the form of 'land improvement' or 'environmental enhancement', where humans want to believe that they can 'manage' Nature to advantage, to meet or achieve some particular goal or use.

The concept is, of course, absurd, because Nature does not need to be managed. 'Management' is required because of poor choices of use, or no choice at all, where beaches exist in *laissez-faire* states until folks perceive that something has gone awry and the system is degraded. Intended uses thus become corrupted and are no longer tenable or morally acceptable. Managers are then called in to put things right with the thought that in due course all will be well. Beach management is thus many things to many people, and it is commendable that this book embraces a holistic point of view in an embattled arena.

An intriguing aspect of this book is its authentic intent, as is evident from its perusal. Human intentions are not easy to decipher, and in a time when governments deliberately deceive their citizens and corporations lie to shareholders and investors, it is important to recognize intentions that are good and authentic. A high level of consciousness runs through the pages of this book to provide a basic understanding of the human context of what beach management really is all about. This book is thus about integration of principles and practices of beach management, within a human perspective of what has gone wrong due to neglect or inattentiveness, and how the errors of omission or commission might be remedied. Mistakes of the past are not uselessly buried in the sand, but studied so that they become lessons learned. This is the value of the book as it elucidates a course for the future where beaches the world over can be used, conserved and protected so that they themselves function as Nature intended, to protect and buffer the shore from intense hydrometeorological events and at the same time provide natural or renourished habitat and recreational value.

To the credit of the authors, royalties resulting from sale of this book will be donated to cancer research. This is a laudable gesture by which a few can benefit the many who are in need of continued research for a cure.

Charles W. Finkl
West Palm Beach, Florida, USA

Preface

This book on beach management was written in order to provide a counterbalance to the many excellent books associated with beach management that emphasize coastal engineering and the variety of techniques associated with this particular field. To that extent we have introduced extremely little coastal engineering apart from some aspects related to beach nourishment. In recognition that considerable efforts in beach management are carried out in an ad hoc manner to correct problems as they occur, this book recognizes that effective beach management needs to be set upon a firmament of sound science, the base from which all management should commence.

The USA 1972 Coastal Zone Management Act probably initiated the concept of integrated coastal management (ICM) and in the intervening years since that landmark act many initiatives have taken place under the umbrella of ICM and its many synonyms, many of which are given in Chapter 1. The knowledge exists but practitioner's judgement is sometimes questionable, as implementation of sound ICM is still a grave cause of concern in many countries – as successful ICM needs a long time span to be truly effective. For effective beach management, extrapolation of pertinent ICM ideas have been absorbed in the various sections of this book.

This book is not about ICM, which is viewed as the umbrella organization under which beach management appears as an offshoot – albeit a very important offshoot. It is about a field of management pertaining purely and simply to beaches, which come in a variety of guises, both in any physical or anthropogenic classification and these are discussed in Chapter 1. The beach has become synonymous with recreation and this, together with the exploding growth in population levels, with more and more people wishing to live on the coast and with the growing impact of climate change (for example sea-level rise and seemingly increasing intensity and number of storms), has meant an escalating stress on the world's beaches. Additionally, beach managers are also experiencing increasing pressure from a variegated measure of beach issues that can lead to conflict, for example lifeguard cover, dog fouling and litter collection, to name just a few. These are dealt with in Chapter 2, which relates to the fundamental concepts associated with beach management, and also in several other chapters. These concepts deal with both theory and practice, for example shoreline management plans, together with legislative issues pertinent to a beach. Many theoretical aspects are based upon the ideas of Carl Sauer, who argued that the environment – in this case the beach, can be represented by integration of a physical fundament on which is superimposed the cultural one (i.e. the human dimension).

Policy, strategy, planning and bathing area management models are addressed in Chapter 3. An innovative model that considers a holistic approach to development of beach management plans is presented, laying down clearly defined steps that lead from national policy to a site-specific beach management plan. Key physical and anthropogenic parameters for successful beach management are presented in Chapter 4, as guidelines for beach managers. Recommendations are presented on, for example ecology, environmental impact statement, varying strategies for different beach types and carrying capacity.

Chapter 5 describes steps taken when using beach questionnaire surveys in order to assess beach users' priorities and preferences. Several examples are given of such surveys, and the pluses and minuses of various survey types (oral, written, postal and so on) are given and commented upon. It is the authors' opinion that all beach managers should be aware of what people on their particular beach think of it, and how, if applicable, it could be improved – bearing in mind that this is not always possible.

Hazards and risk management are important components of any aspect of beach work that concerns itself with people. Among many other parameters, hazards include the water itself (for example waves, currents, fish, jet skis), ultraviolet radiation and rock falls. Chapter 6 discusses these issues and a risk assessment matrix is presented together with a section on beach signage.

Examples of three types of tools that beach managers might utilize are given in Chapter 7. These are dimension analysis, which looks at five types of dimension associated with a beach and a worked example is given on the evaluation and recommendations associated with these dimensions. This is followed by function analysis that helps to place the main thrust of beach usage between the end spectrum points of recreation and conservation. The last section provides an example of utilizing a semi-quantitative environmental risk assessment technique to assess the consequence and consequence magnitude of a revetment construction along a beach.

Chapter 8 relates to a synopsis of a number of differing beach rating and award schemes from various countries that have emerged in answer to the tourism industry's thirst for such schemes. The pros and cons of each are discussed and a summary statement concludes the chapter by identifying disparate approaches that lack consistency regarding classification criteria, for example in definition of beach types, range of focus and cognizance of beach users' preferences and priorities. Most importantly, there appears to be a general failure to develop such ratings schemes into effective beach management tools.

The authors conclude their work by presenting a detailed review of a novel Bathing Area Registration and Evaluation (BARE) scheme that addresses gaps identified in previously described award schemes. It recognizes the importance of establishing a solid beach management base prior to consideration of applying, if this is deemed to be the desired option, for any such awards The technique focuses on achieving improvement in beach quality through effective management, by considering a wide spectrum of beach types, five critical criteria reflecting beach quality (safety, water quality, litter, facilities, scenery) and by integrating into the system's ethos the recognition that the importance of these criteria change with beach type. It further recognizes the value of beach quality evaluation as guidance to ongoing management. It is presented as a beach management tool that facilitates identification of management priorities required for upgrading beach quality.

Various external authors were invited to provide international case studies of good/bad/indifferent beach management practice, as guidance for future work in this field. These case studies also serve to reflect and act as a bridge between theory and field application.

First, Cliff Nelson looks at safety on UK beaches and assesses the risk associated with bathing. He traces the origins of the beach lifeguard movement and introduces a beach management plan from the safety viewpoint, postulating future scenarios associated with the need to create international standards, especially with respect to signage and documentation that evaluates public rescue equipment.

Andrew Cooper and John McKenna discuss problems associated with car driving/parking on a rural beach in Ireland. These include safety aspects (thousands of cars can be parked on a beach), environmental impacts on beach fauna and the sediment exchange between dune and beach. The case study is a sound example of a management authority utilizing a participatory approach in order to achieve management goals. The spatial scale of the area in which participation was invited was the key to successful resolution.

The sole *detailed* aspect of coastal engineering dealt with in this book is beach nourishment i.e. 'soft' engineering and Enzo Pranzini studies its efficiency at two sites in Sardinia, Italy, while Antonio Klein and co-authors looks at ameliorative strategies at a Brazilian beach. In Sardinia, the case study shows how stakeholders' expectations are intermeshed with legal and technical problems for recreational beaches. One beach studied is urban and used mainly by local people, and the other is a completely artificial gravel beach created along a high-energy coast to answer the needs of the tourism industry that is attracting increasing numbers and has an increasing season length. Picarras beach in Brazil is an important tourist centre, and Antonio Klein and his co-authors describe this beach that is sited in an erosional hot spot. Several nourishment projects have been carried out to try to counteract erosion and the lessons learned are outlined.

David Tudor investigates policies ranging from local to global scales. He emphasizes recent legislation in the field, especially from the viewpoint of the UK. This is necessary as different countries have differing legislation and policies. The links between marine management and coastal and terrestrial planning and management, together with integration of policy and management, are stressed as essential requirements for successful beach management.

Deirdre Hart investigates the effectiveness of river mouth lagoon management on beaches located in high-energy mixed sand and gravel coasts, via examination of a spectrum of lagoons and institutional frameworks at Canterbury, New Zealand. This case study demonstrates the need for effective management to be based not only on analysis of coastal environments and associated human use values but also on *practices* that recognize the spatially and temporally variable and open nature of coastal systems. Despite the sound 'sustainable management' purpose and integrated principles of current New Zealand management frameworks, non-cumulative effects-based catchments and activity-focused practices are leading to progressive lagoon degradation.

Karl Nordstrom, Nancy Jackson and Harry de Butts look at actions taken to manage the shorefront at Avalon, New Jersey, USA. Specifically, they refer to attempts to decrease hazards in this wealthy barrier island community by measures such as increasing dune elevations, managing sediment budgets and utilizing educational programmes. The focus was on restoring and maintaining dunes in a community that is active, independent and with a creative beach and dune management programme and this is a very good example of sound beach management.

Marcus Polette concentrates on assessing beach users' preferences and priorities at Balneário Camboriú, Brazil. His findings stress beach comfort, the effects of buildings shadowing the beach, water quality and beach nourishment. He concludes that managing interests from both private and public sectors for the preparation and implementation of an integrated beach management plan to protect and develop the beach area through coastal governance seems to be the only way to avoid technocratic decision making.

Paul Komar provides a personal account of problems associated with housing development for beach areas in Oregon, USA that are prone to landslides. Detailed examples are given of two sites and the case study traces paths taken by engineers, geologists and developers, who provide vastly different interpretations with respect to whether a proposed development site is hazardous or not, hence the 'Bad Apples' in his title.

Ayşen Ergin identifies a totally innovative holistic approach to beach management, using a case study of Çıralı beach, Turkey. In this case, the whole community has rallied around a beach management project, initially concerned with the plight of the *Caretta caretta* turtle, but this has since mushroomed out of all proportion into a village cooperative, organic agriculture and ecotourism.

Silvia Banchini and co-authors look at the new directions being undertaken in two beach areas in Barcelona, Spain, both of which exemplify 'good' beach management. They stress the efforts needed by local, regional and central administrators in order to protect, promote and aid recuperation of beach ecosystem functions. Emphasis is given to long-term cost–benefit planning for socio-ecosystem resilience.

Finally, Michael Phillips highlights beach consequences of industrial development, including the construction of a tidal harbour for importing iron ore and coal at Port Talbot in South Wales, UK. Management responses to significant beach erosion and seawall failure are discussed, including the use of waste material from steel production processes as coastal defence. He subsequently shows that residential and tourism redevelopment, in conjunction with industrial decline, will require new beach management strategies.

Acknowledgements

The people who we would wish to acknowledge are too numerous to mention, but some must be singled out. Professor W. C. (Bill) Bradley, University of Colorado, Boulder, USA, first ignited my love for beaches, to be followed by Professor Dennis Dwyer (University of Hong Kong and latterly Liverpool), who encouraged and pushed me to work in this field. I cannot thank them enough. Beach field work has been a learning curve, made thoroughly enjoyable through the companionship and lifelong friendship of Dr Peter Davies, Dr John Howden and Professor Stephen Leatherman.

Allan Williams

My love of beaches is undoubtedly bound to a Mediterranean heritage that gifted me a childhood blessed with long hot summers, lived within a stone's throw of the sea. While Jacques Cousteau (my childhood hero) kept me enthralled by the ever-close marine environment, it was much later that Professor Allan Williams introduced me to the wonderful world of beaches, from which I have never looked back – and for this I thank him dearly.

Anton Micallef

The friendship and advice offered by Professor Erdal Ozhan, founder and chairman of MEDCOAST, has been a bulwark on which both of us have hopefully built a beach management structure. At various periods, Dr Neil Caldwell, Dr Robert Morgan and Dr Sarah Simmons, in particular, helped create innovative ideas with regard to various beach issues, for which we are especially grateful. Finally, Hilary and Erika suffered the 'toil, tears and sweat' part of writing this book. Words cannot express the gratitude felt by us to them.

Allan Williams and Anton Micallef

The authors of Case Study 3 (A. H. F. Klein, R. S. Araujo, M. Polette, R. M. Sperb, D. Freitas Neto, J. M. Camargo, F. C. Sprovieri, and F. T. Pinto) wish to thank Balneário Piçarras municipal government for the information given; Universidade do Vale do Itajaí (UNIVALI/CTTMar/ Brazil) and the Faculdade de Engenharia of Universidade do Porto (UPorto/FEUP/Portugal) for support on the project ELANCAM (European and Latin American Network on Coastal Area Management); and the fieldwork team (Jonas R. Santos, Liana P. Foerstnow, Lucas Silveira, Marcos P. Berribilli and Tomás Thomé) for the valuable help. A. H. F. Klein and colleagues would also like to acknowledge Professor Charles Finkl (CERF-JCR), Christopher Makowski (CERF-JCR) and Professor Karl Nordstrom (Rutgers University) for the review and helpful discussions and critical readings of the initial manuscript. A. H. F. Klein is appreciative of the support from Brazilian National Council for Science and Technology (CNPQ Research Fellow) under grant no. 307267/2006-7, from the Hanse Institute for Advanced Study (HWK Fellow), Germany, and from Delft University of Technology, The Netherlands (Erasmus Mundus Visiting Scholar). M. Polette is appreciative of the support from Brazilian National Council for Science and Technology (CNPQ Research Fellow). R. S. Araujo, D. Freitas Neto and F. C. Sprovieri are appreciative of the support from PIPG/PROPPEC/UNIVALI.

Deirdre E. Hart (Case Study 5) thanks Paul Bealing for assisting with the production of Figures CS5.2 and CS5.3, to ECAN for providing river flow data and to Derek Todd for useful discussions on hapua management.

The authors of Case Study 7 (Karl F. Nordstrom, Nancy L. Jackson and Harry A. de Butts) are grateful to Linda Camp, Stewart Farrell, Stu Friedman, Tony Geiger and Bruce Tell, for information and insight.

Ayşen Ergin (Case Study 10) would like to thank Atila Uras, Emine Kuzutürk and Mustafa Esen for the support they provided during preparation of the case study.

List of Acronyms and Abbreviations

ABP	Associated British Ports
ACA	Agència Catalana de l'Aigua
AOP	Australia's Ocean Policy
asl	above sea level
BAMM	Bathing Area Management Model
BARE	Bathing Area Registration and Evaluation
BQI	Beach Quality Index
BSMP	beach safety management plan
BTCV	British Trust for Conservation Volunteers
CAM	coastal area management
CAMP	coastal area management plan
CIEH	Chartered Institute of Environmental Health
CM	coastal management
CMP	catchment management plan
CPA	Coastal Protection Authority
CRM	coastal resource management
CZM	coastal zone management
CZMA	Coastal Zone Management Act
DEFRA	Department for Environmental, Food and Rural Affairs
DHKD	Doğal Hayatı Koruma Derneği (Turkish Society for the Protection of Nature)
DoC	depth of closure
DPSIR	drivers-pressures-state–impact–responses
ECAN	Environment Canterbury
EEZ	Exclusive Economic Zone
EHS	erosional hot spot
EIS	environmental impact statement
EMAS	Eco-Management and Audit Scheme
ENCAMS	Environmental Campaigns
EPA	Environmental Protection Agency
ERA	environmental risk assessment
ESSIM	Eastern Scotian Shelf Integrated Management
FEE	Foundation for Environmental Education
FEMA	Federal Emergency Management Agency
FIS	Fédération Internationale de Sauvetage Aquatique
GIS	geographic information system

ICAM	integrated coastal area management
ICM	integrated coastal management
ICZM	integrated coastal zone management
ILS	International Life Saving (Federation)
ILSE	International Life Saving Federation of Europe
IOM	integrated oceans management
LA21	Local Agenda 21
LDIP	Llobregat Delta Infrastructure Plan
MCA	Maritime and Coastguard Agency
MCS	Marine Conservation Society
MSP	marine spatial planning
NALG	National Aquatic Litter Group
NBSC	National Beach Safety Council
NetSyMod	Network Analysis–Creative System Modelling–Decision Support
NGO	non-governmental organization
NHBC	National Healthy Beaches Campaign
NPF	National Planning Framework
NZCPS	New Zealand Coastal Policy Statement
OSPAR	Ministerial Meeting of the Oslo and Paris Commissions
PDUSC	General Plan of the Urban Coastal System
PGO	Planning Guidance Order
RLSS UK	Royal Life Saving Society UK
RMA	Resource Management Act (New Zealand)
RMB	Regional Metropolitan Barcelona
RNLI	Royal National Lifeboat Institution
RoSPA	Royal Society for the Prevention of Accidents
RTR	relative tide range
SCTE	Sistema de Calidad Turística Española
SAC	special areas of conservation
SEA	strategic environmental assessment
SIC	Sito di Importanza Comunitaria
SLB	street-level bureaucrat
SLSA GB	Surf Life Saving Association of Great Britain
SMP	shoreline management plan
SPA	special protected area
SPSS	Statistical Package for the Social Sciences
SVL	Statutory Vegetation Line
SWOT	strengths, weaknesses, opportunities and threats
UNCHS	United Nations Centre for Human Settlements
UNCLOS	United Nations Convention on the Law of the Sea
WAG	Welsh Assembly Government
WHO	World Health Organization
WLS	World Life Saving
WTP	willingness to pay
WTTC	World Travel and Tourist Council
WWF	World Wide Fund for Nature

'People certainly work, or play, hard on the beach. They build the most elaborate sandcastles, construct dams and create lagoons, race the tide in elaborate water games, spend hours skimming pebbles on the sea, lug heavy equipment for miles down cliffs, through sand dunes and up cliffs again. They spend fortunes on elaborate, powered water toys, wait for days for the right wave to surf, make beach camps like nomads, sit in beach huts all day gazing out to sea, or simply take off their shoes and socks and paddle.'

Roger Deakin, from *Waterlog: A Swimmer's Journey through Britain*

'Τής δάρέτης ιδρῶτά θεοί προπάρουθεν ἐθήκάν'
['Achievement? It has to be sweated for; the gods have made sweat the sole way']

Hesiod, from *Works and Days*

'Mir hilft der Geist! auf einmal seh ich Rat
Und schreibe getrost'
['The spirit moves me! All at once I can see the light
and write confidently']

Johann Wolfgang von Goethe, from *Faust*

CHAPTER 1

An Introduction to Beach Management

INTRODUCTION

Coastal zone management (CZM) is a relatively new field and a number of terms are used interchangeably: coastal management (CM), integrated coastal management (ICM), coastal resource management (CRM), coastal area management (CAM), integrated coastal zone management (ICZM) and more. Many common elements regarding ICM represent challenges/themes such as financial sustainability, inadequate capacities, weak law enforcement and a lack of integrated and collaborative efforts. These elements are also common in beach management, which is a subset of the more voluminous ICM literature, but with particular reference to pragmatic local management. When the 1972 USA Coastal Management Act was implemented, it kick-started global ICM programmes in which Clark's (1996) book has provided a fundamental philosophical and practical basis. In this context, Vallejo (1991) has pointed out that the ICM marine dimension may be divided between coastal and ocean areas. The former was defined by Ketchum (1972: 4) as, 'the band of dry land and adjacent ocean space (water and submerged land) in which land ecology and use directly affect ocean space ecology and vice versa. The coastal zone is a band of variable width.' ICM is essentially a broad-brush approach for this coastal zone and traditionally has emphasized fisheries (seemingly with the Tragedy of the Commons in irreversible decline), tourism and recreation and, increasingly, hazards (mainly erosion, flooding, storms, tsunamis and dunes – especially migrating dunes), while corals and mangroves also serve as important markers in the present-day coastal zone.

Many coastal nations have ICM plans, but the numbers who have implemented these plans are extremely small. Leaders in this field are probably the US, The Netherlands and Sri Lanka, which has over 25 years of ICM history (Aeron-Thomas, 2002). Some current ICM problems involve difficulties in obtaining relevant reliable information and its rationalization, the lack of networks for information exchange, lack of long-term planning and low take-up of new techniques, such as information systems. Some of these are applicable to beach management, which exhibits a much more specific local approach to this zone. However both approaches are inter- and trans-disciplinary, but beach management focuses on the local scale

– the outcome level of Olsen et al (1998) – in essence individual beaches, which *should* be managed under the broader overall umbrella of ICM. This exemplifies a recent trend in the subject of scaling ICZM to the local level.

Beaches display a variety of functions, such as coastal defence, recreation (swimming, surfing, sand yachting, fishing, jet skiing and so on) and conservation, and frequently a conflict of interest arises. It should be axiomatic that *effective* beach management fulfils the following condition, first postulated by Sauer (1963) with reference to landscapes, namely the integration of the physical environment – the fundament, with the cultural (anthropogenic) environment – that can be viewed as the superstructure (Williams et al, 2002b) (see Chapter 2). This is a matter that is rarely accomplished in practice. It is essentially a team effort, as one person cannot possibly understand all the demands made for this complex zone. Detailed discussion with all personnel and experts will provide a coherent reference framework, but in reality, it is in essence 'how conflict between user groups is resolved', the phrase used by Olsen et al (1998: 618) to define ICM.

There have been many viewpoints and definitions of the term 'beach management' and two common ones are given here:

> that process of managing a beach, whether by monitoring, simple intervention, recycling, recharge, the construction or maintenance of beach control structures or by some combination of these techniques, in a way that reflects an acceptable compromise in the light of available finance, between the various coastal defence, nature conservation, public amenity and industrial objectives. (Simm et al, 1995: 147)

> Beach management seeks to maintain or improve a beach as a recreational resource and a means of coast protection, while providing facilities that meet the needs and aspirations of those who use the beach. (Bird, 1996: 212)

It includes the framing and policing of any necessary regulations and decisions on the design and location of any structures needed to facilitate the use and enjoyment of the beach environment.

An alternative view is that beach management is about managing humans and the way they interact with the beach environment, with a view to avoiding, remedying or mitigating adverse interactions. This is more a derivative of a hazard model based on the assumption that 'coasts/beaches' would not need 'managing' if there were no humans wanting to use them. This needs knowledge and wisdom before implementation, which should be based on accurate and relevant information appropriate to the prevailing situation, all being influenced by the prevailing political philosophy, socio-economic situation and, at the beach level, emotions. On this point Mills et al (2008) emphasize the importance of long-term research and education. Beach management seeks to achieve optimal physical usage and development of beach resources that respects the natural physical elements of a beach environment while satisfying basic social needs within that environment.

However, sound beach management can lead to:

- effective utilization of an increasingly valuable (socio-economic and in places ecological) national resource;
- encouragement to overseas /local tourism;
- an increase in quality of recreational opportunities;
- a contribution to enhancement of nearby urban settlements;
- enhancement of coastal protection;
- facilitation of monitoring, regulation, planning and decision-making;
- promotion of sustainable coastal development.

The essence of sound beach management is that it is multidisciplinary, having sound aims, objectives and a correct methodological approach. In this respect, sound management should include ongoing training and would involve information on the area's history, description of the area, relationships and so on. Ideally, within any team of beach managers, a range of skills can be found on which to graft common project aims. Research into the natural/cultural beach processes should also be encouraged in conjunction with local academic institutions, as this knowledge can prove invaluable to the beach manager.

Beaches change virtually by the minute, as coastal processes (waves, tides) and even people are dynamic, and frequently irreversible changes occur, which can be natural or anthropogenic in origin (Komar, 1976). Sound management should be based upon sound scientific findings and a beach manager's role would cover a broad spectrum of beaches ranging from resort to remote and wilderness, of which definitions are given later in this chapter and also in Chapter 9. The end points of this range are easily defined but frequently conflict exists as to whether a beach should veer into the recreational (resort) or conservation (remote) field. To help with this viewpoint, a worked example utilizing function analysis is given in Chapter 7. Few academic papers have been written on this technique, but it is straightforward, relatively easy to perform and resolves many beach management conflict issues regarding the future management regime/bias for a particular beach.

KEY MANAGEMENT ELEMENTS

In any management design, elements shown below would be incorporated into plans and in practice managers must be able to identify and/or devise:

- *The range and causes of 'poor/good' beaches.*
- *The strengths, opportunities, weakness and threats unique to their own beaches* (SWOT analysis) (Coelho et al, 2003) and/or the drivers–pressures–state–impact–responses (DPSIR model) (Marin et al, 2007; Satumanatpan and Juntarashote, 2008).
- *Comprehensive, practical and fundable action programmes,* for example award schemes (see Chapter 8).
- *Encouragement of third parties to cooperate in bringing about improved environmental standards and long-term investment.*
- *A high quality product* for visitors, locals and investors alike, whether it is a resort or a remote/wilderness area.
- *Proactive future planning.* Claridge (1987) has provided a sound account of the checklist procedures involved in this matter. Plans are usually drawn up on the prevailing status quo. Knowledge of a change in state, which frequently happens, is vital, and impact assessment can help to define the necessary controls to prevent or limit specific impacts. Judgement is then necessary to reflect the probable best manner in which to proceed. As a result of the explosion in world tourism, linguistic ability should be emphasized. An example of a planned beach state change is given in Chapter 7.
- *Beach user cooperation.* This is essential as this area encompasses diverse groupings and therefore specific approaches are needed. These groupings could include villages, fishermen, planners, engineers, tourist boards, schools, conservationists and so on. An 'adopt a beach' viewpoint could be a first step towards successful beach management. The many coordinated activities between local communities, volunteers and non-governmental organizations (NGOs) that can be found, for example, in coral reef-based sustainable ecotourism, provide sound models. Mu Koh Chang coal reef demonstration site, Trat Province, Thailand is a good case of such successful cooperation, which encourages capacity building within local communities (Yeemin, personal communication). The important principle is to get the local community working together, where ideally the rights and responsibilities of governance are moved to community-based coastal management – a very large step indeed. In Indonesia, traditional community-based management (legally implemented in the Coastal and Small Island Act, 2007 – termed HP-3) has been practised in many parts of the nation for over 200 years, but relates only to utilization of resources in coastal waters. If extended it could prove to be an invaluable asset to ICM in this region. Governance – the key to building good communities – is an elusive ideal involving multiple actors, but management is much broader. Glavovic (2004) emphasizes this point in the transformational practice of consensus building exemplified by the ICM strategy to promote coastal sustainability in South Africa. Smith and Lazarow (2004) have also stressed, as an emerging paradigm, the concept of adaptive learning as a management tool. This

focuses on social learning for a commitment to implement all stages of management, and they have developed an online 'toolbox'. The many Australian CZM plans for the Great Barrier Reef also accentuate this point, which by its very nature, is a costly, long-term initiative, a point also made by Clark (1996) in his seminal book on CZM.

- *Infringements that occur in many guises and at regular intervals*. Persuasion is the main argument, as court cases are usually costly, can give bad publicity and should only be undertaken as a last resort (see Chapter 6).
- *Monitoring via collection of information, recording the condition of the managed area and the effect that management has upon the area*. This is very important. Davies et al (1995a) show that application of the W model (see Chapter 3, 'The Bathing Area Management Model', page 77) for problem solving in dune management is a powerful tool for any subset of managers. This involved conceptual and fieldwork components, and pilot and full-scale field trials, and the technique is equally applicable in the context of beach management (see Chapters 4 and 5). Linkages with academics are of the utmost importance here, as most managers do not have the time and/or necessary expertise to run these exercises. As a result of monitoring, management plans will usually be changed if conditions are such that original objectives are not being achieved. The important questions that must be asked are: *What has gone wrong? Why? And what can management do to resolve the issue?*

Additionally, beach managers should be aware of the environmental impact of:

- *Structural effects*, for example the clearing of pre-existing ecosystems, port development, mariculture and seawalls.
- *Process damage impacts*, for example pollution and the 'Tragedy of the Commons'.
- *Maintenance or amenity value*, which are very difficult to assess, because for a productive diverse environment they involve knowledge of interactions between human populations and sustenance.

Some typical examples of monitored beach-related parameters would include water quality, litter management (which includes adequate litter bins, industrial waste, urban waste and fly tipped material), 'active' management (for example a policy on dogs), availability of fresh water, toilets, telephones, local emergency plans for dealing with any oil spill, safe confinement of any beach construction work, buildings in a high state of repair and so on. Ease of beach access is important, including facilities for less able persons, as are prohibition of unauthorized driving, dumping and camping and the management of competing interests, for example swimmers/boaters, surfers, fishermen and the provision of safe bathing in normal summer conditions.

Some parameters are beyond the control of the beach manager. For example, European water quality was originally determined by EC Bathing Water Directive 76/160/EEC (CEC 1976), recently updated by CEC (2006); but water quality at any one instant relates to water company discharges, combined sewer overflows, ship discharges and so on. On a conceptual basis, beach management is ostensibly straightforward, i.e. impacts relating to any given activity are identified and the problem rectified by suitable controls within the structured management plan. However, problems rarely exist in isolation and synergetic effects usually enter into the scenarios. In practice, almost all management of the beach environment/natural resources consists of assessment of the human impact. As an example, Miami beach with its initial circa US$65 million beach nourishment project, epitomizes this statement, as without the beach area, this part of Florida would succumb to prevailing erosional coastal processes. This anthropogenic initiative brings in over $2 billion in revenue from more than 2 million visitors per annum (Houston, 2002). Federal tax revenues from this beach alone bring in over $130 million (six times the amount spent to restore all US beaches) and it receives more visitors than the combined totals of three major national parks: Yellowstone, Grand Canyon and Yosemite (Houston, 2002). At the Australian Gold Coast, surfing alone brings in 65,000 to 120,000 individuals, who spend some AU$126–233 million per year. This could easily be tripled when non-market values, multipliers and externalities are added (Lazarow, 2009). In addressing *project justification* for a proposed beach nourishment exercise in Malta, Micallef and Cassar (2001) describe how an environmental impact statement (EIS) considered that generation of a sand beach at St George's Bay, Malta, a prime concentration of 5 star hotels and a neighbouring area hosting extensive leisure facilities, bars, restaurants and discos, would result in:

- an anticipated increase in tourist satisfaction visiting the proposed beach area;
- a positive impact of the above on the likelihood of repeat visitors to the Island;
- a 13 per cent increase in nearby public property values and 1 per cent increase in hotel property values. This was calculated to translate to an estimated $6 million increase in local property values.

The EIS also identified a willingness of approximately 50 per cent of existing beach users to pay around US$1.65 per visit for improved beach facilities, resulting in a computed potential annual income flow of $9900 (equivalent to a capital increment of $123,700). It was further postulated that since the proposed beach was designed to cater for about 660 additional beach users, the potential annual revenue from the expressed willingness to pay was $65,500, corresponding to a capital increment of $816,400.

Policy definition must also acknowledge that different beach types exist (see 'Typology' below and Chapter 9), and also that bathing areas exist that are not beaches in the strict definition (see below for definitions). These areas are usually devoid of sediments that form beaches and can include rock ledges used for sunbathing and as diving platforms, natural/artificial shore platforms that people utilize for sunbathing and picnicking (see Figures 1.1 and 1.2), natural and artificial rock pools, and old harbours (see Figures 1.3, 1.4 and 1.5).

BEACH PROCESSES AND TYPOLOGY

Processes

To quote Bascom (1964: 184), 'Every coastal dweller in the world is quite sure what a beach is like. Yet if you were to ask, you would find totally different opinions, and all derived from local knowledge.' A beach to a dweller in the Maldives is sparkling white coral, in the big island of Hawaii it is black basaltic material, in many parts of Great Britain it is pebble/shingle, for example Chesil, while in China, mud constitutes large tracts of the Yangtze estuary in contrast to a large expanse of sand at Number 1 beach, Qingdao.

Figure 1.1 *Natural rocky shore bathing platform, Sliema shorefront, Malta*

Figure 1.2 *Artificial rocky bathing platform in Croatia,*
plus (inset) a typical ladder access facility

Figure 1.3 *Artificial swimming pool on the Madelaine coast*
in the Azores, Portugal

Figure 1.4 *Semi-natural bathing area (boat slip-way), Pocinho, Pico island, Azores, Portugal*

Figure 1.5 *Old harbour bathing areas, Porto das Baixes, San Miguel, Azores, Portugal*

Beaches have been defined as:

the zone of unconsolidated material that extends landward from the low
water line to the place where there is a marked change in material or physio-
graphic form, or to the line of permanent vegetation (usually the effective
limit of storm waves). The seaward limit of a beach – unless otherwise
specified – is the mean low water line. (Shore Protection Manual, 1981: A3)

Note the emphasis on the lower low water position. However, from
a beach manager's perspective, beaches might be better described as
accumulations of unconsolidated materials (for example sands, gravels,
muds – or mixtures) that extend seaward from the landward edge of
the beach, for example a dune scarp or seawall, to the water depth at
which significant sediment motion is absent – the depth of closure (DoC).
This is the zone that a beach manager should understand if he/she is to
comprehend beach dynamics; it is vital to the well-being of a beach, and
is especially crucial for artificial nourished beaches, which since the 1970s
are an increasingly used method for protecting near-shore infrastructures,
rather than 'hard' structures (Finkl and Walker, 2005; Finkl et al, 2006),
together with renovation of degraded beaches and creation of new artificial
beach resources. Unfortunately, many ICM 'experts' and beach managers
tend to fall down with respect to a sound knowledge of coastal processes.
Knowledge of the littoral sediment cell concept based on sediment littoral
drift patterns is one 'must for managers', as this is a basic building block
for adequate management. In the UK this approach has developed very
rapidly (Motyka and Brampton, 1993; Cooper and Pontee, 2006).

DoC is a rather vague concept in an oceanic wave environment and is
time dependent (although sometimes it is event dependent); the longer
the wave period the larger will be the DoC (Leatherman, 1991; Stive et al,
1992; Kraus et al, 1999). It can be estimated using techniques such as grain
size trends (Larson, 1991; Work and Dean, 1991), orientation of offshore
contours and wave statistics (Hallemeier, 1981), and may be defined as
the ratio of change in cross-sectional area divided by advance or retreat of
the high water line, or other convenient contour, and determined from an
analysis of beach profiles, providing they continue far enough underwater
(Simm, 1996). Many formulae have been produced for calculation of this
elusive point (Bodge, 1992; Wang and Davis, 1999; Phillips and Williams,
2007).

Capobianco et al (1997) reviewed the problems associated with DoC,
highlighting the many difficulties of reconciling theory and practice by
scientific evidence. Frequently, insufficient data are available for analysis
and DoC is estimated by experience, using information on beach profiles
at various locations along a coast (Simm, 1996). This concurs with the
observations of Leatherman (2001) who argued that in most developing
countries, active profile width must be estimated by using expert
judgement rather than hard quantitative data. Where gently sloping

platforms occupy much of the nearshore zone and frequently, the inter-
tidal foreshore lower part, they adopt a shallower slope than mobile sand
or gravel under wave action and in this instance the beach underwater
profile usually terminates as a distinct line on the platform (Simm, 1996).
Wang and Davis (1999) examined DoC trends in variation from 555 beach
profiles along a 20km beach at Sand Key, west-central Florida. With respect
to rock platform exposure, they found agreement with theoretical profile
predictions (Dean, 1977; Bodge, 1992), with the greatest discrepancy
between predicted/average profile being at the bar and trough.

All managers should have a grasp of these basic fundamental processes
operating upon their beaches and many books exist that explain them
(Bascom, 1964; Kay and Alder, 1999; Short, 1999; Haslett, 2000; Masselink
and Hughes, 2008). Whatever a beach composition, the governing principles
remain the same, basically a function of waves and currents, and they
occur in any water environment – rivers, lakes, but are more commonly
associated with the sea. Material size determines beach steepness with
sand and mud forming very low gradient beaches, which steepen as
material coarsens in size because wave run-up is able to percolate through
material voids and so limit surface scour. All beaches change in shape and
if regular profiles are taken over time and superimposed on each other, a
'sweep zone' will be produced (a zone delimiting the extent of change, i.e.
by a line drawn to join all profile tops and another the bottoms), which is
indicative of beach stability. If it is narrow, the beach is stable, if wide, it is
unstable. The profiles should extend seawards from the back of the beach
to the depth of closure – Figure 1.6 and Chapter 2, 'Essential Concepts of
Beach Management', page 34).

A storm can disrupt the system ripping material away, flattening a
beach in hours, whereas a long period of gentle waves will build up a
beach and produce a steeper gradient. A shape change can also occur if
artificial structures are introduced into the beach system, for example
groynes and breakwaters, which can interrupt the conveyor-like longshore

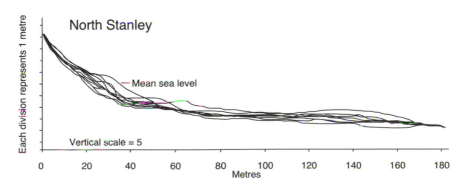

Figure 1.6 *Two-year sweep zone at Stanley Bay, Hong Kong, showing the DoC*

movement of sediment and cause deposition/erosion of material on the updrift/downdrift side respectively. Material movement is accomplished by energy inherent within the system provided by waves, which can be conveniently divided into storm and swell – the former being destructive in character, the latter calm and constructive. The division is a function of the wave period, that is the time taken for consecutive waves to pass a fixed point, some 8–10 seconds being an average arbitrary nodal point.

Waves can usually be divided into two types, namely deep and shallow water, the latter forming when the influence of the sea bottom starts to be felt. This is usually at a half wavelength depth. When deepwater waves move into shallow water, they become unstable and break, as the crest moves faster than the base due to frictional effects. This is a function of wave height, wave period and beach slope. Wave height is the measured distance between the crest (top) and the trough (bottom) of a deepwater wave; wavelength is the distance between consecutive wave crests or troughs. The occurrence of different breaking wave types is a function of deepwater steepness (wave height/wave length) and the bottom slope. Breaking waves can be categorized into:

- *spilling waves* – foam cascading down the wave top, usually associated with waves of large steepness values breaking on a gently sloping beach;
- *plunging waves* – 'the banzai pipeline' so beloved of top surfers, usually found on steep beaches;
- *collapsing waves* – where the wave peaks, as if to plunge but the base rushes up-shore as a thin foaming layer; the category lies between the plunging and surging types;
- *surging waves* – where waves remain smooth with very small air entrainment and simply slide up a beach, usually found when waves with small steepness propagate upon a steep beach.

The long-term beach condition is a function of the supply of material together with loss of littoral material. It has been estimated (Bird, 1996; Heinz Center, 2000) that the majority of the world's beaches are in an erosional phase, as a result of a reduction in natural production of coastal sediments. This process has been anthropologically accelerated due to cutting off river sediment inputs by dams, the 'concretization' of coastlines, sand dredging activities for the construction industry, climate change and sea-level rise. For example, the eastern coastline of the US is dominated by a chain of barrier islands and a broad consensus of wide-ranging work is that apart from a few isolated areas, such as the tips of some islands, erosion is the predominant geomorphological process. This has been confirmed by many reports. Galgano (1998) infers that some 86 per cent of the east coast is in retreat, while the Heinz Center (2000) reports some 90 per cent of the US coastline to be in retreat. This has vast implications with respect to CZM and therefore beach management, particularly when consideration is given to the fact that the bulk of the US population lives along the coastal fringe and property values for the US east and Gulf Coast barriers have been valued at over \$3 trillion (Platt, 1995). Klein et al (2004) show that tourism-related earnings as a percentage of total earnings in the US are concentrated in counties within 40km of the coastline, as these counties have shifted emphasis from traditional maritime activities, such as fishing and boating, to a service-oriented, tourism-dependent economy. Additionally, China, a massive country that has no integrated coastal area management (ICAM) act or any semblance of ICZM at a national level, currently has some 60 per cent of the total population living along its 18,000km coastline (Shuolin Huang, personal communication). In several coastal areas of France, Italy and Spain, the built-up area exceeds 45 per cent (EEA, 2006). In the case of Spain, Piqueras (2005) points out that with only 0.001 per cent of space occupied by Spanish beaches, they generate roughly 10 per cent of the gross national product of the country. To date, over 50 per cent of the world's coastline is threatened by development, and it is estimated that by 2025, around 75 per cent of the world's population will live within 60km of the sea (Small and Nichols, 2003; Finkl and Kruempfel, 2005). Good beaches are worth billions (Clark, 1996), and it is worth noting that when Wilson and Liu (2008: 130) carried out a number of peer-reviewed non-market valuation studies (1970–2006) of coastal-marine ecosystems, beach recreation 'got inordinate attention in the economic literature'.

Typology

Beach systems are dependent upon four factors: Hb – wave height, T – wave period, Ws – sediment size (fall velocity) and TR – spring tide range. All can be quantified using Ω, the dimensionless fall velocity (Short, 1999). Ω = Hb/T Ws, or via the relative tide range (RTR) = TR/Hb (Short, 1999).

Beach state is controlled by the RTR and Ω, and each beach state has a characteristic morphodynamic regime. Based on RTR, beaches may be classified into three beach types:

- wave-dominated, RTR <3;
- tide-modified, RTR 3–10;
- tide-dominated, RTR 10–50+.

Likewise based on Ω, each type can be classified into beach states that are subdivided as: wave-dominated, tide-modified and tide-dominated. However, some beach systems have additional factors that to an extent override waves and tides, such as, inter-tidal coral reefs (tropics only), or inter-tidal rock flats (global). Additional states occur in higher energy sea environments, for example ridge and runnel. All states will be modified in polar environments where frozen beaches and shore-fast sea ice dominate during winter.

Therefore based on the *physical* dimension, beaches could be classed as follows, with each type having different characteristics and subdivisions:

- Covering a spectrum from *dissipative* to *reflective*, essentially characterized by wave climatology (high energy to low energy) and beach material composition, i.e. beaches can consist of a sediment range varying from mud to sands (see Figure 1.7), gravels, cobbles (see Figure 1.8) and boulders (or mixtures).
- Whether they are natural or artificial. Examples of the latter are south beach Miami, USA; many portions of the Italian Adriatic coast (Cammelli et al, 2005; Guerra et al, 2004); and Porthcawl, UK (see Figures 1.11 and 1.12).
- On shape, for example:
  - pocket, which are small beach enclaves ubiquitous around the world, the size of which is debatable but that essentially have onshore–offshore sediment movement, little longshore movement and are enclosed by headlands (see Chapter 4 and Figure 1.9);
  - linear – long straight beaches with a pronounced longshore drift such as the long beaches of the Outer Banks or the eastern seaboard, USA (see Figure 1.7);
  - logarithmic spiral (Zeta curve, hyperbolic tangent), where the beach shape is curved at one end, for example Rhossili, UK (see Figure 1.10) or Half Moon Bay, California, USA, where the headland of Pillar Point protects the beach at the curved end from prevailing northwest swell waves (Moreno, 2005).
- Recently, Jackson and Cooper (2009) have argued that geological controls on beach morphodynamics are under-rated. This probably represents a beach class that exists in a constrained state, operating outside the boundaries of existing unconstrained morphodynamic models.

Based on an *anthropogenic* dimension, beaches may be classified as remote, rural, village, urban or resort, with the last of these being found in any of the previous four beach types (see 'Anthropological Beach Typology' in this chapter; Chapter 4, Figures 4.6, 4.7). Another way of classifying beaches is by usage i.e. heavy, medium and dense, which is the system utilized in Barbados in the Caribbean (CEES, 2006). Ariza et al (2008a) classify Catalan beaches in Spain into three types: urban – located within the main nucleus of a municipality with over 60 per cent of an urbanized hinterland of high density; urbanized – found in residential areas outside the main municipality nucleus with a maximum of 50 per cent urbanized hinterland (low density); and natural beaches – outside the main nucleus located close to very low-density urbanized areas (under 30 per cent of the hinterland being urbanized) or in uninhabited areas. In the UK, the Heritage Coast philosophy covering one third of the England and Wales coastal management framework, classifies beaches ranging from

Figure 1.7 *Typical linear sand beach*

Figure 1.8 *Typical cobble beach*

Figure 1.9 *The 'ultimate' pocket beach at the base of >600m cliff face, Sliabh Liag, Donegal, Ireland*

Figure 1.10 *A Zeta curve beach, Rhossili, Wales, UK*

'honeypots' – geared to recreational activities, to remote (few people involved), with sometimes intermediate categories (Williams and Ergin, 2004).

Some of the above points are discussed in more detail below.

Dissipative to reflective beaches

A basic framework for morphodynamic beach states is invariably inherited from earlier states, each being distinguished by a different association of morphology, circulation and behaviour. Different morphological types relate to stages in erosional or accretional sequences and the two extreme beach types recognized by the scientific community are the end members – *dissipative* (with most energy expended via the breaking process) and *reflective* (with minimum wave energy dissipation) beaches, separated by four intermediate domains (Short, 1991; 1999). The bulk of this work has been developed on *sand* beaches and micro-tidal areas. Average wave energy in one wavelength per unit crest width is given by:

$$E = \varrho g H^2 L / 8$$

where ϱ is the mass density of water, g is the gravitational constant, H is wave height and L the wavelength.

End members of this classification correspond respectively to flat, shallow beaches (dissipative) with relatively large subaqueous sand storage and steep beaches (reflective) with small subaqueous sand storage and this classification is now used worldwide. It works extremely well in micro-tidal regions (tidal range of less than 2m), for example the Mediterranean, but several anomalies occur when transposed to macro-tidal (tidal range of over 4m) areas.

The dissipative–reflective spectrum is based on the surf scaling parameter (ξ), which depends upon wave amplitude a_b (the height distance between the top/bottom of a wave), wave period (T) and beach slope (β):

$$\xi = a_b \sigma^2 / g \tan^2 \beta$$

where: a_b is the wave amplitude, σ is radian frequency (= $2\Pi/T$, where T is the wave period), g is the gravitational acceleration and β is the beach slope.

As the surf scaling parameter value decreases, the surf zone (the area in which waves breaks) narrows and an increasing proportion of wave energy is reflected.

When:

- ξ <1.0 complete reflection occurs;
- ξ <2 to 2.5 strong reflection will continue to permit strong standing wave motion, surging breakers and resonance;
- ξ >2.5 waves begin to plunge, dissipating energy;

- ξ circa 20 spilling breakers occur and the surf zone widens; turbulent dissipation of incident wave energy increases with increasing ξ values;
- ξ varies from 30 to >100, it tends towards the dissipative extreme with these high ξ values extending across the surf zone and beach face.

Four intermediate stages exist and possess coexisting dissipative and reflective elements:

- The longshore bar and trough state can develop from an antecedent dissipative profile in an accretional sequence. Bar–trough relief is much higher and the beach face much steeper than on a dissipative profile. The bar is the locus of initial wave breaking and is moderately dissipative. Waves reform in the 3–4m deep trough after passing over the steep inner bar edge. The steepened beach face tends to be reflective with a ξ of circa 2. Run-up is usually high.
- The 'rhythmic' bar and trough state is similar to the above, but rhythmic longshore undulations of the crescentric bar and subaerial beach occur. Weak to moderate rip circulation exists; embayments are more reflective and horns dissipative. Rip currents – seaward movements of water that cease at the surf line can be prevalent. These currents are fast moving, especially dangerous to bathers and the cause of many beach deaths. Much research is currently being carried out on the dynamics of these currents – for example, Austin et al (2009) and Gallop et al (2009) – as well as the associated deaths (Hartman, 2006).
- The most pronounced segregation is in the region of a 'transverse bar and rip' topography. High dissipation and set-up over shallow, flat transverse bars alternate with reflective conditions, low set-up and higher run-up in embayments that can have strong rips. Bar spacings are usually inherited.
- The 'ridge and runnel' low-tide terrace has a relatively narrow, moderately dissipative and flat accumulation of sand around the low-tide position, backed by a steeper beach face, which is reflective at high tide. Rip currents can occur and shore parallel runnels are often present, formed by shoreward migration of swash bars over flat low-tide terraces.

A fully reflective beach lacks any dissipative elements. Breakers surge and collapse and turbulence is confined to the zone of high run-up on the beach face. Immediately beneath this is usually found a pronounced step of coarser material, whose depth increases with increasing wave height.

Gravels
Gravel beaches, a generic term for beach material with a mean grain size greater than for sand (see Figure 1.8), are found in many parts of the world, for example the UK, Italy and Croatia, and have not in the past

been recognized as suitable for recreational purposes, but recent work by among others Pranzini (2004), has indicated that they are now becoming 'fashionable'. Therefore it is pertinent to mention them in this context. Bluck (1967) was one of the first to produce a major study of such beaches, postulating that in a pebble/gravel ridge, there existed a:

- *large disc zone* at the beach crest full of large-sized discs and small-sized rods and spheres;
- *imbricate zone* with a high disc population of all sizes;
- *infill zone* that is complex but composed mainly of spheres and rods usually with a sand sheet over it, called a 'sand run'; spheres and blades infill the larger pebbles;
- *outer frame* of cobbles and boulders, with a high numbers of spheres, usually one or two items thick.

Pebble ridges are built by storm waves that destroy pre-existing patterns; mixing occurs and these conditions are a major means of onshore transport. Seaward transport takes place by shape/weight either within the beach (this is the most common condition via backwash through the voids, i.e. a sieve-like effect), or on the surface where rods and spheres move fastest and therefore are winnowed away.

Bluck (1967) stressed 'modal' sizes in upper erosion and lower beach deposition, the distinguishing feature being the degree of reworking by waves, and introduced two beach types termed Sker and Newton. Bluck (1967) looked at sediments alone and not the dynamic mechanisms associated with wave processes. Orford (1977) followed up this study and showed that Bluck (1967) had failed to identify a specific facies sequence for storm conditions, and inferred that storm waves could sort out material, dividing the beach configuration into 'step', 'bar' and 'composite' profiles. A scale factor, from daily changes to long-term ones, was introduced showing that it was possible to obtain both Sker and Newton types on the same beach but in different areas. Instead of the two types given by Bluck (1967), Orford (1977) finished with eight types, relying heavily upon profile analyses in order to show that sorting could occur in both an onshore and offshore direction. This was followed in turn by Williams and Caldwell (1988) who produced an inferred energy model, based on the pebble c axis value and standard deviation, showing that in low-energy conditions, particle shape factors were dominant, while size was the main factor in high-energy conditions. With rising sea levels, barrier overtop and breaching of gravel beaches is likely to increase, leading to management of a previously self maintaining barrier (Orford et al, 2002: Gallop et al, 2009; White, 2009).

Nourished beaches
Beach nourishment is an anti-erosion scheme that has been promoted as a safer 'soft' engineering approach when compared to 'hard' engineering,

for example sea-walls and breakwaters (Simm, 1996). In terms of cost it is less expensive and results in restoration of a more natural landscape (Cipriani et al, 2004). Beach nourishment is normally applied to recharge eroded or depleted beaches with imported materials but may also be used to create new beaches. The main purpose served by this management option is to restore/enhance the beach's coastal defence function and/or amenity value. Instances where beach nourishment may be applied as a management option are identified in Box 1.1.

Artificial gravel beaches have in recent years become very popular in places such as Italy (Cammelli et al, 2005). Over 50 per cent of Italian beaches experience large-scale erosion, which until recently was countered by 'hard' engineering projects such as detached breakwaters, groynes and seawalls. At Marina di Pisa, some ten detached breakwaters (fronting over 2km of seawall) have been lowered to -0.5m from mean sea level and a gravel beach (6.25km^2) constructed seaward of the seawall. The aim was primarily coastal defence, so no lifeguards, beach umbrellas or beach cleaning was provided, but gravel beaches (Carrara marble in some instances) have become intensively used for recreation during summer months and a valuable adjunct to the tourist industry.

Box 1.1 *Opportunities for application of beach nourishment as a management option*

1   Sustaining beach systems experiencing a net loss of sand, such as the case presented for Bournemouth beach, UK, by Harlow and Cooper (1995).
2   Increasing sediment volume of a beach having little inputs or outputs of material but where localized redistribution of sediment is occurring, as represented by many pocket beaches.
3   Creating new artificial beaches or replacing ones completely eroded away as in the case of the Spanish beach restoration programme (1993–1998), which included development of a number of completely new beaches (Houston, 1996; 2002). Micallef and Cassar (2001) have described the socio-economic and ecological considerations of a beach nourishment scheme in Malta.
4   Improving natural shoreline protection. An example of such application is the case study presented by Runcie and Fairgrieve (1995) for the Mablethorpe to Skegness coast in the UK, where beach nourishment was implemented as part of a strategy to enhance the Lincolnshire sea defence system.
5   Enhancing the amenity value of a small or narrow beach by enlargement.

Advantages of beach nourishment as a management option (see Box 1.1) are represented by positive aesthetic results that enhance recreational value, creation of additional recreational space and the minimal likelihood of causing downdrift erosion. Disadvantages of beach nourishment include high monitoring and maintenance costs, a potential for changing local sediment characteristics and introducing new biological species through the importation of foreign sediments and problems related to smothering of flora and fauna (Micallef and Cassar, 2001).

In carrying out beach nourishment, management must closely adhere to established guidelines and procedures since the possible repercussions of mismanagement are large-scale changes to local geomorphological and ecological characteristics. In this context, the material used for replenishment should preferably correspond in form and size to existing local beach material (CIRIA, 1996). If it is not possible to obtain an exact material match, it is important that extremes are avoided since new beach material that is too fine will result in local turbidity and water retention problems and result in erosion rates higher than normally applicable to that environment.

Alternatively, materials that are too coarse will result in steeper beach gradients that may prove socially unacceptable. This was shown to be the case by Micallef and Cassar (2001) in their discussion on the hydrodynamic modelling of a number of sediment options as part of an environmental impact assessment of proposed beach nourishment in Malta. Similarly, Breton et al (1996) commented on the negative public perception of coarse sediment beaches off Barcelona that had to undergo profile regrading by the municipality due to what was then considered as unsafe bathing waters for children. In the design of beaches geared to recreation rather than conservation, special attention must therefore be given to the consideration of social preferences and priorities and conservation of local environmental characteristics.

Miami beach, USA, is probably the most cited example of beach nourishment projects and Houston (1996; 2002) has given an excellent account of the benefits produced by this scheme. In the mid-1970s there was almost no beach in existence at Miami and beach nourishment in the late 1970s rejuvenated the area. An expenditure of around $65 million on the project has netted an annual foreign revenue from tourists of some $2.4 billion, i.e. every $1 invested annually to nourish Miami beach has brought a return of about $500 annually in foreign exchange (Houston, 2002). Similarly, the area between Sandy Hook and Barnegat Inlet, New Jersey, USA was extensively nourished between 1989 and 1998, resulting in a viewpoint change of New Jersey people: when polled in 1989, 74 per cent of people thought that the New Jersey shoreline was going 'downhill'; this had fallen to just 27 per cent in 1998 (Zukin, 1998). King (1999) indicated that from 1995–1999, California received some $2 million annually in federal beach nourishment funding, while the government received some $14 billion in tax revenues annually from tourists. He showed that California beaches alone had more tourist visits (567 million) than the combined visits to all National Park Service properties (286 million).

Utilizing sand is expensive as the nearshore profile is deepened due to wave reflection, and very large sand volumes are needed to reconstruct beach profiles extending from nearshore to backshore. Over the past few decades, tens of millions of cubic metres of marine sands have been dredged in many countries for nourishment purposes (Hanson et al, 2002). For example, in Italy, over 20 million cubic metres of marine sand has been used (Pranzini, 2004). As stated, recently, the usage of gravel beaches (a generic term for beach material with a mean grain size greater than that of sand) has come to the fore with respect to coastal protection. In many instances this has involved conversion of old, hard structures into gravel beaches, or placing gravel material in front of old seawalls. Pranzini in Case Study 6 gives an interesting account of this technique, as introduced in many Italian areas, for example Lido di Policoro, Fondi-Sperlonga and Marina di Pisa (Cipriani et al, 2004). Such beaches have lower cost and maintenance factors associated with construction, and gravel is one of nature's best methods of protecting a coastline via diffusion of wave forces. Additionally, they have greater stability due to uprush water infiltration through pore spaces that returns to the sea as a subsurface flow rather than running down a beach surface, as happens on a sand beach.

Novel 'nourished' beaches

Urban These can provide sand beaches within urban cities. For example, in 2002, the mayor of Paris, France, introduced the Paris Plage stretching some 3km along the right bank of the River Seine, where bathers, roller skaters, cyclists and strollers meet. It has a 28m swimming pool, and evening concerts are on the agenda. It cost over €2 million to construct and opens from 8 a.m. to midnight and from 20 July to 19 August. The sand was inserted at three locations between the Ile St Louis and the Jardin des Tuileries: from the Louvre to the Pont de Sully; along the Bassin de la Villette stretching from the Rotonde de Ledoux to the 'anciens Magasins généraux' which concentrates on water sports; and at the national library.

Another example is the free summer 'sand beach' in Chamberlain Square, Birmingham, which lies in the landlocked West Midlands area of the UK, which was one of the most recent cities to follow this trend. It opened on 25 June and closed on 16 September, 2007. Deck chairs and palm trees added to the occasion and sporting attractions included volley ball and cricket matches played on the 'beach', while culture was provided by items such as ballet and opera nights. Management of such beaches is very different to water-based beaches since no lifeguards are needed (although security guards might be involved), no water quality monitoring exists, and the scenery is composed of buildings (old/modern), with chairs replacing traditional sun-loungers. Unfortunately litter invariably exists in large quantities at the end of the day, so cleaning on such artificial beaches is analogous to manual beach-based cleaning.

Depending upon the author, approximately 25–40 per cent of Florida's 1350 mile (2025km) coastline is suffering from erosion and around $80 million is spent annually restoring the beaches (Marlowe, 1999). One county, Broward County with some 24 miles of beaches considered critically eroded, is exploring the utilization of recycled glass, crushed into very small grains and mixed with regular sand. Beach-related activities in this area bring in over $1 billion a year for Broward alone. The origin of the glass-sand idea came from an ocean dump site at Fort Bragg, Northern California where garbage (organics, glass and so on) was deposited into the ocean in 1949. The organic matter decomposed with time and the glass abraded to a smooth texture as a result of surf processes, resulting in a beach known locally as 'Glass Beach'.

Broward County would become the first in the US to combine the disposal of recycled glass (some 15,600 tonnes per annum). Currently some 13 million tonnes of sand has been dredged from the ocean floor in order to replenish beaches in Broward County but sand is becoming scarce and dredging is being carried out further offshore with a consequent rise in costs (Edge et al, 2002). In 2005, dredging brought in about 2.6 million tonnes of sand at a cost of $45 million. A similar operation in 1991 dredged around 1.3 million tonnes of sand for just $9 million. Makowski and Rusenko (2007) have shown in experiments with varying amounts of sand from Broward County, Florida and recycled glass cullet from Fariboult, Minnesota, that the material is biologically inert and therefore very suitable as beach nourishment fill. To date some $600,000 has been spent on testing the 'glass idea' in the US (Skolloff, 2007). Recycled glass has also been used for beaches along Lake Hood in New Zealand, the Dutch Caribbean island of Curacao and Hawaii.

Paved   In the strictest of definitions, these are not really beaches. Reflection of wave energy from a vertical seawall built in 1906 at Porthcawl, UK, resulted by 1932 in the base and pilings being exposed, necessitating the building of a new 450m seawall. By 1942, the mean high water mark intersected the base and a concrete buttress was added to crumbling wall segments. By the 1970s all were worn. A rock revetment, beach nourishment, offshore breakwaters were considered but finally a bitumen grouted revetment was deemed to be the preferred solution and work commenced in 1984/85. The 'beach' is composed of a 15cm thick asphalt-concrete layer poured over a sand/cobble fill, ending in a bitumen grouted toe, 0.7m thick at bedrock and 0.5m at the asphalt-concrete junction (see Figures 1.11 and 1.12). The bedrock to seawall base height is 3.0m and the surface is coated with a tar spray plus a veneer of light chipping. Maintenance is cheap and easy and the area is a renowned sunbathing site in the heart of a coastal resort.

Anthropogenic beach typology

Anthropogenic beach typology is described by the BARE system (see Chapter 9).

Figure 1.11 *Porthcawl seafront, Wales, UK with the 'paved' beach*

Figure 1.12 *Close-up of Porthcawl seafront*

Figure 1.13 *Example of a resort beach (associated/managed by an accommodation complex and offering a wide range of services and recreational activities), Croatia*

Resort   There is a lot of controversy over the term 'resort', as resort beaches come in many guises (see Figure 1.13) and various organizations have differing views, for example the Blue Flag's definition (FEE, 2008) is that a resort beach provides:

> varied facilities and provides varied recreation opportunities. It would normally be adjacent to or within easy and reasonable access to the urban community and typically would include a cafe or restaurant, shop, toilets, supervision, first aid and could be reached by public transport.

The USA Blue Wave initiative (www.cleanbeaches.org) defines it as:

> one that has developed its facilities, actively encourages visitors and provides varied recreational opportunities. The beach should be within easy access to commercial development. It would typically include hotels, resorts, restaurants, shops, toilets, public transportation, municipal supervision, first aid facilities, and public phones. Resort beaches also may include beaches in urban settings, such as New York City or Los Angeles beaches. (Chapter 8)

It is a chameleon of a term that means different things to different people and epitomizes Humpty Dumpty's comment that 'words mean whatever

I want them to mean'. Intuitively most people understand the term but definitions are fraught with difficulty.

The BARE technique defines a resort beach as one that has three distinct aspects:

- A beach adjacent to an accommodation complex, where a substantial proportion of beach users are resident.
- Beach management is the responsibility of the above-mentioned complex. This would include beach cleaning, provision of a plethora of recreational facilities – sun-loungers, pedaloes, jet skis, para-sailing, wind surfing, speedboat towing activities (rings, 'banana' water skiing) sailboats and diving – and responsibility for bars/restaurants for beach users. A good example is the Club Med organization that is a privately run hotel/chalet accommodation complex where facilities galore exist. In certain instances, for example all-inclusive resort holidays, the majority of these facilities would be free for residents.
- The bulk of beach users utilizing a resort beach do so mainly for recreational purposes rather than purely leisure activities i.e. swimming/ sunbathing.

If a locality is private (for use by accommodation complex residents, for example Paradise Island, Maldives) or private with an option for day usage payment by non-residents, it is by definition a resort beach. 'Exclusive resorts' generally tend to be private. In theory, most world beaches are open to the public, but in practical terms, several hotels, private apartments/houses/restaurants illegally/semi-illegally lay claim to the beach in front of the dwellings, for example, the Rimini coastal area of Italy. Here establishments pay yearly fares to the local Comini for the surfaces they rent and all establishments should (but not always) allow public access from the gate to the swash zone. Theoretically this is always a public domain for safety and defence reasons. The problem is acute in winter when kilometres of beach are illegally closed by high fences with no gaps, but complex legislation makes enforcement very difficult.

An alternative type of 'resort' beach found in the literature is one attached to a traditional resort bathing area, for example a number of coastal urban sites in the UK such as Skegness, Blackpool and Brighton. These are popular due to a myriad number of recreational activities such as funfairs, arcades and piers, and even donkey/horse rides may be common. Similar, 'resorts' exist in the US, for example Coney Island, New York; in France, for example St Tropez, Biarritz and Deauville; in Brazil, for example Copacabana in Rio de Janeiro; and in South Africa, for example Camps Bay, Muizenberg main beach.

With respect to BARE, unless a locality satisfies the three above points, they are not classed as resort beaches as such, but by their environment. A good example of this is that in Spain there exist several 'resorts' (Residencia de Tiempo Libre) that cater mainly for two categories of residents – the general public and elderly people. They may be associated with bathing areas. Application for holidaying at such 'resorts' (which are generally less expensive than equivalent hotels) is lottery based. There is no connection between the 'resort' and the adjacent beach, which if present, is usually managed by the municipality. Spain also has the impressive 'Lei de Costa', a law that protects public coastal access so effectively as to prevent establishment of privately owned or operated beaches, which is often encountered in other Mediterranean countries. So no 'resort beaches' exist in Spain.

In essence, a resort beach is a self-contained entity that fulfils all recreational needs of beach users to different degrees. The majority of such users would reside at the beach-associated accommodation complex that is integrally linked to the management of the beach. Resort beach users visit largely for recreational (rather than leisure – sunbathing/swimming) purposes. Resort beaches can be private but may be open to the public for day use for a fee.

Urban   Urban areas serve large populations with well-established public services such as primary schools, religious centres, banks, post offices, internet cafes and a well-marked central business district. In the proximity of urban areas can be found commercial activities such as fishing/boating harbours and marinas. Urban beaches are located within or adjacent to the urban area and are *generally* freely open to the public (see Figure 1.14).

Source: Ministry of Education, Spain

Figure 1.14 *Aerial view of an urban beach, adjacent to or fronting an urban area that serves a large population with well-established public services, la Rada, Spain*

Figure 1.15 *A typical village beach located outside the main urban environment and associated with a small but permanent population reflecting access to organized but small-scale community services*

Figure 1.16 *A typical rural beach located outside the urban/village environment, Ramla Bay, Gozo, Malta*

Figure 1.17 *A typical remote beach, largely defined by difficulty of access, Andalucia, Spain*

Village   A village is located outside the main urban environment and associated with a small but permanent population reflecting access to organized but small-scale community services – such as a primary school(s), religious centre(s) and shop(s). The village environment would also include 'tourist villages', mainly utilized in the summer months as well as 'ribbon development' between urban and rural environments. Arguably, it is the most difficult definition of the five bathing area types (see Figure 1.15). Village beaches may be reached by public or private transport.

Rural   A rural area is located outside the urban/village environment. It is not readily accessible by public transport and has virtually no facilities (see Figure 1.16). However in the Mediterranean context, permanent land-based recreational amenities (such as golf courses) and summertime beach-related recreational facilities (for example banana boats and jet skiing typical of resorts) may be found associated with rural bathing areas. Housing in rural areas is limited in number (generally 0–10 but may be more depending on the size of the coastal stretch) and is of a temporary (summer) or permanent (year-long) nature but without permanent community focal centres (religious centre, primary school, shops, cafes, bars). Rural beaches have little or no beachfront development but may have some residential dwellings. They are valued by beach users for their quietness and natural (unspoilt) qualities.

Remote   Remote areas are largely defined by difficulty of access (largely by boat or on foot – a walk of 300m or more). They may be contiguous to or on the fringe of rural areas and, on occasion, village environments but not urban areas (see Figure 1.17). They are not supported by public transport and have very limited (0–5, if any) temporary summer housing. In the Mediterranean, restaurants and second homes may be found in the summer season, occupied by a few people who may live there permanently.

CHAPTER 2

Fundamental Concepts of Beach Management

THEORETICAL CONCEPTS

Simm et al's (1995) beach management definition (see Chapter 1, 'Introduction') addresses social, economic and environmental aspects of beach use, a catholic spectrum of potential conflict. It is concerned with potential financial limitations often encountered in everyday management practices. Alternatively Bird's (1996) definition lays greater emphasis on beach users' needs. The authors' own interpretation of beach management is that it reflects the taking of decisions to undertake or not undertake actions that reflect governing policy objectives and the socio-economic and environmental capabilities of beach areas, which range from urban to remote. These actions can promote the maximum enjoyment of the beach and/or desired coastal protection measures with the minimum of disturbance to the natural environment. The question may be posed: 'What is the right way to manage a beach/coast, or is there a right way?'. This derives from the school of environmental virtue ethics (Cafaro, 2001) and we are of the opinion that there are ways of achieving sound beach management. Management decisions can be loosely classed into 'good' or 'bad', or 'somewhere in between'. Chapter 4 on beach management guidelines and the Case Study section of this book give many examples of these matters.

The global trend of coastal erosion, identified by Kamphius (1980) as active in approximately 95 per cent of world beaches and more modestly in 70 per cent according to Bird (1996), is a global process influencing beach management policy. As a result of sea-level rise, coastlines of the world are drowning, causing untold damage to coastal communities, for example the 53 per cent of the US population living in the coastal zone (Crossett et al, 2004), or the drowning of Pacific islands (Kaluwin and Smith, 1997). In the US, coastal counties account for some 11 per cent of the land yet hold over 25 per cent of the population (USCB, 2002), and between 1900 and 2000 they were the site of over 18 per cent of the nation's economic loss from natural hazards (HVRI, 2004), which poses huge questions regarding coastal vulnerability (Boruff et al, 2008). However, Crowell et al (2007) indicate that most published data on coastal demographics are limited and represent the upper boundaries of coastal population statistics. Changes in sediment availability induced by the Holocene sea-

Figure 2.1 *Marsalforn Bay in Gozo, Malta –*
an example of anthropogenic development common to many
Mediterranean coastlines and those of other regions

level rise as well as the more recent impact of insensitive anthropogenic activity such as construction of seawalls, dwellings and roads on the beach backshore have been the main causes for this global trend in beach erosion. Figure 2.1 reflects such insensitive development at Marsalforn Bay on the Island of Gozo (Malta). Excavation to reconstruct one of the seafront houses unearthed beach sand foundations, suggesting that this area once supported a much larger sand beach/dune system (Micallef, 2002). This is a fairly common phenomenon among coastal areas.

The need to prioritize issues in competing socio-economic and environmental interests is a function of ultimate ICM and beach management objectives, for example the conservation versus recreation debate. Cost justification for effective beach management may be represented by:

1 *Higher financial returns* via:
   – *Increased beach use* – increased opportunities for beach recreational activities and educational purposes resulting from a well laid-out beach space, particularly in urban/resort locations. A well-planned beach layout can provide improved environment-related information and appropriate hazard warning notices where needed

(RNLI, 2005). Enhanced beach access and/or area will result in an increase in the number of beach users, including bathers, fishing enthusiasts and other leisure seekers. In this context, increasing trends of beach-associated tourism represents one of the highest revenue-generating industries and as such, justifies high capital investment necessary for example with beach nourishment. In this context, Houston (1996; 2002) has described how federal tax revenues from foreign tourists who visit Miami beach, Florida, represented over 75 times the federal budget for beach management in Florida, well justifying such investment. An added value of this beach nourishment has been the school educational system that benefits directly from taxes generated by the influx of visitors.

–   *Reduced maintenance/restoration costs* – beach management practice, concerned primarily with prevention of environmental degradation will result in a reduction of maintenance/restoration costs. At Elmer Beach, West Sussex (UK) pre-emptive work carried out in expectation of predicted future impacts from shore stabilization works resulted in a financial saving of otherwise expensive restoration costs. In this instance beach nourishment was carried out in support of construction of eight shore-parallel breakwaters and a downdrift rock groyne along a 2km frontage; subsequent coastal restoration costs were saved due to this pre-emptive work (Cooper et al, 1996).

–   *Improved coastal defence* – beach management has been promoted as improving coastal defence through the provision of a natural buffer for storm impact on the coast. Along the south coast of England, a strategy that effectively anticipated active beach management was to minimize local sediment disruption caused by extreme storm events (Holmes and Beverstock, 1996). The scope of such a strategy was to strengthen coastal defences. In considering the function of beaches as natural coastal protection features, beach management can also be considered as contributing to overall ICM shoreline management plans.

2   *Increased conservation value and socio-economic quality of the surrounding area.* With respect to vegetation cover, beach management can improve several beach attributes, such as those represented by species diversity and aesthetically enhanced beach sediment, layout and access. Morgan et al (1995) carried out beach user opinion and beach rating surveys in a pilot study on the Turkish Aegean coast; those values considered as particularly important and desirable by beach users were recorded. Findings suggested that people visiting different coastal environments had varying expectations and requirements from their leisure surroundings. Of beach users preferring to visit commercialized beaches, a higher priority was placed on those aspects normally associated with good beach management practice, such as the provision of lifeguards, facilities and protection of areas having

high environmental quality. In addition, well-managed beaches have a high positive contribution to the socio-economic and environmental qualities of a coastal stretch and as such represent a sound example of good ICAM practice. The biological function of a coastal area may also be improved through good beach management practice in the form of associated dune management and non-mechanical beach cleaning operations that serve to enhance the diversity of flora and fauna within a beach system (Llewellyn and Shackley, 1996).

3 *High multiplier effect on the socio-economic structure of the beach environment.* Nelson and Williams (1997) discuss the need to better manage beaches in respect of bathing water quality and health implications and argue for a need for more scientifically based water quality criteria, emphasizing the risk of 'intellectual arrogance'. Blakemore et al (2002) studied the economic concepts for indigenous beach user and foreign tourist's perceptions, attitudes and behaviour with regard to their willingness to pay (WTP) at three locations: St George's bay, Malta; Mamaia beach, Romania; and Olu Deniz, Turkey. The amounts calculated via contingent valuation methodology together with their consumer surpluses via the travel cost methodology were found to be similar. WTP values were GB£1.41 for the UK; £1.07 for Turkey and £0.39 for Romania and overwhelmingly the preferred payment was per visit. In general the consumer surplus and WTP of locals were less than those of non-indigenous tourists. Similar results have been recorded elsewhere, for example, Ahmed et al (2006) examine recreational/ conservation benefits of coral reef conservation in the Philippines.

Essential concepts of beach management

Simm et al (1995) identify the essential concepts of beach management as:

- *Sound management philosophy.* This involves working with nature rather than against it. In this context the UK's National Trust organization, which owns over 700 miles (1050km) of coastline, made a binding decision in 2007 to 'let nature rule if possible'. For optimization of beach resources, potential management strategies and the socio-economic value of resources have to be identified. Among the criteria used for justifying beach improvement schemes, the need for enhanced beach space, restoration of lost or eroding beaches and conservation-oriented management schemes should also be considered.
- *An understanding of coastal processes.* This includes knowledge of, for example, the early Tanner ABC model and its derivatives (involving sources, transport pathways and sinks), sediment budgets and cells, which have important repercussions not only regarding erosion/ deposition processes but also litter (Tanner, 1976).

- *Data collection and establishment of baseline criteria followed by long-term monitoring.* Monitoring should be considered an essential component of data collection and serve the purpose of accumulating a time series database to facilitate management plan evaluation and identify possible trends and beach changes. A monitoring programme should highlight important baseline survey findings and be of sufficient duration (particularly in beach environments) to identify potential seasonal, annual or multi-annual changes and trends. For example, Phillips (2007) showed through the collection of data spanning more than ten years that erosion of Penarth Beach in Wales was an unexpected result of a three-year wind shift, rather than the more commonly perceived culprit of dredging activities. The problem here is who pays for the monitoring?
- *Use of expert personnel and appropriate techniques* (see Chapter 7 and the Case Study section).
- *Provision of legislation and, more importantly, enforcement mechanisms* for the establishment of environment-related standards and objectives and definition of the roles of different government bodies and their responsibilities. For example, UK local authorities were empowered in 1996 through the Dogs (Fouling of Land) Act to designate land (including beach) areas in which unremoved dog litter became a fineable offence (with a maximum fine of £1000). More importantly, local authorities were also given power to employ authorized officers who could issue these penalties (Williams and Tudor, 2006).

To these critical organization problems may be added: resource decisions that in the past have been made primarily on the basis of economic considerations to the exclusion of ecological considerations and with a lack of coordination among public agencies; insufficient databases and lack of information for decision making. This involves short- rather than long-range planning, little public participation and poorly educated management, confusing laws and goals, and a lack of public funding.

While the suggestion of a 'sound management philosophy' may appear as a fairly obvious strategy, this has not always been the practice and many past human coastal interventions have been carried out in a manner opposing natural processes with the consequence of, for example, exacerbating beach erosion. Examples of this may be seen on coasts across the world in the form of extensive groyne and seawall constructions (Ergin and Balas, 2002; 2006). With application of environmentally sound management, optimum use of beach resources may be achieved within their scope for providing coastal defence, recreation and/or environmental conservation. In criteria determination justifying beach improvement schemes, high priority should also be given to the identification of beach user preferences and priorities, reflecting a social consideration in the management of natural resources (Williams and Morgan, 1995; Leatherman, 1997).

An example of sound management philosophy has been described by Breton and Esteban (1995) and Breton (1998). Environmentally sensitive beach management works carried out in Catalonia, Spain, were shown to enhance regeneration of previously degraded dune systems, partly due to increased vegetation cover of the backshore beach area. The case study referred to a 1.5km length of coast where, in 1988, the local council of El Prat implemented a beach management project, which had as a main objective the integration of public beach use with conservation considerations related to the area's flora and fauna (see Case Study 11). Of actions implemented by the beach management plan, area designation as a preservation site was one of the initial steps in securing better protection for the site. Access was seasonally controlled in conjunction with the use of designated pathways so as to reduce trampling damage. Litter collection by hand was employed to replace mechanical beach cleaning. Some of the more sensitive backshore areas were left without access while other less sensitive areas had regulated access imposed, information signs and managed pathways. A public educational campaign was employed to indicate habitat value, and the benefits accrued by this approach are presented in Box 2.1.

Box 2.1 *Benefits of the beach management strategy in Catalonia*

Benefits are:

- establishment of native flora following decreased human disturbance;
- better representation of natural plant distribution typical of this part of the coast;
- reconstruction of dune systems as a by-product of increased vegetation cover;
- contribution to a community-based management approach through the involvement of the public in litter collection;
- academic value from data recorded on the ability of 'sand-loving' plants to adapt to low water, high temperature and substrate mobility and poor soil conditions;
- opportunities to utilize this area for educational purposes for both academic users and the general public;
- data generation for use in future beach management and rehabilitation programmes;
- development of a beach management strategy utilizing low levels of human and financial resources.

Souce: adapted from Breton (1998)

The case study presented by Breton and Esteban (1995) is a particularly good example of sound beach management practice that considered both socio-economic as well as environmental interests related to beach use. Of particular note is that through the application of sound management, the previously defined objective of integrating beach use with environmental considerations was clearly achieved. However, Ariza et al (2008a) have pointed out that the main concern on the Catalan coast appears to be erosion-induced problems, and as three different administrations have different jurisdictional powers over a narrow strip of land, the end results have produced very complex administrative schemes.

Many of the principles used by the management plan are reflected in beach management guidelines proposed by Micallef (1996) and Williams and Davies (1999). Sound beach management intervention schemes (which change in scale of application from site to site according to specific needs) are represented by longshore sediment recycling, profile regrading, maintenance of natural physical features, improvement of the beach amenity value and monitoring of environmental criteria, and identification of user preferences and priorities. An example of extensive beach profile regrading is work that took place in the mid-1990s on the coast off Barcelona, Spain (Morgan et al, 1996). In this instance, artificially constructed steep beach slopes arising from previous coarse sediment nourishment works were considered dangerous for children's swimming and were regraded to improve safety considerations.

In addressing sediment transport pathways, local geology, climate change and sea-level rise, coastal protection structures and any form of sediment removal or interruption activity must be considered. In this connection, longshore sediment transport, the net effect of which is responsible for long-term beach changes and cross-shore sediment transport, which normally acts in the shorter term (such as tidal and storm events) but which can also lead to long-term beach erosion, are the main sediment transport mechanisms involved. Other essential elements in the understanding of coastal sediment transport processes are identification and quantification of sediment sources and sinks, sediment budgets and sediment cells. In England and Wales, a national shoreline management plan (SMP) is based on 11 main sediment cells identified in the early 1990s by Motyka and Brampton (1993). A sediment cell has been defined as 'a length of coastline which is relatively self-contained as far as the movement of sand or shingle is concerned and where interruption to such movement should not have a significant effect on adjacent sediment cells' (MAFF, 1995: 1).

An SMP (see detailed discussion below) is a strategy plan that sets out a coastal defence strategy for a specified coastal length taking cognizance of both natural and human activities, essentially: coastal processes and defences; land use and the built environment; the natural environment, especially in the UK with respect to special protected areas (SPAs) and special areas of conservation (SAC). Their length is usually controlled by a natural boundary such as a prominent headland. In Europe, the EUROSION project running from 2002 to 2004 concerned itself with pilot projects for erosion management and identified the potential of strategic environmental assessment (SEA) to incorporate key erosion concerns, particularly for small-scale developments that are frequently overlooked. SEA, as part of the environmental policy initiated by the European Commission, effectively integrates coastal erosion concerns on coastal planning processes and addresses the cumulative impacts of developments, notably with regard to political influences that often influence management decisions (EC, 2001). Finkl and Kruempfel (2005) are adamant that recognition of the socio-economic consequences of strategic decision making is crucial. SEA emphasizes early identification and prevention of development plans that could have an adverse coastal impact and it came into force in July 2004. In common with other European edicts (for example the Water Framework Directive, 2000, and the EU National Conservation Policy – Birds Directive in 1979 and the 1992 Habitat Directive that created the European ecological network of SAC called NATURA 2000, which integrated nature protection into EU policies) and CAM initiatives, it is broad-based in its approach and forms part of the main building blocks regarding ICAM, the umbrella under which beach management should take place. SEA is a regulatory requirement for development in many countries.

While it is recommended that SMPs should address entire cells, often boundaries of major sediment cells, normally representing large estuaries or prominent headlands include a number of smaller sub-cells that could be more practical for the application of shoreline (or in this case) beach management plans. Cooper and Pethick (2005) demonstrate this approach to addressing erosion problems in the Channel Islands, but Cooper and Pontee (2006) point out some limitations of this approach, especially where influenced by estuarine processes, the different transport processes associated with grain size, and the spatial and temporal nature of sediment transport processes. The viewpoint has implications regarding coastal defence and van Vuren et al (2004) have shown how this in turn has many sociological consequences.

Sound beach management is largely dependent on the availability of baseline data concerning the beach system and associated cliff and dune environments and on erosion processes and sediment sinks influencing beach sediments. Data on beach processes serve to identify trends, their implications and origin, and provide a basis on which to design beach management plans, subsequent evaluation and possible redesign of strategy.

Therefore sound beach management practice necessitates the collection of data on:

- physical aspects, represented by beach attributes, profiles and sediment characteristics, geo-technical data, nearshore and offshore sediment, wave and current characteristics, tides and tidal currents and local wind regime;

- environmental aspects identified as beach flora, fauna and water/sediment quality criteria;
- socio-economic aspects including beach user preferences and priorities, economic evaluation of beach resources and WTP.

Although the recommendation by Simm et al (1995) to apply appropriate techniques and personnel as sound management practice may seem at first glance as self-evident, it is well founded on past mismanagement practice. This subject is discussed by Williams et al (2002a) who describe the use of an inappropriate water-jetting scheme to address the problem of cliff erosion at Southerndown beach, South Wales in the UK. The project was instigated as a consequence of loose rocks causing injury to beach users. Coastal cliff recession was around 8cm per annum but as a result of the pilot £10,000 water-jetting scheme, the erosion rate was tripled. As well as removing loose blocks, the water jet removed soil and vegetation that previously contributed to cliff stability. On the same subject, Ozhan (1996) noted that a basic tenet of good beach management practice is that it is dependent on expertise and local knowledge. Once a problem has arisen, a beach manager should clearly identify its source and determine the natural processes influencing it. If it is not possible to mitigate the problem source then it is necessary to identify potential solutions, appraise options based on a number of socio-economic and environmental criteria and select the preferred option. In management of an existing or planned artificial beach for example, it is also important to be able to predict (using physical scale and/or numerical empirical simulation models) the likely long-term changes of the beach in question (HR Wallingford, 2000; Balas and Tunaboylu, 2007). These changes should be predicted not only in response to potential extreme events (storm or sea-level rise) but also to normally occurring coastal processes and seasonal (winter/summer) forcing.

Numerical empirical/physical simulation models play an important role in the development of management plans and understanding of the natural processes addressed by such plans. These models allow analysis of existing data in an extensive manner thereby adding considerably to the value of often limited data (Aagaard and Greenwood, 1995; Balas et al, 2004; Tian-Jian Hsu et al, 2006; Balas and Tunaboylu, 2007; Li et al, 2007). Sediment transport numerical models may be used to define and quantify nearshore sediment transport by evaluating hydrodynamical forces (primarily waves and currents) in association with known seabed characteristics. In Malta this was clearly demonstrated by Hydraulic Research Wallingford (HR Wallingford, 2000) in their simulation of beach sediment movement related to a planned nourishment exercise (Micallef and Cassar, 2001). Knowledge of these techniques, however, is usually beyond the remit of any beach manager.

LEGISLATIVE ASPECTS OF BEACH MANAGEMENT

With respect to legislative and enforcement mechanisms necessary for sound management, both common law and statutory legislation influence the application of beach management regulations (WHO, 2000). In the case of common law, the concept of 'duty of care' is applicable to many countries where liability and negligence may be attributed to infringement by either private operators or members of the public. In this instance the responsibility involves 'acting with reasonable care' and as applied to beach management safety, the onus of responsibility lies with the operator (see Chapter 6). The operator is therefore held responsible for bringing to the attention of the general public any hazards or dangerous practices related to beach use.

Examples of this were identified in Malta at Ghajn Tuffieha Bay where a local NGO used information boards to provide information to the public on potentially dangerous rip currents. Similarly, activities performed by the public are subject to the same legal concept and would be deemed liable if not considered as acting with reasonable care. The other main body of legislation influencing beach management is that encompassing statutory law, which is often much more comprehensive and deals with:

- health and safety at work;
- public health;
- rights of the disabled;
- navigation for pleasure and commercial craft;
- aquatic sports;
- fishing activities;
- concession of land belonging to the state;
- trade activities on public land.

In the context of this legislation it may therefore be seen that not only are beach users and related recreational activities subject to statutory Law, but so are marine activities that may in any way impinge on the beach or public using that beach.

A literature search on existing coast-related legislation shows that in many countries local authorities are empowered to make by-laws relating to public bathing and beach management. Examples can be found in the UK where district councils (rather than the county councils) have responsibilities that include local plans, environmental health and coast protection (see Case Study 4). In Australia, local councils have direct responsibilities for generation of coastal management plans, coastline hazard mitigation, hazard awareness and beach management, while in the US, the Coastal Zone Management Act of 1972 allows all 35 coastal states to devise their own CZM programmes for submission to the Office of CZM for evaluation and approval (US National Research Council, 1990). In the Mediterranean, French law dealing with the coastal area (*loi littorale*) states that every modification of the form, landscape or use of the coastal area depends on the state that has the responsibility of managing such coasts. In this context, the *loi littorale* of 1976 states that:

- the mayor of a coastal town or village is responsible for and has to take decisions about the inland area but not coastal waters;
- for the seabed and as far as the boundary of the territorial waters, the Commissionaire de la Republique is responsible;
- all forms of sea transport are the responsibility of the admiralty.

In Italy, by contrast the Ministry for Public Works is responsible for the authorization of any maritime-related development proposed by local councils (Bartoletti et al, 1995). In Turkey, beach management falls under the influence of the Shore Law (1990) and responsibility for enforcement is given to municipalities in urban areas and to provincial governors in rural areas (Eke, 1997; Ozhan et al, 1993; 2005). On the Island of Malta, beach management is regulated by aspects of the Environment Protection Act 1991, the Development Planning Act 1992 and more specifically by the Sand Preservation Act 1949. As in other countries, local councils are able to pass by-laws regarding shore use under their jurisdiction.

This legislative review clearly demonstrates that given the appropriate resources, local authorities are empowered to play a very important role in facilitating beach management by ensuring the availability of all necessary legislative, regulatory and implementation mechanisms for effective beach management. However, it should be noted that a common problem identified by many authors concerns the frequent lack of coordination between authorities involved in coastal management issues that results in a fragmented application of regulations over what is intrinsically a continuous shoreline.

To reiterate, beach management plans should be considered as part of, or implemented in line with, other coast-related management plans such as national structure and local area plans and coastal zone, shoreline and catchment management plans, which are implemented in many countries. Beach management plans may also be related to the management of specific conservation or designated areas. It is important to note that all coastal-related plans can potentially influence or interact with a beach management plan for the same coast.

While beaches are generally considered to be public areas there are many instances of privatization (extensive on the coasts of the US), either arising from titular ownership or (more commonly) through illegal erection of barriers preventing public access (Bird, 1996). This is still a problem in some countries. Though less frequent, similar conditions may also be found in Italy and France where coastal zone and shoreline management issues reached the political agenda only after the building boom of the 1960s and 1970s that scrambled to meet the rising demand for coastal development as a result of increasing world tourism (Goldberg, 1994).

Due mainly to the physical influence of a large oceanic swell and high tidal regimes, beach management in Europe is principally seen as a means of coastal protection and defence against erosion and flooding. In the UK, this responsibility is borne by local district councils under directives from the Department for Environmental, Food and Rural Affairs (DEFRA). In contrast, the Mediterranean has a much-reduced tidal range and a much higher demand for coastal tourism. Consequently, in this region, beach management is much more likely to reflect a desire to enhance tourism or local recreational potential of an area as directed by ministries for tourism and related planning/maritime authorities. In a more complex manner, beach management in regions such as the Caribbean has to address both high tourism pressure and pressing coastal protection needs from recurrent hurricane events.

Multiple purpose beach use in the form of tourism, conservation, boat berthing/fishing and land filling can result in a number of conflicts such as:

- Conflict with nature and natural processes that arise when develop-ment takes place too near or on the beach or a component of it, such as construction on or removal of sand from beach and dune systems. Examples of such practice were common at the global level up to a decade ago ranging from, for example, sand removal from the Welsh coast (Merthyr Mawr) prior to being banned in the 1970s, to coastal overdevelopment in Faro, Portugal (Morgan et al, 1996). This type of conflict will often result in beach erosion and migration of sand into human habitation areas. An excellent example of this has been described by Mannoni and Pranzini (2004) who showed that a change in occupation from agriculture to tourism caused beach erosion in Italian regions. They studied two pocket beaches on the island of Elba. At Procchio, shoreline retreat was 12m between 1940 and 1997; at Lacuna beach it was 11m. During the same period, crops that used to cover 25 per cent of the Lacuna basin area were reduced to 10 per cent. At Procchio the figures were 28 per cent and 2 per cent. Reduction of crop areas meant an increase in forest and shrubs, so that land use was less prone to soil erosion, thereby reducing sediment input that in turn caused beach erosion. This is deemed irreversible as tourism is a relatively easy means of making a living.
- Coastal degradation resulting from deposition of building rubble at the coast. This practice decreases the aesthetic value of an area and is likely to change the sediment characteristics of beach systems.
- Conflict can also result from bad or misinformed management practice, which is often the case when human interference is above the desired level. Llewellyn and Shackley (1996) describe such a case where mechanical beach cleaning at Swansea Bay, Port Eynon and Pembrey in Wales resulted in the decimation of animal (invertebrate) populations. Indiscriminate use of beach cleaning equipment and compaction

of beach face resulting in loss of local ecology and increased beach erosion are also discussed by Breton and Esteban (1995), who describe the management plan for beach restoration on the Llobregat Delta in southern Spain. Bad or poor beach management can in itself lead to consequences that will in turn require further human intervention. Numerous examples of mismanagement exist in many countries, with some having particularly large-scale negative repercussions. In the Mediterranean, Nir (2004) describes large-scale beach erosion along the Israeli coast, resulting from pre-1964 exploitation of beach sand for construction purposes, the impact of which was still visible over 40 years later. The damming of the Nile in Egypt resulted in coastal/beach erosion along the Egyptian delta and adjacent countries, as well as the collapse of the sardine fishing industry in the region (Jernelov, 1990).

Apart from the beach itself, the backshore, which is often instrumental in determining the health of the beach, is also susceptible to inherent danger of encroachment from urban, suburban, commercial and industrial development. It is unfortunate but true that such activity is invited and fuelled by the very attraction of an unspoilt natural beach setting in the first place, i.e. 'the killing of the goose that lays the golden egg'! Examples of backshore despoliation can be seen along large sections of the Costa del Sol in Spain. These occurred in the 1970s and 1980s as a result of short-sighted (and possibly uninformed) national tourism and development plans. However, as a result of increased awareness and understanding of coastal processes and a realization that degraded environments lead to reduced tourism, present-day actions at the coast are beginning to lend themselves to adapting to and supplementing natural coastal processes. It is through such policy changes that sustainable coastal/beach management may be achieved. One of the first concerted national efforts at integrated coastal management in the Mediterranean was the Spanish Coastal Act (22/1988) (Costa de Ley), introduced following large-scale mismanagement on the Spanish coast. The Public Maritime – Terrestrial Domain Coastal Act defined:

- a strip of land parallel to the coast (*zona de servidumbre de transito*) devoted to the transit of persons extending 6–20m landward from the coastline, depending on coastal features;
- a zone of total protection (*zona de servidumbre*) extending landward from the coastline by 20–100m. In this area it is not possible to build any kind of construction;
- an influence zone (planning/building in this area regulated by local authorities) extending 500m inland from the coastline.

In other words, the sequence going landward from the coastline is a transit-devoted area, a zone of total protection and an influence zone.

On the understanding that both erosion and accretion phenomena influence the area addressed by beach management, Bird (1996) states that the landward boundary of the area addressed by a beach manager may or may not include parts of the backshore. Seaward boundaries will always include (in theory) the nearshore area up to depth of closure. In practice, however, the extent of management coverage is often determined by the technical and human resources available to a beach manager.

Effective beach management should serve to facilitate resource management in a manner that is able to cater for socio-economic and environmental interests as part of an overall long-term coastal area management approach determined by policy-makers' goals and priorities. While the foundation of beach management guidelines is based on a complete understanding of coastal processes supported by data collection and analysis, formulation of beach management guidelines must also consider the ability to cater for different interests and needs, and changing priorities and attitudes reflected by policy-makers and beach users.

Effective beach management must therefore include a better understanding of local and regional geology and geomorphology and its influence on beaches, which as mentioned in Chapter 1, includes aspects of sediment origin, sources and beach loss as well as a comprehension of the forces driving beach erosion and deposition represented by winds, tides and currents. The large variety of beach management issues shown in Figure 2.2 also reflects the potentially complex interaction with the surrounding wider coastal environment. The interrelationships between the physical aspects, socio-economic criteria and biological content of beach systems and their wider surrounding coastal area must also be considered by beach management.

STRATEGIC MANAGEMENT

A vacuum seemingly exists with respect to beach management theory. Current management is essentially practical, and problem solving has to possess clearly defined dimensions and limits. Five primarily beach-dimensional elements exist: substantive (including factors such as whether something being done should be stopped/modified/introduced); spatial (for example assessment of boundary problems); temporal (whether the problem is long or short term); quantitative (whether there is a single or multiple cause); and qualitative (which looks to instigate a philosophy of worth and values).

Effective beach management must cover a wide variety of beach types (see Chapter 1, 'Typology', page 13; Chapter 9, 'The Bathing Area Registration and Evaluation System', page 192; and Chapter 9, Annex 1, 'The Bathing Area Registration and Evaluation Form', page 202), all of which require different sets of skills. Usually, retroactive management is a result of cultural action within the physical environment, i.e. it is people

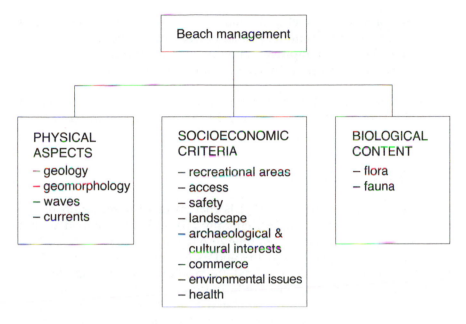

Source: adapted from MAFF (1995)

Figure 2.2 *Breakdown of beach management aspects*

oriented, but processes such as storms, tsunamis and hurricanes can exact a large toll on the beach physique.

The goals for most beach managers should be:

- to assess the causes of any beach degradation/accumulation tendencies (Nordstrom et al, 2004);
- to bring the ideas of local communities and other concerned agencies into management plans, together with practical involvement i.e. the 'adopt a beach' idea as advocated by the Green Seas Campaign (see Chapter 8);
- to devise a comprehensive package of practical proposals regarding the above;
- to ensure long-term monitoring;
- to make sure that plans fit into any national/international directive frameworks. For example, the UK Heritage Coast philosophy for 45 different coastal zones all follow the same aim, but each area is left to decide how best to achieve these aims (Williams et al, 2002a):
    - to conserve scenic quality and foster leisure activities that rely on natural scenery and not on man-made activities, and provide for the sustainable usage of the coast for public enjoyment and recreation;

- to conserve, protect and enhance the coastal environment and foster awareness and understanding of conservation;
- to maintain and improve community involvement;
- to identify the finest stretches of undeveloped coast.

A theoretical structure for understanding landscapes development, based on the ideas of Sauer (1963) is shown in the equation (in the context of beaches, it can be represented as Figure 2.3):

$$L_n = \sum_{t_0}^{t_p} f\,(G,\,V,\,C,\,U \text{ or } X)_t$$

where the present landscape (L_n) is the result of summation of the geognostic (G), vegetation (V), climatic (C) and unexplained or not understood (U or X) factors from time zero (t_0) to time (t_p) .

It is not easy to quantify/qualify and assess objectively several of the parameters in this formula. If solved, the result would be a high level of landscape understanding that could underpin the beach management process. A structured approach related to analysis, planning, implementation and control is the basis of many classic models of management strategy. However, Barwise (1996) suggests that many managers tend to be strongly oriented to action rather than reflective activities, as they needed to be adaptable, innovative and able to work as a team having the ability to learn from events. Successful strategies do evolve with time and Mintzberg (1994), in a memorable paper, shows that while planning strategy is associated with conscious prior intention, it can also have hidden agendas.

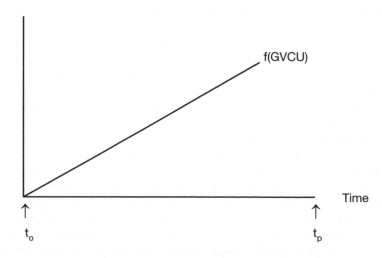

Figure 2.3 *Development of the natural beach landscape L_n*

Figure 2.4 summarizes Mintzberg's (1994) view. He emphasizes that any realized management strategy is a combination of strategies that could be deliberate (i.e. intended) and/or emergent (i.e. related to events that were not originally part of the intended strategy). This frequently involves crisis management – a high risk/cost strategy, which should be avoided by anticipation and nipping a crisis in the bud before it grows.

In essence, strategic management is a direction-setting exercise that leads to a structured approach to address management problems. Johnson and Scholes (1988) have described strategic management as involving:

- *analysis,* where one tries to understand the system's content, the existing management philosophy and aims, if any, and decide what action, if any, to take;
- *choice* of the different courses of action available;
- *implementation,* where whatever option is chosen, is put into effect. It is in this area that the largest problems appear to exist (van der Meulen, 2005).

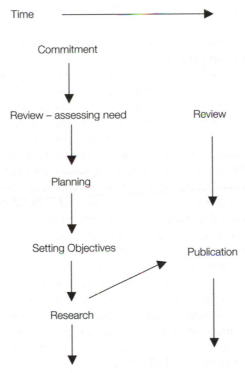

Source: adapted from Mintzberg (1994)

Figure 2.4 *A beach management strategy*

Mintzberg and Waters (1989) described four main types of strategic planning approaches available to an environmental manager:

1   *Deliberate planning*, which can be used in environments that are understood and that can therefore be controlled by the manager. For example, the creation of an artificial slope in a simple and predictable coastal geological setting, such as beach slope regrading (Bennett et al, 2003). This type of planning gives rise to proactive management – the most desirable sort of management. An example of this was the transfer of monies from the UK Treasury Department to local authorities as a consequence of the introduction of the Local Government Act (2003) relating to fixed penalty notices for littering and dog fouling.
2   *Imposed planning*, where appropriate responses are made to change. This is more often the case due to uncertainty in the knowledge of many environmental processes resulting in poor prediction capabilities. Imposed planning may also be utilized with systems that are predictable but where management action is nonetheless responsive rather than proactive, either due to policy or in the absence of effective management plans, for example stabilization of a rock slope or shore platform.
3   *Umbrella-type planning*, relating mainly to systems that contain uncontrollable and unpredictable elements. An example could be an attempt to stabilize a large-scale natural coastal slope in a complex geological setting by installing drainage systems to reduce pore water pressures and increase shear strength, and/or building containing structures at boundaries of slope failure. At the coast, this technique has been used to stabilize otherwise erosion-prone shore slopes (see for example Davos, 2000). The effectiveness of this approach depends upon a number of factors such as the accuracy of subsurface data on soil/rock mechanics structures, knowledge of mechanism of movement, scale of investment in structures and future intensity of rainfall events. In this instance, only general guidelines can be set, such as the definition of boundaries within which environmental processes may be influenced by management actions. With this form of planning, a delicate balance between proactive and reactive management is required.
4   *Emergent planning* is one used in more complex and unstable environments on which very limited data is known and where environmental processes are poorly understood (Kahn and Gowdy, 2000). A good example of this type of planning is represented by the reactive responses to the devastation imposed by catastrophic tsunamis (see for example Yalciner et al, 2005; Yalciner and Synolakis, 2007).

Short-term immediate responses include clearance and evacuation while longer-term planning would refer to stricter planning (zonation) of land use. In the Boxing Day tsunami of 2004, mangroves and coral areas suffered much less damage than areas where these had been removed, usually for hotel/recreational development purposes (Yalciner and Synolakis, 2007). The success of this strategy will be affected by a number of limitations, i.e. in the understanding of natural phenomena such as rock-fall mechanisms, the effect of possible climate change/global warming, and economic pressures of tourism that relate to carrying capacity problems (Pereira da Silva, 2002; McCool and Lime, 2003). Such planning is totally reactive in character.

The type of planning adopted from the possibilities described by Mintzberg and Waters (1989) is obviously very much dependent on availability of clear objectives, quality data and process comprehension, related to the environment addressed.

Johnson and Scholes (1988) and Williams and Davies (1999) identify problems encountered with environmental/beach management as:

- Changing objectives and/or environment arising from strategic drift, for example opening limited access to previously strictly controlled sites. Nir (2004) shows that Israel had lost some 33 per cent of the Israeli sand reserves to construction exploitation. Prior to 1964, more than 12 million cubic metres were removed, necessitating a government law that caused total cessation of this activity.
- Problems of goal diversity, informational quality, limited expertise and experience, and psychology of the manager. These can lead to irrational or wrong decisions. At Colhuw beach in the UK a revetment was constructed across a recreational beach in order to protect a café and lifeguard station. It was a wrong decision and construction was eventually halted by the Welsh Office (Williams et al, 2002a).
- Environmental qualitative variables that produce disagreement regarding acceptable standards, for example on water quality criteria and sampling strategy, and impede logical decision making, i.e. the debate on EC 76/160 regarding bathing water quality that 31 years later resulted in a proposed revision enshrined in the CEC (2006) directive, where compliance to the new directive is envisioned for 2015.

New data and knowledge, for example generated by new expertise and data sets can dispute the basis of existing policies, which may therefore change. For example, many European dune systems are now changing into pastures and there is a trend among dune researchers to move away from planting marram (*Ammophila arenaria* in the European context) to actually bulldozing portions of the dune in order to have a mobile sand supply, as dunes need fresh sand in order to thrive. Geelen et al (1985) demonstrate how two stabilized parabolic dunes near Zandvoort in The Netherlands were reactivated by removal of vegetation and humic topsoil in order to restore blowouts.

Quinn (1980) argues that managers often adjust policy via a learning process termed 'logical incrementalism' – a learning and adjustment sequence by which policy is synonymous with environmental change. This assumes a tension between the environment and reality of management practice due to non-objective management viewpoints. Strategic management is here considered to involve the following:

- *Analysis* – this would address the existing situation, identify problems and determine the desired results.
- *Planning* – the planning step would consider where and how change could be implemented, together with what techniques should be utilized and what planning strategy to use.
- *Management* – at this level, decisions taken during the planning phase would be implemented. Action would also be taken to ensure completion of the adopted action plan.
- *Monitoring* – the final phase must consider how best to monitor the environment, and results and progress achieved by the management plan, through the setting of milestones and comparison with baseline data.

Many of these components are generally absent from standard management practice. As a consequence and in view of their importance to a structured development of strategic management, these principles have been applied in the development of the Bathing Area Management Model (Micallef, 2002) (see Chapter 3, 'The Bathing Area Management Model', page 77).

MANAGEMENT OF LOW-LYING ROCKY SHORES

Apart for a few specialized manuals that focus on aspects of engineering (Shore Protection Manual, 1984; Simm, 1996) or for example on monitoring of bathing waters (WHO, 2000) very little research work has *specifically* addressed management needs of beaches and related recreational areas. While recent textbooks address a plethora of coast-related subjects such as catchment, estuarine, coastal and shoreline management plans, none have been identified that address beach management in a specific or comprehensive manner. In this regard, while beach management is given scant attention, the management of low-lying rocky shores appears to be given even less attention.

In coastal recreation, the generally more extensive and accessible low-lying rocky coastlines, compared to that area occupied by sand beaches, would suggest that management needs for such coasts are greater. In reality, the more popular beaches result in a greater human presence and related impact, justifying concern over limited beach resources (Mastronuzzi et al, 1992; Morgan and Micallef, 1999). Rocky coasts are nonetheless subject to increased land-use conflict due to increasing trends in coastal urbanization and vacationing at coastal resorts. For example, in Italy the coastal population density has increased from 297 individuals per km^2 in 1951 to 402 individuals per km^2 in 1989, while 30 per cent of the

Italian coast is eroding (Cipriani et al, 2004). In addition, this population density is augmented by 14 million visitors during the peak holiday season (Marson, 1994). Despite this global trend, management of low-lying rocky shores is virtually unaddressed.

Scientific researchers' lack of consideration of management needs for these shores is reflected by a literature survey (1990–2002) of coast-related research presented in scientific journals and at international conferences addressing coastal management issues. Of 902 research works, only 0.33 per cent (3) were identified as specifically addressing management aspects of low-lying rocky coasts (Micallef, 2002). In comparison, 9.8 per cent (88) dealt with beach-related issues, while 6.2 per cent (56) were concerned with bathing water quality. In the UK, indirect reference to low-lying rocky coasts was identified in studies concerning shoreline management plans but these dealt largely with coastal defence strategies and the protection of wildlife habitats such as wetlands.

Due to what appears to be a preconceived idea that bathing and vacationing in general occurs only in connection with beaches, most field research has been specifically oriented to beaches and related environments. This is clearly illustrated by research addressing bathing water quality and litter that has been largely related to beach use but that may be equally applicable to low-lying rocky shores used for recreational purposes (Kay et al, 1990; Pike, 1994; 1997; Rees, 1997; Williams and Davies, 1999). Other aspects of coastal studies are similarly oriented, as for example in-depth studies on economic valuation of the coastline (Edwards, 1987; Dharmaratne and Braithwaite, 1994; Blakemore and Williams, 2008) that refer either solely to beach valuation or to beaches in conjunction with other resources such as water quality and tourism in general. Coastal erosion works have also largely focused on beach studies and to a lesser extent on cliff recession with the only work related to low-lying rocky shores indirectly addressed in works investigating shore platform development (Trenhaile, 1987; Sunamura, 1992). General studies on integrated coastal management were also identified as failing to sufficiently consider recreational aspects of low-lying rocky shores. At the Mediterranean regional level for example, UNEP guidelines on Integrated Management of Coastal and Marine Areas (UNEP, 1995) make general recommendations with some specific reference to sandy beaches and cliffs but completely omit reference to accessible rocky shores.

Various national legislation cover general land-use issues that may be perceived as having specific relevance to low-lying rocky shores. The Lei de Costas of 1988 of Spain, for example, refers to rights of public passage over a 6m wide strip adjacent to the shoreline and to specified development that can take place in the first 100m inland from the shore (Montoya, 1990). However no specific reference is made to recreation-related management of accessible shores. Similarly, in Italy, national coastal management policy includes reference to rocky coasts but aspects of recreational use are not addressed. This is reflected by the description given by Marson (1994) of the objectives of the section of the Italian 'National Plan for the Defence of the Sea and Coastal Areas' dealing specifically with shoreline and maritime aspects. This plan addressed promotion of research on coastal erosion, environmental protection works and restoration of sediment equilibrium to disrupted shorelines but omits reference to management issues concerning recreational use of accessible rocky shorelines. Some government agencies were entrusted with its implementation, but very little use was made of its ideals and philosophy and its aims were never realized.

SHORELINE MANAGEMENT PLANS

Of the coastal management plans currently in use, SMPs are very applicable to the broad-brush integrated management approach of coastal zones and in particular low-lying rocky shores. They are a major ICM tool and as such exert an influence on beach management. In the UK, the Ministry for Agriculture, Food and Fisheries and Welsh Office (MAFF/Welsh Office, 1993) publication was the initiating document for SMPs, which are high-level, non-statutory documents. They represent large-scale assessments of the risks associated with coastal evolution in both cultural and natural environments. Essentially, they are planning process guidance documents that identify constraints to coastal dynamics and with respect to this, identify potential areas at risk together with the consequences associated with decisions producing differing future scenarios, especially in the realm of coastal engineering. In the past decade, studies such as 'Futurecoast' (DEFRA, 2002a) and 'Foresight' (DEFRA, 2004) and legislative changes have paved the way for initiation of a second generation of SMPs (DEFRA, 2006).

Early plans were developed as a planned framework for decision making and management of coastal defences, using historical and recent evidence of recurrent flooding events and trends of erosion. The aim was to arrive at a sustainable defence policy within each sediment cell and to set objectives for future management. The need for such plans grew with increased frequency of extreme storm event phenomena and a more widespread (and often permanent) urban and industrial settlement at the coast. Purnell (1995) initially reviewed the national objectives and implementation of shoreline management plans, and this in turn was followed by MAFF (2000).

In the case of the UK, Powell and Brampton (1995) reflect that strategic development of SMPs in southern England necessitated a clear understanding of the forcing processes active in particular sediment cells and as such offered an important opportunity to model such processes at regional level. Ash et al (1995), Pos et al (1995) and Holmes and Beverstock (1996) also review case studies for SMP development for the north Norfolk coast, Lizard Point to Land's End (southwest coast of Cornwall) and Lancing and Shoreham (all in the UK), respectively. In the last of these, the plan was seen to have additional value in raising and maintaining public awareness of the need for sea defence measures, the options available and the development of a management strategy in an area with a long history of erosion. Such case studies are instrumental in highlighting important findings that reveal the benefits of SMPs to the overall coastal management process.

Although such case studies do not address the recreational potential of low-lying rock shores, SMPs have been shown to benefit the overall coastal management process and ultimately beach management through:

- increasing the possibility for coastal defence authorities to work closer with environmental organizations;
- maintaining wildlife habitats through management of coastal defence strategies;
- provision of an opportunity for data collection, therefore improving the possibility of process modelling and consequently more realistic predictions of future coastal development;
- development of management plans at regional or coastal sediment cell level, allowing a better understanding of coastal resources through the identification of their distribution and abundance, and establishment of priorities for habitat conservation;
- increasing the possibility of resolving conflict mainly arising between coastal protection and environmental conservation and coastal defence strategies and landownership requirements;
- enabling authorities to bring together diverse parties operating at the coast and to develop an integrated management approach to shoreline management;
- increasing the potential for community consensus and involvement through the process of integrating diverse coastal management initiatives that is essential for effective management. In this respect, Williams et al (1992) carried out psychological profile analysis of beach and dune users in South Wales in an attempt to distinguish and therefore better understand the different coastal visitor groups and their make-up;
- implementing questionnaire surveys (Morgan et al, 1995; Morgan and Williams, 1995; Morgan and Micallef, 1999) that are particularly valuable in subsequent application of community-based management schemes since they are able to reflect user perceptions and priorities;
- providing a framework for development or improvement of other coast-related management plans such as coastal area management plans (CAMPs), local plans, estuarine and catchment management plans (CMPs) and beach management plans;

Source: Malta Environment and Planning Authority

Figure 2.5 *Aerial image of Ramla beach in Gozo, Malta showing severe precipitation and sea storm damage to sand dune remnants on the left of the image and on the central and right side of the beach*

- allowing planners to better prepare for likely changes resulting from past and ongoing climate change and therefore better mitigate some of the potential hazards of erosion, flooding and coastal storms (see Figure 2.5).

Purnell (1995) argues that SMPs consist of a holistic and integrated approach to project appraisal through which options, cost efficiency and justification may be determined; and a sustainable management approach based on sound policy and strategic planning. The integrated approach suggested by Purnell (1995) presents the case for adopting a wide-angled approach to SMPs where various (internal and external) influences are assessed holistically, enabling a better understanding of the system. In this manner a more effective choice may be made of various management options available based on their cost efficiency and justification. In this context, Dharmaratne and Braithwaite (1994), Spurgeon and Brooke (1995) Goodman et al (1996) and Blakemore and Williams (2008) discuss the use of economic valuation methods (such as the revealed preference and contingent valuation methods) and public surveys as tools for environmental resource evaluation. The revealed preference method evaluates the value of non-marketable resources such as beaches, parks and scenic value by assessing the value of marketable goods related to their use, such as travel, food and lodging. The contingent valuation method, by contrast, is an indirect assessment of the value of natural resources, such as clean air and wildlife, which are utilized without consumption of marketable goods. Therefore, as an example, the value of beaches may be calculated by estimating the total value of all recreational activities of visitors since no direct cost is incurred solely for beach use. In this respect, beach use is considered as just one component of the estimated total value. The same is applicable to recreational use of rocky shores.

Purnell's (1995) reference to sustainable management necessarily included aspects of environmental protection needs, particularly of scientifically important and/or protected sites. A case in point was the rethinking by Holderness District Council of applying hard coastal protection structures on the East Anglian coast in the UK in response to alarming local coastal erosion that threatened the village of Easington and a neighbouring major gas distribution plant (BBC, 1993). Consideration of the need to change strategy resulted from concern over potential erosion of a neighbouring protected wetland area as a consequence of the planned hard structure protection scheme.

The concept of zonation for coastal management purposes has been used in the development of many management plans. While regional cells are often representative of political planning boundaries (at municipal level), it is preferable that they reflect coastal and biological processes. Such coastal parameters would refer to currents, water levels, bathymetry, wave climate, sediment transport, and ecosystem and territorial limits. This zonation concept within a study area and development of management strategies for individual 'coastal units' is important in coastal and shoreline management plans, as it reflects the clear need to consider issues at a number of scales, with beach management being the base (Hutchinson and Leafe, 1995).

McCue (1995) proposes a classification structure to manage coastal areas based on a hierarchical subdivision of the coastal environment that reflects the extent of natural ecosystem boundaries. This approach is particularly well suited to management of low-lying rocky shores, as it allows clear, objective strategies to be assigned to distinct geographical areas (such as accessible shorelines) that may effectively be used for bathing and related recreational activities. The proposed subdivision of coastal management identified zones reflecting regional, sub-regional and local levels.

At the regional level, 'regional cells' divide the coastal zone and territorial waters into manageable sectors, representing regions of national, political and geographical significance. At the sub-regional level, coastal cells are deemed to be representative of integral cells based on marine habitat extent and coastal hydrodynamics. The definition of coastal cells would therefore require accurate assessment of ecosystem boundaries through detailed oceanographic and environmental surveys that would consider, in addition to the parameters listed for regional cells, land- and sea-use characteristics, coastal morphology, ecology and geology, development limits, fishing areas and water quality parameters. At the local level, 'shoreline and offshore units' are identified as having individual management strategies; the boundaries of the former reflecting changes in landownership, land usage and shoreline characteristics.

McCue (1995) also considers that in cases where policy determined different management options for similar shoreline stretches, then separate shoreline units would be defined. Offshore units were considered to represent areas of particular use or desired future development within the offshore or nearshore zone, as in the case of marine conservation areas. While these are essentially equivalent to shoreline units and related by biological and physical processes, offshore units do not have the same spatial restrictions, being more complicated to administer due to more complex interrelationships of hydrodynamics and energy and nutrient exchange mechanisms.

In order to guide management, strategic policy must be determined at the regional cell level, addressing aspects of marine ecosystem conservation, water quality and multiple use options and controlled coastal development (see Figure 2.6). Such policy statements would in turn guide strategies adopted for offshore and shoreline units. In considering low-lying rocky shores as shoreline units, it is possible to apply this approach for beach management purposes. Since coastal use is segmented through this method, it is also possible to consider management needs of individual stretches of low-lying rocky shores for different purposes, minimizing environmental degradation by diverting environmentally incompatible activities from sensitive areas.

Most first-generation SMPs had five-year revision cycles and Beech and Nunn (1996) discuss issues that needed to be addressed in preparation of the next generation of SMPs. They considered it important to complete ongoing plans in order to identify unresolved issues and conflicts that may be better addressed in the future. Monitoring systems and data logging mechanisms in particular are identified as necessary in order to learn as much as possible from current plans and to fill in information gaps, particularly those regarding sediment transport mechanisms in regional and sub-regional sediment cells. Beech and Nunn (1996) also consider the need to update present land-use and planning policies to ensure the participation of all interested parties and to promote better integration of future SMPs with other coastal management plans.

In 2000, the UK's Ministry of Agriculture, Food and Fisheries (MAFF, 2000) recommended that in future UK SMPs:

- would have a policy consideration of 100 rather than 50 years;
- should involve stakeholders;

Figure 2.6 *A largely degraded beach at Balluta Bay, under severe anthropogenic pressure from physical development on the northern coast of Malta, where beach nourishment is under consideration by the Malta Ministry for Tourism*

- as a result of the Water Framework Directive, river basin plans should involve analysis of the pressures and impacts on the water environment and communication lines laid down.

These recommendations were further refined in 2003 and finally implemented in 2006 (DEFRA, 2006). These second-generation SMPs are in their infancy, with the Medway Estuary and Swale SMP being the first estuaries to follow DEFRA's revised SMP guidance of 2006, with the Isle of Grain foreland SMP being one of the first 'open coast SMPs'. These second-generation SMPs will consider longer-term implications, i.e. 50–100 years of climate, coastal change and so on, and also have a more involved and focused consultation with stakeholders. Theoretically they should learn from past lessons about problems garnered from technical, managerial and stakeholder issues, for example with reference to dialogue expectations, one single person should be responsible for multiple SMPs, as this increases efficiency; the shear volume of paper work associated with an SMP shows that understanding SMPs is difficult.

In 2005, the UK government's (DEFRA, 2005b) aim for coastal management was to manage flooding and coastal erosion risks by using an integrated portfolio approach reflecting national and local priorities in order to reduce the threats to people and their property; and deliver the greatest environmental, social and economic benefits, consistent with the government's sustainable development principles.

There exists a three-tiered hierarchy from policy to defence management based on SMPs. The second generation of SMPs (DEFRA, 2005b) put forward the view that policy decisions are initially based upon the appraisal of achievement of objectives and not on any economic appraisals. These are only undertaken to provide a check on the availability of selected preferred policies. This is an important factor in delivering the best sustainable answer, rather than an economically driven solution. Currently (April 2008) in the UK, the Environment Agency has taken on the role of implementing a strategic overview of the coast, concerned with flood and coastal erosion flood management. It is a new way of working, with government, the Environment Agency, local authorities and coastal flooding groups having bigger, more-focused and strategic roles. The Environment Agency will grant aid coastal erosion capital costs (giving permission to go ahead with the various schemes, the standard required and so on), while the local authorities will be accountable for delivery of the works. The Environment Agency will have strategic oversight of all SMPs and quality control on behalf of DEFRA.

It is worthy of note that in the US and Europe especially, coastal zone strategies to tackle coastal issues are now on the political agenda (OCRM, 2004).

CHAPTER 3

Theoretical Models for Determining Beach Management Strategy and Management Plans

INTRODUCTION

Development of a beach management master plan involves a number of logical and sequential steps that include:

- development/identification of a national policy for ICZM with a clear set of objectives which can provide an overall umbrella for local/state/county beach management;
- identification of national/county bathing area resources and types and associated risks/hazards;
- identification of bathing area issues/management guidelines;
- adoption of a strategy with which to achieve policy/objectives;
- development/adoption of beach management plans that are largely dependent on beach typology and desired goals (in accord with the second point above).

BEACH MANAGEMENT POLICY

A fundamental beach management policy objective should include achievement of optimal physical usage and development of beach resources that respect the natural physical elements of a beach environment while satisfying basic social needs within that environment. Beach environment policy, being a subset of a broader CZM regime, would follow and reflect the wider-scoped coastal management policies. Beach management plans should be considered as part of, or implemented and in line with, other coast-related management plans such as national structure and local area plans for the coastal zone, shoreline and CMPs.

Effective beach management should provide a way of balancing the social and economic demands of the beach if possible, with protection of coastal ecosystems. Beach management should integrate the different

This chapter is based on material from *Beach Management Guidelines, 2009*, by Anton Micallef and Allan Williams, published by the UNEP/Mediterranean Action Plan's Priorities Action Programme/Regional Activity Centre, Split, Croatia (Micallef and Williams, 2009).

policies that affect the area and bring together all stakeholders affected by those policies, as it is the place where natural and anthropogenic patterns coalesce. Limiting resources in the coastal strip generates special issues and demands for a variety of beach types.

Negative impacts of policies insensitive to specific beach user needs are evident: i.e. wholesale exploitation of limited resources, during which process significant pollution of land and coastal waters can be generated. Fencing off beaches for tourism is also a common feature, for example many beach/dune areas on the western coast of France (see Figure 3.1), but in all probability, the gravest task facing beaches is the threat of sea-level rise, as an adjunct to global warming, plus the inordinate number of people who use popular resort/urban beaches, which frequently exceed carrying capacity. So new indicator tools are needed that consider different variables (e.g. economic, environment and social), with special reference to beach user perception (Jurado et al, 2009). Ariza et al (2008b) showed that no periodic quantitative evaluation of beach user levels was carried out at any Spanish municipality, and if beach carrying capacity was exceeded it was classed as normal. This is not an unusual occurrence on many world beaches.

Beach management policy requires a balanced scientific assessment of the environment (natural and cultural), and managers need to understand the variety of discipline perspectives and processes operating within the system. The first of these is a sound environmental database, which is essential for any satisfactory solution of management problems. An effective management strategy depends upon availability of essential information, objectively measured if possible rather than anecdotal, as the quality of decision making suffers if data on the system's controlling parameters are not systematically collected and analysed. This is particularly critical in assessment of beach vulnerability and determination of management policies because of the range of processes operating, some of which are sporadic in occurrence. Policy management relates to diagnosis and direction setting. To be effective and rational, managers need to be aware of a broad range of useful knowledge, as well as being suspicious of claims that 'promise too much, but there is much we do not know!' Managing man–nature relationships involves mutual interactions and feedback based on power differentials, conflicting values and competing interests and expectations. A procedure of structured data collection is needed that is incorporated into management policy with clear objectives. So one crucial aim of a beach management programme is to set structured data collection within the context of a sound methodological and theoretical perspective; currently the latter is sadly lacking within most beach management strategies and procedures.

Figure 3.1 *Fencing and rubberized access mat of beach/dune areas on the western coast of France*

BEACH MANAGEMENT STRATEGY

While meeting guidelines set by national policy, management plans should provide for individual shore needs and predominant use characteristics as well as catering for both environmental and recreational user needs. The last of these should be identified though surveys aimed at defining beach user perceptions and priorities as reported by, for example, Morgan et al (1993; 1996), Micallef et al (1999) and Nelson et al (2000). Resources at the coast should be partitioned, with some managed by placing an emphasis on conservation, while others would be mainly oriented for heavier tourist use. In this regard, existing classifications of specific coastal areas having particular ecological or/and scientific importance, or as nature reserves, should serve as useful guidelines for appropriate management orientations. Last but not least, it is imperative that political decisions are firmly taken to determine *one* decision-making body with responsibility for environmental protection and planning. If this is not possible, then it is necessary to harmonize the roles where more than one agency exists. Effective beach management is a relatively young discipline, ICM is only about 40 years of age, in which, as already stated (in Chapter 2), a theoretical foundation has yet to be fully established. Previously it was driven by resolution of practical issues, essentially carried out on an ad hoc basis.

Bathing area quality evaluation systems

Beach classification is as an extremely effective management tool, not only allowing a better-informed option for potential beach users, but moreover presenting a technique for identifying those aspects that require upgrading in order to further improve this recreational product's quality. In this connection, *the adoption of a rigorous beach quality evaluation scheme is an effective strategy through which improvements in beach quality and beach user satisfaction may be achieved*.

Participation at any level of a number of such schemes may serve an educational purpose through highlighting public awareness of the issues at stake. Programmes of this type may also be considered to provide a practical contribution to impartial monitoring of the environment. Award schemes may also serve to encourage effective or stricter adherence to beach management guidelines by stipulating a number of criteria that must be attained to enable qualification for the award (Williams and Davies, 1999). In this context, however, it is important that beach managers should monitor *'opinions and perceptions'* regarding beach user priorities from which recommendations may be made to shape and influence beach management policy guidelines (Morgan et al, 1993; Williams and Morgan, 1995). It is also necessary that, in practice, criteria used by such award schemes are assessed to determine their (scientific) reliability and (practical) applicability to beach management practice (see Chapter 8). There seems to be a current viewpoint that perhaps award schemes have run their course because, if a beach has been 'improved', local councils need no longer pay money to obtain the award as the beach user is invariably unaware of the meaning of such awards and they play an insignificant role in motivation to visit beaches. Perhaps awarding bodies have become too successful for their own good; their distinctive 'brand identity' being lost as the improvements demanded became an accepted standard. In 2006, Ards Borough Council, a local authority in Northern Ireland, decided to withdraw from Blue Flag status for Millisle, a recreational beach, as it considered the effort and expense involved was not cost effective.

A variety of works concerning bathing area management have focused on development of management guidelines, awards and classification systems: Costa Rica Award Scheme in Chaverri (1989); classification of Australian surf beaches in Short (1993); the Beach Rating Scheme in Williams et al (1993b) and Williams and Morgan (1995); monitoring and assessment of recreational water quality in WHO (2000); the Welsh Green Coast Award in Nelson and Botterill (2002); the Blue Flag Award scheme in FEE (2009); and the BARE system. A thorough review of such schemes is given in Chapters 8 and 9.

Adoption of a general strategy for beach management

Further to the adoption of a beach quality evaluation and classification system, a *general strategy for beach management* may consist of four main phases, namely the identification of areas suitable for bathing and related recreational activities, data collection, establishment of a management plan and committee, and application of relevant management guidelines.

Figure 3.2 *Low-lying rocky shore reflecting an ideal bathing platform requiring basic management intervention such as improved access to the shore, safe access to and from the sea, litter bins and information boards indicating nearest public toilet and emergency telephone facilities*

Phase I: Identification of areas suitable for bathing and related recreational activities
The general ethos of beach management policy identifies the need to maximize the recreational potential of beaches in keeping with current environmental protection strategy. In addressing bathing areas rather than beaches per se, bathing resources in the form of gently sloping rocky shores should also be considered if suitable for development as *bathing platforms* (see Figure 3.2), particularly as a means of reducing the pressure on sandy beaches where these are limited.

Phase II: Data collection
Using survey questionnaires aimed at local and overseas tourists, the more popular rocky sites may be identified together with user preferences and priorities. Also related to the identification of suitable bathing areas is national policy regarding beach nourishment of existing small or degraded beaches and/or creation of new artificial beaches.

Prior to the generation of a management plan, a wide variety of information regarding the beach/rocky shore and its immediate environment should be collected from the field as well as from desktop studies of existing records and research projects. Such data should preferably be incorporated into an appropriate geographic information system (GIS). Phase II of the management strategy should therefore address:

- a site survey to identify boundaries, distinct components (such as sand dunes and shore platforms) and their physical attributes such as location, dimensions, sediment characteristics and likely source, geomorphologic description and any facilities on or linked to the locality;
- morphodynamic analysis of beaches, which would involve profiling and analysis of the beach forcing factors such as wave and inshore current regime and erosion-related studies of rocky shores;
- identification of the possibility of and need for zonation and protection needs of any special (rare, threatened) components;
- identification and understanding of natural processes active on the coast and their interaction with local human activities. Particularly where local coastal resources are size-restricted, it is important to identify quick-acting processes that could lead to a rapid deterioration of the system, for example nearby sewage and industrial outfalls prone to faults/accidental discharge. In addition, any temporal and geographic variations, including historical written or memory records of such phenomena and possible user interactions and potential conflicts, should be identified to achieve best allocation of site zonation and management priority;
- evaluation of the importance of the three main use categories, i.e. social (recreational), economic (commercial activities) and environmental (nature and landscape), at international, national, regional and local levels;
- evaluation of the level and type of activities to be allowed in different identified zones; these should be based on the conservation/recreation value of the area, user preferences and priorities and overriding shore-use function, i.e. whether used mainly for bathing or conservation;
- identification of official and non-binding regulations and by-laws that may be applicable to the bathing and surrounding areas and that may be used to further strengthen management strategy.

Phase III: Establishment of a beach management plan/SMP and committee
The management committee must reflect an inter-sectoral representation of coast-associated official and NGO bodies. These could include representatives from the environment, planning, tourism, maritime and local council sectors, an NGO and, importantly, a person with expertise in beach management. The main function of such a committee would be to identify and resolve issues and to design, implement and review a management plan that should address:

- identification of funds necessary for appropriate management and subsequent monitoring;

- design and implementation of an appropriate education campaign for the public, bathing area users and local council members through appropriate information signs, public lectures, exhibitions, seminars and publications;
- identification of specific criteria and indicators of coastal environmental quality in line with national policy; these should reflect not only environmental concerns, for example water quality, rare species and habitats, but also socio-economic interests, for example cultural heritage, user preferences and priorities and tourist-related needs.
- identification of qualified governmental, non-governmental and/ or public sector personnel who may be able to contribute to the responsibility of implementing the management plan(s);
- employment of a site(s) manager or warden to ensure that regulations set down by the management plan are enforced;
- consideration of suitable bathing area management guidelines.

Phase IV: Application of relevant management guidelines
A number of essential beach management issues (based on US bathing water standards, see Health Education Service, 1990) and a review of the work on beach management guidelines by Micallef (1996; 2002) and Williams and Davies (1999) are provided in Chapter 4.

BEACH MANAGEMENT PLANS

In describing the potential content of a typical beach and shoreline management plan and related guidelines, it should be stressed that each bathing area, depending on its characteristics, content and general use pattern (i.e. beach typology), merits special consideration to cater for any particular needs. The specific management plan adopted will also depend largely on the desired objectives of the responsible government authority, or if delegated, a management committee, and the economic resources available. In this context, the Bathing Area Management Model (see page 77) was developed to cater for both recreational and environmental conservation needs. It is recommended that unless effective zonation is feasible, particular areas of use be given priority according to specific circumstances, i.e. a management bias is predetermined. This would be the case for small islands, whose majority of beaches and low-lying rocky shores suitable as bathing platforms are small and restricted in size (see Figure 3.3).

Prime aspects of a beach management plan would consist (in no particular order) of:

- adoption, if desired, of quality standards through a beach quality evaluation scheme that considers specific quality-related parameters, for example water quality criteria, safety, litter;

Figure 3.3 *Bathing area comprising small sand beach and extensive low-lying rocky shore platform*

- identification of current beach quality status, for example via a beach rating scheme;
- identification and improvement of priority management issues required to improve beach quality;
- application of beach management guidelines (see Chapter 4);
- integration of beach management actions within a holistic beach management model (see below);
- identification of beach stability or erosion trends arising from both natural and human-generated sediment supply diminution, for example sand mining, river/water course damming and coastal construction;
- consideration of the need for environmentally sensitive beach litter collection schemes;
- incorporation of techniques for problem analysis (for example dimension analysis – see Chapter 7, 'Dimension Analysis', page 139);
- identification of natural, artificial and political beach boundaries, i.e. identification of management area;
- application of incentives for user participation in overall management regime, for example public education/awareness campaigns;
- understanding of the natural system's behaviour;

- consideration of national/international directives and guidelines on beach management, for example ICZM directives;
- identification of the natural functions of a beach (for example through function analysis – see Chapter 7, 'Function Analysis', page 153) to determine conservation or development bias in management.

Plans that may enhance any of the above-mentioned attributes should not result from ad hoc reactions to local problems, though this may occasionally be necessary if, for example, coastal stability is at stake. Beach management should form part of an overall long-term action plan that postulates beach behaviour over future years. Additionally, beach management plans should be flexible enough to allow revision where necessary to adapt to changing circumstances not predicted at the plan's inception. While a beach management plan is often the result of a desire to improve beach facilities or the function it serves, such as defence or conservation, it may also be in reaction to a planned activity that is anticipated to influence the beach in question. For example, effective beach management should actively consider alternative solutions to planned mechanical beach cleaning. Some of the more important questions that need to be asked by effective beach management regimes should refer to the level to which individual beaches should be developed, i.e. from the end points of a spectrum of beaches (remote to large-scale urban – see Figures 3.4 and 3.5), whether they should be left undisturbed or be fully

Figure 3.4 *An example of a small, remote pocket beach in Tibouda, Tunisia*

Source: Ministry of Education, Spain

Figure 3.5 *An example of a large-scale urban beach at Torre del Mar, Spain*

developed for mass tourism, what the requirements and preferences of beach users are, and what level of disturbance should be tolerated? In this respect, it has been shown that some of these questions may be answered using techniques such as function analysis that permit an evaluation and comparison of the conservation and use development values of a beach/coastal environment (see Figure 3.11 and Chapter 7, 'Function Analysis', page 153).

Beach management plans have to follow national guidelines (if any exist) associated with ICM. Most countries have a policy relating to these matters. If not, then beach management will tend to be carried out on an ad hoc piecemeal basis, usually relating to artificial boundary constraints and irrespective of sediment cell boundaries. The UK for example has over 80 sets of legislation relating to the coast and currently (2009) the proposed Marine Bill is moving to put all these under one act – as well as proposing a host of other measures in order to clear up the current piecemeal approaches to beach management. Within a national framework, regional/local plans may be formulated. At the regional level, preparation of statutory beach plans by local authorities should be done in conjunction with adjacent authorities and all relevant/interested bodies should be consulted and involved. Conferences and groupings of the local authorities should ensure improved knowledge of coastal processes, define key issues for planning, coordinate policies for conservation, coastal defence and development. At the local level, i.e. where beach management is carried out, the following are deemed to be essential for formulating a management plan:

- All stakeholders should be consulted.
- Plans should be aimed at seeking ways to reconcile competing demands made on beaches.
- Plans should reflect a balanced approach.
- If needed, an 'adopt a beach' campaign is a tried and tested approach.
- Plans need to be flexible and not rigidly cast as 'tablets of stone'.

Plans have to take into account what the beach is geared for, for example whether it is basically for recreation as a resort, an urban beach or a remote one where 'no management' represents a management decision. This is one of the bulwarks and strengths of the BARE scheme (see Chapter 9), in that beaches are delineated according to these terms.

Implementation of a beach management plan can stimulate and guide coastal area sustainable development. It can minimize natural system degradation, provide a framework for management of multi-sectoral activities and maintain options for future uses of resources, ultimately contributing to the protection and sustainable use of a region's coastal resources. The growing realization of the relevance of coastal dynamics to the understanding of the health and well-being of the general environment, and the need to further study and understand different systems as representative of the whole, have now been accepted by virtually all scientific personnel.

Emphasis should be given to building and increasing human capabilities/resources and the transfer of appropriate technologies, i.e. a bottom-up approach, which necessitates a long, iterative and cyclical process, proceeding on the basis of a good information system concerning the driving characteristics, the building of technical capacity and the development of appropriate methodologies and, if needed, rating schemes.

In reality many of the above-mentioned components and/or concepts, for example development of strategy/management plans, are at best fragmented in management practice. As a consequence and in view of their importance to a structured development of strategic beach management, these principles have been applied in the development of an innovative beach management model that is considered as instrumental to achieving a set strategy.

A sound example of a beach management plan is the strategic one produced by Cornwall Council, UK. A two-stage plan incorporates a broad holistic view, similar to a Strategic Environmental Assessment (SEA), which then provides the backbone for site-specific beach plans, focused upon individual unique site requirements. Essentially the aims are as follows.

- To put in place management techniques, in order to sustain economic, cultural and environmental values of beaches. This will be mainly carried out by a Public Spaces Team together with the Beach Ranger Service.
- To improve/diversify participation involvement and cooperation and to obtain wider stakeholder involvement, especially at the local level. As beach management plans continuously evolve, this is a flexible process.
- To promote the importance of the coastline with regard to values and opportunities in view of the current opportunities and threats (i.e. society and the economy are interlinked and interdependent functions of the ecosystem and a balance needs to be obtained).
- To provide guidance and direction for beach activities via voluntary agreements/legislation. The broad diversity of beach activities can cause conflict if left uncontrolled, especially with regard to public safety (e.g. surfing/kite flying/jet skis vs. swimmers).
- To improve beach access, both physical and intellectual. Education and awareness are important parameters here, varying from guided activities and on-site interpretation to web interpretation.

To this end the document addresses issues such as involvement and participation (e.g. questionnaires), ranger services (e.g. litter, education), safety (e.g. water quality, hazards), facilities (e.g. litter bins, toilets, shower provision), policy and legislation (Cornwall Council, 2009). It is emphasized that the above are not Mosaic tablets of stone.

BEACH MANAGEMENT MODELS

A conceptual modelling regime for beach management proposed by Nelson et al (2003) is reviewed below. This model embraces a holistic viewpoint of the delineating functions that comprise the complex and dynamic nature of interactions of a wide spectrum of variables acting upon the beach environment.

Figure 3.6 describes stakeholders, issues and management implications related to beach management:

- Phase 1: (input stage) reflecting the stakeholders, main issues and resolutions;
- Phase 2: the research process to quantify the main issues;
- Phase 3: (output stage) presents objectives to achieve sustainable management planning.

Most models have a 'top-down' approach (see Figure 3.6) at both intel-lectual and institutional levels, and regulations are formulated at various hierarchical levels with sometimes very little interaction. In Model 2 (see

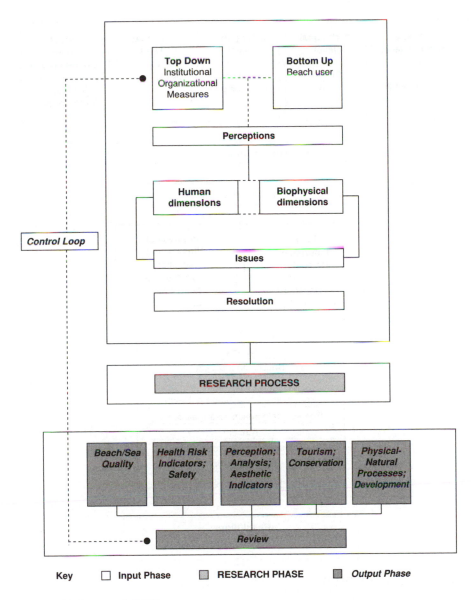

Source: Nelson et al (2003)

Figure 3.6 *Model 1: Conceptual model of beach management, providing a control loop to feed back information to decision-makers*

Figure 3.7), which represents the input phase of Model 1, some issues arising from interaction of human and biophysical processes are presented. Methodological options for resolution, such as Delphi techniques and

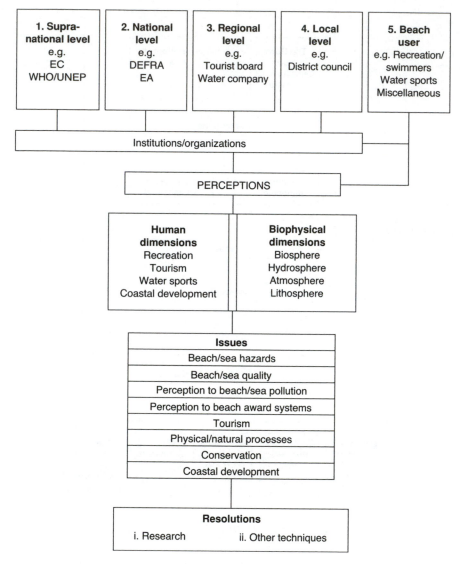

Source: Nelson et al (2003)

Figure 3.7 *Model 2: Regulation, dimensions and issues*

focus groups, can be carried out but research is probably by far the best option.

The input phase to Model 1 emphasizes and identifies that stakeholders involved in beach management – supranational, for example the European Community, World Health Organization (WHO); national, for example DEFRA; regional, for example tourist boards; and local levels of management and beach users – need both vertical and horizontal integration and communication links between organizational/institutional levels (see Figure 3.7).

Within a European context, supranational levels of management would include European Commission directives, beach quality and award/rating schemes and protocols for beach management research, for example on epidemiological-microbiological investigations and the European Commission's Urban Waste Water Directive. A national level of management may be represented by governmental agencies and non-governmental bodies responsible for implementing European directives, for example relevant environment agencies. Regional-level management include authorities (regional agencies) responsible for regional economic development, such as tourist boards and those responsible for ensuring high quality bathing waters. The local level is represented by those responsible for practical aspects of beach management (for example beach cleaning and provision of safety). The beach user group would include a plethora of users from swimmers, fisherman to ornithologists and more, and it is vital to have their perceptions/views early on in any planning process.

In the research phase of the conceptual model in Figure 3.6 issues may be measured and quantified, paving the way for management of critical issues (output phase in Model 1), that will lead to an improvement of beach quality. The provision of a review process (of the output phase) also provides an opportunity to feed back critical information to the institutional/organizational level that may result in adapting planning and regulation processes to any flux in the natural system resulting from human/natural process interactions.

Other models include the NetSyMod (Network Analysis–Creative System Modelling–Decision Support), which is described in Box 3.1 and Figure 3.8. The DPSIR model involves various indicators of which some are shown in Figure 3.8; the reader is directed to the works of Venturelli and Galli (2006) and Svarstad et al (2008) for further information. The original implementation model was mainly concerned with the legislative approach of any policy and Mazmanian and Sabatier (1978), working in coastal conservation in California, set out a conceptual framework of variables in order to help explain implementation. The variables were both dependent and independent and affected achievement of legal objectives.

House and Phillips (2007) (see Figure 3.9) adapted this model in their analysis of policy processes in the coastal zone, South Wales. Data were obtained from semi-structured interviews with officials from several administrations and institutions (supranational, national, local/regional government, quasi and non-governmental organizations) to establish the different approaches to both policy formulation and implementation. They conclude that there is a strong need to complement scientific process theory with implementation theory. Goggin et al (1990) propose a 'variegated polyphasic' empirical methodology for testing and developing

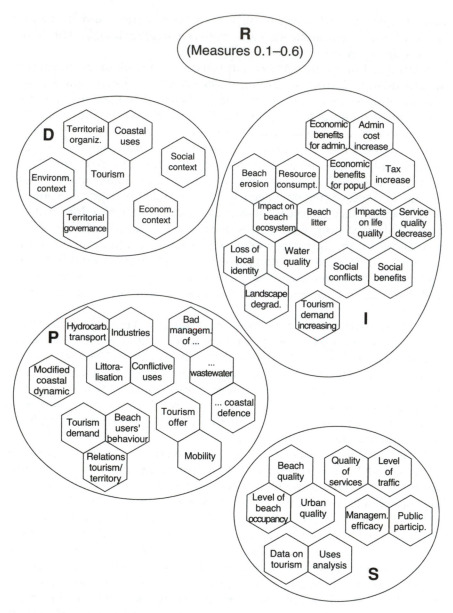

Souce: Marin et al (2007)

Figure 3.8 *DPSIR framework*

implementation theory, emphasizing the dynamic nature plus constraints
that stakeholders are under, together with the power of committee
chairmen, and that choices available in the implementation process are
made via a subsystem of actors.

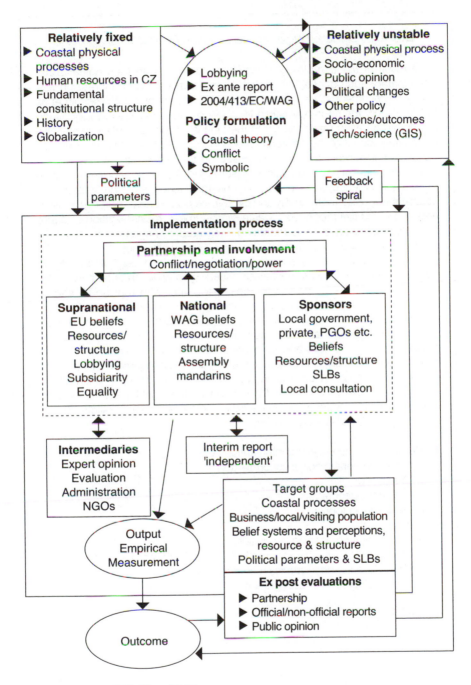

Souce: House and Phillips (2007)

Figure 3.9 *Implementation model: CZM*

Box 3.1 *Application of participatory method for beach management*

As a result of the complexity of issues associated with the coastal zone, participatory approaches with stakeholders have played an increasing role in any management strategies put forward (Buanes et al, 2005; Peterlin et al, 2005). A new methodology called NetSyMod was conceived in Italy aimed at improving beach management in the Liguria region. Essentially, a specific conceptual model of the environmental and socio-economic framework was developed specifically for beaches, based on the DPSIR (drivers–pressures–states–impacts–responses) framework (see Figure 3.8), together with evaluation of 10 management options, 5 current – coastal defence, environmental quality, sustainable tourism (both quality and cycle tracks), stakeholder information and education, and five proposed – waste management, reclassification of public funding, application of tools regarding integrated management of beaches, tourism networking and a mobility plan for improved efficiency.

'Brainstorming' sessions resulted in model building as a result of focusing on two questions, i.e. causes/mechanisms leading to environmental and socio-economic problems in the Liguria region, together with the modifications/impacts (environmental and socio-economic) that would be derived from the processes. Answers were clustered in Hodgson hexagons (Hodgson, 1992).

Results indicated that linking actions (responses) with the main causes of coastal unrest (drivers and pressures) was the way forward rather than focusing on mitigation of single problems (impacts). Management interventions in the Liguria region encompassed eight criteria (EEA, 2001) of which after a weighting exercise, starred items (*) were ranked the most important. Different stakeholder categories in Liguria agreed on the exercise's validity, which supported the DPSIR categorization:

- Relevance, coherence and interventions of:
    - environmental/biodiversity protection;*
    - life quality;
    - coastal defence;*
    - sustainable tourism.
- Adequacy of:
    - management/planning capacities;
    - interventions associated with the territorial identity of the region;
    - financial and administrative resources available;*
    - stakeholder level of acceptance.

Source: Marin et al (2007)

Simultaneously, Winter (1990) examines the integration problem arguing that models come first, with methodology as a secondary aim. Winter identifies four socio-political conditions that interact with one another to give outcomes – the most relevant variable. These are:

1   the character of the policy process prior to the law or decision to be implemented;
2   the organizational and inter-organizational implementation behaviour;
3   street-level bureaucratic behaviour;
4   the response by target groups and other changes in society.

The Bathing Area Management Model

In conjunction with development of BARE technique, the Bathing Area Management Model (BAMM) was developed (Micallef, 2002) as a management tool related in particular to any proposed management plan for local bathing areas, but also applicable to coastal area management plans in general. BAMM (see Figure 3.10) had its origins in the KJ method (Anon, 1994). The method was originally used in 1967 for structuring data from anthropological fieldwork and is popular mainly in Japan. It has since been applied to numerous other fields, mainly as a management tool in governmental administration but also for dune management (the W diagram – see Figure 5.1) by Davies et al (1995b). The KJ method is a tool for data sorting and problem solving by repeatedly applying the method using a cyclical iterative model. This consists of successive phases of problem exploration, field observation, hypothesis making, evaluation, experimental design, laboratory observation and verification, operating at two main levels, namely, the field and conceptual levels. This model consists of seven main phases: data gathering, policy definition, planning, implementation, analysis, evaluation and review, and monitoring/control.

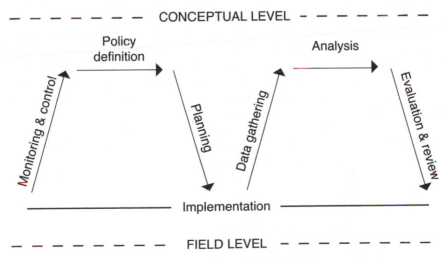

Figure 3.10 *The Bathing Area Management Model:*
Concept and implementation

Figure 3.10 describes how a BAMM envisages policy definition and analysis phases at the conceptual level and implementation of the management plan at the field level. The remaining phases naturally involve both conceptual and field application. For example, the data-gathering phase involves both fieldwork as well as desk studies and consideration of innovative data-gathering strategies, such as the design of beach registration schemes.

The first phase of policy definition in the model proposed in Figure 3.10 involves setting up a management committee whose first task should be to identify, through desk studies, current national policy related to bathing area and coastal management. Policy addressing bathing areas should include socio-economic and environmental considerations as well as a definition of desired objectives for particular beaches and rocky shores identified as suitable for recreational/conservation purposes. The policy definition phase would therefore also include determination of a desire or otherwise to having beach-specific management bias through the spectrum of conservation to recreation. Quality standards are also a policy consideration. For example, adoption of particular bathing area awards/ rating systems (for example BARE or Flags – see Chapters 8 and 9), water quality criteria (for example the Barcelona Convention, the European Union Bathing Water Directive or national standards) and carrying capacity, the last of these referring to how crowded one is prepared to allow individual beaches to become. It is also recommended that data collected by questionnaire surveys on beach user preferences and priorities are used to allow more effective and site-specific policy definition and where necessary, development of recommendations for revision.

Policy definition must acknowledge that different beach types exist i.e. physical/cultural dimensions (see Chapter 1). For example in the US, the federal government lays down a broad-scale coastal policy for the entire country and individual states implement their own policies in line with government directives, i.e. they cannot go against federal governmental policy dictates. In the UK, a government-backed authority, the Countryside Commission, now disbanded into English Nature in England and the Countryside Council in Wales, set up three pilot schemes in 1972–1973 in Glamorgan, Dorset and Suffolk, termed Heritage Coasts. This was expanded into 27 Heritage Coasts and the number has since been increased to 45, covering 34 per cent of the England/Wales coastline (Williams and Ergin, 2004; Radic et al, 2006; Williams et al, 2007). The concept broke new ground in coastal conservation and planning (see Chapter 2, 'Strategic Management', page 44)

Management guiding principles that formed the basis for Heritage Coast planning and management were:

- determination of acceptable levels of usage;
- a zonation policy that covered intense, intermediate and remote areas;

- developmental control;
- regulation of access, i.e. car parks and footpaths;
- landscape improvement;
- diversification of activities with an emphasis on passive (walking, fishing) rather than active (motor cycling);
- provision of interpretation services to promote public understanding and interest;
- no purchase of land but landowners 'volunteer' parcels of coastal land for the good of the scheme;
- to take into account the needs of agriculture, forestry and fishing, and the social needs of small coastal communities.

Scheme management was left to individual councils/municipalities who zoned them according to a philosophy of 'honeypots' (recreational usage), remote (conservation) and intermediate (any falling between these two end members) beach types. The beauty of the scheme was that conservation interests were well served as the bulk of the populace went to recreational areas thereby 'saving' the other stretches of coast. Conservation was written off in recreational areas.

The BAMM policy definition phase refers to an exercise by a government-approved body to define a desired development/conservation usage of the country's bathing area resources.

In the second phase of planning, management strategies and beach management plans (based on set policies and objectives) are adopted. To this end, the management committee should identify a working hypothesis through evaluation of possible options/solutions and identification of appropriate bathing area management guidelines through which to achieve set policy. In this context, recommendations emanating from application of, for example, function analysis (gaining a holistic understanding of the main development potential/conservation value of a beach system, thereby allowing the setting of policy on management bias – see Figure 3.11 and Chapter 7, 'Function Analysis', page 153) together with identification of beach typology should be considered, so as to allow site-specific planning.

The management committee's work would also include development of a public educational campaign and engagement of a site manager/warden/ranger. On remote coasts it would not be envisaged that a site manager be engaged for each individual site but rather he/she would be responsible for a number of beaches along a stretch of coastline. On resort/urban beaches, a site manager could be expected on individual sites. This, however, may be a function of beach size and available financial/human resources.

The third proposed phase of data gathering (registration) involves information collection of the entire bathing area (that area generally visible from the beach and within walking distance of the beach). This is relevant since the experience of a bather or beach user is generally influenced by

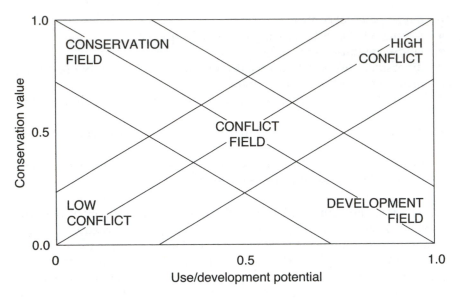

Note: see Chapter 7

Figure 3.11 *Conservation/use development matrix utilized by function analysis that may be applied to describe beach management bias requirements*

various aspects within the bathing area and *not* limited to the beach or in the case of a rocky shore, the bathing platform. It is envisaged that beach registration would collect background information (for example data on beach type, size, shape, granulometry, access, beach responsible authority, staff engaged and beach occupancy rates), as well as important data on beach parameters that may be related to beach quality (for example safety, water quality, facilities, scenery and litter). It is recommended that this phase also include morphodynamic analysis (for example erosion, shore/ backshore type), dimension analysis for problem/issue identification, and questionnaire surveys for identification of beach user preferences and priorities.

The fourth phase of the model is analysis and involves processing/ analysis of preliminary data collected during the data-gathering phase and/ or by ongoing research. It is recommended that suitable data-processing techniques and software are identified or developed in advance so as to facilitate this phase of the model. Development of questionnaires survey and usage of specific software packages, such as the Statistical Package for the Social Sciences (SPSS) or Minitab are recommended as particularly well adapted for gathering and processing data related to beach and rocky shore user preferences and priorities.

Data analysis would also involve site mapping, i.e. transfer of data either to hard-copy maps, or preferably to a GIS that enhances the potential for data access, manipulation, analysis and presentation.

The fifth phase of the model, evaluation and review of the proposed BAMM (see Figure 3.10), allows evaluation and verification of preliminary results emanating from data analysis, in particular evaluation of beach-related quality parameters (with whatever award/rating scheme, if adopted) and development of the pilot-scale management plan into a full-scale plan, applying modifications where necessary through the processes of innovation and incrementalization. In this phase, site evaluation using a beach quality evaluation technique (such as the BARE system – see Chapter 9) would allow identification of priority management needs in order to enhance bathing area quality. In addition, evaluation of the performance of the bathing area's environmental functions, through for example application of function analysis (de Groot, 1992; van der Weide et al, 1999; Micallef and Williams, 2003a) would allow confirmation or otherwise of whether desired beach-use functions and/or improvements were attained through past management.

The sixth phase is implementation and involves setting into motion a pilot-scale project of the management plan based on priority management issues identified through prior beach quality evaluation carried out in the evaluation and review phase (for example application of the BARE technique – see Chapter 9), and the beach management guidelines identified in the planning phase.

The plan adopted should address issues related to various beach types, for example:

- restricted access where necessary to protect environmentally sensitive areas;
- prevention of vehicular access to the beach;
- provision of adequate service facilities, parking and safety measures;
- provision/or not of appropriate beach cleaning techniques;
- implementation of monitoring programmes to ensure adherence to water quality criteria and to detect signs of environmental change.

During this phase, particular emphasis should be given to implementation of the educational campaign adopted in the planning phase. This should be aimed at improving the general public's awareness not only of the natural beach attributes and relevant by-laws (for example prohibited beach activities), but also of the management plan being implemented. The implementation process is enhanced by information generated by the questionnaire surveys related to user perceptions and priorities that ensure consideration of user needs and therefore increase the chances of acceptance and cooperation by the general public (see Chapter 5 and Appendix 1).

In the seventh phase of monitoring and control, beach classifications achieved through prior beach quality evaluation, for example through BARE or some other award/rating scheme, are reassessed. This allows adoption/ revision of the management plan developed in Phase V of the model. This serves as a control mechanism to check the adopted management plan's effectiveness and to identify at an early stage any changes in environmental behaviour outside set limits of normal fluctuation through, for example, the use of beach profile sweep zones and comparison with baseline data and historical records to monitor beach erosion. Application of function analysis (van der Weide et al, 1999; Micallef and Williams, 2003a) is recommended at this stage as it presents an opportunity to graphically view achievement or otherwise of any desired shift in beach function. Monitoring and control allows the opportunity to scrutinize known issues that have been highlighted through the implementation phase and/or to identify unknown issues.

While this novel model for bathing area management has a predetermined start and finish point, it has been developed in such a manner so as to allow maximum flexibility. In this context, model initiation can take place at a number of points, depending on the degree of management already implemented in a particular bathing area. As an example, in the case where current management practice is not yielding the desired objectives, entry into the model could take place at the planning phase where adjustments may be made to the adopted management plan. Alternatively, when a problem is obvious, for example erosion, where environmental dynamics appear outside known normal limits of behaviour and need better definition and problem solving, the model may be initiated at the data-gathering phase.

In the context of BAMM, it would follow that beach management may be described as being a product (a set of actions) derived from the *planning, implementation* and *monitoring* processes that form part of an overall management model. To better describe the interrelationship between beach management policy, strategy and beach management plans, the model proposed by Micallef (2002) has been revised into a single framework encompassing all three issues/components (see Figure 3.12). A more detailed description of each phase of the revised BAMM is provided below:

- Identification/formulation of beach management policy:
    - define the desired development/conservation usage for the nation's beach resources (taking into account social, economic and environmental considerations);
    - largely determined by national CZM policy;
    - an exercise by a government-approved body or representative (for example an inter-sectorial beach management committee or local/ county council).

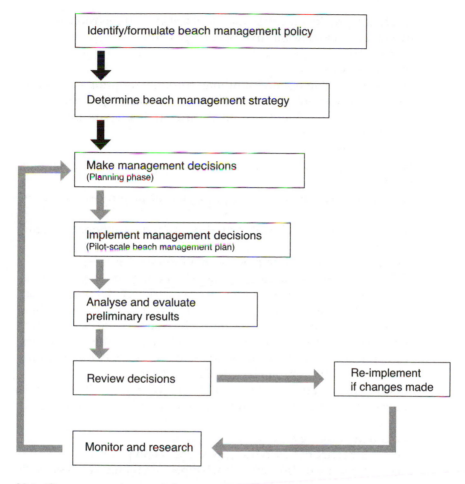

Note: Grey arrows represent the management plan component.

Figure 3.12 *Bathing Area Management Model:*
Planning, implementation and monitoring framework

- Determination of beach management strategy (how to achieve policy):
  - register beaches (data collection on general beach-related background information and more importantly on beach quality-related parameters);
  - identify beach types;
  - identify overall bathing area quality standards through a beach quality evaluation scheme (for example BARE or some other award/rating scheme);
  - identify beach-related issues/problem areas, for example through public consultation process, beach user surveys, risk assessment

exercises, problem identification tools, such as dimension analysis (Chapter 7, 'Dimension Analysis', page 139);
- verify issues;
- prioritize issues;
- evaluate possible options/solutions through adoption of relevant beach management guidelines (for example carrying capacity);
- delineate management responsibilities (engage site managers/wardens and so on);
- identify applicable by-laws.
- Making management decisions (the planning phase or do something/nothing option):
  - design a beach management plan/plan of action (i.e. what one wants);
  - identify current beach status/quality through any adopted rating scheme;
  - design actions to maintain beach quality-related issues;
  - design actions to implement beach management guidelines/standards (see Chapter 4) identified in strategy definition phase above; these would include applying restricted access where necessary to protect environmentally sensitive areas, limiting beach vehicular access to emergency vehicles and those providing essential services, provision of adequate service facilities, parking facilities and appropriate beach cleaning techniques;
  - develop public education campaigns in order to sensitize users to policy, strategy and so on, for example restricted beach access to dogs;
  - design monitoring scheme and frequency;
  - take cognizance of beach user preferences and priorities;
  - take cognizance of difference beach types and therefore site-specific needs;
  - identify need/desire for site-specific management bias (through identification of development potential/conservation value – function analysis).
- Implementation of management decisions (through pilot-scale beach management plan):
  - implement actions to maintain beach quality-related issues identified in the planning phase (for example safety, water quality, facilities/services, litter control, aesthetics) according to specific beach-type requirements/expectations;
  - implement actions to address priority management needs identified through any adopted award/rating scheme;
  - implement applicable beach management guidelines/standards identified in the planning phase;
  - implement monitoring programmes to ensure adherence to water quality criteria and to detect signs of environmental change;
  - implement public education campaigns (on natural beach attributes, applicable by-laws, proposed beach management plan and so on).

- Analysis and evaluation of preliminary results:
  - process/analyse data collected during strategy definition phase and by ongoing research;
  - site mapping (data transfer to hard-copy maps or preferably a GIS);
  - evaluate beach quality parameters, for example using BARE or some other award/rating scheme;
  - identify unaddressed priority management needs using adopted quality evaluation scheme.
- Review of decisions and re-implemention of plan (if changes are made):
  - modify beach management plan if necessary,
  - evaluate environmental functions to confirm achievement or otherwise of objectives;
  - adopt pilot-scale beach management plan to full scale.
- Monitoring and research:
  - reassess beach quality through adopted beach quality evaluation system, for example BARE or some other award/rating scheme, to assess performance of beach quality-related parameters;
  - application of function analysis (see Chapter 7) is strongly recommended at this stage as it presents an opportunity to graphically view achievement or otherwise of any desired shift in beach function;
  - scrutinize known issues that have been highlighted through the beach management plan implementation phase and/or to identify unknown issues.

Monitoring serves as a control mechanism to check the effectiveness of the adopted management plan and to identify at an early stage any changes in environmental behaviour outside set limits of normal fluctuation through, for example the use of beach profile sweep zones and comparison with baseline data and historical records to monitor beach erosion.

Issues to be addressed within a beach monitoring programme can include:

- overall bathing area quality (safety, water quality, services, litter and so on);
- beach user preferences and priorities, visitor satisfaction, use patterns, visitor background, expenditure and aspects of WTP and so on;
- public adherence to regulations/legal infringements;
- natural beach attributes – erosion studies (beach profiles, dune stability studies and ecological surveys), flora and faunal studies including bathymetric studies;
- beach-related phenomena (wave studies, dangerous currents, wind patterns, storm events and so on).

CHAPTER 4

Beach Management Guidelines

INTRODUCTION

Of the qualities that enhance beach attraction or potential for tourism, many authors, for example Micallef et al (1999) and Jones and Phillips (2008), have identified as key parameters: physical aspects such as local geology and geomorphology, biological attributes such as flora and fauna, and a number of socio-economic criteria represented by recreational amenities, access, safety, landscape (aesthetics), archaeology, commercial interests and environmental quality criteria, for example cleanliness, hygiene and toilets facilities. Many award schemes relate to these parameters (see Chapter 8).

APPROPRIATE BEACH MANAGEMENT GUIDELINES

Some of the more important questions that need to be asked by *effective* beach management regimes should refer to the level to which individual beaches should be developed. For example, from the end points of a spectrum of beaches, ranging from whether they should be left undisturbed or be fully developed for mass/resort tourism, what are the requirements and preferences of beach users? What level of disturbance should be tolerated? In this respect, it has been shown that some of these questions may be answered using beach questionnaire surveys and rating techniques (Morgan et al, 1993; Williams and Morgan, 1995) (see Chapters 5 and 8).

Williams and Davies (1999) provide a concise and practical set of beach management guidelines. As priorities, these include the need to:

- clearly establish beach area and desired/permissible management boundaries;
- identify all coastal resources related to the beach;
- identify quick-acting processes particularly in small beach systems that could lead to rapid deterioration, for example local sewage outlets or industry prone to faults;
- identify potential problems and select specific criteria/indicators of coastal quality on which monitoring programmes can be based;

these should include not only physical (for example natural habitats, anthropogenic presence, area coverage) and biological criteria (for example diversity and rare species), but also social indicators such as views held by indigenous populations and local customs;

- identify all official, as well as non-binding regulations that relate to the general protection of the coast and that can therefore assist in protection of the beach amenity;
- identify and understand natural processes active at the coast as well as the interaction of local human activities with these processes;
- clearly establish the responsibilities of beach managers since subsequent questions regarding application or otherwise of the rule of negligence may cause considerable and unnecessary legal complications;
- identify local land-use patterns, including those of a recreational nature and their potential influence on the beach in question; for example, these would include large visitor numbers that may result in trampling of vegetation and its destruction along unmarked dune footpaths;
- identify the necessary funding for appropriate management purposes.

In addition to the above guidelines, one may also consider the need to:

- acknowledge aspects of spatial coastal continuity and the problems raised by artificial boundaries in the form of district borders and limits of authority;
- apply zonation of conflicting beach uses;
- identify sediment cells;
- identify problems related to enforcement of beach-related by-laws and regulations.

Based on currently adopted principles of integrated coastal and shoreline management plans (see for example UNEP, 1995; 1996; DEFRA, 2005b; 2006), a number of beach management guidelines are presented as an aid to effective beach management and as a contribution to sustainable use of the beach and related environment:

- Anthropogenic interventions should not disrupt sediment transport pathways that supply marine and beach systems, in part compensating for natural beach sediment transport losses through aeolian, marine and precipitation storm-induced sediment transport. In this connection, natural coastal recession should be allowed to proceed unimpeded wherever possible. This presumes the absence of any large urban settlement, protected conservation area or significant energy-generating installation that would otherwise justify coastal defence mechanisms. The large coastal cities of Alicante, Corunna, Barcelona and Malaga in Spain are examples where the threat to human safety

Figure 4.1 *Tree debris at the mouth of the Kano River, Fuji, Japan*

and personal property resulting from active erosion of the beach
fronting these settlements justified extensive beach nourishment
programmes during the early 1990s (Ministry of Works, Transport and
the Environment, 1993).

Accretion is, for example, often found to be the consequence of
catchment area tree stripping, as shown in Figure 4.1, where tree
thinning in the catchment basin of the Kano River, Japan, has not only
resulted in river mouth accretion, but also huge amounts of sapling
fragments that cover river mouth beaches.

The case of erosion is typified by the damming of the River Nile
in Egypt, where erosion of both anthropogenic (roads, dwellings)
and natural systems (beaches, deltas) has occurred (Abu Zed, 2006).
El Sayed et al (2007) discusses as a counter to shoreline erosion, the
shoreline protection works at Rosetta (where erosion rates of up to
5m/year have been measured) on the northeast coast of Egypt, and
deltaic loss of up to 871 acres/year at the Rosetta promontory alone,
which was aggravated by the 1964 Aswan High Dam construction,
as well as aggradation problems due to silting resulting from an
absence of water outflow from the Rosetta branch of the Nile Delta.
The solution was nourishment and hard engineering structures to
counter erosion, together with jetty construction and dredging for the

silting. Additionally, of the more negative impacts of this development, Jernelov (1990) listed saltwater intrusion and a decline in Nile floods that previously brought high nutrient and sediment loads (about 140 million tonnes/year) to the coast. A decline of Levant basin sardine fisheries (from 10,000–20,000 tonnes prior to 1965 to 554 tonnes in 1966) was also linked to this decline of the sediment-associated nutrient load.

- Planners of beach-related activities should recognize, understand and work with, rather than impede in any way the spatial integrity (marine sediment cells and terrestrial catchment areas) of natural coastal sediment transport systems.

- Beach management should take cognizance of problems raised by artificial coastal boundaries imposed by neighbouring national coastal authorities, primarily by taking a holistic view and approach to the coastal system. This practice is well reflected in the UK, where major coastal sediment cells have been identified at a national scale for use in a number of coastal management-related plans (including estuarine, catchment and SMPs). While these cells often reflect natural coastal features such as major headlands (MAFF, 1995), they do not always agree with the jurisdiction of local authorities, therefore encouraging (and sometimes necessitating) cooperation on coastal management issues.

- Human activities on the coast should preferably be limited in scale with minimum impact on their environment and having short-term economic recovery potential. Such environmentally sensitive development with visible socio-economic benefits will encourage support at both government and local community levels. The negative socio-economic reaction to unsustainable coastal development (including a drop in quality tourism) has been exemplified by insensitive development on the Costa del Sol, Spain, Cote d'Azur, France, or the Costa Esmeralda in Sardinia, Italy, and has served as a sobering lesson from which a new more sustainable approach to coastal and beach management has emerged (Montoya, 1990; Butcher, 2003).

- If unavoidable, large-scale human activity on the coast should preferably be focused in areas having a positive sediment budget but having utmost regard for the ecological and functional integrity of natural systems such as beaches, dunes, wetlands and other sediment-rich areas. In this respect, *functions of nature* and *environmental function analysis* have been addressed by de Groot (1992), van der Weide et al (1999), Micallef and Williams (2003a) and Phillips et al (2007), who applied a man–environment model in which 'the function provided by the environment' was the central concept (see Chapter 7, 'Function Analysis', page 153).

- Local authorities could be encouraged to participate in award schemes such as the European Blue Flag Award and the Clean Beach Campaign in the US, and in public participation survey programmes such as Coastwatch in the UK (see Chapter 8). Rees and Pond (1995) and

Pond and Rees (2000) conclude that programmes such as Coastwatch provide an important opportunity for the public to participate directly in coastal management and to increase their awareness of important coastal issues. Nelson et al (2000) describe the UK national seaside award standards, and in a review of the Coastwatch UK programme, express doubt regarding the utility of beach award schemes (see Chapter 8).

- Development should not be permitted to encroach on the beach and backshore areas, and the immediate coastal strip should remain free of construction and be recognized as far as possible as rightfully open to public access (UNEP, 1995). This principle has in recent years been well integrated by Spain in its 22/1988 Shores Act of coastal legislation that clearly caters for public access to a coastal strip stretching as far inland as the waves reach during the worst storms for that area. This and aspects such as safety issues and beach plans involved in local and regional plans, constitute the core regulatory framework for Spanish beach systems (Ariza et al, 2008a). It also includes beaches, dunes, cliffs, swamps and other low wetlands. The law as described by the Ministry for Works, Transport and the Environment (1993) allows no type of trade or activity in this immediate coastal strip (defined as the first 100m from the water's edge), only allowing public use that is in harmony with the environment. To reiterate, three levels of administration exist: national (the coastal public domain), regional (land-use planning) and local (municipalities), which experience most of the benefits and problems pertinent to beach management. In March 2008, the Spanish government announced a €4.47 billion initiative to try to save the ravaged coastline extending from the Costa del Sol to the Costa Brava from further development, basically by knocking down properties constructed with illegal building licences and retrospectively applying the law. It will be interesting to see what progresses. The law does not guarantee ICM or beach management and currently a master plan for coastal sustainability is being generated that will implement ICM in Spain according to the EU recommendation of ICM (413.2002/EC). Similarly, the Turkish Shore Law identifies the *shore strip* as occupying the area stretching 100m inland from the shore-edge line, which has been defined as the natural inland limit of beaches, wetlands and rocks associated with coastal waters (Eke, 1997; Ozhan, 2005).
- Information signs on local natural characteristics, health and safety aspects and regulations should be an important tool for effective beach management practice (Williams and Williams, 1991) (see Chapter 6).
- Beach management should resist the ubiquitous influence of political and economic pressure for proposed coastal development, which will often attempt to bypass such management guidelines. This could be achieved through:
  - Constant reference to, and strict enforcement of, regulations and legislation.

  - Integration of national policy based on sustainable development principles into practical operational procedure. James (2000) has shown how a sustainable ICM plan could be a first step in modifying current beach management practices. This would indicate shortcomings in, for example, legal and administrative frameworks, the definition of resources, local processes and stakeholder profiles, so that beach management is essentially proactive rather than reactive.
  - Development of realistic predictive models and scenarios showing the most likely impacts and repercussions of planning decisions that conflict against the above-mentioned principles.
  - Attribution of realistic economic values to beaches and related coastal resources based on the most recent environmental economics theory and cost–benefit analysis that can be used as a strong argument for protection. This is a form of reasoning often better understood by policy-makers and other government planning authorities.

Effective beach management may often be hampered by:

● Limited baseline data on the coastal environment that may be dated, insufficient and/or largely limited to scientific research/development project application, environmental impact statements and/or

Figure 4.2 *Well-balanced and informative signs at Santander municipal beach, Spain*

development of local/regional development plans. This may be related to limited funding/opportunities for research institutes to engage in long-term coastal studies.

- Poorly developed public environmental awareness and/or low acceptance of related legislation. This may be linked to a low priority given to environmental education at primary and secondary school levels and low quality public information signs concerning environmental issues (see Chapter 6).
- Insufficient government personnel addressing coastal management resulting in inefficient environmental monitoring, poor enforcement of legislation and implementation of policies. The last of these is particularly the case in small island environments plagued with 'everyone knows everyone else' syndrome. The unrecognized/ underutilized potential of NGOs to assist in this field may also contribute to this.
- Absent or poorly defined national CZM plans providing insufficient consideration to beach management issues.
- Poorly developed/lack of 'chartered status' of national expertise in coastal/beach management. This may be linked to inadequate institutionalized training opportunities at both local and regional levels.
- Absence of a single authority with overall responsibility for coastal management, or poor cooperation between government entities having partial responsibility within this zone.

On the basis of a literature review, a number of bathing area management recommendations can be made:

- Ecological qualities should be carefully considered in the adoption of shore cleaning guidelines and techniques (Schembri and Lanfranco, 1994; Llewellyn and Shackley, 1996; Micallef, 1996; Williams and Davies, 1999; de Araujo and Costa, 2005). In this respect, the study reported earlier by Breton and Esteban (1995) on a Spanish pilot programme of information and conservation for beaches on the Llobregat Delta in Catalonia, provides useful guidelines that may be applied to any beach cleaning strategy. Selective beach cleaning was identified as a particularly useful opportunity to include community participation as part of beach management strategy. Mechanical cleaning of the more sensitive (and therefore protected) part of the beaches concerned was replaced by a manual approach. Positive impacts recorded referred to a dramatic increase in native flora establishment representing a natural (rather than opportunistic dominated) distribution of species and a consequential regeneration of otherwise eroded dune systems, due in part to the increase in vegetation cover.
- Management of bathing areas, particularly those of an environmentally sensitive or protected nature should be preferably carried out by

specialized agencies. If this is not possible, then it may be appropriate that such management is carried out under supervision or guidance of specialists. Edwards (1994) questions the sufficiency of the voluntary approach for management of environmentally sensitive areas and strongly argues the need for appropriate legislative, financial and expert human resource support to assist such management needs.

• Management of bathing areas should include programmes for educating not only bathers and recreational users but also managers and authorities responsible for coastal management. Morgan and Williams (1995) and Morgan et al (1996) have described this process as a difficult and complex issue as a consequence of different socio-demographic variables that result in varying user perceptions.

• Environmental impact statements and risk assessments should be carried out, not only with proposed developments on or near to bathing areas, but also to assess the management strategy itself so as to probe likely long-term impacts on the shore. Unlike construction development, adoption of a management strategy is often not bound by legislation and many examples of misinformed or misdirected unwise management practice exist, leading to considerable environmental degradation. For example, Yerli and Demirayak (1996) consider the need for an effective beach management plan to mitigate what they and the Turkish Society for the Protection of Nature and the World Wide Fund for Nature (WWF) consider as inappropriate aspects of a Turkish Tourism Master Plan for the Belek region. Some 25 proposed sites selected for large hotel complexes and around 4000 duplex units, included construction on Belek beach and associated sand dunes in Istanbul. These were deemed as threatening to both landscape and turtle nesting sites in Belek, as it is a biodiversity hot spot with a unique highly complex ecosystem and the second most important marine turtle rookery in the Mediterranean. Of approximately 800 nesting sites of *C. caretta* and *C. mydas*, Yerli and Demirayak (1996) estimate that Belek supported some 260. Despite its importance, only a small beach area – the sand spit of the Acisu River – has been designated within a specially protected area and expanded use for beach recreational has prevented consistent long-term monitoring.

• Different management strategies should be considered for different beach types rather than taking a blanket management approach (Schembri and Lanfranco, 1994; McCue, 1995). In the UK, planning policy guidance notes, for example PPG20 (DoE, 1996), do a similar task for coastlines, differentiating between *undeveloped with landscape and conservation values, other undeveloped* and *poorly developed* coasts, *developed* coasts (having large urban areas, ports, energy installations and so on), and *despoiled* coasts. It is necessary to cater for conservation and representation of the diverse habitats and functions offered by different coastal environments. However, this consideration should not be limited to variable beach characteristics but should also be applied to deviant user perceptions and priorities as well as emphasis on use patterns. Such an approach should facilitate identification of management priorities in cases where financial or human and technical resource limitations impose such decision making. Therefore bathing areas frequented mainly by those seeking solitude and a desire to experience a natural environment should have conservation-oriented priorities as an integral part of their management strategy. Avis (1995) addresses these issues in a study of three urban beaches in South Africa, where he concludes that socio-political changes and increasing population numbers influence beach utilization trends and preferences. In line with the proposed application of different management strategies to different beaches, Vogt (1979) some 30 years ago recommended that a country's resource base should be partitioned into different '*use zones*'. The author further suggested that this would be particularly applicable where establishing a balance of conflicting interests (such as those often presented by mass tourism and conservation) is found to be practically unfeasible. Rather more dramatically, Villares et al (1997: 622) suggest the sobering concept that environmental, aesthetic and physical qualities resulting from a (coastal/beach) management action are 'nothing more than a series of services that the citizen expects as a consequence of the price, the image and the reputation of the service'.

- Wherever possible, highest priorities should be given to maintenance or restoration of dunes as these, without fail, form an integral part of beach systems and are subject to a battery of assaults from golf courses, military training grounds, urbanization and so on (Bird, 1996; Cassar, 1996; Nordstrom, 2000). While public awareness concerning the importance of protecting dune systems has risen in recent years and a plethora of environmental protection-related legislation has been passed and conventions signed, dune systems remain threatened by the ever present and financially attractive coastal construction industry. In proposing a semi-quantitative assessment of the interrelationships between coastal dune vulnerability and protection measures, Williams et al (2001) include 'beach condition' as one of four groups of indicators to be featured in a checklist technique developed for rapid assessment of dune vulnerability. Doody (1995, 2008) considers that protecting dunes from activities that destroy their surface should be one of the highest priorities in related management strategy. In this connection, Davies et al (1995a) note that many instances of dune degradation on the French coast have been recorded arising from uncontrolled visitor pressure, including camping activities.
- Where vegetation or other natural habitats are associated with bathing areas, entry of heavy or other vehicles should be limited to emergency and rescue services, as the potential damage to vegetation can be extensive. In describing the impact of trampling, Ugolini et al (2006; 2007) demonstrate a clear correlation between bather numbers

on selected beach areas along the Italian coast of Tuscany and the population density of sandhoppers (*Talitrius saltator*), a supra-littoral amphipod found on those beaches.

● Particularly on environmental conservation-oriented beaches, accumulated seagrass (*Posidonia oceanica) banquettes* (see Figure 4.3) should not be cleared until the beginning of the summer season (if at all), as these provide a medium for beach fauna physical protection from the erosive impact of storm waves and water runoff following intense wind and precipitation storm events, and reduce unintentional removal of beach sediment trapped within the seagrass *banquettes* (Schembri and Lanfranco, 1994) (see Figure 4.4). While the last of these aspects appears as yet unconfirmed in scientific literature, it would seem very likely

Figure 4.3 Posidonia banquette *accumulations*

Figure 4.4 *Cross-section of a* Posidonia oceanica banquette *showing accumulation of sand and pebble beach material*

that the often thick (1–1.5m) and well-matted form of such a protective layer will offer considerable protection to the beach. On beaches with little or no conservation value and largely utilized for recreational activities, accumulated dead seagrass should be removed throughout the year as this increases recreational potential and reduces the likelihood of marine pollution from increased nutrient levels. In Italy, *Posidonia* shoaled detritus, if collected on urban beaches, is usually sent to an industrial treatment plant to create new products (lamp shades, building materials, insulation mats, biodegradable injection moulded pieces) or to be incinerated, and at other times is used as a fertilizer (see below).

With respect to rocky shores, a number of management options have also been identified for improving the use-potential of rocky shores through:

- employment of wardens (Buttigieg et al, 1997), to monitor recreation-related shore use;
- a cleaning strategy for regular collection of litter, for example through the provision of strategically placed litter bins and clean-up of other pollutants, for example oil contamination;
- establishment of set-aside (development-free) zones (Buttigieg et al, 1997);
- establishment of a public educational campaign regarding potential use of rocky shores for bathing and other recreational activities;
- identification of rocky shores particularly well suited as bathing platforms and focusing of management effort on these areas;
- consideration of the most appropriate engineering interventions for improvement of rocky shore presently considered unsuitable as bathing platforms, for example installation of temporary wooden decking;
- demarcation of rocky shores for environmental conservation purposes;
- identification of user perceptions and priorities and use patterns for inclusion in SMPs;
- provision of sanitary facilities close to popular areas; this is particularly important where older persons are concerned (Tudor and Williams, 2006);
- consideration of strategic car parking facilities; this can be a sound way of managing inputs to rural beaches with low carrying capacities that are within easy reach of populous urban centres;
- establishment of a long-term environmentally sound maintenance programme to improve access to rocky shores and enhance their use for recreational purposes.

A number of the management guidelines listed in Table 4.1 are discussed in more detail below.

Table 4.1 *Some proposed bathing area management guidelines*

Issues	Recommended strategy
Bathing area carrying capacity	A minimum of circa 3m² of beach space per user.
Beach/rocky shore slope	For water depths of up to 1.2m, a slope not exceeding 1:10 is considered as safe while for greater depth, the slope should not exceed 1:3.
Zone allocation	Mainly separating bathing and boating/ski jetting-related activities using lines with marker buoys but also to specify land-use sub-zones such as dog-free zones and conservation areas. Other recreational activities such as picnicking and camping should also be controlled.
Access	Adequate parking facilities should be provided off the bathing area but preferably not further than 500m. Vehicular access should be restricted to emergency cases. While public access should be facilitated by signposted footpaths, access to sensitive areas should be restricted or prohibited.
Drinking water	To counter the potential problems of dehydration, drinking water should be supplied from municipal supplies according to national standards.
Toilet and shower/ changing room facilities	Adequate numbers to be provided particularly for bathing areas receiving large number of visitors. All facilities should be sited away from sensitive areas to encourage better zonation. With respect to the potential problems of disposing of sewage from portable toilets that utilize chemical treatment, it is recommended that urban/village beaches (as well as highly frequented rural beaches) should have permanent toilets located at the back of the beach linked to the main sewerage system.
Beach cleaning	Adequate and appropriate beach cleaning services should be provided. Mechanized beach cleaning should be prohibited particularly in environmentally sensitive areas. These are usually areas designated by the competent authorities in individual countries as a result of some natural or cultural phenomena that are either unique, under threat or have a value that may be difficult to quantify but that is nevertheless important either to ecology, culture or science (for example dunes or turtle breeding sites).
Litter bins	A minimum of one per 150 beach users is recommended, having covers to minimize insect nuisance and health hazards. It is essential that litter bins are regularly emptied since full or overflowing litter bins may discourage use.

Issues	Recommended strategy
Hazardous items	Glass and other potentially hazardous material should ideally be prohibited from the beach and service facilities encouraged (through incentives) to use alternatives. In addressing issues of concern relating to health and safety, beach managers should also consider aspects of bacterial contamination present in most sand beaches and the recommendation is that wherever possible beach users should utilize a towel when lying on a beach so as to reduce the risk of skin contamination.
Barbeques	On popular bathing areas, BBQ areas should be set aside with facilities provided as a permanent fixture at the back of the beach. This would be an effective means to control the negative impacts and haphazard practice of such activities, such as the spread of charcoal residues and potentially hazardous debris (for example broken glass) across the beach. People would be encouraged to cook in a communal area, which would also provide adequate refuse depositories.
Information boards	These should be constructed and sited to facilitate visibility and understanding, addressing hazards (such as storms and dangerous currents), regulations and by-laws, environmental concerns and information on the bathing area management plan, where implemented. In particular, they should be erected at beach and water entry sites so as to maximize visibility.
Wardens	The engagement of suitably trained wardens is considered essential for application of guidelines for effective management of bathing areas. In particular, wardens should have the necessary legal status for enforcement of regulations and local by-laws.
By-laws	By-laws should address all issues of concern to shore use including generation of noise, unpleasant behaviour, fires, dog fouling and litter.
Lifeguards	These should have specialist training and access to further training and updating courses. They should be aware of both natural and man-made features/hazards of the area as well as access to further medical assistance. Volunteer lifeguard services, when utilized, should have a clear contract delineating their responsibilities. Blue Flag guidelines recommend a minimum of two lifeguards at appropriate intervals, 200m being the suggested figure (FEE, 2008).
Patrol towers	These should be ideally placed either at the centre of the bathing area or in that area where bathers tend to concentrate.

Table 4.1 *(Continued)*

Issues	Recommended strategy
Public rescue facilities and emergency/public telephones	Ring buoys and/or similar devices should be available, particularly on non-supervised bathing areas, having at least 30m of throw-line and being no more than 100m apart. Emergency telephones (particularly on rural/remote beaches) should be available with easily visible contact numbers for emergency services.
Monitoring	A long-term monitoring programme related to baseline studies should be implemented to detect early signs of environmental change.
Beach concessions	The granting of beach concessions to private operators offering facilities on or near to bathing areas should consider the need to protect unencumbered public use of the space.
Management	A system should be established to monitor the implementation of the management plan. The plan should also be regularly reviewed with a view to modification as a consequence of changing local circumstances.
Dogs	A strict dog ban should be in operation at recreational beaches. Dog notices and bins should be conspicuously displayed around the bathing area (see Figure 4.5).

Source: adapted from USA bathing water standards (Health Education Service, 1990) and a review of the work on beach management guidelines by Micallef (1996; 2002) and Williams and Davies (1999)

Discussion

Getz (1987) identifies six issues to be considered when addressing carrying capacity, namely resource limits, tolerance of the changes by locals (think of the huge changes in Dubai since 1990), visitor satisfaction, excessive growth rate, cost–benefit evaluations and utilization of a systems approach. Tools that may be used to implement carrying capacity involve:

- Regulatory approaches, for example siting car parks, environmental impact assessments, eco-labelling and planning (for example the provision of 'honeypot' areas such as the Heritage Coast concept in the UK (Williams and Ergin, 2004) that attract people thereby leaving other parts of the coast unscathed, or as protected areas (Nepal, 2000)).
- Economic considerations, for example differently set scales of pricing so that tourists pay more than locals. This may well be a form of discrimination but is common in many areas of the world. Another economic tactic is to provide initiatives to transfer some of the high

Figure 4.5 *Typical dog waste bin*

season tourism load to the low season, for example special air travel/
accommodation rates.
- Organizational initiatives, for example where tour operators manage a
  spread of tour routes to include underutilized areas.

Values given for the bathing area carrying capacity provided in Table
4.1 are general. While carrying capacity issues of sustainable tourism
have been largely elucidated with specific attention given to the *coastal*
environment, there is less experience in assessing *beach* carrying capacity.
Beach users, which are part of a burgeoning market in coastal tourism,
exert 'pressure' on the resource commodity – the beach – and thresholds
of population densities – the carrying capacity – has been deemed an apt
choice for limiting such numbers (Pereira da Silva, 2002). The pressure
caused by high user numbers may be of a physical nature, for example
trampling of dune and other ecologically sensitive areas, or one resulting
in a lowering of the quality of beach user experience. In this connection,
apart from applying fixed beach area per user, a number of systems
additionally consider carrying capacity as a function of beach type (see
BARE system, Chapter 9).

Several interlinked parameters make up beach carrying capacity. These
are physical/ecological, socio-demographic and the political/economic,
which have different weightings as a function of place characteristics and

tourism type. For example, there is a vast difference between the carrying capacity management of a pure recreational beach (see Figure 4.6) and a small pocket beach (see Figure 4.7). Similarly mass tourism markets, such as the Costa del Sol, Spain, which has many package holiday tourists, as well as cruise ships and many second (coastal) homeowners, will have very different carrying capacity to, for example, upmarket tourism expressed by gulet journeys along the Turkish coastline, where passengers can swim on near-deserted island beaches, or to an ecotourism coastal holiday in India.

Most estimates of carrying capacity give a single number. For example, all Portuguese bathing areas have a formula that gives a single carrying capacity value to such a locality (Pereira da Silva, 2002). Due to the huge variability within both user groups as well as locality, the carrying capacity concept is very fluid, and it has been suggested that it might be more appropriate to give upper and lower carrying capacity values and the essential limits considered as guidelines (Saveriades, 2000; Pereira da Silva, 2002).

In a case study of beaches on the southwest coast of Portugal, Pereira da Silva (2002) identified important differences between physical carrying capacity (reflecting the number of users a beach can physically accommodate) and social carrying capacity (expressing the perception of crowding, i.e. the concentration of beach users above which individuals become uncomfortable). One may consider that social carrying capacity may also include the issue of beach user satisfaction or overall recreational experience, tying in the need for effective beach management as a prerequisite for enhanced beach carrying capacity. In this context it may be seen that apart from the beach area, the carrying capacity of a beach would also be influenced by the distance travelled to the beach, ease and state of beach access, car park facilities, presence of lifeguards, restaurants, leisure facilities and infrastructural quality (roads, water, electricity and so on). In addition, beach user sex, age and socio-economic and cultural background would obviously play a strong role in levels of satisfaction or otherwise (Morgan and Williams, 1995).

The *slope safety* guideline (see Table 4.1) is considered as a particularly useful parameter for delineation of low-lying rocky shores suitable for bathing purposes. Where bathing areas are limited in size and/or number, *zoning* may be impractical and management should emphasize one particular use. However, restricted access and zoning as proposed in Table 4.1 are particularly applicable for scheduled areas representing important environmental habitats such as clay slopes, sand dune remnants, saline marshlands and coastal wetlands.

The guideline addressing *provision of drinking water* so as to counter the problem of dehydration (Table 4.1) is particularly relevant to northern European tourists visiting Mediterranean shores or US citizens to the Caribbean, who consequently are unacquainted with locally high temperatures characteristic of the summer months. In certain areas the

Figure 4.6 *Copacabana beach, Rio de Janeiro, Brazil – pure recreation*

Figure 4.7 *A small pocket beach, Gower, UK*

provision of permanent toilet and shower facilities may not always be feasible due to the very small and remote nature of some bathing areas. In this instance, the use of portable facilities is recommended and where bathing areas are particularly small and remote, such facilities may be limited to toilets. However utmost consideration must be given to ensuring that the disposal of drainage wastes emanating from such services may be achieved with no risk of pollution. In bathing areas where restaurants/lidos are granted beach-related concessions or are located particularly close-by, they should be encouraged through incentives to offer toilet and shower facilities so as to decrease the need for additional construction near to the bathing area.

In addressing guidelines concerning *beach cleaning* (Table 4.1) the practice of removal of dead seagrass from sand beaches throughout the winter season should be carefully considered in view of the potential protection from storm erosion that the seagrass *banquettes* may offer to beaches and their contribution to littoral biodiversity. This is particularly applicable to beaches where environmental conservation is one of the prime management objectives. However the pros and cons of removing seagrass *banquettes* whether seasonally or throughout the year appear to be insufficiently researched and as a consequence different country practices may be found. As part of a wider dune stabilization project in the south of Rosignano Solvay or south of San Vicenzo (Provincia di Livorno) in central Tuscany, Italy, seagrass is also used as a mulch that is deposited in a backshore trench dug by bulldozers and provides a basis for increasing, as well as helping commence, any new dune formation (Beachmed, 2009). In Ireland, seaweed ('*dulche*') has been used as a fertilizer for generations as it improves poor soils. Vegetation washed in by storms, contains many nutrients that can, for example, encourage dune growth. Dunes provide a critical niche on the coastal zone, not only being a source of sediment for beaches (and vice versa) but also a protection for the phreatic stratum from seawater entry. Overwash frequently brings such vegetation debris into an overwash fan, providing fertile ground for embryo dune development. These dunes, in turn, build up as surrounding dunes erode further, so that on this minor scale Bryan's (1940) principle of gully gravure takes place. In Malta, the practice of seagrass *banquette* removal in winter months appears to be decreasing as a consequence of revised government policy and increased public awareness. However, popular bathing beaches are regularly cleaned of such debris during the spring and summer months (Mifsud et al, 2002–2003).

In considering the provision of *information boards*, use of notices as a template of good management practice is strongly recommended. In addressing management guidelines concerning by-laws, close cooperation with local councils is recommended for identification and, where necessary, formulation of appropriate by-laws.

Application of guidelines concerning engagement of *wardens and lifeguards* should consider the generally small size of local bathing areas, optimization of limited resources and the need for an integrated management approach. In this context, integration of warden/lifeguard responsibilities where appropriate and enlargement of the area managed to include the environment surrounding the bathing area is recommended. Management guidelines concerning *beach concessions*, refers to the practice where operators tend to occupy a large majority of the beach prior to the arrival of the local public. An example of such bad practice is the provision of umbrellas and sun beds prior to requests by beach visitors that results in a gross reduction of beach space for use by the local public.

CHAPTER 5

Beach User Questionnaire Surveys

INTRODUCTION

While beach management addresses a number of physical issues represented by beach processes, erosion problems, protection measures and beach nourishment, recent work in the past decade has related to socio-economic aspects of beach management and in particular the use of questionnaires relating to beach user perceptions and priorities (Breton et al, 1996; Micallef et al, 1999; Sardá et al, 2005; Villares and Roca, 2007). These authors have suggested that other beach aspects, such as facilities, litter, odour, sediment colour, scenery, size and so on should also be regarded as important beach management issues. For example, in the case of scenery, the design of beach management plans should give careful consideration to local aesthetics due to the synergistic association that exists between aesthetics and management (Ergin et al, 2004). It is arguable that while beach management may directly influence beach aesthetics and determine future use capabilities of the beach area, the latter will subsequently influence the cost effectiveness of any management/ restoration costs. Williams et al (1993a), Leatherman (1997) and Ergin et al (2004) describe the relevance of taking into account a variety of features when considering beach area aesthetic values. Such features are represented by the human element (numbers and physical development), physical values (for example beach slope, pocket, broad or narrow beaches) and biological features (such as presence/absence of endangered species).

There is considerable value in identifying beach-related socio-economic data sets, as inclusion of such information in beach management plans might encourage beach user compliance by the general public with management policies. Identification of beach user preferences and priorities could also pre-empt management measures addressed to beach aspects subject to high user pressure. Despite this growing awareness of the need to clearly identify a wide range of socio-economic data sets relating to beach use that can be applied to beach management guidelines, a literature search identified relatively few authors who have addressed this novel field of work (for example Lockhart and Ashton, 1991; Williams et al, 1993a; Morgan et al, 1993; 1996; Goodman et al, 1996; Young et al, 1996; Leatherman, 1997; Nelson and Williams, 1997; Ball, 2003; Peterlin et al, 2005; Villares et al, 2006).

In an effort to distinguish and better comprehend different visitor group composition and characteristics, Williams et al, (1992) developed a survey questionnaire to identify psychological profile analysis of beach and dune users in South Wales, UK. Morgan et al (1995) carried out beach user opinion and beach rating surveys in a study on the Turkish Aegean coast, where they identified user preferences and priorities, as did Blakemore et al (2002) for beaches in Turkey, Rumania and Malta. Leatherman (1997) devised a US beach rating scheme with questionnaires based on 50 criteria related to physical, biological and human use (see Chapter 8). Micallef et al (1999) utilized questionnaire surveys to identify beach user needs/priorities and rating schemes for beach management strategy and long-term policy determination. Pendleton et al (2001) investigated perception of Californian beach users, Marin (2006) at Italian beaches, Villares et al (2006) at Catalan beaches, Villares and Roca (2007) at beaches in the Costa Brava, Spain, and Blakemore and Williams (2008) investigated WTP of Turkish beach users. Among many diverse results identified by these studies, it is implied that different coastal environments attract visitors with different values, which is considered important and desirable. Three examples of questionnaires currently in use are presented in Appendix 1.

QUESTIONNAIRE DESIGN

The classic books for this topic are Kidder and Judd (1986), Malhotra and Birks (1999) and Gregoire and Valentine (2008) and the reader is referred to these. Question framing and overall questionnaire design has to be seen in the context of the aims and objectives of any research proposal, and questions should usually contain a mixture of factual and subjective questions. The former theoretically should be easier to answer, but experience has shown that respondents frequently misinterpret questions or are reluctant to answer. Opinions/beliefs of a respondent should be looked at via subjective questions and should cover a response range reflecting divergent viewpoints. The time taken to cover a questionnaire set is also very important, and the rule is quicker is usually better, with a beach-based maximum time of the order of 15 minutes. For these interviews, non-verbal cues can be observed that aid in formulating an answer, as well as clarifying terms that are unclear to the person being questioned (Robson, 1995). An interview is defined by Cannell and Kahn (1968: 530, our emphasis) as:

a two person conversation initiated by the interviewer for the specific purpose of obtaining research-relevant information and focused by *him* on content specified by research objectives of systematic description, prediction or explanation.

This definition encompasses the entire range of any research interview (Willemyns et al, 1997). However, the major plus of a personal beach interview is the fact that a high response rate (over 95 per cent) is virtually guaranteed. It is a costly form of interview but one that produces excellent data quality. People sitting on a beach are invariably happy to answer posed questions, as they are relaxed, sitting comfortably and are intrigued to be actually doing something, so the interviewer basically has a captive audience. Visual aids can be used and rapport, motivation and interview context control can be established quickly. Frequently, people on either side of the person being interviewed ask to be interviewed but beware of these (see below) as the sampling strategy must be followed.

Many sampling strategies and books exist, for example the seminal book of Malhotra and Birks (1999). In their review of questionnaire design strategy, Kidder and Judd (1986) identified the need to consider several issues culminating in what may be described in a ten-step process that should be considered as a basis for all questionnaire designs:

- **Step 1** Crucial to effective questionnaire design is *specification of required information*. This is often defined in a research project's objectives. In considering information required, it is also important to consider the likely *characteristics of the target respondent* group since an increasingly diversified respondent group will increase the difficulty of developing a single questionnaire to address the entire group.

  In the design of bathing area-related questionnaires, *specific inform-ation requirements* would concern identification of user preferences and priorities for both beaches and rock shores and the socio-economic value that beach users attribute to beach environments. Due to the multiple nature of these information requirements and the diverse nature of beaches (sand, gravel and so on) and rock shores, different questionnaires may be designed to address user preferences and priorities on sand/gravel beaches and rock shores and the evaluation of their economic importance.

  In considering the *characteristics of targeted respondents* (for example employment, country of origin, type of accommodation used) and the potential influence of respondent background to their stated perceptions, reference should be made to work relating to the development of questionnaires that address beach user preferences and priorities (Lockhart and Ashton, 1991; Williams et al, 1993a; Morgan et al, 1995; Ball, 2003; Villares and Roca, 2007).

- **Step 2** Questionnaire design should consider adoption of an appro-priate interviewing method. Options may include personal, tele-phone, mail or electronic questionnaires. The interviewing method naturally influences questionnaire design due to different methods of administration dictated by different interviewing methods. Many beach user questionnaires developed have been designed to reflect a conversational style due to the personal (face-to-face) interviewing method chosen. The method is usually chosen as a consequence of the public and recreational nature of beach environments (obviously negating telephone, mail and electronic options) and to the increased scope for respondents to ask, if needed, lengthy, complex or varied questions.

- **Step 3** This concerns determination of individual question content – usually preordained in a sequential manner. The strategy used should consider two main aspects, namely the *necessity* of the question and whether a single question is *sufficient* or may require additional related questions. The necessity of the question is largely ascertained by previously determined information requirements. However, it is possible that an interviewer may wish to include a number of neutral questions in the questionnaire either to establish involvement and rapport with the respondent or to generate support for the survey being undertaken.

  The issue of asking several questions rather than one is related to the need to obtain complete information. While the number of questions should be sufficient to ensure a meaningful evaluation of responses, it is important to avoid unnecessary or double-barrelled and multiple questions embedded in a single question and unnecessary level of detail. Question content should also address the value (to the researcher) of identifying the importance allocated to a particular issue by respondents. In this instance, respondents may be either asked directly to rate the importance of x or y, or can be asked open-ended questions that reflect the allocated importance. It is also relevant to consider that in many instances question content may need to be different for different respondent sub-groups. The issue of *question necessity* may also be addressed by ensuring that the majority of questions contribute directly or indirectly to questionnaire objectives. The issue of *question sufficiency* may be addressed by asking a second question related to a preceding one, where respondents are provided with the opportunity to clarify their position if their answer to the previous question was in the negative.

- **Step 4** A researcher should consider and address the potential inability of the respondent to answer. This may arise when not all respondents are likely to be informed about the subject, in which case, unless the research objectives include measurement of uninformed reactions, inclusion of 'no opinion' or 'do not know' answer options is suggested. However, since more 'do not know' responses are generated when this answer option is explicitly mentioned than when it is not, filter questions (that reflect the familiarity or otherwise of the respondent with the subject being addressed) can be inserted into the questionnaire to filter out unsuitable respondents, i.e. those not adequately informed.

  Schuman and Presser (1981) show that up to 25 per cent of respondents who give a 'do not know' response, when a filter question provides the opportunity, will also provide a substantive opinion to an unfiltered question. The recommendation on this controversy by Schuman and Presser (1981: 312) was that:

> filters should be used to screen out uninformed respondents if the measurement of only informed opinion on the issue is the goal but to use standard (unfiltered) questions if basic values, ideologies or general attitudes are desired.

A factor influencing respondent capability to answer is their ability to remember. This has been associated with errors related to not recalling an event that occurred, time compression and remembering events that did not take place. Although subject to *'reply biasing'*, this problem may be addressed by adopting an *'aided recall approach'* that tries to stimulate a respondent's memory by providing cues. A further factor influencing respondent capability to answer is their ability to articulate. This potential obstacle may be addressed by providing aid in the form of pictures, maps and alternative answers that may stimulate the respondent to provide an answer.

- **Step 5** This should address a potential respondent's unwillingness to answer. This may arise when respondents consider that too much effort is required, for example a questionnaire that has many pages, or the question context is inappropriate, has no legitimate purpose and/or is sensitive information. To avoid such circumstances, questionnaire designers should ensure they consider all options regarding a question's format and choose those proving the greatest assistance to the respondent, manipulate context where necessary to maximize appropriateness and explain why data are needed, so as to increase question legitimacy. In addition, a number of techniques are available to increase the likelihood of obtaining information that respondents consider too sensitive. These include placing the question at the end of the questionnaire, leading the question with a statement reflecting a common interest, using the third person to ask questions and providing a number of response options rather than expecting specific figures. However, if a respondent is unwilling to answer any questions, it is better to courteously thank him or her and move on (see below).

- **Step 6** This considers question structure options (unstructured or structured):
  - *Unstructured* (free response) questions are generally open-ended, allowing respondents to answer freely and in their own words and may therefore be more motivating to respondents and could introduce a measure of observer subjectivity. They are particularly useful in pilot studies since they provide a researcher with insights on the target respondents, for example attitude position, intensity, issue awareness and involvement, education and ability to communicate. Unstructured questions are also useful as opening

questions, as they provide respondents with the opportunity to express general opinions and attitudes. Disadvantages with unstructured questions include their tendency to elicit shorter responses if questionnaires are self-administered and an increased complexity with response coding in data evaluation. Responses to unstructured questions are often incongruous, difficult to understand, unrelated and difficult to code meaningfully.

– *Structured questions*, by contrast, pre-specify a set of response alternatives and the response format (for example multiple choice, dichotomous and scale-related questions). Such *closed-ended* (or fixed alternative) questions are easily coded, thereby providing meaningful results for analysis and need less motivation to communicate views and '*non-response*' answers tend to be given less frequently (Frankfort-Nachmias and Nachmias, 1992). Answers are usually quick, as no wordy response is usually required and analysis is straightforward. However, the major problem is that these questions could introduce bias by forcing respondents to choose from fixed answers or by making the respondent pick alternatives that they had not thought of – so an '*other*' category is essential. While dichotomous questions are used where 'yes/no' or 'agree/disagree' type responses are expected (thereby reflecting a large degree of certainty), multiple choice questions are introduced where the decision-making process reflects a degree of uncertainty. Multiple choice questions also assist respondents to understand question scope and sometimes to jog their memory. The question of whether to include a third (neutral) alternative to dichotomous questions may be decided by whether the overriding percentage of respondents are expected to take a neutral stand on the issue or not. Although easiest to code, dichotomous questions are subject to increased likelihood of influencing response by question format and particular care to avoid this must be taken. Ranking of questions answers to indicate priorities is recommended.

Questionnaire design often attempts to optimize use of both open- and closed-ended questions by providing a combination of both fixed response alternatives together with an open-ended '*other*' response option. This allows respondents to provide their own response if they disagree with the given alternatives. Unfortunately, this approach rarely obtains sufficient '*other*' responses to validate analysis and Schuman and Presser (1981) suggest that an ideal option may be to initiate a pilot study with open-ended questions to identify likely responses on which closed-ended questions may be formulated.

• **Step 7** This concerns the choice of *question wording*, which is probably the most difficult task of questionnaire construction since a poorly worded question may result in either a non-response (increasing the complexity of data analysis) or incorrect answering (introducing serious result bias). Correct question wording is considered of particular importance in the questionnaire design process. Avoidance of double-barrelled questions, long questions and jargon is important. Payne (1951) has given an excellent account of factors involved in formulating a sound survey. In pursuit of appropriately worded questionnaires, it is suggested that close attention be given to recommendations put forward by Kidder and Judd (1986) and Malhotra and Birks (1999), namely to:

- provide clear issue definition;
- use ordinary and unambiguous words;
- avoid leading questions;
- preclude implicit alternatives and assumptions; unwarranted assumptions are often generated by double-barrelled questions and may be avoided by asking a preliminary, confirmatory question,
- avoid generalizations and estimates;
- utilize both positive and negative statements;
- design response categories that reflect an appropriate balance between vagueness and over-precision where mutually exclusive ranges of numbers are often an acceptable solution;
- design response categories that, where necessary, are properly balanced to avoid creation of bias.

In addition, to ensure the quality of wide-scoped beach user questionnaire surveys, question format and wording should be subjected to rigorous assessment by coastal research personnel, sociologists and psychologists, as a basis for pilot and then further full-scale field studies.

- **Step 8** This concerns question ordering. This should reflect logical connections between questions as perceived by respondents and attempt to overcome respondent doubts about their ability to answer the questionnaire. Initial questions should be interesting, having clear social importance and relevance to the survey purpose. Questions that are considered difficult, for example sensitive, embarrassing or complex, should preferably appear late in the questionnaire, thereby allowing a preliminary confidence to be generated between interviewer and respondent. This reflects the accepted basis on which valid replies to all questions depends, namely the interviewer's rapport with the respondents that is normally gained by a professional approach, a confident expectation of an answer, and the use of transition statements prior to sensitive topics to clarify their relationship to the research topic.

In considering the best question order, questionnaire designers should consider that certain questions may influence the answer provided for others and should therefore not precede them. An easy guide to avoid this problem is that general, easy questions should be fielded first, followed by increasingly specific and detailed questions, i.e. the 'funnel down' approach. Naturally, questions dealing with different topics should be placed in distinct sections and ideally separated by a statement introducing the new topic. While such transitional statements should at a minimum, indicate that one topic has been completed and a new topic is being addressed, it is preferable that clear and meaningful statements are provided that reflect the relevance of new topics to survey objectives. By reflecting a sense of order, the respondent's comprehension and ability to answer are increased.

In order to avoid influencing answers, questionnaire design should ensure that general questions precede more specific ones. In establishing questionnaire design, questions should also be sorted to reflect a logical and issue order. In addition, for more expansive questionnaires, questions may be clearly subdivided into different sections, each addressing different aspects of the questionnaire, for example respondent-related data, beach user preferences and priorities, and beach-specific data.

- **Step 9** This considers form and layout. In this stage, a researcher should consider the most professional appearance possible, subdivisions of the questionnaire (reflecting distinct questionnaire sections), aspects of question numbering, avoiding question crowding, and providing of clear, easy to follow directions and instructions. Questionnaires should be pre-coded and serially numbered.
- **Step 10** This involves execution of a pilot survey (Figure 5.1) where the efficacy or otherwise of *all* aspects considered in the design so far is tested. Further to pilot surveying, problems are identified and addressed through questionnaire revision. Additional pilot surveys are only suggested following significant revision of the questionnaire. Pilot surveys are invariably necessary, to find out if any changes (question additions, ordering and so on) need to be carried out prior to the main survey.

After the ten steps, it just remains to begin the full survey. Figure 5.1 indicates the logical sequence of the above steps.

The above ten steps refer to surveys that are generally undertaken in situ on beaches. However, some questionnaires need a follow-up, for example health issues such as the effects of swimming and ingesting sea water on health (Nelson et al, 1999). This would necessitate a telephone number/ address to be given. This immediately cuts down replies by respondents by perhaps 50 per cent, as people are loath to give out such information. Interviews done by phone can be long, i.e. one hour plus with little loss of data quality. Such interviews also cut down on interviewer bias and have the advantage of interviewer supervision, as the overall team leader can be available for immediate problem resolution. The non-usage of maps/ figures is a drawback.

For beach surveys, paper colour is not very important, but for postal surveys, coloured paper increases response rates by around 9 per cent

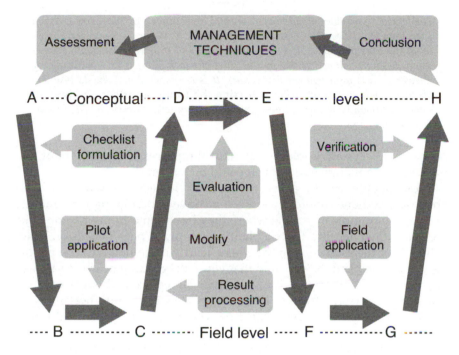

Source: Davies et al (1995a)

Figure 5.1 *The W checklist diagram*

(Fox et al, 1988). This brings into play an unknown bias as a result of large population non-responses. Many excellent papers/books have been written on the topic of postal questionnaires, for example Futrell (1994), Fink (1995) and Robson (1995). The advantage of this means of eliciting data is that very large numbers of people can be targeted and data accumulated in a very short time. This survey also allows a respondent to answer in their own time, so pressure is minimized and anonymity is assured (Potts, 1999). As there is separation between interviewer and interviewee, often a more critical response can be obtained, but it does mean that there is no rapport between interviewer and interviewee and there is no guarantee that the selected person was the only person to fill in the questionnaire – other family members could have helped.

THE INTERVIEW

What is frequently forgotten in assessing beach questionnaires is the actual interview procedure. It cannot be stressed enough that a clean, happy countenance and courteous manner is mandatory when dealing with the public (see Figure 5.2). For example:

*A cheerful 'good morning/afternoon', should be followed by 'my name is X and I am from the University/Council/Organization of Y. We are doing research work on Z (for example public perception of beaches) and wonder if you could answer some questions that are written on this sheet of paper. There is no right or wrong answer, as it is **your** opinion that counts. It is confidential and should take you about five minutes or so'. After collecting the forms, a further chat should ensue, as usually the interviewee asks some general questions. Always be courteous.*

Note, it is always advisable to state that the process will take about five minutes, even though you know it could be longer!

Most people would agree to be interviewed following such an approach, and one should try to keep a conversation going for a minute or two, for example by asking where they have come from or if they like the beach/town/locality. Have a plentiful supply of pens/pencils on hand. If time is of the essence, it may be beneficial if up to half a dozen people are approached and they are told that you will be sitting nearby to answer any questions. This approach can produce 50 replies in about two hours. If a selected person refuses to take part, politely thank him/her and walk away. In our experience, less than 5 per cent of people questioned refuse to participate.

Moser and Kalton (1983) have argued that three essential conditions have to be fulfilled for interview success:

- accessibility – selection of respondents;
- cognition – the interviewee must understand what is required;
- motivation – the establishment of a rapport.

Figure 5.2 *Interviewing people who have been selected by random numbers along a row of 'tiki' huts at Olu Deniz beach, Turkey*

Figure 5.3 *Face-to-face interviews at Aberaeron, Wales, UK*

Ball (2003) suggests another condition – that of perception, which is not merely listening to and interpreting a respondent's answer, but relates also to the implied meanings of the response, evident via body language, voice intonations or long silent periods (see Figure 5.3).

Breakwell (1990) argues that there is no golden rule about interview sample sizes. On small pocket beaches in rural/remote areas, trying to obtain a subtotal of 30 – which is adequate for a pilot survey (although we suggest a sample size of 50) – could take a considerable time as few people go to these beaches, especially remote ones. However, the advantage is that one can cover all beach users at that site.

For urban/resort beaches where numbers of potential respondents could be thousands, it is important to decide on a sampling strategy that selects people for interview without bias. This is not a trivial matter, depending on the size and nature of the site. For example, interviewees should be selected from the whole beach area, not clustered near the access point or along the shoreline. A stratified sampling strategy involves subdividing the area with respect to any natural features that affect people's distribution, for example landward to seaward zones, close to an access point or more remote. Such factors may influence the type of respondent encountered in different areas of the site. For example, if parallel rows of 'tiki' huts/sun-loungers are characteristic of a beach – common throughout the Mediterranean and Caribbean – equal numbers of respondents should be selected from rows alongside the shoreline as well as inland, since people arriving early to occupy the 'prime sites' (it is inherently cooler the nearer the sea) may have different views to those in less 'desirable spots' behind the first row. Within each sub-area of the site (stratum), interviewees may be selected systematically throughout the sampling frame, or, ideally, using random number tables. For example, working along a row of sun-loungers, people at every nth point (where n could be 2, 3, 4 etc.) could be asked to contribute to the survey. If a refusal is met, go to the next set. Alternatively, random numbers can be selected and the interviewer moves along rows and addresses the person at the particular number selected. People who are in the sea or walking about should be avoided as they are *'doing things'* and usually loath to be interviewed.

Random selection is preferable in statistical terms to systematic because each person on the whole site has an equal chance of being selected, but in practice this is often difficult to manage on a crowded beach. The important thing is that selecting the individual for interview should be unbiased, i.e. adopt a scheme in advance and approach only those people who are selected arbitrarily – do not be drawn towards those who are particularly attractive or kindly looking. The sub-areas of the site (strata) may be equal in size, for example five rows of sun-loungers, or arbitrary zones along the beach away from the access point. If the numbers of people occupying different strata are not equal, for example all sun-loungers by the sea may be occupied whereas there may be few people using those inland, or there may be a high density of people near the access point and fewer in more remote areas, then the sampling intensity should be adjusted so that equal numbers of respondents are sampled from all strata, for example interview only one in ten in a high-density area, but one in three where people are sparse (see Figure 5.4). As every site is different, a pilot survey is valuable to determine the best sampling strategy given the desired sample size and the time available for the survey.

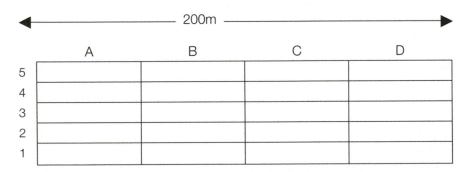

Note: Stratified sampling. A 200m stretch of beach has been subdivided (A–D at 50m widths) and down the beach are lines of sun-loungers ranged in rows 1–5. Row 1 could be the nearest to the sea. For a sample size of n=400, one would need 20 responses in each of the segments, i.e. 20 in each of rows 1–5 for each of segments A–D. Random number tables will indicate which people should be selected in each row.

Figure 5.4 *Sample grid for a beach survey*

Table 5.1 *Sampling error margins*

Acceptable sampling error (%)	Sample size
(p<0.05)	
1	10,000
2	2500
3	1100
4	625
5	400
6	277
7	204
8	256
9	123
10	100

Source: De Vaus (1986)

For larger samples undertaken after the pilot survey, De Vaus (1986) produces a table for sampling error margins, for example the 5 percentile figure would be reached after 400 interviews (see Table 5.1). After all data have been gathered, standard computer statistical packages (for example SPSS or Minitab) can cross-tabulate items at will to produce quantitative results in line with the aims/objectives of the project. For example, Villares and Roca (2007) working from 42,000 responses to 590 questionnaires on the Costa Brava in Spain found, via SPSS cluster analysis, that two opinion groups existed regarding evaluation of beach quality. The 'Demanding' group expressed dissatisfaction with general beach cleanliness, while the 'Satisfied' group were more pleased with their choice and use of beach.

Interviewers should be aware that whatever questionnaires are used, the measured variables are only approximations to abstractions/constructs. The questionnaire answers relate to specific questions geared to measure these abstractions/constructs (Kidder and Judd, 1986).

CHAPTER 6

Environmental Risk Management

INTRODUCTION

Coastal and beach planners/managers are starting to use risk assessment techniques (for hazards, vulnerability and suchlike) when faced with complex multidisciplinary problems that have to be solved in short time periods (DoE, 1995). With respect to emergency management in a bathing environment, hazards are considered as sources of damage, and damage reduction is the core of *hazard mitigation*, defined as the cost-effective measures taken to reduce the potential for damage on a community from the hazard impact. In simple terms, humanity is generally ignorant about its *vulnerability* (Latin *vulnare* – to wound), especially with respect to the adverse effects of water hazards. Therefore it behoves beach managers to utilize vulnerability assessment as a tool to reduce the potential for damage from impact of these hazards. Truly effective mitigation – *hazard damage reduction* – must be based on a clear understanding of the causes of damage gained by applying a *vulnerability assessment* methodology applicable regardless of the specific hazard type. Assessment takes place at three levels: *hazard identification* defines the magnitudes and probabilities of the hazard that threatens anthropogenic interests; *vulnerability assessment* characterizes the population exposed to the hazard and the damage/injuries resulting; and *risk analyses* incorporates the probability of damage/injury.

Specifically, a *hazard* is a set of circumstances, usually physical environmental elements but sometimes human induced, that could lead to harm i.e. death, injury or an illness of a person, and that are caused by extraneous forces (Smith, 2004). They come in various guises, i.e. natural/anthropogenic, rapid/slow, intense/diffuse, rare/chronic, high/low energy. Hazard is a function of risk, exposure and response and if there is no human interaction, there is no hazard. The *risk* of an event happening is the probability that it will occur due to exposure to a defined hazard degree, i.e. = f (probability of occurrence, vulnerability) or sometimes as = f (hazard, vulnerability), and this causes loss. Risk analysis is concerned with chance, consequences and context (Elms, 1992), while risk management reduces adverse events identified by risk analysis. The *rate of incidence* (frequency of recurrence) can be viewed as the expected number of events that occur for this defined hazard amount. Probabilities and rates obey different mathematical laws, but if events are independent and probabilities small, the two values are essentially the same. Risks can vary from negligible – an adverse event occurring at a frequency of one per million plus, for example an asteroid hitting the Earth – to very high, that is fairly regular events such as bathers in difficulty. Hazard is an abstract idea but disaster is its realization (Mitchell, 1988). Two types of vulnerability exist, of which only *relative vulnerability* concerns bathing area hazards. This results from specific factors present in any given location/site that may affect or modify how the hazard impacts the area and is the rationale behind risk assessment studies carried out in the UK by, for example, the Royal Life Saving Society (RLSS, 2008a, b) and the Chartered Institute of Environmental Health (CIEH, 2002). These organizations have developed a checklist system of risk assessment and this field is of growing concern to beach managers (see Box 6.1).

HAZARDS

The growth of risk management as a discipline has many subjective elements, and value judgements have to be made as to the seriousness of any hazard, especially as beaches vary in usage as well as physical characteristics. Hazard research essentially commenced in the context of flood studies in the US in the 1950s and 1960s with the behavioural school of geographers (Kates, 1962; Saarinen, 1966; White and Haas, 1975), which emphasized the interaction of man and natural events and used feedback loops implying rational responses as adjustments to the events. They placed great emphasis on events (that are not necessarily unusual) and the decision maker, i.e. the individual. Among others, Hewitt (1997) criticizes this approach because of its emphasis on geophysical events (hazard impact is not solely determined by these), lack of scientific understanding and the fact that disaster response planning was frequently in the hands of the military. Such criticisms gave rise to the structural approach to hazard research. This emphasized the fact that disasters are almost regular events in developing countries where populations are poor and vulnerable, for example along the Bangladesh coastline. Rapid environmental/social change can occur here with only limited responses available. The more balanced viewpoint of the contextual approach followed, suggesting that both approaches should be considered and postulating that two subsystems make up the hazard system: components, i.e. the physical processes, populations, processes and costs; and contexts, i.e. the exogenous factors that can affect the components.

The assessment benchmark is a summary statement obtained from parameters shown in Box 6.1. What is a *'significant'* hazard (natural or artificial) on beaches that are in an inherently hazardous environment? A beach manager's aim must be to identify *key* hazards that would be dangerous and pose significant risks.

On a beach, many hazards occur as people are close to a water hazard zone for example rip currents, large wave heights, dangerous rock areas, large tidal ranges, in some areas dangerous marine species (sharks, crocodiles, stonefish, stingrays, snakes), jet skis and rock falls, many of which can require urgent medical attention. In addition, there can exist overcrowding with respect to carrying capacity, lifeguard shortages and harmful UV exposure. In Northern Europe, shoals of jellyfish are now becoming increasingly familiar in coastal waters and first aid is frequently needed for stings. These are more commonly found in warmer waters when heat waves occur. For example, in the shallow waters off Praia Grande, Brazil on 30 December 2007, some 300 people were treated at clinics for stings. Mediterranean beaches have in recent years been plagued by the mauve stinger jellyfish (*Pelagia noctiluca*), which tend to live some 10km offshore but now appear to actively proliferate in winter months prior to assaulting central and northern Mediterranean shore beaches. Between November 2007 and January 2008, densities of four to ten creatures per cubic metre were routinely recorded, with some as high as 100 per cubic metre. Mild temperatures, no icy wind blasts and low rainfall have proved to be ideal breeding conditions. Small nets termed '*pelicanes*' have been used to collect surface drifting jellyfish; on submergence in fresh water for 48 hours their poison drains away and they can be recycled as protein-rich fertilizer. It is important to catch them without causing damage as the tentacles remain poisonous even when detached.

Overfishing (especially of tuna and swordfish) is a major cause of these blooms as there are fewer fish to feed on the jellyfish. Numbers of their other main predator, the turtle *Caretta careta*, are also diminishing as tourists lay claim to their traditional nesting sites. Adding to the problem is the fact that jellyfish gorge themselves on fish eggs and larvae, especially the *Aurelia Aurita* species. The salty lagoons of the Mar Menor, near La Manga, Spain, are rich in fertilizer-based nutrients associated with the many plastic greenhouses in the region, and frequently nearby waters are turned into a creamy soup colour by the jellyfish species *Cortylorhiza tuberculata* (the 'fried egg' species). Global disequilibrium due to overfishing is not only confined to the Mediterranean; spectacular jellyfish growth has been found in Japan, Namibia, Alaska, Peru and Australia and so is an international ecological problem. In addition, one must not forget about beaches located in freshwater areas, where leptospirosis can occur.

Almost by definition, family-orientated beaches may have many small children splashing about in the water and this can influence the hazard degree. Excessively large wave heights might trigger an action level response of reducing patrol coverage, as few swimmers are in the water, or even forbidding bathing, an act totally inappropriate on a typical surfing beach. Definitions of these terms (accidents/incidents) are essential, as they mean different things to different people and, with the risk of increasing litigation, these should be mandatory. A more thorough assessment should follow the pattern shown in Boxes 6.1 and 6.2.

Grenfell and Ross (1992) found in an Australian study of beach injuries, that beach litter accounted for 19 per cent of all injuries. Further studies by Santos et al (2005) in Brazil showed that beach users were of the opinion that the main beach injury to humans is caused by hazardous litter. UNEP (2005) also finds that marine litter has a negative effect on health. The topic of risk assessment is currently extremely important, but is one that in the past has been subjective and consisted of making value judgements concerning the seriousness of any hazard. Physical hazards should be readily perceptible, unlike microbiological, chemical and biological ones, which are far beyond the remit of a beach manager and require specialized laboratories. There is ever-increasing need for such assessments, especially as beaches vary in usage as well as physique and an in spite of European-wide safety regulations, rule adherence is often flouted. In 2005, Hannah Sutton died as a result of a jet ski accident in Cyprus. She was under the legal age (18 years of age) for hiring such a vehicle. Aristos Ioannou of Chris Watersports did not check ages of Ms Sutton and her friend James Dudley, who crashed into her causing her death. After the tragedy, Dudley was briefly jailed and fined some £2000. In 2007, after the 12th court hearing, Ioannou was fined £523 at Limassol district court. A jet ski can reach speeds of up to 60 knots (BMIF, 1999).

Less obvious health risks can feature on beaches, namely medical waste and sewage-related debris and:

> whilst the risk of infection by serious disease is small, the visible presence of faecal and other offensive materials carried by the sewerage system can mean serious loss of amenity and is therefore an unacceptable form of pollution. (HCEC, 1990: xvii)

Even though risks are low (Rees and Pond, 1995; Nelson and Williams, 1997; Nelson et al, 1999) contact/ingestion with infected sanitary products, syringes and fluids can cause disease. Garrity and Levings (1993) in Panama found significant levels of medical waste on beaches. Sharps containers have been issued to lifeguards in the UK, who are advised not to go barefoot. In the UK, 40 needle-stick accidents on bathing beaches were reported to the UK Public Health Laboratory Service Communicable Disease Surveillance Centre between 1988 and 1991 (Philipp et al, 1995). Sewage-related debris suggests that adjacent waters are contaminated, which means a health risk to beach users, with bathers having a higher risk of skin and ear infections (McIntyre, 1990). In 1990, it was reported to the UK House of Commons that the aesthetic quality of recreational waters, as represented by hazardous litter such as dog faeces and sewage debris, is 'becoming increasingly important as the public become more aware of, and sensitive to, the risks' (HCEC, 1990). This is still true today.

Box 6.1 *Coastal hazards considered by risk assessment*

Environmental hazards:
1   Local geography
2   Beach configuration (expanded as Box 6.2)
3   Beach composition
4   Tides and currents
5   Waves
6   Weather
7   Water quality

Man-made hazards:
1   Structures – piers, harbours, jetties
2   Coastal defences – seawalls, wave breaks, groynes
3   Hazardous substances

Equipment hazards:
For example winches, transport and so on

Human hazards:
1   Activity hazards – *what people 'do'*, for example swimming, surfing and
    wind surfing
2   Behavioural hazards – *how people 'do'*, for example alcohol, bravado, and
    ignorance
3   Vulnerable groups

Lifeguard/employee hazards:
1   Normal operations
2   Emergency operations

Summary assessment: Hazard/risk profile:
Severity; likelihood; action rating

Assessment updates

Source: RLSS UK (2008b); CIEH (2002)

An assessment benchmark – a summary statement obtained from
parameters shown in Box 6.1 giving a dossier of the risks associated with
any beach – should be drawn up, with Box 6.2 being an example of an
expanded category from Box 6.1. This is to be recommended as essential
work to be carried out at all recognized bathing beaches and follows a
similar road to the work of Kenyon et al (2006), who argue for *'vertical
knowledge'*, i.e. a deep understanding of the system. Accident analysis
(Figure 6.1) will give a very clear idea as to what major hazards exist
at any particular beach, and a risk analysis, as outlined above, should

be carried out first. The guiding principles for the RLSS UK (2008a) and CIEH (2002) risk assessment protocol are given in Box 6.3. From Box 6.1, the summary assessment 'Severity; likelihood; action rating' is the end point of the assessment, found after 47 pages of assessment. This could easily be incorporated within the Associated British Ports environmental risk assessment package (ABP, 1997; see Chapter 7, 'Environmental Risk Assessment Method', page 161).

Box 6.2 *Risk assessment matrix – expansion of point 2, beach configuration, in Box 6.1*

2) Beach Configuration

The area covered by this assessment has the following configuration

☐ Abrupt changes in depth/shelving/troughs

☐ A gradient of 1:10 or less

☐ Sand bars interceded by deep troughs

☐ Rip channels

A. Summarize/describe/other

....
....
....
....

B. Significant hazards presented

....
....
....
....

C. Which could cause harm if/by

....
....
....
....

D. People/property/equipment at risk

....
....
....
....

E. Specialized risk assessment required ?   ☐ YES   ☐ NO
Details...
....

F)   Rating   Severity   Likelihood   Action rating

G)   Current control measures

....

....

....

....

....

                    Are these adequate?   Yes   No

H)   Action levels identified?   Yes   No

Detail..

....

....

....

I)   Further control measures recommended

....

....

....

....

J)   Other personnel/departments/agencies involved

....

....

K)   Target dates for achievement of further controls

....

....

L)   Information and training needs

....

....

....

Completed on...

By..

M)   Monitoring
      a)   Frequency...
      b)   Person responsible..

N)   Review dates

....

....

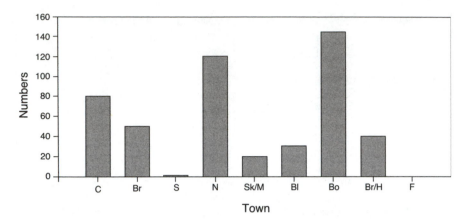

Note: C, Cleethorpes; Br, Brighton; S, Southend; N, Newquay; Sk/M, Skegness and Maplethorpe; Bl, Blackpool; Bo, Bournemouth; Br/H, Brighouse and Hornsea; F, Felixstowe

Source: NELC (2007)

Figure 6.1 *Typical graph of incidents/accidents per year*

Box 6.3 *Risk assessment matrix*

General guidelines

This matrix is designed for use by holders of the RLSS UK/CIEH 'Risk Assessment Principles and Practice' Programme certificate. The matrix suggests a structure for conducting risk assessments. It is *not* the 'one right way'. The matrix may be used 'as is' or may be modified or amended to suit the needs of a particular environment.

The subjectivity of risk assessment requires that assessors have a clear grasp of parameters, which constitute the seriousness of a hazard and the extent of risk. They must also understand that these parameters can be different from one beach to another and can change from day to day.

Changing weather

This is particularly true in the beach environment because of the *variability* of and *interaction* between hazard and risk factors. Variability refers to the way in which factors which affect the outcome of the assessment, such as the weather, the shape of the beach or the number of visitors, can change.

The beach environment is *constantly* changing. Tides alone dictate this. There is almost always an interaction between these changes and the relationship between hazard and risk, which in turn affects the hazard rating.

Interaction then is the term used to describe the way these variable factors act upon each other.

To allow for these changes, operators are recommended to formulate a 'summary' assessment which provides a typical or 'snapshot' hazard/risk profile. The 'summary' assessment will need to be updated to account for significant changes and therefore 'assessment updates' are recommended. Example summary and update assessment sheets can be found at the back of the matrix.

No magic formulas

How then, can we be sure that our assessment is 'suitable and sufficient'? Well there is no easy formula. First, the process must be considered. This is to say properly and demonstrably 'thought through'. Second, a formula or format will obviously be helpful in avoiding omissions. The formula followed in this pack is just one suggested by RLSS/CIEH. It is not necessarily the only right way. It is, however, the result of extensive research into best practice.

Making it manageable

By breaking the assessment into definable areas, e.g. 'Environment' and 'Equipment Hazards' the process is simply made more manageable. The intention of working through the checklists is to create a *summary assessment*. This is a benchmark or starting point which forms the foundation of the overall assessment and from which basic control measures may be formulated.

Simple checklists

This *summary assessment* must be updated as appropriate, the frequency being determined by local conditions and may be hourly/daily and may depend on the variability of conditions on any particular day. Risk assessment *updates* take the form of simple checklists to assist the operator in ensuring that control measures are adequate and suitable for any change in conditions. As regards 'grey areas', assessors judge, using their experience and skill, taking external advice if necessary for hazards requiring special attention.

Souce: RLSS UK (2008b)

Determining a beach as safe/unsafe has many connotations, with most beaches falling into a gradient between the end members of this spectrum. Excessive microbiological counts, for example the presence of excessive *Faecal streptococci* in water samples, usually means that bathing is unsafe, and entrance to the water not recommended. This is 'hard' science. On the other hand prolonged exposure to the sun's UV rays is harmful, so a 'safe' beach would have signage and educational campaigns, such as *'slip, slop and slap'* regarding sunscreen creams to protect against harsh sunlight exposure, which was carried out originally in Australia. This can change beach behavioural patterns regarding skin cancers and photo-aging

(Harvey, 1995). The United Nations Environment Programme (UNEP, 2005) estimated that some 2 million non-melanoma skin cancers occur annually, plus some 200,000 malignant ones, mostly originating from exposure on beaches.

A recent beach classification system proposed by the WHO and co-sponsored by the United States Environmental Protection Agency provided an alternative approach to monitoring and assessment of recreational water quality (WHO, 2000). Beach classification is in this case related to a single group of issues, i.e. health risks, which are assessed as a consequence of a combination of a microbiological indicator of faecal contamination and inspection-based assessment of bathing area susceptibility (to such contamination). In so doing, the system addressed current concerns with existing regulatory schemes that rely solely on microbiological indicators representative of a single moment. Based upon health risk, beaches are assigned a class (very poor, poor, fair, good or excellent) (see Figure 6.2).

This approach could also be conjoined with the environmental risk assessment package (see Chapter 7, 'Environmental Risk Assessment Method', page 161). However, beach hazard assessment tends to be poorly developed/implemented, especially when compared with the wealth of information about the microbiology associated with bathing waters.

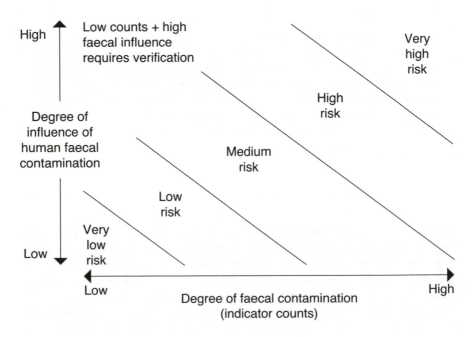

Source: WHO (2000)

Figure 6.2 *Representation of health risk*

Hazard effects can range from death, for example drowning (see Box 6.4), to major impact injuries, for example paraplegia, fractures, cuts and grazes, punctures and so on. King-sized lobsters can also come into this category! A 50-year-old, 1m lobster attacked a person at Weymouth jetty in the UK (*The Guardian*, 10 July 2007). It is now in a nearby sea life park. Male deaths via drowning are more likely than females, due usually to more exposure and sometimes alcohol consumption (WHO, 1998), but many more near-drowning experiences occur. Diving accidents – usually by diving into a wave and crashing into the beach bottom – constitute the main cause of beach-based spinal injuries, with a resulting high financial cost to society (Blanksby et al, 1997).

Recent 'crazes' include '*tombstoning*', where thrill-seeking people leap into the sea off cliffs, piers or any coastal structure. In the UK this causes some 15 deaths per year and around 200 serious injuries per year have occurred from this 'sport'. For example, at Berry Head, Torbay, Devon in the UK, in June 2007, a 46-year-old man jumped 10m into the sea at low tide and was killed. In July 2007 another male jumped from Clacton Pier, Essex, UK and died after being rescued by lifeboat crews and airlifted to hospital. On 2 August 2007, a 16-year-old died after jumping from the harbour wall at Minehead, UK; on 17 August 2007, a 25-year-old man leaped into the sea from the harbour wall at Hugh Town, Saint Mary's in the Isles of Scilly, and will probably not walk again. On 11 May 2008, a man jumped 8m from a Southsea pier (in the UK) into 1m of water and is now confined to a wheelchair. A BBC interview given by him is now being shown to children warning them of the dangers associated with this craze. However, it is usually cuts and grazes that are legion on beaches; as are, unfortunately, a growing number of incidents caused by discarded syringes and hypodermic needles. Additionally, Australian lifeguards (who rescue around 5000 people each summer) are now being trained to handle outbreaks of '*surf rage*' – abuse from belligerent beach users who object to being told when/ where to swim, and anger caused by the banning of dogs and such like – even though the rules are geared to best beach management practice. Workplace violence specialists are teaching lifeguards how to defuse hostile situations.

Beach hazard assessment is critical in order that safety can be ensured. It must embrace natural (cliffs, water and so on) and artificial (groynes and seawalls) hazards, the hazard severity, area usage, density of people and type of beach. A typical assessment scenario by a beach manager would be production of graphs of accidents/incidents per year at bathing beaches, as shown in Figure 6.1. A classic litter case regarding beach closure, as a result of the reporting of medical waste (syringes, catheters) occurred on beaches in New Jersey in 1987 and Long Island in 1988, which resulted in an estimated loss of 37–121 million beach users and an expenditure loss of $1.3–5.4 billion (Valle-Levinson and Swanson, 1991). The reduction in glass from bottles and the rise of plastics, has, however, lessened amounts of glass to be found on beaches, with a corresponding reduction in the chances of being cut by glass. Ironically, recycled glass – particularly car windscreens and bottles, is now considered suitable for beach nourishment projects, especially in 'hot spots' (Edge et al, 2002; see Chapter 1).

Box 6.4 *Brighton beach, UK*

Mr Paul Cooke on 28 July 2001 visited Brighton, UK, for the first time with two other persons and went for a swim near the marina end of the beach. No signs or flags indicated that it was dangerous for swimming and that it was not an area zoned for lifeguard cover, lying between two such zones termed Dolphin 1 and Dolphin 2. Additionally, there were no signs indicating which areas of the beach had lifeguard cover and which did not. There was no such duty to erect them over the majority of 7 miles of beach. Mr Cooke swam approximately 50m into the sea and soon was in need of urgent assistance. The tide was incoming, the weather clear, hot and sunny and the sea calm.

Brighton and Hove City Council has around 7 miles (10km) of potential beach to cover (an unreasonable if not impossible task). Their policy is to concentrate service provision at specified points of highest usage and risk, demarcated with flags and uniformed, trained staff at surveillance points. As no lifeguard was present in or near the area in question, fellow swimmers brought Mr Cooke ashore where he was found to be in cardiac arrest. Cardiopulmonary resuscitation was initially provided by a recently qualified dentist, continued by paramedics and later the Sussex Ambulance Service transported him to the intensive care unit of the Royal Sussex County Hospital, where he stayed for over three weeks. The near-drowning episode resulted in irreversible hypoxic brain injury, leaving Mr Cooke with spastic tetraplegia and confined to bed/wheelchair.

Mr Cooke had the benefit of a Public Finding Certificate, and the case of *Paul Cooke* v. *Brighton and Hove City Council* was finally brought to court in 2006. The verdict was that no offers were to be made apart from a 'drop hands agreement' i.e. each party bear its own costs.

According to Lord Hoffman on free will:

> It is of course understandable that organisations like the Royal Society for the Prevention of Accidents should favour policies which require people to be prevented from taking risks. Their function is to prevent accidents and that is one way of doing so. But they do not have to consider the cost, not only in money but also in deprivation of liberty, which such restrictions entail. The courts will naturally respect the technical expertise of such organisations in drawing attention to what can be done to prevent accidents. But the balance between risk on the one hand and individual autonomy on the other is not a matter of expert opinion. It is a judgment which the courts must make and which in England reflects the individualist values of the common law. (*Tomlinson* v. *Congleton Borough Council and Another*, House of Lords, 31 July 2003, [2002] EWCA Civ 309, [2004] 1 A.C. 46)

Litter as mentioned previously, is of growing concern in most countries, and Australia with its many pristine beaches stands out as one nation that really prizes its beach culture. Beach users would not dare to leave an Australian beach littered with the usual paraphernalia associated with many European beaches (for example beer cans, water bottles and food containers)! The draconian laws of Singapore also mean that beaches remain renowned for being clean of litter and therefore one key risk factor is alleviated. Clean beaches not only mean a lowering of the risk factor but produce viable income, as beach users want such beaches – even if some users leave all their litter behind (Balance et al, 2000).

HAZARD SIGNAGE

The danger associated with rock-fall hazard is particularly marked when cliffs occur around/adjacent a beach area and is used below as an example to describe appropriate hazard signage. Beach users invariably sit close to cliffs as they provide a convenient warm back rest and users are sheltered from winds (see Figure 6.3). A plethora of signs usually exist indicating the danger of staying close to a cliff base (and near a cliff edge at a cliff top), but the general public apparently do not perceive these signs. Maintenance is crucial to signage, as is the siting of such signs. From a sample population of 125 beach users, only 34 per cent correctly recalled the sign and its message content indicating the danger of rock falls. The signs were sited some 200m from the beach on an approach road to a car park in Wales, UK (Williams and Williams, 1991). The remaining percentage had either not seen the sign or had seen it but could not recall the message. Yet signs

Figure 6.3 *Beach users at a cliff base*

placed at the car park entrance were seen and understood by 84 per cent of users.

Sign colour is important as 85 per cent of respondents remembered the sign was coloured red; this being statistically significant at the 0.01 level. This confirmed the standard international layout of warning signs as being red in colour with a white frame and white lettering (see Figure 6.4). Note the colour coding in Figure 6.5, which is the opposite! A valid question concerns the nature of the message: should it be pictorial, written or both? With short viewing times, written verbal signs are less efficient than symbolic signs.

Note: This sign is red with a white frame and white lettering

Figure 6.4 *Beach sign with correct colour coding*

Note: This sign is white with a red frame and red lettering

Figure 6.5 *Beach sign with incorrect colour coding*

Individual differences examined (age, sex, education, distance travelled, frequency of visits) were not significant to sign perception. However, trends did exist, for example users with basic education levels perceived signs to a lesser degree than those with higher educational attainment – only 19 per cent of the former perceived signs, in comparison to 44 per cent of the latter. Some 67 per cent of first-time visitors perceived the signs, possibly because they were looking for directional signs rather than warning ones. A classic paper by Szlichicinski (1979) shows that symbolic signs are a very useful way of conveying messages and can perform better than word signs. Testing sign efficiency can be carried out by a simple semantic differential scale comprising bipolar adjectives ranging from excellent to bad (see Table 6.1). If a sign is deemed to be good, the subject being tested would indicate a strong level of association towards the 'good' end of the scale, which varies with respect to the parameter being measured. In testing a variety of word/picture signs, including signs currently utilized on a cliffed coastline, Williams and Williams (1991) show that current signs (words only with the standard international colour code) scored well on 'understandability' and 'evaluative' factors but less on 'potency' and 'activity'. The 'best' tested sign was that shown in Figure 6.6. An interesting account of signage and *'unusual danger'*, is given in Box 6.5.

Table 6.1 *Semantic-differential test*

Adjective	Scores							Adjective	Factor
Good	1						7	Bad	E
Weak	7						1	Strong	P
Active	1						7	Passive	A
Unpredictable	7						1	Predictable	U
Clean	1						7	Dirty	E
Slow	7						1	Fast	A
Worthless	7						1	Valuable	E
Rugged	1						7	Delicate	P
Strange	7						1	Familiar	U
Simple	1						7	Complicated	U
Light	7						1	Heavy	P
Sharp	1						7	Dull	A

Note: E – evaluative, attitude, opinion; U – understandability, comprehension, understanding; p – Potency, power; a – Activity, energy. A low score indicates a high degree of meaning.

Box 6.5 *Subordinate Courts of the Republic of Singapore*

The plaintiff claimed damages as a result of a poisonous stonefish sting while wading in 1.5m of water off Janjong beach, Sentosa island, Singapore, arguing that the defendants breached a duty of care owed him by virtue of their being the occupiers of Sentosa island. The trial hinged on the issues/liabilities quantum of damages. The plaintiff had been going to the beach since 2000 and claimed not to have seen two warning signs placed there by the defendants, resulting in medical expenses of $17,629, as a result of three operations while in hospital care. Defendants argued that they had no control over 'the existence of marine creatures in the said waters'. The following issues were considered:

- **Whether the defendants were the occupiers of Janjong island, and in particular the waters off the beach.** Unlike UK law where the law on occupier's liability is encapsulated in the Occupier's Liability Act, 1957, the liability in tort incurred by an occupier is governed solely by common law. What is an occupier? The general principle is Lord Denning in *Wheat* v. *E Lacon and Co Ltd*:

  > whether a person has a sufficient degree of control over premises that he ought to realise that any failure on his part to use care may result in an injury to a person coming lawfully there, then he is an 'occupier' and the person coming lawfully there is a 'visitor', and the 'occupier' is under a duty to the visitor, to use reasonable care.

  The crux of an occupier's liability is physical or occupational control. The defence council argued that there was nothing in legislation that conferred on them the control/management of the foreshore, seabed, territorial waters and biological resources of the sea. However, they had instigated 'trawling' operations via nets and fish traps to help clear seaweed and fish from the area, and so had the power to exercise supervision and control over the area.
  Court Ruling: The defendants had sufficient de facto physical control over the said waters.

- **Whether the defendants fulfilled their duty as occupiers, vis-à-vis the plaintiff, a beach visitor.** The duty of an occupier to a visitor would be to prevent damage/injury from any 'unusual danger' in the premises, which he knows or ought to know and which the invitee does not. Were stonefish an *'unusual danger'*, as many other dangers lurked in the sea (sharks, jellyfish, sea urchins) in their natural habitat? The defendants were aware of stonefish in the nearby waters and one sign specifically referred to this danger and argued that the chances of being stung were 0.000033 per cent. Signs had been placed on the beach control tower, as this was a focal point for visitor traffic flow. However, the key factor for 'unusual danger', is that it must be one that an objective person would not reasonably expect to be there.
  Court ruling: stonefish did not present an 'unusual danger' and no breach of duty by the defendants had occurred by virtue of a lack of warning signs or other measures to prevent damage from the *'unusual danger'*. The stonefish encounter was a misfortune.

Source: Subordinate Courts of the Republic of Singapore (2006)

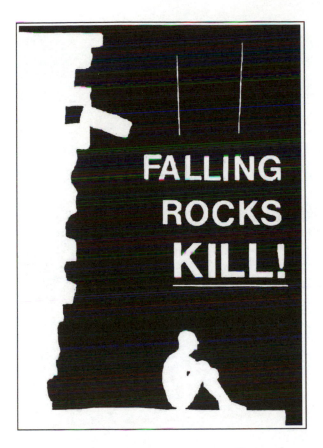

Note: The sign should be red with a white border and white lettering (and cliff shading)

Figure 6.6 *Sign voted the best of 15 tested signs*

Therefore a risk analysis framework is a conceptual planning tool (see Chapter 3) that a beach manager can use to downgrade the risk of death/injury. Risk/vulnerability results from both natural and socio-economic conditions. The population at risk is *all* beach users, although the chances are that the vast majority will not incur any encounters with a hazard. The physical environment (especially water) is a potential hazard for all users and mitigation through education, lifeguards and a risk assessment should be the common-sense and only viable approach.

CHAPTER 7

Innovative Application of Selected Management Tools to the Beach Environment

INTRODUCTION

Many tools exist that can help beach managers, and this chapter gives but three that are deemed of exceptional interest to managers. All have been gleaned from outside literature, but all have been shown to have utility in solving problems that managers experience in the normal running of their work tasks.

DIMENSION ANALYSIS

Dimension analysis is an evaluation technique that has not been specifically developed for beach or coastal management. However, it is a very effective scoping technique that is extremely adaptable in obtaining essential facts so that problem definition is clarified and areas are indicated that need further analysis. The technique grew out of the '5 Ws and an H model' approach to problem solving, i.e. who (person/department), what (what is wrong/happened), when (time aspect/how often), where (location), why (why did it happen – diagnosis of personnel) and how (how did it happen). This evaluation tool can be used during the problem definition phase of a proposed bathing area management model (see Chapter 3, 'The Bathing Area Management Model', page 77). It is a problem-solving strategy that approaches an issue by thoroughly characterizing information into *five dimensions* (Jensen, 1978). These dimensions are of social and psychological concern and in considering them for beach management they almost take the form of an advanced structured checklist that keeps track of any information flow. The five dimensions are substantive, spatial, temporal, quantitative and qualitative, where the first three terms relate to the 'what, where, when' of the '5Ws and an H model'. Each dimension consists of several aspects that are used to approach the problem from the respective angle of that dimension. Dimension analysis is a *'problem definition'* management tool able to better define problem scale and scope and, through such considerations, to contribute to formulation of effective management strategy. The term was initiated by van Grundy (1988) after he was influenced by Jensen's (1978) paper. In the worked example given later in this chapter, descriptions of these dimensions and their aspects are considered strictly in terms of beach management.

The first beach-related aspect considered is the *substantive dimension*, i.e. what is the problem, which involves the question of existence or viability of current management practices and whether or not these practices should be continued or amended, for example, coastal engineering practices such as steel netting on dangerous cliffs. The second aspect of the substantive dimension brings into question the need to provide beach users with information concerning the beach area (notice boards and such like). The third substantive aspect considers the level at which suitable measures should be taken to remedy different problems at the beach. The final aspect serves as an editing function, as it questions whether or not all problems of a beach have been addressed.

The *temporal aspect* of dimensional analysis involves aspects concerning the effect of time on bathing area-related problems. The first aspect considers whether or not a problem is of recent origin, for example bathing water quality. The second aspect is concerned with the need to recognize trends and patterns in practice and whether or not they are having an adverse effect on a beach, while the third aspect involves natural trends or cycles. The final aspect addresses time-related variables in implementation of beach management practices, so that they might be conducive to natural trends or correct problematic patterns.

The *spatial dimension* involves defining problem boundaries. The first aspect assesses the actual need to clarify the issues of boundaries – political or natural. The second aspect considers adaptation of sampling strategies according to site-applicable criteria. The final aspect hinges upon the ethos that, as with any other environmental system, beaches need to be addressed in a holistic prospective, particularly when designing a management plan.

The *quantitative dimension* involves identification of aspects that provide pertinent knowledge to problem solving. In addressing beach environments, the first aspect considers the need to identify the number of sources giving rise to a problem and whether or not they might have synergistic effects. For example, while Dixon (1995) suggests that around 70 per cent of beach litter in the UK is generated by maritime shipping and related craft, one would have to query whether these statistics reflect a bias generated by the author's sampling of generally remote areas where marine litter would indeed be largely expected to predominate. The second aspect involves identifying threshold levels for various problem parameters, while the final aspect queries the number of beach user groups affected by a particular problem.

The *qualitative dimension*, as its name implies, is concerned with addressing the quality of various components of a problem. The first beach-related aspect identifies a need to allocate values to socio-economic and environmental parameters affected by a problem or conflict. The second aspect augments the first by addressing the need to establish a scale of quality to provide beach managers with practical optional alternatives. The final aspect considered brings into question the acceptability of established beach and bathing water quality criteria.

Both documented reports and field visits should be utilized for data collection. However, unlike the application of beach registration (see Chapter 9), the data required by this technique depend much more on desk studies and personal interviews than collection through field visits, for example with planning and environment government officers and local council representatives. Personal experience and knowledge gained from working with the beach environment for several years is also invaluable for completing the dimension analysis *registration form*.

Few researchers have employed this technique to coastal/beach areas, but Williams and Davies (1999) and Micallef (2002) consider the theory supporting dimension analysis and its value to elucidation of beach management guidelines. Their findings indicated that data analysis and evaluation reflect the strong potential for application of this technique to bathing area management.

A worked example of two contrasting beaches on the Mediterranean island of Malta – (Ghajn Tuffieha rural beach (see Figure 7.1) versus St Georges' urban beach (see Figure 7.2) – is presented in Tables 7.1–7.10. This

Figure 7.1 *Backed by limestone plateaus and (boulder-strewn) clay slopes, Ghajn Tuffieha beach is set in a typically Maltese rural environment*

Figure 7.2 *Beach-facing view of St George's Bay, Malta, reflecting a concentration of hotels and recreation-related facilities in the area*

example reflects the type of pertinent beach questions that would evaluate commonalities and differences arising in subsequent beach management.

The *spatial dimension* considered the availability of beach registration and bathing area quality classification data (see Table 7.1). Beach-related system boundaries were identified as having been defined only at Ghajn Tuffieha (see Table 7.1) and not at St George's beach (see Table 7.2). Available data reflected a general absence of accurate data on sediment budgets and sediment cell characteristics and a generally poor understanding of external influences on beach quality. In this context, consideration of the spatial dimension recommended use of novel environmental evaluation tools examined by this study for effective site management together with the establishment of sediment cell-related studies. Site-specific recommendations concerned the need to evaluate the impact of anthropogenic shoreline structures on sediment transport at St George's beach (see Table 7.2). For St George's Bay, the recommendation was implementation of mitigation efforts as indicated by an environmental impact assessment study (Micallef and Cassar, 2001).

Examination of the *temporal dimension* identified common beach-related issues concerning the generation of annual bathing-water quality reports by the national health authorities and availability of general data

Table 7.1 *Dimensional analysis of Ghajn Tuffieha considering spatial management aspects*

Spatial dimension	Current evaluation	Measures/recommendations
1. Have the site boundaries been identified, with interaction of beach system, sediment cells and adjacent areas considered?	Site management has included studies identifying site/ ecosystem boundaries as well as terrestrial vegetation cover and conservation value. Sediment exchange with adjacent beaches and sediment cells are largely undefined.	Sediment surveys should be carried out to identify locally dominant sediment cell, area of influence and depth of closure for this beach.
2. Have the cause and effect of internal and external influences been considered holistically?	The management approach implemented by the GAIA Foundation is appropriately holistic.	Site management should assess applicability of novel environmental evaluation tools evaluated by this study (beach registration/classification system, dimension and function analysis).
3. Have facilities associated with bathing and related recreational activities been evaluated for this site?	The impact on bathing area quality by available facilities and the surrounding area was evaluated as part of this study through the development of a bathing area register and site evaluation system.	The adoption of beach registration and evaluation within the existing management plan is strongly recommended.

on Maltese and other Euro-Mediterranean beach user preferences and priorities (see Tables 7.3 and 7.4). From a negative aspect, absence in both beaches of long-term beach profile monitoring programmes and beach user health-related studies were identified. Recommendations emanating from evaluation of this dimension included the need for long-term monitoring programmes on beach sediment dynamics at both bays and in the case of Ghajn Tuffieha Bay, clay slope stability studies.

The scouring impact by storm water runoff and potential sewage pollution were problem areas raised specifically for St George's Bay, and increased efforts to raise public awareness were also recommended for this beach. The need to better identify site-specific trends in beach

Table 7.2 *Dimensional analysis of St George's Bay considering spatial management aspects*

Spatial dimension	Current evaluation	Measures/recommendations
1. Have bathing area and related system boundaries been identified? Has interaction between beach, sediment cells and adjacent areas been considered?	Bathing area and related system boundaries have been identified. Aerial photography indicating absence of beach change over the last 43 years suggests a stable sediment cell. While local sediment cell is unidentified, the depth of closure has been determined at approximatley 2.6m.	Prior to beach nourishment, sediment resources should be identified. Following nourishment, a monitoring programme of beach sediment fluctuations should be implemented.
2. Have the cause and effect of internal and external influences been considered holistically?	Yes, through an extensive environmental impact assessment study on proposed beach nourishment (Micallef and Cassar, 2001).	The impact assessment findings should be reflected in the beach management plan. Novel environmental evaluation tools proposed by this study should be considered for site management.
3. Have facilities associated with bathing and related recreational activities been evaluated?	Yes, as part of this study through a bathing area registration and classification system.	Bathing area classification and registration are recommended as a programme monitoring beach status.

user preferences and priorities was recommended for both beaches. Establishment of baseline studies in conjunction with the use of historical records was recommended for Ghajn Tuffieha but not for St George's Bay, where recent comprehensive studies had been undertaken as part of a local environmental impact assessment in order to determine any evidence of beach change over time.

In contrast to the previously considered dimensions, evaluation of the *substantive dimension* (see Tables 7.5 and 7.6) reflected the fact that the issues considered were highly specific to the individual beaches due to an NGO (GAIA Foundation) pilot management project at Ghajn Tuffieha and an environmental impact assessment at St George's Bay. Ghajn Tuffieha beach reflected the strong management role played by the GAIA Foundation,

Table 7.3 *Dimensional analysis of Ghajn Tuffieha considering temporal management aspects*

Temporal dimension	Current evaluation	Measures/recommendations
1. Are past records available? Is it possible to identify past problems or activities that have given rise to current problems/ concerns?	Only short-term beach profiling records are available with clay slope erosion being a prime concern. Past aerial photographs have not been used.	Establishment of baseline studies where past records are unavailable. Use of past maps and aerial photographs is recommended.
2. Have present beach-use patterns been identified? What are they? What are predictions for the future?	Questionnaire surveys on beach user preferences and priorities have been carried out.	More site/user group-specific beach user questionnaire surveys and on the bathing area carrying capacity are required to allow more effective management practice.
3. Have short- and long-term health analysis been considered?	National health authority annual bathing water quality reports are produced but no health-related studies are known.	Health authorities should undertake studies on local and overseas bathers to evaluate the impact on health of bathing in local waters.
4. Is there evidence of change of the beach over time?	While short-term beach profiling does not indicate any serious erosional trends, there are concerns of the impact of clay slope slippage over this very narrow beach.	Monitoring of short-term (seasonal trends) and long-term (rates) fluxes in beach sediment and clay slope stability/movement should be integrated with studies on beach sediment dynamics.

with a recommendation to include seagrass clearance within the current management plan administered by the NGO (see Table 7.5). While the information provided to the general public was considered sufficient, it was recommended that a first aid and information centre (as proposed by NGO management) should be established at this site. In the absence of suitable baseline studies on clay slope and beach erosion, long-term monitoring was also recommended to allow subsequent identification of trends and problem extent. For both beaches there was a need to identify sediment exchange mechanisms between the different sediment cell

Table 7.4 *Dimensional analysis of St George's Bay considering temporal management aspects*

Temporal dimension	Current evaluation	Measures/recommendations
1. Are past records available? Is it possible to identify past problems or activities that have given rise to current problems/concerns?	Past aerial photos are available. Increased urban development has altered water flow patterns to this beachhead and minor sewage leaks resulted in pollution. Replacement of one of the rocky shores forming the embayment with a concrete platform and the construction of a seawall to support a road across the back of the beach have altered wave dynamics and increased beach sediment scouring.	Storm water runoff from the highly developed urban area must be managed so as to prevent direct scouring of the beach. Further construction on rocky shore platforms should be prohibited. Beach nourishment should be considered.
2. Have present beach-use patterns been identified? What are they? What are predictions for the future?	Continued use of this largely eroded beach reflects its popularity. Questionnaire surveys on beach user preferences and priorities reflect the desire for a nourished beach with adequate facilities and a WTP.	More and longer-term studies on beach user preferences and priorities should be carried out to identify any emergent trends in beach-use patterns and user needs post-nourishment.
3. Have short- and long-term health analysis been considered?	Annual water quality reports are produced. A recent environmental impact assessment has considered health aspects without long-term health studies.	Long-term studies concerning beach user health and increased public awareness raising are recommended.
4. Is there evidence of beach change over time?	Past aerial photography shows that the current degraded state of the beach dates back over the last 50 years.	In the event of beach nourishment, careful consideration of natural sediment dynamics should be made to mitigate the causes of beach erosion.

Table 7.5 *Dimensional analysis of Ghajn Tuffieha considering substantive management aspects*

Substantive dimension	Current evaluation	Measures/recommendations
1. Do any active management practices exist? If yes, should they be continued, stopped or amended?	While an NGO is responsible for overall conservation, wardening and safety aspects, the Local Council undertakes seagrass banquette clearance operations.	Better integration between Local Council seagrass clearance and NGO management activities is desirable.
2. Is there any information provided to the beach users? What type?	Information boards are provided by NGO on sea state leading to dangerous undercurrents and on its general management objectives.	The measures for a first aid and information centre, proposed by the NGO (GAIA Foundation) should be implemented.
3. Have any studies been carried out to determine what level of suitable measures should be taken? (facilities, structures, etc.)	• Measures to remedy the problem of clay slope erosion implemented. • Dimension/function analysis and beach register/classification applied • Absence of bar/toilet and emergency telephone facilities.	Sediment exchange mechanisms between beach, sediment cell and adjacent beaches should be identified.
4. Have any studies been conducted concerning extent of beach problems?	• Short-term beach profiling indicating general beach stability. • Unconfirmed beach erosion baseline studies prevent evaluation of extent of problems.	• Confirm technique suitability to enable identification of trends and extent of problem. • Implementation of long-term monitoring studies to evaluate extent of problems.

components active in each area, and particularly at Ghajn Tuffieha Bay sediment interaction with adjacent beaches should be investigated.

Quantitative dimension analysis for both beaches highlighted the bathing-related thresholds of water quality and carrying capacity (see Tables 7.7 and 7.8). European bathing water quality standards (CEC, 2006) were identified as being applied to all monitored bathing areas. For both

Table 7.6 *Dimensional analysis of St George's Bay considering substantive management aspects*

Substantive dimension	Current evaluation	Measures/recommendations
1. Do any active management practices exist? If yes, should they be continued, stopped or amended?	Limited to mechanical collection of seagrass *banquettes* and hand collection of litter debris.	Under present circumstances, these practices should continue. However, if the beach is nourished, a comprehensive management plan is required.
2. Is there any information provided to the beach users? What type?	None.	Information boards regarding aspects of management, locally applicable by-laws and regulations, and on water quality standards/safety parameters.
3. Have any studies been carried out to determine what level of suitable measures should be taken (facilities, structures and so on)?	An environmental impact assessment considering beach nourishment identified the suitability of a pedestrian promenade located behind a 25m wide sandy beach, better regulation of water sports, redirection of storm water runoff, upgrading of the sewage system, improvement of bathing-related facilities and application of Blue Flag criteria.	Include a mechanism within the monitoring proposal adopted for the beach to review progress of implementation of recommended measures. Determine sediment exchange mechanisms active in the area.
4. Have any studies been conducted concerning the extent of problems of the beach?	Yes, through the above-mentioned environmental impact assessment.	Application of mitigation measures recommended by the impact assessment and establishment of a long-term monitoring programme to compare with baseline studies established by the assessment.

Table 7.7 *Dimensional analysis of Ghajn Tuffieha considering quantitative management aspects*

Quantitative aspect	Current evaluation	Measures/recommendations
1. Have problems been identified having single/ multiple sources? If so, what are they?	Existing management plan has addressed the anthropogenic pressure resulting in clay slope destabilization. Litter and absence of toilet, bar and emergency telephone facilities noted. Aesthetic quality of the area is impacted by a dilapidated hotel on the escarpment overlooking the bay.	Retain current management plan but determine sediment budget and rates of sediment flux. Increase efforts to obtain planning permission for toilet, bar and emergency telephone facilities. Increase off-season beach cleaning efforts particularly in clay slope undergrowth. Demolition/re-siting of dilapidated hotel is recommended.
2. Are there threshold levels (for example beach loss, water quality, beach population, air quality, dune erosion)? If threshold levels have been defined, have they been applied?	Bathing water quality and beach capacity thresholds (2006/7 EC and 3m^2/person) (Planning Services Division, 1990) are established but only bathing water quality criteria are applied.	All existing national policies concerning bathing quality-related thresholds should be identified and applied. Recommendations should be made on absent threshold levels (for example on acceptable rates of beach sediment fluctuations).
3. Are data on preferences and priorities for different beach user groups available?	General data on Maltese and other Euro-Mediterranean beach users have been collected.	More site/user group-specific data are required to ascertain site-specific data and emergent trends in beach-use patterns.

beaches, an absence of applied carrying capacity thresholds was identified. Similarly, an absence of extensive site and user group-specific information on beach user preferences and priorities was indicated for all examined beaches. Recommendations stressed the need for determination at both sites of sediment budgets and flux rates, updating and implementation of beach-related thresholds and identification of site and group-specific beach user preferences and priorities. The development of holistic beach management plans was recommended for St George's Bay.

Table 7.8 *Dimensional analysis of St George's Bay considering quantitative management aspects*

Quantitative dimension	Current evaluation	Measures/recommendations
1. Have problems having single/multiple sources been identified? If so, what are they?	Beach erosion has been attributed to increased urban runoff from a large catchment area, altered wave dynamics and limited/poor quality sediment supply. Outflow from cracked sewage pipes, the coast road along the back of the beach and heavy construction activity impact on water quality and recreational potential.	Beach nourishment must ensure the mitigation of existing problems as well as of any problems it might generate itself. A holistic bathing area management plan should precede nourishment. Determination of sediment budget and rates of sediment flux is recommended.
2. Are there threshold levels (for example beach loss, water quality, beach carrying capacity, air quality, dune erosion)? If threshold levels have been defined, have they been applied?	While levels for water quality and beach capacity have been identified, only the former are currently applied. In the case of St George's Bay, air, noise, water quality and beach sediment fluctuation thresholds are of particular relevance.	Identify and apply set threshold levels and make recommendations on undefined thresholds (for example bathing area quality, safety parameters and acceptable sediment fluctuation rates).
3. Are data on preferences and priorities for different beach user sectors available for this site?	General beach user questionnaire surveys on preferences and priorities have been carried out for several sites in Malta and Gozo (including this site).	Data determined from beach user questionnaires should be used to maximize effectiveness of beach management plan. More site/user group-specific surveys are recommended.

Evaluation of the *qualitative* dimension is normally noted for its difficulty in interpretation (Jensen, 1978; Williams and Davies, 1999) and in this respect application of a number of evaluation techniques (for example beach user questionnaire surveys (see Chapters 5 and 9) greatly facilitated site evaluation. It is recommended that these evaluation techniques form part of adopted beach management plans. Through information provided

Table 7.9 *Dimensional analysis of Ghajn Tuffieha considering qualitative management aspects*

Qualitative dimension	Current evaluation	Measures/recommendations
1. Have beach-related socio-economic and environmental values been evaluated?	Function analysis revealed that Ghajn Tuffieha has less development potential than all other beaches studied while having the second highest conservation value after Ramla Bay, Gozo (see 'Environmental Risk Assessment Method', page 161).	Environmental evaluation by a number of techniques applied to this site suggested development of a management policy with a strong conservation bias.
2. Has the bathing area quality rating been evaluated?	Beach quality evaluation identified the absence of toilet, bar and emergency telephone facilities as influencing the class of this bathing area (for year 2000) to a 4 star rating.	Bathing area quality evaluation should form part of regular monitoring. Although a rural site with high conservation value, provision of absent toilet, bar and emergency telephone facilities is desirable.
3. Are sampling and analysis strategies scientifically sound?	The methodology used for beach profiling may be questionable as it was restricted to subaerial beach sediments. Scientific literature criticizes European-wide established sampling procedure used for water quality evaluation (see Chapter 8, 'The Blue Flag', page 169).	Review methodology used for assessment of beach sediment fluctuations so as to consider depth of closure. Water quality sampling and monitoring strategy should keep abreast of ongoing debate in this field.
4. Does the beach meet acceptable bathing water criteria?	The bathing water quality for year 2000 was evaluated as Blue Quality, based on the EU's Bathing Water Directive (CEC, 2006).	In the absence of onsite potential sources of pollution, the management plan should ensure that the influence of the entire water catchment is adequately evaluated.

Table 7.10 *Dimensional analysis of St George's Bay considering qualitative management aspects*

Qualitative dimension	Current evaluation	Measures/recommendations
1. Have beach-related socio-economic and environmental attributes been evaluated?	Function analysis rated St George's Bay as having the lowest conservation value and highest potential for development among the four beaches investigated. Socio-economic questionnaire surveys indicate a need for the provision of well-managed beach-related facilities.	Function analysis should be integrated into the beach management model to update beach status and confirm suitability of management orientation. The management objectives should reflect a development/recreational bias with well-managed bathing and related facilities.
2. Has bathing area quality rating been evaluated for this site?	A 1 star bathing area quality rating was attributed for year 2000. This was largely influenced by the degraded state of the beach, incidents of sewage pollution and very poor safety-related facilities.	Bathing area quality rating (and other novel evaluation tools) should preferably form part of regular monitoring. Results indicate the need for beach nourishment, development of an extensive management plan and full sanitary and safety-related facilities.
3. Are sampling and analysis strategies scientifically sound?	Water quality analytical procedure follows widely used Euro-Mediterranean standards, but recent scientific debate criticizes current sampling techniques.	Sampling strategy should follow current scientific debate in this field. Analytical strategy should additionally consider water quality before discharge into the bay.
4. Does the beach meet acceptable bathing water criteria?	For bathing period 2000, a rating of blue/green quality was achieved (based on CEC, 1976 standards). A breached sewer mains pipe was identified and repaired.	To ensure improvement in water quality, continued monitoring and a consideration of water quality prior to discharge into the bay (for example storm water runoff) is required.

by other techniques, the *qualitative dimension* of dimension analysis was therefore able to make specific recommendations for management policy bias for each beach (see Tables 7.9 and 7.10). It was recommended that management policy at Ghajn Tuffieha should have a conservation bias and a recreational bias at St George's Bay. With regards to bathing area water quality issues, the qualitative dimension highlighted the need to keep abreast of the ongoing political/scientific debate regarding acceptable sampling procedure (Pike, 1997; Rees, 1997; WHO, 2000). It was also observed that for a representative evaluation of trends in beach sediment fluctuations, the methodology may need revision to include underwater profiling up to depth of closure.

Dimension analysis has been presented as a structured step-by-step approach supporting intuitive judgement and having an ability to contribute to the determination of the scale and scope of beach problems, to assess relevant beach characteristics and therefore facilitate formulation of an effective management strategy. Practical results obtained suggest that it represents a valuable tool for beach managers through facilitating identification of the scope and origins of issues influencing beach quality, better evaluation of the bathing environment's natural and anthropogenically influenced resources and for the generation of more effective management plans. It is a very adaptable tool with a long information-gathering phase.

FUNCTION ANALYSIS

It is evident that indicators or tools are required to achieve both sustainable development and ICM/beach management due to the complexity and conflicts of interest between stakeholders (Ketchum, 1972; Coelho et al, 2003). In the context of beach management, various interest groups would include: parents with children (safety being pre-eminent), surfers (waves being their main concern), swimmers, shore fishermen, jet ski/power boat people, wind surfers and so on. Van der Maarel (1979) and de Groot (1992) promote a management strategy by considering the goods and services or functions that the environment provides by addressing the characteristics of that environment. This method is known as *function analysis* and is an excellent tool that may be utilized by beach managers in conjunction with ICM. Beach managers on their own would normally not be able to implement this policy but their input is *essential*. This would be a good example of synergy within the coastal community.

The idea is taken further by Cendrero and Fischer (1997) who, in a classic paper, propose indicators that could be used to assess both environmental quality and the development potential of an area by a scoring and weighting system. In essence, an ecological and social score can then be plotted graphically against each other to identify whether areas are within a conservation zone, development zone or in conflict.

Areas with high ecological value but low social score should be placed in the conservation zone, whereas those with high social value and low ecological score should be placed in the development zone. Areas with high ecological and social scores would be placed in the high conflict zone, and the lower the score the lower the level of conflict.

Van der Weide et al (1999) argue that the method is too complex for easy application by beach managers within ICM strategies. Therefore, the authors adopt the work of Cendrero and Fischer (1997), using a simplified methodology for application in coastal regions. The simplified methodology does not use a weighting system, but instead assesses each indicator that is relevant to the area being studied and allocates a score that can subsequently be normalized. The results are then used to assess conservation and development potential and assess conflict.

Methodology

Micallef (2002) uses indicators established by Cendrero and Fischer (1997) for use in the Maltese coastal environment but bases them on the underlying principles given by van der Weide et al (1999), i.e. using only parameters that are relevant to the Maltese coastal environment. Micallef (2002) uses this technique to value conservation and development potential, values ranging from 1 to 3 for each indicator, 1 being the lowest value and 3 being the highest value (see Table 7.11). For example, if a water quality sample exceeds the requirements by law then a score of 3 could be given but if it is under the quality set by law then a score of 1 could be given. Normalizing the total score of the ecological and socio-economic values to give a parameter score between 0 and 1 is carried out by dividing the *collective* score of the parameters by the *total* possible score. These two figures are then plotted graphically to determine distinct conservation and development values for certain areas in question (see Figure 7.3).

Beach-relevant environmental functions (adapted from the work of Cendrero and Fisher, 1997) are identified by Micallef (2002) as including:

- Production functions:
  - genetic resources (as supported by seagrass meadows, where present);
  - medicinal resources (from beach-associated seagrasses and algae);
  - raw materials for building/construction;
  - fertilizer (as provided by seagrass *banquettes*).
- Carrier functions:
  - energy conversion;
  - recreation and tourism;
  - nature protection.
- Information functions:
  - aesthetic information;

- – historic information (of heritage value);
- – cultural and artistic inspiration;
- – scientific and educational information.
- ● Regulation functions:
  - – regulation of the local energy balance (related to beach migration of wave energy);
  - – regulation of runoff and flood protection (watershed protection);
  - – water catchment and groundwater recharge;
  - – prevention of erosion and sediment control;
  - – formation of topsoil and maintenance of soil fertility (through aeolian transport of beach sediments);
  - – fixation of solar energy and biomass production (by beach associated seagrass meadows, where present);
  - – storage and recycling of nutrients (by beach-associated seagrass meadows where present);
  - – maintenance of migration and nursery habitats (by beach-associated seagrass meadows where present);
  - – maintenance of biological and genetic diversity (by beach-associated seagrass meadows, where present).

Reviews

Micallef (2002) assesses four bathing areas in the Maltese islands: St George, Mellieha, Ramla Bay and Ghajn Tuffieha. Like van der Weide et al (1999), he uses indicators relevant to the Maltese islands (see Table 7.11 and Figure 7.3) taken from the list suggested by Cendrero and Fischer (1997). This more accurately reflects the coastline as aspects such as tsunamis, earthquakes and volcanic eruptions are omitted due to Malta not experiencing these hazards in recent years. In addition, there are no rivers, river flooding, open fresh waters, timber as a resource and little presence of sedimentation. Consequently, all these are omitted. Moreover, certain indicators proposed by Cendrero and Fischer (1997) are replaced by Micallef (2002) to better describe the Maltese bathing perspective, and include replacing red tides with eutrophication, pollution level assessment evaluated with respect to runoff, and coastal and soil erosion measured as beach erosion. In addition, the process of reclamation is substituted for nourishment with positive results.

Table 7.11 *Environmental components, value allocation and calculation of normalized scores for bathing area-relevant coastal parameters in Malta*

Environmental component	Characteristic	Indicators	Evaluation of characteristics			
			St George	Mellieha	Ramla Bay	Ghajn Tuffieha
Ecological values						
Air	Pollution	Gravity	1	3	2	3
		Visibility	3	3	3	3
		Effect on humans	1	2	2	3
	Noise	Intensity	2	2	3	3
	Normalized score		0.583	0.833	0.833	1.000
Coastal waters	Quality	Microbiological pollution	2	2	3	3
	Aesthetic condition	Turbidity	3	3	3	2
		Floating debris	3	2	3	3
	Normalized score		0.889	0.778	1.000	0.889
Fresh water	Supply	Rainfall	1	2	3	2
	Normalized score		0.333	0.667	1.000	0.667
Terrestrial biota		Natural vegetation cover	1	2	3	3
	Quantity	Biological productivity	1	1	3	3
		Biological diversity	1	2	3	3
		Species of special interest	1	3	3	3
	Normalized score		0.333	0.667	1.000	1.000
Marine biota	Quantity	Biomass	1	3	2	2
		Biological productivity	1	3	2	2
	Diversity	Biological diversity	3	3	3	3
		Species of special interest	2	No data	No data	No data
	Normalized score		0.583	1.000	0.778	0.778
Geological and topographical features		Lithological	1	2	3	3
		Size of bathing area	1	3	2	2
	Normalized score		0.333	0.833	0.833	0.833
Hazards		Coastal erosion	1	2	2	3
		Coastal flooding	2	3	3	3
		Storms	1	3	2	1
		Cliff/slope instability	3	3	2	1
		Soil erosion	3	3	2	2
		Torrential rains	1	3	2	2

	Normalized score		0.611	0.944	0.722	0.667
Resources	Non-renewable	Minerals, rocks, construction materials, fuels	1	1	1	1
		Soil	1	2	3	2
	Renewable	Fish	1	1	1	1
		Visual quality	1	2	3	3
	Landscape	Uniqueness	1	3	3	3
	Normalized score		0.333	0.600	0.733	0.667
		Total	46.000	65.000	68.000	65.000
	Normalized score of ecological value		0.511	0.802	0.840	0.802

Human component	Characteristic	Indicators	Evaluation of characteristics			
			St George	Mellieha	Ramla Bay	Ghajn Tuffieha
Social values						
	Potential for use	Historic, artistic, archaeological sites	1	2	3	2
		Public recreation facilities	1	3	2	1
		Hotels, restaurants	3	3	1	1
		Utilities	3	3	1	1
		Parking	1	3	2	2
		Accessibility	3	3	3	1
		Land use	3	3	1	1
		Extent of development	3	3	1	1
		Population density	3	2	1	1
		Intensity of use	2	3	2	2
		Extent of reclamation (with nourishment)	2	1	1	1
		Public health	1	3	2	2
		Opportunity for employment	3	3	1	1
		Perception of the quality of the environment	1	2	3	3
Total			30	37	24	20
	Normalized score for social values		0.714	0.881	0.571	0.476

Note: On the scale used for total score allocation for ecological and social values, 1 = minimum and 3 = maximum

Source: Environmental components, value allocation and calculation of normalized scores from Micallef and Williams (2003). Scale used for total score allocation for ecological and social values adapted from Cendrero and Fisher (1997)

With respect to Figure 7.3, values situated to the left side of the matrix on the X axis, enshrine low economic potential and areas situated to the matrix right indicate high development potential. Y axis values located at the base will have low conservation values while those placed in the upper part of the figure will have a high conservation value. The outcome of the matrix diagram has previously determined appropriate management strategies for certain areas (van der Weide et al, 1999; Micallef, 2002). Areas positioned on the figure's bottom-right quadrant should be developed first. Conversely, those areas located at the figure's top-left quadrant should be given a high level of protection through conservation. Difficulty arises when areas are positioned in the centre of the diagram – the conflict zone – as this indicates that the conservation and development potential are at similar levels. In such an instance, van der Weide et al (1999) propose that conflicts be identified by utilizing in-depth functional analysis studies to aid an appropriate management strategy by moving out of the conflict zone towards the conservation or development fields, or alternatively and if possible, by achieving a balance between the two in the conflict.

Much time was dedicated to the issues and problems surrounding the development of particular indices for the purpose of assessing environmental quality and development potential. These problems included:

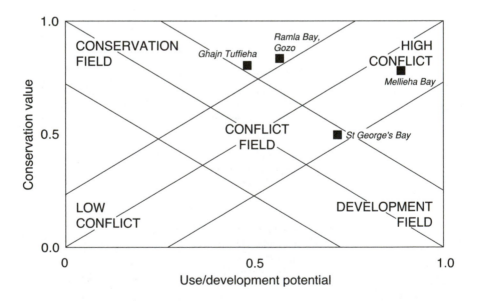

Source: Micallef and Williams (2003)

Figure 7.3 *Maltese beaches evaluated within the conservation/use development matrix developed by Cendrero and Fisher (1997)*

- finding the relevant elements;
- limiting assessment to the most relevant elements;
- assessing the measurement but being careful in the choice of units;
- finding a common scaling to measure all coastal characteristics;
- determining the level of importance for each index for weighting.

Problems encountered were considered in depth. Consequently, indicators developed by Cendrero and Fischer (1997) were based on the presence of stakeholder interest in any coastal area relating to law, jurisdiction, ownership, economic, social and environmental issues. Furthermore, the stakeholders concerned included scientists, landowners, developers, governments, residents, users and potential users.

To limit the indicators to those most relevant, if elements were duplicated or tended to overlap, then one indicator of these characteristics was chosen. It is asserted that there is no practical method that could accurately achieve a plausible system for integrating one measurement for all indices, and the most appropriate measurement unit for each indicator in a quantitative sense was taken. Weighting of respective importance was determined by a professional evaluation team using a multifaceted weighting system.

The rationale for the exclusion or adaptation of the indicators proposed by Cendrero and Fischer (1997) goes further than simplicity. The in-depth studies proposed in the original paper relate to aspects such as the impact of atmospheric pollution on ecological and human entities and employment issues. Measurements and figures on such subjects, however, can often be unclear, time consuming, not readily available and difficult to interpret. Furthermore, obtaining such details will frequently be impractical for coastal managers developing ICM plans.

Despite the subjective nature within the methodology used in Turkey, van der Weide et al (1999) conclude that results were positive in that the end diagram, with only slight differences, correctly mirrored the areas. The authors are confident that if more analysis and objective measurements were used then results would more accurately reflect a coastal area. Additionally, it is suggested that the environmental components in the original paper by Cendrero and Fischer (1997) were overemphasized in comparison with social components and it is proposed that more importance should be given to social indicators (van der Weide et al, 1999).

Comparison between a 3- and 5-point scale scoring matrix

The above examples are on a 3-point scale (see Table 7.11). However, it appears that a 5-point scale would give even better results, and this is backed by evidence from Wales, UK, where 15 beaches were analysed on both a 3- and 5-point scale scoring system (Phillips et al, 2007a).

Using the 5-point scale, four of the analysed beaches moved further within the *development field* of the function analysis matrix (Barry Island and Aberavon are given as two examples in Figure 7.4). The resulting shift of Barry Island from the conflict field of the matrix to the development field (as a consequence of applying a 5-point scale) reflects its similarity to the Aberavon site. This is likely to better categorize the areas as both Barry Island and Aberavon are typical seaside resort destinations with plenty of facilities and have a low ecological value. They are situated near large cities or towns that are already highly developed, putting pressure to further develop beaches for increased economic growth. It appears that there is likely to be more benefit from development of these areas rather than conservation, as there are nearby beaches that would be better suited for conservation (i.e. Oxwich – see below) to achieve a balance of development and conservation.

Similarly, of the six investigated beaches located within the *conservation* field (Merthyr Mawr and Oxwich are given as examples in Figure 7.4), all moved further towards the high ecological conservation field. Oxwich and Merthyr Mawr are both National Nature Reserves and therefore conservation is an extremely high priority in both systems. Oxwich was also the first area in England and Wales to be classed as an Area of Outstanding Beauty. Both areas have also been designated as Heritage Coasts (Williams and Ergin, 2004; see Chapter 3, 'The Bathing Area Management Model', page 77).

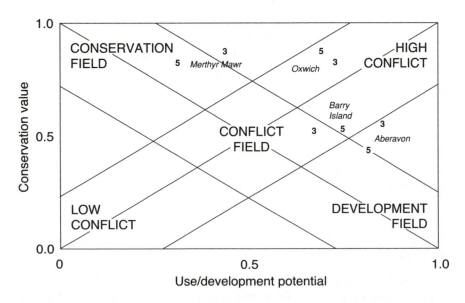

Figure 7.4 *Conservation/use development matrix utilized by function analysis for four beaches in Wales on 3- and 5-point scales*

This strongly suggests that the 5-point scale scoring system gives a clearer picture of the selected beaches.

ENVIRONMENTAL RISK ASSESSMENT METHOD

Associated British Ports' (ABP) research environmental risk assessment (ERA) system is an eight-step online software package that provides a framework for assessing the consequences of environmental impacts of events of a given project affecting a coastal area (ABP, 1997). It was first developed for application in specially protected conservation areas. The aim of the ERA model is to formalize and document the assessment process for any proposed development, allowing judgements to be made on a case-by-case basis, carried out by quantifying impacts as much as possible and so providing a basis on which decisions can be made in determining significant project effects (ABP, 1997). This is achieved through semi-quantitative and statistical weighting of probabilities to provide a consistent qualitative assessment of impact effects. Information regarding the proposed development and the assessment of the project's impacts and consequences is entered by the project supervisors and assessors. It formalizes and documents professional and expert knowledge; assesses magnitudes, probabilities, relevance and risk; and produces estimated probability values for each magnitude (severe, high, mild and negligible).

The ERA model provides:

- a structured framework for data entry and assessment of impacts and consequences of proposed development projects;
- a database facility for storing project descriptions and assessments;
- semi-quantitative and statistical weighting of probabilities to provide a consistent qualitative assessment of impact effects;
- a standard reporting format for the above results.

The ABP (1997) model's eight-step approach to risk assessment of development projects involves:

1 *Description of project or plan*
   Project description requires provision of information under the following headings:
   - situation prior to development (environmental characteristics, social setting, location of sites and so on);
   - proposed development, its aims and objectives;
   - operations and activities required to carry out development;
   - likely changes to operations and activities as a result of development.

2   *Identification of possible impacts*
    Each feature of the development that may cause an environmental
    effect is listed in the impact record. These may be changes to physical
    processes and to water, soil and air quality, changes affecting an
    ecosystem function, potential for accidental incidents and long-term
    effects on the environment.

3   *Identification of consequences*
    For each of the impacts defined, the consequences likely to occur are
    entered (see Box 7.1). Consequences arising from an impact may be
    very wide ranging, affecting the living and non-living environment
    directly or indirectly over the short or long term.

4   *Estimation of magnitude of consequences*
    When estimating the magnitude of each consequence, magnitude
    is defined as severe, high, mild or negligible (see Table 7.12). An
    explanation should be given by the assessor for the reasoning behind
    the estimated magnitude of the consequence. In some cases, in
    addition to the magnitude of the consequence, a monetary value could
    be assigned to quantify the consequence. The magnitude is assigned to
    both living and non-living environments.

5   *Estimation of probability of consequences*
    For each consequence, estimation is made for the probability of an
    effect being realized (see Box 7.1).The aim here is to quantify as much
    as possible so that the need for judgement is reduced.

6   *Relevance of consequences*
    A decision has to be made on whether a consequence affects, directly
    or indirectly, the habitats or species for which the site was classified or
    designated.

7   *Assessment of risk*
    For each consequence, combination of its magnitude and probability
    results in an estimation of the environmental risk (see Box 7.1). No
    single formula can combine these two quantitative estimates so a
    matrix, as shown in Table 7.12, is used for risk estimation. However,
    such a matrix is a simplification, as it does not represent the true
    complexity of detail by assigning numerical values.

8   *Overall assessment*
    When the ERA technique is applied, two matrices are normally
    produced. The first summarizes estimated magnitude and probability
    of all possible consequences while a second matrix (see Table 7.12)
    identifies a subset of those relevant consequences that affect the
    habitats and species typical to the particular site being classified. The
    matrix supports the judgement of whether a proposed development is
    likely to have a significant impact on an area.

Box 7.1 *Example of ERA report format for impacts considered*

Impact number and type

Impact explanation

Consequence number and type
Magnitude
Probability
Relevance
Risk
Estimated probability values for each magnitude
Severe   High   Mild   Negligible

Consequence number and type
Magnitude
Probability
Relevance
Risk
Estimated probability values for each magnitude
Severe   High   Mild   Negligible

Despite the simplicity of this approach, clarity and consistency are very important requirements. Risk assessment at every stage should be quantified as much as possible so as to reduce the need for judgement. In addition, when using the model, the following key points are important for a representative assessment of impacts and consequences of a proposed development:

- At every stage assumptions should be made explicit and recorded.
- The intrinsic characteristics of the situation before and after the proposed development should be described.
- In probability estimation, the event under consideration must be defined.

Table 7.12 *Estimation of risk from consideration of magnitude of consequences and probabilities relevant to a particular site*

Probability	Consequences			
	Severe	*High*	*Mild*	*Negligible*
High	High	High	Medium/Low	Near zero
Medium	High	High/Medium	Low	Near zero
Low	High/Medium	Medium/Low	Low	Near zero
Negligible	High/Medium/Low	Medium/Low	Low	Near zero

Boxes 7.2–7.4 give a worked example for the effects of revetment construction along a section of beach in South Wales, UK. In essence, a revetment structure was built along half of a beach in order to provide protection to a café and surf lifesaving station. Post-construction analysis indicated a high probability impact factor that would have severe to high negative consequences on the beach (Box 7.4).

Box 7.2 *Impacts selected for assessment*

1   Hydrodynamic change
2   Geomorphology (see Box 7.3)
3   Inter-tidal communities
4   Landscape
5   Beach users
6   Cultural sites
7   Local economy

Source: Williams et al (2000)

Box 7.3 *Environmental risk assessment report*

Impact no 2: effects on geomorphology (see Box 7.2)
Consequence No 1: Erosion of upper beach deposits

Magnitude	high
Probability	high
Relevance	yes
Risk	high

Estimated probability values for each magnitude

Severe	High	Mild	Negligible
0.6	0.3	0.05	0.05

Consequence No 2: Lowering of beach elevation

Magnitude	high
Probability	high
Relevance	yes
Risk	high

Estimated probability values for each magnitude

Severe	High	Mild	Negligible
0.6	0.3	0.05	0.05

Consequence No 3: Erosion of cliffs on eastern side due to changes in sediment supply and wave currents

Magnitude   severe
Probability   high
Relevance   yes
Risk   high
Estimated probability values for each magnitude

Severe	High	Mild	Negligible
0.3	0.3	0.2	0.2

Consequence No 4: Erosion of cliffs on western side

Magnitude   medium
Probability   high
Relevance   yes
Risk   medium/low
Estimated probability values for each magnitude

Severe	High	Mild	Negligible
0.5	0.3	0.15	0.05

Consequence No 5: Protection of landward sites in moderate sea conditions

Magnitude   severe
Probability   high
Relevance   yes
Risk   high
Estimated probability values for each magnitude

Severe	High	Mild	Negligible
0.5	0.3	0.2	0.1

Consequence No 6: Erosion of downdrift sites under severe high-tide storms

Magnitude   severe
Probability   high
Relevance   yes
Risk   high
Estimated probability values for each magnitude

Severe	High	Mild	Negligible
0.5	0.3	0.1	0.1

Consequence No 7: Erosion of deltaic deposits

Magnitude   mild
Probability   negligible
Relevance   yes
Risk   low
Estimated probability values for each magnitude

Severe	High	Mild	Negligible
0.3	0.3	0.3	0.1

Source: Williams et al (2000)

Box 7.4 *Count matrix for all relevant consequences*

Consequence probability	Consequence magnitude			
	Severe	High	Mild	Negligible
High	4	4	1	0
medium	0	1	1	0
low	0	1	3	0
negligible	0	0	1	0

Probability of a relevant consequence magnitude occurring
Severe 0.05   High 0.80   Mild 0.10   Negligible 0.05

Source: Williams et al (2000)

CHAPTER 8

Beach Awards and Rating Schemes

INTRODUCTION

There exist many different beach rating systems and the main characteristics of several of these are discussed below. Detail is provided for a new approach, the BARE system, which is considered to benefit from having a very strong management-oriented bias, making it a particularly applicable system (see Chapter 9). This takes into account not only physical and water quality parameters but has a multifaceted approach relating to anthropocentric parameters, based on what a bathing area user desires. This point is frequently glossed over by planners and managers, who impose a top-down approach, i.e. the 'experts know best', rather than bottom-up approach. To date there is no universally applied award, and even the front runner – the Blue Flag – changes its criteria depending in which part of the world it is operating.

One of the prime responsibilities of beach managers is to facilitate the bathing area so as to maximize its potential on a scale that ranges through strict conservation to full recreation (see Chapter 7, 'Environmental Risk Assessment Method', page 161). This is done in accordance with the primary aim/objective to which the bathing area has been designated. In practice, a balance is aimed for, between developing recreation too far (so that conservation is impaired) and conserving absolutely (so that tourism declines). The coastal tourist industry apparently relishes a variety of aesthetic scales, rating recreational areas (especially) and remote areas (on a lesser scale) with the aim of informing the general public where the 'best beaches' occur. The Oxford English Dictionary defines *aesthetic* as 'concerned with beauty or the appreciation of beauty', but what is this beauty? Does it lie, in Margaret Wolfe Hungerford's famous phrase, in the 'eye of the beholder'? If so, how much cognizance is taken of the beholder's viewpoint? A dearth of work exists with respect to this point (Cutter et al, 1979; Morgan et al, 1993). Ratings exist, so in essence they should be objective and cover many aspects of the relevant topic rather than just one or two – as sometimes happens. It should be an axiom that physical, human and biological parameters be covered in any rating scale, but in some instances these aspects are dealt with (if at all) very lightly, and virtually all are not weighted. The following is a synopsis of some current schemes and further information may be obtained from the internet addresses given.

SOME RATING SCHEMES

As stated, many schemes exist. A century or so ago, word of mouth probably brought certain beaches to the fore, as wealthy people made the 'Grand Tour' of Europe. For example, Deauville, Monte Carlo and Nice in France, the Amalfi coast in Italy and the Algarve in Portugal were all on the itinerary of travellers. The 19th-century railway boom in the UK brought coastal resorts to the fore, enabling working masses to spend holidays at the coast and stimulating the development of resorts such as Blackpool and Skegness. Now over 40 per cent of tourism in the UK is motivated by the coast (ETC/WTB/STB, 2004).

More generally, improved road networks and a changing social fabric resulted in increased leisure time, and since the 1960s air travel has become feasible for the masses. As a consequence, more people are now living and holidaying at the coast, thereby having greater access to the beach environment. Olsen et al (1997) estimate that by 2025, the world population will be 8.5 billion and of this number, 75 per cent will be living on the coast. Kullenberg (2001) states that over 50 per cent of the world's population lives within 200km of the coast and this number is on the increase.

The EU Environment Agency indicates that the biggest driver in European coastal zone development in recent years has been tourism, and the largest holiday destination is Europe (60 per cent of all international tourists), with 3.8 per cent business growth per year. Greatest activity is in France, Spain and Italy (79 million, 59 million and 40 million tourists, respectively), with increases of around 50 per cent since 1990. Malta, for instance receives over 1 million visitors per year, three times its permanent population. In French coastal areas, tourism provides approximately 43 per cent of the jobs – giving more revenue than fishing or shipping, with peak densities reaching 2300 tourists per km^2 in Mediterranean Spain and France, i.e. double the winter population (Epaedia, 2008). Jones and Phillips (2008: 375) point out that 'Tourism growth trends and consequent demands are showing continued signs of exponential growth which will ultimately exacerbate current demands and impacts.' It remains to be seen what effect the current global recession will have on these figures.

Following on from the above patterns, there have been a number of award schemes set up to provide indicators of quality. The following are but a few examples of current bathing area rating schemes.

Costa Rica

This is probably the oldest scheme of the modern era and the Marine and Terrestrial Act (Ley Maritimo Terrestre) in Coast Rica was used by Chaverri (1989) to identify beaches suitable for governmental/private tourist development. He identified 113 factors, split into 'positive' and

Table 8.1 *The positive/negative factors involved for three groups in the Costa Rican checklist*

Water		Sand shores		Physical environment	
Positive	*Negative*	*Positive*	*Negative*	*Positive*	*Negative*
Clarity	Sudden large	Dry beach	Rubbish	Immediate	Marsh/estuary
Temperature	waves	size	Entangled	access	fragility
Wave type	Undercurrent/	Vegetation	vegetation	Distant	Obstruction of
Surf	rips	quality	Thorny	access	infrastructure
regularity	Heavy swell/	Vegetation	vegetation	Area scene	Presence of
Substratum	rough seas	extent	Poisonous	variety	urban network
density	Submerged	Substrate	vegetation	Tourist	Private areas/
(below water	obstacles	Hardness	Hot supra-	image	private use
line)	Weak edges	Slope angle	littoral area	Space	of grounds
Submerged	Ridges/		Gentle area	availability	(resorts)
coast depth	troughs		Blowing		Supportive
Coastal area	Longshore		sand		capacity
wealth	currents		No		(carrying
Salinity	Oceanic litter		vegetation		capacity)
Substrate	Dangerous		Dunes		
type (below	litter		Irregular		
water line)	Muddy		relief		
	bottom				
	Algae/				
	seaweed				
	Floating				
	leaves,				
	driftwood				
	Bad smells				
	Bad tastes				
	Suspended				
	sediments				
	Suspended				
	contaminants				

'negative' parameters divided into six groups, each of which was given a score ranging from 0 ('bad') to 4 ('good'), with three of the groups being shown in Table 8.1. The rating of any particular beach was obtained by summing scores for the 'negatives' and 'positives', for the six groups, subtracting to find a total and then summing these final scores. This division was very subjective and of doubtful validity. The groupings are:

- water (10 and 16);
- beach (9 and 7);
- sand (6 and 10);
- rock (11 and 11);

- general beach environment (11 and 12);
- the surrounding area (5 and 5).

The bracketed figures relate respectively to 'positive' and 'negative' parameter numbers.

As an example, Los Leones 1 beach in Guanacaste, La Cruz Province, scored 26, 11, 4, 0, 12 and 9 respectively for the above bulleted points, giving a total rating of 62. But what does this mean? Nothing quantitative was attempted and the score reflected the subjective viewpoint of the investigator. No weighting with respect to importance was attempted – a common trait in most of the following rating schemes. A brief glimpse at Table 8.1 shows how difficult it is to give a value to parameters such as 'vegetation quality', 'tourist image', 'weak edges', 'blowing sand' and 'coastal area wealth'. Some of these parameters are ephemeral; others lack any quantitative bite at all.

The Blue Flag

The Blue Flag (www.blueflag.org) is probably the most well known of European award schemes. It is geared to both beaches and marinas, and run by the non-profit Foundation for Environmental Education (FEE), based in Denmark (FEE, 2008). A beach is eligible if it is nationally or internally designated as a bathing area, with at least one sampling point for water quality analysis and also has the necessary facilities and standards needed to comply with the criteria needed. It was launched in 1985 in France and commenced operations outside Europe in 2001 when South Africa was included; 35 countries now participate. Its aim is to promote coastal sustainability at local, regional and national levels via high standards in water quality, safety and environmental management, together with environmental education, and is awarded for only one season. Two criteria need emphasizing. The FEE places great store on what are termed Imperative (I) and Guideline (G) standards for total coliform, faecal coliform and faecal streptococci counts (see Table 8.2). Total coliform counts are only applicable to European sites. Imperative standards means that a beach *must* comply with them in order to receive an award; Guidelines standards infers that these standards *should* be achieved, i.e. they are not mandatory. In the context of water quality, the following comment by Rees (1997: 1) should be noted:

> Current bathing water quality monitoring standards are so fundamentally flawed that we can have little or no confidence in the accuracy of respective arbitrary and an almost limitless variable set of statistics. It is impossible to guarantee the quality of bathing water as a beach award.

Non-applicable criteria exist in some parts of the world. National criteria can often be stricter than the demands of Blue Flag, as in Turkey for

Table 8.2 *Blue Flag and ENCAMS water quality values*

Test for:	Limit values/100mL	% test values >limit values
Total coliforms	500 G	20
	10,000 I	5
Faecal coliforms	100 G	20
	2000 I	5
Faecal streptococci	100 G	0
	0 I	

Note: G = Guideline standard; I = Imperative standard

example. In some areas, for example the Caribbean, East Africa, South Pacific, some of the Guideline restrictions have been lowered to the Imperative standards. National/international juries approve the award and the cost for an award is £300 plus VAT.

Aspects covered for a Blue Flag are in four main areas in which different criteria are given. The number of criteria has changed slightly over time, but currently 27 exist and they must cover:

- *Environmental education and information.* This relates to information concerning coastal ecosystems and sensitive areas of the coast; bathing water quality (minimum of five samples taken weekly or, at most, fortnightly intervals); the Blue Flag campaign aims; a code of conduct; and a minimum of five environmental activities must be offered, for example leaflets, books, exhibitions, films, conferences and guided tours. In Italy, environmental education courses for municipalities are run; at Loutraki beach, Greece, a colourful brochure gives a history/ overview of the Flag. All these groupings are for the Imperative standard.
- *Water quality.* This relates to compliance with the standards and requirements for excellent water quality (CEC, 2006); no industrial/ sewage discharges to the beach; monitoring of the health of any coral reefs in the vicinity (within 500m of the beach); algae and suchlike should be left to decay on the beach unless it is a nuisance. These are all Imperative standards but there are also Guideline standards relating to compliance with the requirements for sewage treatment and effluent quality.
- *Environmental management.* The beach should: conform to coastal zone planning and legislation; be clean; have adequate bins available that are regularly emptied; have recycling waste facilities on/by the beach; have adequate and clean sanitary facilities with controlled sewage disposal; no camping, driving, dumping or dogs; and have all buildings properly maintained. All these are Imperative, while the Guidelines relate to sustainable transport in the area and the existence of a beach management committee.

- *Safety and services.* The beach must have: an adequate number of lifeguards/lifesaving equipment; first aid equipment; beach management for different users, for example swimmers and surfers; safe access; a map showing facilities; and a minimum of one beach per locality must have access and toilet facilities for the disabled. These are all Imperative standards, while Guideline standards relate to potable water and the existence of patrols.

Environmental Campaigns

Environmental Campaigns (ENCAMS) (www.encams.org) is an organization based in Wigan, UK, which historically (until 2006) distinguished between resort and rural beaches. Its criteria for Seaside Resort Awards in the main followed that of the Blue Flag – which it administers in England. For example, in the case of toilets, both awards demanded they be provided, occur in adequate numbers for visitors and disabled people, and be cleaned and regularly maintained throughout the day. Small deviations occur, i.e. dog refuse bins were needed, dogs on promenades had to be leashed and records kept of all emergencies for Seaside Resort Awards, but not for the Blue Flag. Similarly both awards required adequate litter bins that were emptied and maintained regularly, but in addition, ENCAMS asked for them to be about 25m apart and in an appropriate style. Parameters needed for a Seaside Resort Award covered: water quality; the beach and inter-tidal areas; safety (including a risk assessment – see Chapter 6); management; cleaning; and information and education.

ENCAMS recognized clean and relatively safe well-managed beaches. There were two award categories: resort (fulfilling 29 criteria) and rural (fulfilling 13) (the criteria numbers changed over time). One crucial criterion needed for the resort beaches was water quality, which had to comply with the mandatory standard of the Bathing Water Directive (CEC, 1976) in the previous year. Other parameters measured included phenols, mineral oils and transparency.

In 2006, the two categories were dissolved and a new Quality Coast award was introduced in 2007. The purpose of the new award is to recognize well-managed and quality beaches but also diverse parts of a coastline available to different users. It is open to all beaches even if water quality is not monitored.

The award recognizes four categories:

- 'Fun in the sea' – essentially water sport activities. Clean water is imperative.
- 'Away from it all' – the need to get away from the city, appreciate wildlife, scenic beauty and so on. Essentially rural beaches.
- 'Bucket and spade' – for day-trippers/holiday-makers who build sand castles, often children with grandparents, and who need car parks.

Beach entertainment for children for example cricket, football and kite flying is important. Safety and water cleanliness are important.

- 'Relaxed recreation' – a nice day out at the seaside. Food outlets, car parks, toilets and so on are needed. Often people have dogs and like long walks.

Certain elements have to be in place before inspection (for example assessment of carrying capacity, ensuring that the beach is clear of dog fouling) and during inspection (for example signage is of an acceptable standard). It is strongly recommended that a beach management plan is in place. An area wanting up to three awards is charged at £350 (plus VAT). This drops to £325 (plus VAT) for four to six beaches, and for over seven beaches it reduces further to £300 (plus VAT). An overview of this award may be found at www.qcaguide.co.uk

The Good Beach Guide

The Good Beach Guide (www.goodbeachguide.co.uk) a book published annually by the Marine Conservation Society (MCS), an NGO based at Ross on the Wales/England border. It also has an internet-based site. The Guide is divided into two main sections, with the first relating to water quality criteria:

- Recommended – minimum sewage contamination;
- Marine Conservation Society Guideline Pass – sewage-affected in heavy rain/certain tides;
- EU Guideline Pass (G) – fails EU mandatory test 5 per cent of the time;
- EU Mandatory Pass (P) – passes but large pollution risk;
- European Mandatory Fail (F) – contaminated.

The second section provides a range of information such as beach descriptions, safety, litter, facilities, wildlife, seaside activities, accessibility and parking, and public and tourist information. In order to pass, beaches have to pass (100 per cent of) the EU Bathing Water Directive (CEC, 2006). The beaches are graded (on a 1–5 scale, the symbol used being 'dolphins') and a beach has to reach a minimum grade of '3 dolphins' to be recommended and described in the Guide book. Beaches can reach a '4 dolphin' standard but fail due to factors such as insufficient information, adjacent sewage outfalls, difficult access, adverse newspapers reports, litter or unsuitability for bathing due to rocks and such like.

The Green Sea Initiative

The Green Sea Initiative (www.dwrcymru.com) is named after a poem by Dylan Thomas, written in 1930 when he was 16, 'Here is the bright green sea'. It is a major national project dedicated to the protection and improvement of the coastal waters and beaches around Wales, UK. It is backed by over 30 public and private organizations including local authorities, statutory agencies, the private sector, environmental and voluntary organizations. Key elements of the beach management policy are: commitment to important issues, mechanisms for stakeholder dialogue, designation of roles and responsibilities, objectives and targets identified, staff training needs identified, internal/external auditing of performance and a management system review process. It requires community-based management involving consultation – on litter, beach cleaning, waste facilities (including for animals), safety, access and water safety), together with information and education (wildlife considerations, environmental activities and events, beach guardianship and management).

It was set up by the Welsh Tourist Board and Welsh Water (the sixth largest water and sewerage company in England and Wales), in order to make the Welsh coastline, 'the pride of Europe' and capitalize on Welsh Water's £600 million capital investment 'in improving the water quality around the Wales coastline' (Nelson and Botterill, 2002: 158). Piloted in 1999, it was specifically geared to the many rural beaches in Wales having high environmental quality and that did not have the intense management enjoyed by resort/urban beaches. It is administered by Keep Wales Tidy (www.keepwalestidy.org). Strong emphasis is placed on community involvement and environmental activities. Stakeholders must get together to form a management team, who catalogue the area's beaches and delineate which should be put forward for an award. Local issues are paramount in the discussions, so this is an instance of the local (and tourist) beach user having a say in the management of the locality's beaches. Management plans involve such matters as beach description, ownership, partnerships, inventory, constraints, issues and objectives, tasks and reviews.

The beach operator must demonstrate best practice in the selection of beach management techniques. These may vary considerably between beaches due to their individual environmental sensitivity, volume of use and so on. The community is involved in the sustainable management of their local environment and the benefits of the scheme may be summarized as:

- responsibility and training;
- networking and linkage with other projects;
- meeting local agenda objectives, for example Local Agenda 21 (LA21);
- accessing community grants to improve coastal management;
- improving relationships between the community and other organizations.

The National Healthy Beaches Campaign

The National Healthy Beaches Campaign (NHBC) (www.nhbc.fiu.edu) was set up by Professor Stephen Leatherman of Florida International University, Miami, and is an annual list that rates the best major public recreational (swimming) beaches in the US. A book, *America's Best Beaches*, is also periodically produced of these beaches (Leatherman, 1998). Around 650 beaches are evaluated each year according to 60 stringent questions based on a sliding scale of 1–5, i.e. 'bad' to 'good'. It specifically singles out water quality (following Environmental Protection Agency (EPA) guidelines – see Table 8.3) as the primary concern of beach users. Other criteria assessed include beach cleanliness, safety, environmental quality, management and auxiliary services. Not surprisingly, Hawaiian beaches seem to dominate the rankings, and the list evaluates beaches by regions – the Northeast, Southeast, Gulf, Southwest, Northwest and Hawaii. Winners of the award are not eligible to be represented in the following year's list. While the questionnaires are designed to address beaches used primarily for swimming purposes, the author suggests that beaches used for other categories (for example scenic, walking, wildlife and sports) could also be rated using this scheme

Table 8.3 *EPA water quality criteria*

Bacteriological indicators	Recommended guideline
Enterococci (marine) *Escherichia coli* (freshwater)	1986 EPA Ambient Water Quality Criteria for Bacteria

Physical factors, biological factors, human impact and use represent the generic headings, and a variety of questions relate to specific parameters. Respondents place a tick in the relevant box, the totals are summed, and the higher the total for all three groupings, the 'better' the beach. An example of biological parameter groupings is given in Table 8.4.

Clean Beaches Council – the Blue Wave

The Blue Wave of the Clean Beaches Council (www.cleanbeaches.org) is an enterprise formed in 1998 in the US that divides beaches into resort and rural. The former has 33 assessed criteria, the latter 27. Standard parameters investigated include water quality, hazards, services, habitat conservation, public information/education and erosion management. Water quality criteria for this award (and for the NHBC award) are geared to the USA 1986 Ambient Water Quality Criteria for Bacteria guidelines recommended by EPA (see Table 8.3) during the high-use season.

Table 8.4 *NHBC beach rating questionnaire*

Parameter	Rating scale				
	1	2	3	4	5
Turbidity	Turbid		to		Clear
Water colour	Grey		to		Aqua/blue
Floating/suspended material	Plentiful		to		None
Algae in water	Infested		to		Absent
Red tide	Common		to		None
Smell (rotting fish/ seaweed)	Bad Odours		to		Fresh salty air
Wildlife (birds etc.)	None		to		Plentiful
Pests (flies, ticks, mosquitoes)	Common		to		No problem
Presence of sewage outfalls on beach	Several		to		None
Seaweed/jellyfish on beach	Many		to		None

The Blue Wave initiative defines a resort beach as:

> one that has developed its facilities, actively encourages visitors and provides varied recreational opportunities. The beach should be within easy access to commercial development. It would typically include hotels, resorts, restaurants, shops, toilets, public transportation, municipal supervision, first aid facilities, and public phones. Resort beaches also may include beaches in urban settings, such as New York City or Los Angeles beaches. (www.gea. com.uy/playas/Criterios_Blue_Wave_english.pdf)

A rural beach is defined as:

> one that has limited facilities and has not been developed as a resort. Rural beaches are generally more remote than resort beaches, with virtually no commercial beachfront development. However, they may be populated with residential dwellings. Rural beaches also include park facilities. Rural beaches are visited and enjoyed for their intrinsic qualities. Local management maintains a clean environment while promoting considerate use by visitors. (www.gea.com.uy/playas/Criterios_Blue_Wave_english. pdf)

See Chapter 9, Table 9.1 and 'Guidelines for Determining Beach Types According to the BARE Scheme' for alternative definitions of the above and other beach types.

The draft criteria are reviewed every two years by an expert panel. A total of 53 US beaches are members, 43 being in Florida alone, and a fee of $2500 is charged for the first year and $1250 for the second, the year commencing on the last Sunday of May. The goal of the Blue Wave Campaign is to promote public awareness and voluntary participation in maintaining clean and healthy beaches. Two inspections per beach are carried out and applications cover many matters (see parameters mentioned above). Interestingly, county-level destination certification can be obtained that includes the services listed below (up to 20 beaches) as well as the following additional services:

- additional consultation with destination staff related to water conservation promotion;
- pledge materials for water conservation partners;
- a comprehensive destination report summarizing the individual beach audits and overall destination analysis.

The fee for Clean Beach Destination certification is $15,000 and this involves: two site inspections, an environmental audit, consultation, an audit report and recommendations, blue wave flags (two per beach, boundary markers (entry and exit); information kiosk sign, a toll-free public feedback line, a certificate of achievement, national and international media campaigns, logo/trademark privileges and outreach media reports

Green Globe Awards

The Green Globe Awards were set up in 1994 by the World Travel and Tourist Council (WTTC), with the aim of implementing the Agenda 21 objectives of the Rio Summit in 1992. In 1998 it became an independent organization run by an international advisory council formed of tourist organizations, NGOs and environmental consultancies, and renamed Green Globe 21 (www.ec3global.com/products-programs/green-globe/Default.aspx). The aim changed with the name change from environmental education to a formal accreditation scheme (Griffin and De Lacey, 2002) whose main objective is to provide a low-cost, practical means for all travel and tourism companies to undertake improvements in environmental practice. It emphasizes best practice via benchmarking, culminating in 2001 with a new three-stage (affiliate, benchmarking and full certification) quantification standard based upon:

- environmental and social sustainability policy;
- environmental and social sustainability performance;
- regulatory framework;
- environmental management system;
- stakeholder consultation and communication.

The awards are either a distinction or commendation. It is a long-term process that is industry driven and that focuses on tourism rather than beaches. It is probably the most global and cross-sectoral approach to industrial self-regulation that exists. However, membership is low, being of the order of 700 (low in comparison to tourist industry numbers).

UK Environment Agency

This assessment is based on the work of the National Aquatic Litter Group (NALG) (www.environment-agency.co.uk) and rates beaches based on the amounts of litter present on a 100m stretch (50m either side of the access point) of beach from the tide line to the back of the beach. Litter is analysed and counted as per the categories given in Table 8.5 and the beach is graded A–D, the rule being that the lowest grade given is the final grade. For example, an A grade could be given for all categories apart from a D grade given to gross litter, and the final grade would be a D grade (see Appendix 2).

Table 8.5 *NALG beach grading via litter*

Category	Type	A	B	C	D
Sewage-related	General	0	0	1–5	6+
debris	Cotton buds	0	1–9	10–49	50+
Gross litter		0	1–5	10–24	25+
General litter		0–49	50–99	100–999	1000+
Harmful litter		0	0	1–3	4+
Accumulations	Number	0	0	1–3	4+
	Total items	0	1–5	4–49	50+
Oil		Absent	Trace	Some	Objectionable
Faeces		0	1	2–9	10+

Beach Safety – Australia

Beach Safety in Australia (www.surflifesaving.com.au) is concerned with saving lives. Over 530,000 people have been saved from drowning in the past 100 years by Australian lifesavers (www.lifesavingfoundation.com. au). Additionally, there exists a series of books published by the Australian Beach Safety and Management Programme via Surf Life Saving Australia. These are written by Professor Andy Short of the Coastal Studies Unit of the University of Sydney. They are 'benchmarks' books providing descriptions of beaches for the whole of Australia based almost wholly on safety parameters. It gives the public information on the origin and nature of beaches plus information on beach hazards and safety. In particular it comments on the beach's suitability for surfing, bathing and fishing. Based on physical hazards, all beaches are rated in terms of their public beach safety and scaled from 1 (safe) to 10 (least safe) (see Table 8.6).

Details are given on the coastal environment (geology, coastal, climate, ocean and biological processes), beaches (morphology, dynamics, types,

Table 8.6 *Beach safety in Australia*

Beach state	Wave height							
	<0.5m	0.5m	1.0m	1.5m	2.0m	2.5m	3.0m	>3.0m
Dissipative	4	5	6	7	8	9	10	10
Longshore bar trough	4	5	6	7	7	8	9	10
Rhythmic bar beach	4	5	6	6	7	8	9	10
Transverse bar rip	4	4	5	6	7	8	9	10
Low-tide terrace	3	3	4	5	6	7	8	10
Reflective	2	3	4	5	6	7	8	10

SAFETY RATING:
Safest: 1–3
Moderately safe: 4–6
Low safety: 7–8
Least safe: 9–10

KEY TO HAZARDS:
☐ Water depth and/or weak currents
▨ Shorebreak
▨ Rips and surf-zone currents
■ Rips, currents and large breakers

Notes: All safety level ratings are based on a bather being in the surf zone and will increase with increasing wave height or with the presence of features such as inlets, headlands or reef-induced rips and currents. Rips also become stronger with a falling tide.

changes), usage and hazards (usage, safety – beaches, fishing and surf). This is followed by detailed maps and descriptions of all beaches in the areas being investigated. The books are mammoth tomes and represent what can and should be done for *all* beaches.

Spain

Spain has a plethora of award schemes: LA21; the European Eco-Management and Audit Scheme (EMAS) (EC Council Regulation 761/2001) (http://ec.europa.eu/environment/emas/index_en.htm); the Sistema de Gestión Ambiental (Guia para la Implantación de Sistemas de Gestión Ambiental Confrome à la Norma UNE-EN ISO 14001 en Playas – www. aenor.es/desarrollo/centroinformacion/servicios/presentacion.asp); and Información General SCTE (Sistema de Calidad Turística Española) (www. calidadturistica.es/index.aspx). These are based on local communities committing themselves to implementing sustainable development plans in their own regions. EMAS started in an attempt to implement LA21, and was originally developed as an aid in improving the environmental performance of industrial companies but has now been extended to include organizations such as local authorities providing services. EMAS and LA21 both involve an initial environmental review or eco-audit consensus plus feedbacks and especially public participation, with the public forming sectoral and neighbourhood committees – the former debating local issues that are then fed to the latter. This is especially so for LA21, which prioritizes sustainable development in environmental, economic and social spheres. EMAS has a more systematic agenda and deals only with the environmental aspects, exercising more independent and objective control of the process (Campillo-Besses et al, 2004).

The schemes run in parallel. Environmental reviews cover the environmental quality assessment, their problems and identification of the risks. At Sitges, Spain, a sustainability commission and committee were set up and agreement reached regarding the structure and responsibilities of these committees. For example, specific goals must be identified, with indicators, benchmarks, work plans and control correction mechanisms put in place. Internal and external audits eventually lead to attainment of the eco-label EMAS validation, which is highly regarded by the tourist industry. The scheme is still in its early stages and problems are evident, such as converting proposals into action. The schemes seem to be substitutes for processes associated with local and government resource management acts, and tend to operate at different levels to the other rating schemes mentioned. ISO 14001, recognized internationally as a quality standard, requires three general objectives to be met: commitment to an environmental policy, steady improvement and compliance with legal and other regulations, and these together with some beach-specific factors are now being considered for implementation on Spanish beaches (AENOR, 2003). Marin et al (2004) also found during research at Ligurian beaches in Italy, that from 528 interviews, 81 per cent of people questioned stated that they knew what a Blue Flag was, yet only 8 per cent could give an exact definition and this dropped to 4 per cent for EMAS.

A recent award is the 'Q' for Quality tourism that has been granted by the Spanish Tourism Administration to 29 beaches in Andalusia, 9 each in Murcia and the Valencian communities, 5 in Catalonia, 3 in Asturias and 2 in the Balearic Islands. It is based upon the Spanish Tourist Quality System (SCTE) for assessing housing and apartment quality (Ariza et al, 2008a).

The Agéncia Catalana de l'Aigua's (ACA's) main role is to give information regarding compliance with water quality requirements of the European Bathing Water Directive, applied to Spain through the Real Decreto 734/88. In addition, aspects of water and sand quality, facilities, appearance and oceanographic and climate factors are considered (ACA, 2002). A simple numerical index obtained from five categories – poor (0), deficient (1), moderate (2), good (3) and very good (4)) – gives a final index varying from 0 (bad) to 12 (very good).

The Centro de Estúdios y Experimentación (CEDEX) Obras Públicas index, formulated in 1996, is aggregated from several performance indicators, based upon beach opinion polls geared to identifying factors considered to be most important to beach users and it uses a weighting index. It ignores managerial issues (general and emergency plans) and the natural functions (e.g. dunes and ecosystems) of a beach, addressing the protective (e.g. width, erosion, slope, grain size and beach form) and recreational functions, water quality (CEC, 2006), sand quality (e.g. visual aspects), beach comfort (e.g. structures), access (e.g. safe access and access for the disabled), services (e.g. information) and activities (e.g. animals and annoying sports) of any beach. The beach quality index is:

$$4ICAG + 3ICSO + 2ICFA + 3ICG + 2ICE + ICCS + ICAC/16$$

where: ICAG = microbiological and chemical water quality, ICSO = sand quality, ICFA = water physical quality, ICG = geomorphological quality, ICE = aesthetic quality, ICCS = service quality and ICAC = activity quality (Breton et al, 1996; AB, 2005; Sardá et al, 2005).

In Catalonia, Ariza et al (2008b) introduced the Beach Quality Index (BQI), designed to include the three main functional aspects of a beach ecosystem (natural, protective and recreational), which correspond to three sub-indices: the Natural Function Index (NFI), the Protective Function Index (PFI) and the Recreational Function Index (RFI), such that:

$$BQI = NFI + PFI + RFI$$

A host of sub-indices were included in each of the above functions (such as beach crowding, activities, parking, etc. for the Recreational Function Index) and weightings were carried out. The individual components were obtained from literature surveys regarding beach quality assessment (Breton et al, 1996; Morgan et al, 1996; Buceta, 2000; Nelson et al, 2000; Yepes et al, 2004), and were a pioneering attempt to evaluate the integral quality of Catalan coast beaches.

GuidaBlu, Italy

The 'GuidaBlu' (Blue Guide) (www.legambiente.it) is an Italian quality labelling system for some coastal localities. It is carried out by Legambiente, an Italian NGO for the municipal administrative level. Evaluation is based on a matrix that considers many weighted attributes. There are seven categories of evaluation, and each of them is given by a symbol. Evaluation uses different databases, via the Eviews programme, which provides estimations and model simulations.

Evaluation of the different specific parameters provides a scale ranging from 1–100, summarized together in a number of 'sails' (from one to five), the number of sails indicating the *overall condition* of the coast at that locality. In 2008, 286 sites were considered and the complicated computer algorithm gave the following results:

- 10 localities were given five sails (81.41–76.03 per cent);
- 43 localities were given four sails (75.90–68.04 per cent);

- 102 localities were given three sails (67.94–62.01 per cent);
- 74 localities were given two sails (61.95–55.00 per cent);
- 53 localities were given one sail (54.97–36.20 per cent).

The seven specific categories have specific attributes such as 'stars', 'waves' and 'petals'. In the first two categories, each symbol has one to five attributes, with each attribute indicating that one of the five parameters has received a positive evaluation:

- environment (one to five stars) – based on natural landscape, coastal landscape, urban landscape, buildings quality and quality of living;
- welcoming (from one to five petals) – based on welcoming capacity, tourism services, mobility, programmes for treating/managing waste, recycling facilities, and the sewage collection/treatment/disposal.

For the remaining five categories, the symbol (given in brackets) is either present or absent:

- sea and beach (waves) – this symbol indicates the best places regarding clean sea water and beach quality, the presence of 'free beaches' (see below), beach crowding and safety services;
- beyond the sea (castle) – indicating places of historical interest, quality handcrafts, museums and archaeological sites;
- sub (bubbles) – indicating the presence of a seabed that is of particular interest to those who practice scuba diving and the presence of land-based services (scuba-diving centre and scuba schools);
- disabled (special symbol) – indicating the presence of facilities for disabled people;
- sustainability (tree) – indicating that a municipality has promoted in the preceding year initiatives for improving environmental sustainability (cycling tracks, pedestrian islands, public transportation between seashore and the urban centre and so on) and where there is record of reduced energy consumption.

In Italy many beaches are privately exploited by means of state concessions given to the private sector (the so-called *'bagni'*), and their use by bathers and other users is subject to a fee. In such cases, people have free access along the first 5m from the waterline. Beaches that are not subject to this type of commercial exploitation are considered 'free beaches'.

The Dolphin Scale, Romania

Romanian legislative framework concerning beach management includes two regulations (MOR 1996; 2004) and water quality must reach EC mandatory standards (CEC, 2006) for the microbiological parameters of total and faecal coliforms and faecal streptococci. MOR (1996) provides

Table 8.7 *Minimum criteria for a tourist beach rating on the Romanian 'Dolphin' beach scale*

No	Criteria	3 dolphins category	2 dolphins category	1 dolphin category
I Beach natural qualities				
1	Sand quality	Sand with a uniform granule size, without foreign bodies	Sand must not contain foreign bodies	Sand must not contain dangerous foreign bodies
2	Average sand level (m)	0.5	0.4	0.25
3	Bathing water must not contain tarry residues and floating materials	Daily cleaning of beach	Daily cleaning of beach	Weekly cleaning of beach
4	Slope angle of the bathing area	Up to 15°	Up to 25°	Up to 30°
5	Submerged beach quality	Bathing area without pebbles, stones, rocks or submerged bodies	Removal of submerged bodies	Removal of submerged bodies at the start of season
II Beach facilities				
6	Showers	One shower per max. 15 persons	One shower per max. 20 persons	At least 4 showers
7	Dressing cabins	One cabin per max. 15 persons	One cabin per max. 20 persons	–
8	WC	Clean toilet facilities (one toilet per max. 15 persons)	Clean toilet facilities (one cabin per max. 20 persons)	Minimum 4 cabins
9	First aid posts	X	X	–
10	Lifeguards	X	X	X
11	Bathing water safety warning notices	Special and conventional notifications (flag)	Conventional notifications (flag)	Conventional notifications (flag)
12	Umbrellas on beach	Provision of (approx. 4–5 m) spaced fixed umbrellas	–	–
13	Renting of beach facilities (umbrellas, sun-loungers etc.)	X	X	–

Table 8.7 *(Continued)*

14	Loud speakers	Autonomous	X	–
15	Phone	Minimum 3	Minimum 1	–
16	Litter bins	Under each umbrella	1 per 30m^2	1 per 60m^2
17	Recreational facilities for children, pedaloes, wind surfing, jet skis, boating, nautical and parasailing clubs	Minimum 3 facilities	Minimum 2 facilities	–

III Other criteria

18	Beach area allocated per beach user (m^2)	Minimum 4	Minimum 3	–
19	Spaced (max. 50m) bather/ boating zonation buoys	X	X	X
20	Beach maintenance	Daily levelling and regularly cleaning	Levelling and daily cleaning	Levelling and daily cleaning
21	Regularly emptied litter bins	Whenever necessary	Whenever necessary	Daily

the 'Norms concerning beach tourist use', namely the main rating criteria on a one to three dolphin scale, primary responsibilities of beach managers and requirements stating specific beach facilities that could be provided. The last of these stipulates that catering facilities providing beverages, ice-creams and such like could continue to operate on beaches for one year after the passing of the law, but after that they have to operate near the beach. The rating criteria are considered imperative ('minimum criteria') and are different for each dolphin category beach. The Romanian beaches must comply with 21 minimum criteria covering aspects given in Table 8.7 (Chiotoroiu et al, 2006).

MOR (2004) stipulates the conditions for granting tourism operating licences and defines mandatory responsibilities for beach concessions. The minimum criteria stipulated by this regulation (which has to be complied with by tourism operators for concessions) endorses only some of the criteria established in MOR (1996).

Portugal: Gold award quality beaches

The environmental organization Quercus (National Association of Conservation of Nature) awarded 196 out of a total of 508 bathing areas (422 coastal and 86 inland) a 'Gold quality award' in 2007 (http://snirh. pt). This award recognized Portuguese bathing areas that over a period of five years have obtained a 'good' grade in water quality standards (CEC, 2006). The rating scheme is much more limited in scope than others mentioned, as water quality is the only criterion and it is based on annual data provided by the Portuguese Institute of Water. The county with the largest number of beaches with 'gold standard' water quality is Albufeira (15 bathing areas), followed by Vila do Bispo (10 bathing areas), Almada (9 bathing areas) and Grândola and Vila Nova de Gaia (7 bathing areas). In 2007, for the first time one interior bathing area – Montargil was selected.

COMMENTS

The above schemes are indicative of what Parkin (2000: 224) wrote regarding science: 'Science is performed within paradigms which are quasi-ideologies imposed by elite scientists. New paradigms replace the old, but none is more representative of the truth than the other'. While policy-makers seem to have the pick of an abundance of awards, such disparate approaches to beach rating and award schemes were identified by Micallef and Williams (2002; 2004) as lacking in consistency of classification criteria by:

- being either too narrow in focus by addressing single (for example health-related) issues or while adopting a wider scoped approach, nonetheless omit inclusion of issues considered by this study as important elements for a holistic bathing area classification system;
- not recognizing the influence of beach user preferences and priorities in defining a selected set of criteria that may be used for quality evaluation purposes;
- having often focused on the beach itself, failing to adequately consider the wider-scoped nature of a *bathing area* that should include the surrounding environment – the quality of which has been shown to influence beach user satisfaction (Morgan et al, 1993; Micallef et al, 1999);
- failing to provide a clear understanding to beach users of the rationale used for their beach rating. Nelson et al (2000) describe how 17 per cent of beach users interviewed at South Wales beaches in the UK associated a Blue Flag with danger!
- ignoring the nature of varying beach types and individual beach type requirements;
- stopping short of integrating concerns into an effective beach management tool.

Williams and Morgan (1995), Morgan et al (1995), Micallef et al (1999) and Micallef (2002) identify a wide range of physical (local geology and geomorphology), biological (flora and fauna), socio-economic (recreational amenities, access, safety, landscape, archaeology, commercial interests) and environmental quality criteria (cleanliness, hygiene and toilets facilities) of particular interest to beach users (Micallef and Williams, 2002). These were utilized in the development of the novel Bathing Area Registration and Evaluation (BARE) system. This system acknowledges five beach types, namely resort, urban, village, rural and remote. Recent research carried out in the Euro-Mediterranean region and the US concerned with beach user preferences and priorities, has identified five main issues of concern. These are safety, water quality, facilities, scenery and litter (Morgan and Williams, 1995; Micallef et al, 1999; Morgan et al, 1996) and they provide the building blocks of the technique. Unlike the previous award schemes, BARE is predominantly a management technique and a full description is given in Chapter 9.

A Bathing Area Registration and Classification Scheme

INTRODUCTION

By virtue of their high potential for recreation for both local and overseas tourism, bathing areas represent valuable national resources requiring effective management. At the same time that increased leisure enhances the desirability of such recreational areas, increased public awareness of health and safety issues and recreational opportunities raises expectations of quality and desire of choice, thereby raising the need for effective bathing area evaluation and management schemes. To date, most approaches consider single or a limited number of issues such as safety or health and fail to address the variety of bathing area types represented in the field.

In addressing a recognized gap in our knowledge base and any information concerning bathing areas, the generation of an inventory of beaches, through *registration, quality evaluation* and *identification of priority management issues* is highly desirable. Such a study would obviously make a very useful contribution to a wide spectrum of end users including, planners, tourism, management and the public sector.

BEACH REGISTRATION

While the creation of inventories of natural coastal habitats and environments is not at all a novel concept, very few authors have specifically referred to the development of beach registers as a means of formal registration of such resources (Short, 1993; Figueras et al, 2000; Pond et al, 2000) However, in considering issues related to beach rating, several scientific works have referred to the use of checklists (Chaverri, 1989; Williams and Morgan, 1995; Leatherman, 1997; Micallef et al, 1999) and in so doing have indirectly considered many of the components of beach registration (see Chapter 8).

A beach register is in essence a checklist that is easy to use and adapt for cost-effective management. For example, it may be used for identification of swimming hazards, development of beach tourism or development of comprehensive management plans. A beach register is useful for storing information and would represent a particularly effective checklist that may be used to assist coastal managers to better manage beach resources through:

- identification of the range and causes of coastal problems resulting in environmental degradation;
- identification of coastal resources and conservation/recreation opportunities that they represent;
- the selection of beaches to be developed and how they should be developed;
- development of efficient beach management programmes addressing both national and local priorities;
- assisting in the development of appropriate monitoring programmes;
- development of beach classification systems.

Pond et al (2000) describe the composition of a beach register, referring to four main components:

1 *Beach description*
   In describing a beach area, the following parameters are noted:
   – area of the beach (described as length and width);
   – beach material (including sand, gravel, mud, other kinds);
   – litter survey – a number of criteria may be used to survey beach litter (Dixon, 1995; Rees and Pond, 1995; Earll et al, 2000), for example the UK Environmental Authority's National Aquatic Litter Group litter assessment technique (EA/NALG, 2000);
   – visitors per day – an estimate of the peak numbers according to season, whole bathing season, main holiday period, on weekdays and weekends has been recommended for this purpose.
2 *Description of the surroundings*
   Beach environment surroundings are described in the form of a number of hinterland, access and facility-related aspects:
   – hinterland (within walking distance and visible from the beach);
   – forests, fields, meadows, steppe, deserts, mountains, industries, power plants, urban area, harbours, military areas, airports, hills, rural area, river outlets and swamps;
   – accessibility (roads, tracks, public transport, absence of access);
   – facilities (restaurants, hotels, bars, toilets, drinking water, litter bins, parking lots, camping grounds, information signs and information sources, lifeguards, summer resorts, showers, first aid posts, swimming safety warnings, diving platforms).
3 *Description of the bathing environment*
   A checklist proposed by Chaverri (1989) identifies an exhaustive and rather unwieldy list of over 100 parameters describing a typical bathing environment, resulting in frequent overlap and sometimes ambiguity.

In a more selective approach, Pond et al (2000) suggest that the bathing environment may be best described by considering the:

- bathing zone, for example sea current (direction and speed), slope, sea bottom material (sand, stones, gravel, rock in percentage coverage);
- usage, for example fishing, jet skis, intensive yachting;
- water quality, for example monitoring programme results, potential influences (river mouths, sewage outlets, harbour area, other outlets);
- shore type, for example sandy beach, rocky shore, cliff (expressed as a percentage of the bathing area).

4   *Designated sensitive areas*

The final parameter recommended for inclusion in a beach register's description of the bathing area's surrounding is that of designated sensitive areas. These may include a resting place for waterfowl, breeding place for rare birds, sanctuary, conservation area and other kinds of protected area (for example military area) where admittance of the public is prohibited.

The beach registration process described by Pond et al (2000) also refers to the most appropriate method of data acquisition (through desk studies, field surveys and accessing valuable information held by the local community) and the importance of annual rechecking/updating of the generated database. The collection of data describing the beach and water environments is also an important prerequisite for evaluation of beach quality.

This format follows that adopted by Short (1993) in his extensive classification of Australian beaches. In the context of this study, it was considered that such a beach register, particularly one developed on a national basis and in a computer-based GIS format, presents an ideal bathing area management tool by reflecting the most appropriate use-policy best suited for individual beaches (for example based on issues such as safety, facilities and/or use value, such as conservation and recreation). Since the information held in such a beach register may also be used for the determination of beach quality, it was also proposed that a beach register may be used for the development of a beach classification system.

Two examples of such an approach to beach registration are given for Brighton beach in the UK (see Box 9.1) and evaluation of Mhlathuze beaches in South Africa (Box 9.2). These reflect facts and figures that augment any management system utilized to capture elements that make up a 'beach'.

Box 9.1 *Beach registration information for Brighton beach, UK*

Local Authority: Brighton and Hove City Council.
Blue Flag Award: Not held previously, but they have applied for two this year.
Previous holdings of Seaside Award (now superseded by Quality Coast Awards): Never been applied for.
Quality Coast Awards: Not applied for. It was felt that Blue Flag was more appropriate to them as they did not fit any of the Quality Coast Award headings.
Number of visitors per annum: 8 million. This is calculated by overnight bed bookings, coach travel and visitor numbers.
Number of accidents/incidents per annum: Brighton and Hove record accidents and incidents throughout the summer via the lifeguards and seafront team. They use the same recording system as the RNLI and send the data to them, which is then held on the national database. They agreed to do this as they are part of the National Beach Safety Council and wanted to help build a picture of what is happening around the coast of the UK. They had 493 emergency responses in 2006, including first aid, rescues at sea, lost children, antisocial behaviour, searches, liaison with emergency services and injured animals.
Cost of resort management: £375,000. This is the total for the seafront and includes planned maintenance and beach safety. The staffing budget of £250,000 includes all summer staff including beach lifeguards and a recreation assistant.
Staffing numbers: Recently restructured and lost the resort services manager. Currently one manager of sports development, one seafront officer, four assistant seafront officers, 27 lifeguards (May to September), two seasonal office staff and one recreation assistant.
Beach safety team: The beach is manned from 9.30am to 7pm every day from 22 May until 10 September. They are looking to start manning the beach from 1 May until the end of September soon as this seems to be the norm elsewhere.
Public toilets: There are nine sets of toilets spread over 13km. They are managed by an external contractor and have various opening times. Three sets are attended all year round and the others are serviced three times a day. Toilets are open 7am until 9pm in the summer and 8am to 5pm in the winter.
Beach cleaning: The whole stretch of beach is cleaned every day.
Further information: Brighton and Hove are members of two relevant groups – the National Beach Safety Council, which is administered through the RNLI in Poole, and the UK Beach Managers Forum.

Source: Brighton and Hove Councils

Box 9.2 *Beach data registration in connection with beach rating and classification at Mhlathuze beaches in South Africa*

The South African Council for Scientific and Industrial Research (Saltau and Theron, 2006) were commissioned by the city of Mhlathuze to determine a 100-year setback development line for the northern beaches in the Richards Bay area, as these beaches were undergoing erosion. Additionally, the study was asked to include an evaluation of the Mhlathuze beaches. In their evaluation of beach rating and classification, the CSIR utilized a point rating system that reflected beach safety and development suitability, used to register and differentiate different recreational beach groupings in set administrative localities. The scores were based on a maximum of 100 points for each category. The total points awarded for safety and development suitability allowed beach ranking according to three categories – Best, Acceptable, Least acceptable (<50 per cent). For example, a beach scoring 100 points for 'development suitability' implies one perfectly suitable for development while one scoring zero points implies a beach extremely unsuitable for development. The points were recorded in tables such as the one below.

	RELATIVE WEIGHTING OF FACTORS	SCORE
A. BEACH SAFETY FACTORS		
Wave climate[a]	15	
Nearshore currents[b]	14	
Beach slopes	15	
Presence and extent of rocks	15	
Presence and extent of river mouths, streams, pipes/outfalls	15	
Surf climate[c]	10	
Total points scored (A)		
B. DEVELOPMENT SUITABILITY		
Potential wind-blown sand[d]	6	
Beach profiles[e]	20	
Beach and backshore space[f]	20	
Presence and extent of rocks	5	
Presence and extent of river mouths, streams, pipes/outfalls	15	
Shoreline stability[g]	20	
Total points scored (B)		
Grand Total Rating (A + B)		
Beach Ranking (Best; Acceptable; Least acceptable)		

a   Wave heights for selected conditions as determined from the wave refraction modeling.
b   Wave angle, cusps, rip currents, gullies/bars and troughs.
c   Number of re-breaks, surf zone width.
d   Dry beach width, wind direction.
e   Beach slope, dune slope.
f   Cross-shore beach width, upper beach and backshore width.
g   Prograding/stable/eroding or slumping.

The points awarded to factors influencing beach safety and development suitability reflected the magnitude of their influence. For each factor considered, the beach at which that factor was most favourable was awarded the maximum points available for that factor. All the other beaches in the beach set considered were then awarded points between zero and the maximum in relation to the specific value. For example, in the safety section, a beach with higher waves will obtain a lower rating as this produces less safe bathing conditions.

The structure of the table reflects how, in the case of Mhlathuze beaches, the relative weighting of factors considered resulted in the 'best' beach being awarded a score of 20, the worst 0 and those in between are scales relative to the number, i.e. maximum 20, minimum 0. The absolute values of the total points are less important than the relative beach ratings, and as the system is a relative comparison, only factors that differ in the region are taken into account, For example, as tidal range is constant in this area, it is not considered.

Source: adapted from Soltau and Theron (2006)

BEACH CLASSIFICATION

A number of authors have considered the management value of beach classification or rating, but the majority are either too narrow in their scope, by addressing single (for example health-related) issues or, although adopting a wider scoped approach, nonetheless omit inclusion of issues considered as important elements for a holistic bathing area classification system (see Chapter 8). In this context, Williams and Morgan (1995) and van Maele et al (2000) reviewed beach award schemes (including the European Blue Flag and other schemes prevalent in the UK) and conclude that the majority do not consider the beach itself and important beach user satisfaction with, for example, issues related to surrounding environment and facilities.

THE BATHING AREA REGISTRATION AND EVALUATION SYSTEM

The BARE system developed by Micallef and Williams (2003b, 2004, 2005) acknowledges five beach types, namely resort, urban, village, rural and remote (see Chapter 1). These occupy a continuous spectrum of beach types and occasionally some difficulty may be experienced in differentiation, as no universally accepted definitions exist. Recently, research carried out in the Euro-Mediterranean region and the US on beach user preferences and priorities, identified five main issues of concern: safety, water quality, facilities, scenery and litter (Morgan and Williams, 1995; Micallef et al, 1999; Morgan et al, 1996; 2000; Tudor and Williams, 2006; House and Phillips, 2007; Marin et al, 2007).

The novel BARE approach (see Figure 9.1) addresses the shortcomings of existing systems. It provides an approach with enhanced scope for management intervention. This is achieved through the development of a scheme able to:

- evaluate not only the beach itself but the bathing area as a whole: the beach together with that area within walking distance (300–500m) and generally visible from the beach and any facility (for example camping area) beyond this distance but clearly serving the beach;
- class bathing areas according to a rating system that focuses on five main beach-related issues that have been shown to rate highly in beach user preferences and priorities;
- prioritize the five beach-related issues of concern according to beach type-specific requirements;
- provide a final bathing area classification primarily as a management tool to assist local management in identifying issues requiring priority intervention leading to upgrading of beach quality.

Further, the scheme:

- promotes a holistic approach to bathing area management that considers the beach and surrounding environment;
- provides beach users with an opportunity to make a better-informed choice of bathing areas;
- provides local authorities with a tool to better gauge the quality of their bathing areas that may be used for both management as well as more effective promotion of the bathing areas under their jurisdiction;
- recognizes a wider selection of beach types (see Chapter 1) that allows selective application of importance to beach-related criteria used for quality evaluation;
- provides a much less rigid system that progresses from pass/fail award options (as in the case of flag award schemes) to an improved management-oriented tool;
- provides a system that groups a number of important beach-related parameters under five main issues of concern to beach users. This has clear benefits not only for ease of site classification but also for adapting the technique to suit individual regional preferences and priorities, where these differ from other areas, by adjusting their parameter rating order of priority within the beach type classification tables.

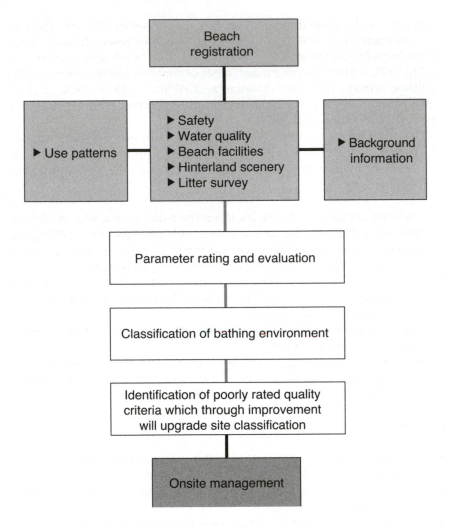

Figure 9.1 *BARE flow chart*

It should be stressed that the BARE technique was developed to cater for beach parameters found in the Euro-Mediterranean region. The authors have no doubt that appropriate adjustments of individual parameters, particularly those criteria related to beach user preferences and priorities (used for quality evaluation but which may change regionally due to cultural backgrounds) and also beach typology may be required for the technique to suit different regions. Despite these comments, the authors would like to stress that it is the ethos of having a solid management scheme in place prior to attempting to register for any award or rating that is the fulcrum of this work and that makes the BARE approach universally applicable.

A full description of the BARE system together with the registration and evaluation forms utilized for beach quality and beach type evaluation are provided in Annex 1 of this chapter.

The BARE technique allows the development of an *action-oriented strategy* through the:

- collection of essential baseline information on which to base beach management policy and strategy;
- production of an inventory of beaches through individual site registration (see below);
- application of a bathing area quality evaluation scheme to each beach site (see below);
- development of site-specific beach management plans based on the identification of priority management issues particular for each beach site (see also Chapter 3, 'Beach Management Plans' and 'Beach Management Models', pages 65–85).

The BARE system is not intended to provide a quality-based comparison between the five main beach types recognized by the system (for example comparison of resort with rural beaches) or indeed between beaches in different countries, but to provide an evaluation of any beach type, allowing quality ratings within countries and regions and more importantly, an identification of management priorities required to improve the quality of individual beaches.

The proposed technique focuses on *achieving improvement in beach quality through effective beach management* by consideration of a wide spectrum of beach types (resort, urban, village, rural and remote beaches – see Chapter 1, 'Typology', page 13, and the criteria and guidelines described below) and beach quality (reflected by a beach's ability to provide levels of safety, water quality, facilities, scenery and litter). Since the five beach types recognized by the technique are considered to require different levels of management and intervention, the value of considering a wider variety of beach types is that management plans will be more site-specific and therefore more effective. It also enables a prioritization of the five main beach-related issues that are rated according to beach type.

Guidelines for application of the BARE form

Through the BARE approach, a wide range of bathing area related data is collected via the BARE Registration Form (Annex 1, page 202). The form is structured as follows:

- *Section I* covers background information.
- *Section II* concerns the five main issues of concern to beach users.
- *Section III* addresses evaluation of registered data that enables parameter rating on a four-scale system (A–D).

- *Section IV* **provides** subsequent analysis of ratings scored for the five issues, using a 1–5 star classification.

NB: In reproducing the BARE Registration Form (Annex 1) for fieldwork application, it is only necessary to consider Sections I and II.

Background information
The BARE technique involves collection of a wide variety of data on:

- beach type, size and shape;
- sea-floor sediment characteristics and shore type;
- backshore information;
- information on the local administration and responsibilities;
- access type to beach and bathing water;
- beach erosion, occupancy rates and carrying capacity (see Annex 1, Table 1.2), beach-use orientation (see Annex 1, Table 1.3);
- designated sensitive areas (see Annex 1, Table 1.4).

Data collection for Section I is largely through a field-based presence/absence checklist procedure in addition to desk studies of existing public reports (for example hard-copy maps and GIS data sets, erosion-related studies and ecological reports for biodiversity/conservation-related data). The identification in Section I of the beach type is *crucial* to the entire exercise since subsequent beach quality evaluation and rating is *beach-type specific*. To this end, particular attention should be given to the determination of beach type based on the definitions provided in the sections below on critical criteria and guidelines (see also Chapter 1, 'Typology', page 13). Where any data are unknown, inaccessible or uncertain, this should be so indicated.

Collection of data on rated parameters
Data on the five main issues of concern to beach users are collected via:

- Annex 1, Table 2.1 (Safety);
- Annex 1, Table 2.2 (Water quality);
- Annex 1, Table 2.3 (Facilities);
- Annex 1, Table 2.4 (Scenery);
- Annex 1, Table 2.5 (Litter).

As with Section I of the BARE Form, data for Section II is collected via a combination of desk studies (for example official bathing water quality reports) and a field-based checklist procedure for safety, facilities, scenery and litter-related data. Current proposals by the European Commission indicate that beach onsite information on bathing water quality will, in the near future, be a requirement and therefore available for field registration. For facilities and safety, data are collected for the entire beach. For litter, the NALG protocol (see Appendix 2) is utilized by the BARE technique. For hinterland scenery, the coastal scenic evaluation system carries out an overall bathing area classification from the beach (Ergin et al, 2004; 2006a).

Scenic assessment is based upon a checklist that itemizes 26 parameters (comprising physical and human parameters), as a first step in quantifying scenery. These parameters were obtained by consultation (700) with coastal experts and beach users. Each parameter was rated on a five-point scale, essentially covering presence/absence or poor quality (1), to excellent/ outstanding (5). Ratings subjected to fuzzy logic matrices and weightings reflected the importance of the various parameters, enabling histograms of weighted averages for the various attributes to be produced. This can give graphs for membership degree attributes for any site and even country. Membership degree figures gave the overall result of scenic assessment over attributes. High weighted averages for attributes 4 and 5 (excellent/ outstanding) reflect high scenic quality; vice versa for attributes 1 and 2. A 'decision parameter criteria' (D) enabled scenic values for any site to be calculated, graphed and five categories of scenery recognized:

$$D = \frac{(-2.A_{12}) + (-1.A_{23}) + (1.A_{34}) + (2.A_{45})}{\text{Total area under curve}}$$

where A_{12} = total area under the curve between attributes 1 and 2. Similarly, areas under the curve may be calculated for $A_{23,}$ $A_{34,}$ A_{45}. Details can be obtained from Ergin et al (2004, 2006a).

Evaluation of ratings allocated to the five beach user priority issues
The evaluation system is based on the ratings allocated to parameters pertaining to each of the five main priority issues of concern to beach users (safety, water quality, facilities, scenery and litter). Rating involves allocation of a scale (A–D) based on the presence/absence of the issue-related parameters (see Annex 1, Tables 3.1–3.4).

Classification
Beach classification is based on an evaluation of the rating results obtained for each of the five main issues (see Annex 1, Tables 4.1–4.3). This results in an overall bathing area classification, ranging from 1 (low) to 5 (high) stars.

Guidelines for determining beach types according to the BARE scheme

Remote, rural, village and urban beaches are defined primarily by their *cultural environment*. Resort beaches are usually defined primarily by their *private nature*. (see also Chapter 1, 'Typology', page 13). Therefore:

Table 9.1 Critical criteria for beach type definition

	Environment	Accessibility	Habitation/ accommodation	Facilities/safety equipment
Remote	May be contiguous to/on the fringe of rural areas and on occasion to village environments but not with urban areas.	*Remote beaches are found in a rural environment but accessible only on foot (a walk of 300–500m) or by boat.* No entry payment fee.	Uninhabited for a radius of at least 500m. May have very limited (0–5 if any) temporary summer housing.	None expected. If present, consider classing as rural.
Rural	*Located outside the urban/village environment, having an absence of a community focal centre (religious centre, primary school, shops, cafes, bars).*	Not readily accessible by public transport. But accessible by private transport. No entry payment fee.	Housing is limited (generally 0–10) but may be more depending on the size of the coastal stretch). May be of temporary (summer) or permanent (year-long) nature.	None expected but many exceptions encountered. If present, consider classing as village but be guided by the *type of environment*.
Village	*Located outside the main urban environment and is associated with a small but permanent population reflecting access to organized but small-scale community services (such as a primary school(s), religious centre(s) and shop(s)).* *The beach may be sited within or adjacent to the village.*	Accessible by both public and private transport. No entry payment fee but use of facilities e.g. sun beds/ umbrellas are normally against payment.	Small-scale residential accommodation plus bed & breakfast for visitors. A village environment would also include 'tourist villages', mainly utilized in the summer months as well as 'ribbon development' between urban and rural environments.	Facilities are expected to be limited to clean public showers and toilets, restaurants, adequate parking and good access, regularly cleaned litter bins, and bed & breakfast accommodation. Safety facilities expected include bather/boating zonation buoys, fixed safety equipment, beach safety-related warning notices and emergency telephones.

	Characteristics	Access	Accommodation	Facilities	Safety
Urban	*Urban areas serve large populations with well-established public services such as a primary school(s), religious centre(s), banks, post office, internet cafes and a well-marked central business district. In the proximity of urban areas, one may find commercial activities such as fishing/boating harbours and marinas. Urban beaches are located within the urban area or adjacent to it.*	Accessible by both public and private transport. Generally freely open to the public but entrance fee may be encountered. Use of facilities e.g. sun beds/umbrellas is normally against payment.	Large-scale residential accommodation units plus hotel/apartment complex accommodation for visitors.	Restaurants, public toilets, showers and litter bins, parking space and good access.	A variety of safety measures (safe bathing environment, lifeguards, bather/boating zonation buoys, fixed safety equipment, first aid posts, beach safety warning notices and emergency telephones.
Resort	A resort may be sited within any type of environment but as a rule has no nearby industrial activities.	*Resort beaches are generally utilized by residents staying at beach-associated hotel/apartment complex/camping resort that manages the beach.* *May be open to the public against payment.*	Associated hotel/apartment/camping complex.	Hotels, restaurants, good camping grounds, beach showers, toilets, clean litter bins, adequate parking and good access; the widest possible range of beach-related recreational activities for hire or freely available for resort residents.	Widest possible range of safety measures (safe bathing environment, lifeguards, bather/boating zonation buoys, fixed safety equipment, first aid posts, beach safety warning notices and emergency vehicle access.

Notes: **Bold italics** represent the critical criteria. See Chapter 1, 'Typology', page 13.

1   A remote beach is found in a rural environment but accessible *only* on
     foot or by boat. (Normally remoteness infers a distance from habitation,
     but for beaches we understand remoteness to include a distance from
     the closest road access point of not less than 300m and up to 500m.) If
     the beach is accessible by private car or by bus or the walk is short, then
     it is NOT a remote beach.
         In remote beach bathing areas, the provision of services (facilities) is
     not expected and hinterland scenery and litter criteria take on added
     importance as quality criteria. Where the average bathing season
     occupancy rate is under 40 per cent of the beach carrying capacity,
     safety-related provisions (for example lifeguards) are also not
     expected and water quality monitoring is limited to visual observation
     techniques (see Annex 1 of this chapter, Table 2.2). However at remote
     beaches where the average bathing season occupancy rate > 40 per cent
     of the beach carrying capacity, safety and water quality criteria are also
     evaluated (see notes to Table 4.3 of Annex 1 of this chapter).
2   A rural beach is located outside the urban/village environment, having
     an *absence* of a community focal centre (religious centre, primary school,
     shops. Sometimes cafes or bars may be found). If there is a school or a
     church and large shopping centre, then it is not a rural area.
         At rural bathing areas, the provision of services (facilities) is not
     expected and hinterland scenery and litter criteria take on added
     importance as quality criteria. Where the average bathing season
     occupancy rate is under 40 per cent of the beach carrying capacity,
     safety-related provisions (for example lifeguards) are also not expected
     and water quality monitoring is limited to visual observation techniques
     (see Annex 1, Table 2.2). However, at rural beaches where the average
     bathing season occupancy rate is over 40 per cent of the beach carrying
     capacity, safety and water quality criteria are also evaluated (see Annex
     1, note to Table 4.3).
3   A village beach is located outside the main urban environment and
     is associated with a *small but permanent population reflecting access to
     organized but small-scale community services,* such as a primary school(s),
     religious centre(s) and shop(s). The beach may be sited within or
     adjacent to the village. If there are no primary schools, churches, shops
     serving a small permanent population then it is a rural area, while
     if the community is large and services include banks, a post office,
     internet cafes and a central business district, then its an urban area.
         Top scoring 'scale A', village beaches are expected to offer basic
     safety facilities such as a safe bathing environment, bather/boating
     zonation buoys, fixed safety equipment, beach safety-related warning
     notices and emergency telephone facilities (see Annex 1, Table 3.1b)
     and strict water quality monitoring (see Annex 1, Table 3.2). Facilities at
     village bathing areas are expected to be limited to clean public showers
     and toilets, restaurants, adequate parking and good access, regularly
     cleaned litter bins, and bed & breakfast accommodation (Annex

1, Table 3.3b). These beaches would also be expected to be cleaned regularly. Absence of parameters as defined for scale A beaches results in a lowering of scale (B–D).

4   Urban areas serve *large* populations with *well-established public services* such as a primary school(s), religious centre(s) banks, a post office, internet cafes and a well-marked central business district. Urban beaches are located within the urban area or adjacent to it. This is probably the easiest to define. A beach in an urban area is an urban beach, unless it is a resort.

Top scoring (scale A) urban bathing areas will include stringent safety-related facilities and water quality testing (as in resort beaches; see Annex 1, Tables 3.1a and 3.2 respectively), hotel/apartment complex accommodation (not integrally linked to the beach as in the case of resorts), restaurants, regularly cleaned public toilets, showers and litter bins, parking spaces and good access and daily cleaning (see Annex 1, Table 3.3a). Absence of parameters as defined for scale A beaches results in a lowering of scale (B–D).

5   Resort beaches are self-contained entities that fulfil all recreational needs of beach users to different degrees, the majority of such users would reside at the beach-associated accommodation complex that is integrally linked to the management of the beach. Resort beach users visit largely for recreational (rather than leisure, for example sunbathing/swimming) purposes. Resort beaches can be private but may be open to the public for day use against payment.

A top-scoring resort beach (scale A) is served by a variety of safety measures (safe bathing environment, lifeguards, bather/boating zonation buoys, fixed safety equipment, first aid posts, beach safety warning notices and emergency telephones) (see Annex 1, Table 3.1a); regular water quality monitoring by competent authorities (see Annex 1, Table 3.2); a wide variety of facilities (hotels, restaurants, good camping grounds, beach showers, toilets, clean litter bins, adequate parking and good access); a variety of beach-related recreational activities for hire or freely available for resort residents (for example beach sports such as wind surfing, jet skiing, paragliding, diving, speedboat activities, pedaloes and aqua-parks) (see Annex 1, Table 3.3a). Resort beaches are also subject to daily beach cleaning. Absence of parameters as defined for scale A beaches results in a lowering of the scale (B–D).

Bathing Area Registration and Evaluation Form

SECTION 1 BACKGROUND INFORMATION

Name of bathing area:...............**Current classification:** ....

Type: *Natural beach* ☐ *Nourished beach* ☐ *Rocky shore* ☐
Resort ☐ *Urban* ☐ *Village* ☐ *Rural* ☐ *Remote* ☐

Length: ....(m) **Width:**............. (m) **Shape:**........ **Slope:** ....(°)

Length is measured along the shoreline and width is measured from water's edge at low tide to back of beach.

Rough sketch/digital image of bathing area

Table 1.1 *Beach sediment characteristics**

Colour:		Geological composition:			
	% cover	Size		% cover	Size
Sand			Cobble		
Gravel			Rocks		
Pebble			Other (e.g. concrete)		

Sea floor: *Sand*......% *Stones*.......% *Cobble/Pebble* ....% *Rock*.......%
Shore type**: *Sand beach* ....% *Gravel beach*.......% *Pebble beach* .... %
   Cobble beach ....% *Rocky shore*........% *Concrete quay*...... %
Backshore type: *Wooded* ....% *Cliff* .... % *Other* .... %

* *beach sediment characteristics* refers to the beach itself that either forms a limited part of the shore (e.g. in a pocket beach environment having boulder or rocky shore edges) or is representative of the entire/large part of shore (as in the case of long linear beaches).
** *shore type* refers to the entire shore visible to the beach user which may include boulder shore, concrete piers, shore platforms etc.

Responsible authority: ....   **Municipality:** ....

Number of staff engaged with beach management: ☐

Date of initial registration: **Date of field survey:**

Accessibility:
   To site: Public beach: By road ☐   By walking ☐   Public transport ☐

   Private beach: Ownership type ☐   Entrance fee ☐

... To water environment: Gentle/steep underwater slope ☐

Beach erosion:
Are there obvious signs of erosion/deposition ?   Yes ☐   No ☐

Is there present or past monitoring of erosion?   Yes ☐   No ☐

If so, by whom? ....

Are there known records or erosion maps available?   Yes ☐   No ☐

If so, where? ....

Table 1.2 *Beach occupancy rates and carrying capacity*

Time of year	Number of bathers (11.00 hrs) ***	Number of bathers (16.00 hrs) ***	% beach occupancy
Whole bathing season			
Bathing season weekday			
Bathing season weekends			
Non-bathing season			

Note: *** beach users on beach and in water.

Method for calculation of beach carrying capacity:
It is recommended that beach carrying capacity assessments should never incorporate dunes where present, as they are very vulnerable sites. Dunes should be preserved and restored if possible.

1. Measure length and width of beach.
2. Calculate area (calculation of beach area for non-linear/pocket beaches may vary from simple width x length calculation).

3. For a beach less than 50m long, subtract the area allocated for emergency services access (i.e. a 3m wide strip across the width of the beach from the back shore to the water's edge). It is recommended that for a beach 50m long or more, one should consider two such access strips of 3m width each (with a third access strip for each second 50m in beach length (i.e. for a beach of 100m, one would consider three access strips from the backshore to the water's edge – one on each edge of the beach and one down the centre).

4. Subtract another area represented by a 3m wide strip along the length of the beach (i.e. along the water's edge) reserved for public access. This may change according to country specific legislation that may stipulate different distances from the water's edge where beach concession deck chairs and umbrellas may be placed. For beaches over 50m wide, these '*across the beach length access strips*' would need to be increased in number with a minimum of two such strips every 50m in beach width.

5. Estimate the carrying capacity of the concession by dividing the remaining area by 16 and multiplying the result by 2 (this assumes a 4m x 4m area per umbrella and two sun-loungers (i.e. 4 x 4m per two persons).

In the estimation of beach area per beach user, field trials and current literature citing acceptable beach area per beach user (Health Education Service, 1990; van der Salm and Unal, 2001; Pereira da Silva, 2003) were considered.

Estimated beach carrying capacity: ☐

Beach-use orientation:

Table 1.3 *Main usage*

Jet skiing		Sailing		Motor boating	
Fishing (shore/boat)		Kite flying		Wind surfing	
Walking		Diving		Surfing	
Sunbathing		Swimming		Picnicking	
Tourism yachting/day cruises		Other sporting activities			

Table 1.4 *Designated sensitive area in the bathing area*

	YES	NO
Resting place for waterfowl/mammals		
Breeding place for rare birds/mammals		
Sanctuary		
Conservation area		
Area having high biodiversity/ecologically sensitive area		
Archaeological sites		
Other kind of protected area, e.g. heritage sites		

SECTION II RATING OF PARAMETERS

Table 2.1 *Safety parameters*

Safe bathing environment including: • a bathing environment slope < 1:10; • wave height < 0.5m for at least 80% of the bathing season	
Lifeguards (inclusive of sea craft-based lifeguards).	
Bather/boating zonation markers	
Fixed safety equipment	
First aid posts	
Beach safety information notices (on safe code of conduct, presence of rip currents or any other, telephone number and location of nearest health centre, latest records for water quality monitoring, other). Provision of warning flag in case of unsafe bathing conditions	
Access for emergency vehicles	

Table 2.2 *Water quality*

National bathing season monitoring programme results (Year .... report)					
Barcelona Convention criteria		**EU Bathing Water Directive (2000)**			
Passed		Blue Quality			
		Green Quality			
		Orange/Red Quality			
Failed		Black Quality			
Potential influences of poor water quality		Sewage outlet			
		Sewage pipes			
		River mouth			
		Harbour areas			
		Other, e.g. known absence of sewerage system			
Visual observations along 100m of shoreline (for rural/remote beaches where average bathing season occupancy rates < 40% of beach carrying capacity)			**A**	**B**	**C**	**D**
Floating debris	Sewage related		0	1–5	6–14	> 14
	Other, e.g. plastics, wood		0–10	11–20	21–30	> 30
Oil			0	1–5	6–14	> 14
Sea-bottom debris			0–10	11–20	21–30	> 30

Table 2.3 *Beach facilities (tick where present and indicate number where possible)*

Toilet facilities	Public		Clean		Apartment complexes	
	Restaurant		Poorly managed *		Camping grounds	
Shower facilities	Public		Clean		Highest hotel star rating	
	Restaurant		Poorly managed *			
Litter bins			Regularly emptied		Summer houses for rent	
			Poorly managed *			
Cigarette receptacles					Bed & Breakfast accommodation	
Restaurants			Snack bars			
Information notice			Security boxes		Freshwater tap	
Adequate parking facilities (see beach carrying capacity)			Wheelchair access		Tiki-huts/umbrellas	
Sun beds	Mattress		Legal/policy restrictions to water-based sport facilities		Speedboat towing activities (e.g. banana boat, tubing, skiing)	
	Nylon					
	Wood/ plastic					
Sail boating			Scuba-diving		Wind surfing	
Pedaloes			Para-sailing		Jet skiing	
Other						

Note: *Poorly managed facilities are facilities that are dirty, non-functioning, or not easily accessible.

Table 2.4 is for the evaluation of hinterland scenery within walking distance and generally visible from the beach. In the context of bathing area quality evaluation, scenery is the only parameter that takes cognizance of a wider range of aspects outside the bathing area. To this end, a coastal scenic evaluation technique is applied (Ergin et al, 2004).

Table 2.4 *Coastal scenic evaluation system*

Site Name :

No:	Physical Parameters		RATING				
			1	2	3	4	5
1	CLIFF	Height	Absent	5–30m	30–60m	60–90m	>90m
2		Slope	45°–55°	55°–65°	65°–75°	75°–85°	Circa vertical
3		Special features*	Absent	1	2	3	Many >3
4	BEACH FACE	Type	Absent	Mud	Cobble/ boulder	Pebble/gravel (±sand)	Sand
5		Width	Absent	<5m	5–25m	25–50m	50–100m
6		Colour	Absent	Dark	Dark tan	Light tan/ beached	White/gold
7	ROCKY SHORE	Slope	Absent	<5°	5–10°	10–20°	20–45°
8		Extent	Absent	<5m	5–10m	10–20m	>20m
9		Roughness	Absent	Distinctly jagged	Deeply pitted and/or irregular (uneven)	Shallow pitted	Smooth
10	DUNES		Absent	Remnants	Foredune	Secondary ridge	Several
11	VALLEY		Absent	Dry valley	(<1m) Stream	(1m–4m) Stream	River/ limestone gorge
12	SKYLINE LANDFORM		Not visible	Flat	Undulating	Highly undulating	Mountainous
13	TIDES		Macro (>4m)		Meso (2–4m)		Micro (<2m)
14	COASTAL LANDSCAPE FEATURES **		None	1	2	3	>3
15	VISTAS		Open on one side	Open on two sides		Open on three sides	Open on four sides
16	WATER COLOUR & CLARITY		Muddy brown/ grey	Milky blue/ green; opaque	Green/grey blue	Clear blue/ dark blue	Very clear turquoise
17	NATURAL VEGETATION COVER		Bare (< 10% vegetation only)	Scrub/garigue/ grass (marram/ gorse/ferns, bramble/ meadow etc.)	Bushes, coppices, maquis	Wetland ± mature trees	Variety of mature trees/ forest – a 'patchwork quilt'
18	VEGETATION DEBRIS		Continuous >50cm high	Full strand line	Single accumulation	Few scattered items	None

Site Name :

	Human Parameters	1	2	3	4	5
19	NOISE DISTURBANCE	Intolerable	Tolerable		Little	None
20	LITTER	Continuous accumulations	Full strand line	Single accumulation	Few scattered items	Virtually absent
21	SEWAGE DISCHARGE EVIDENCE	Sewage evidence		Some evidence (1–3 items)		No evidence of sewage
22	AGRICULTURE***	None, bare (>10% vegetation) greenhouses	Field crops (wheat, corn etc.) hedgerows, monoculture	Vineyards, terracing, tea, etc.	Shrub type plants – date palm, pineapples, etc.	Orchards – apples, cherries etc.
23	BUILT ENVIRONMENT****	Heavy industry	Heavy tourism and/or urban	Light tourism and/or urban and/or sensitive industry	Sensitive tourism and/or urban	Historic and/ or none
24	ACCESS TYPE	No buffer zone/heavy traffic	No buffer zone/light traffic		Parking lot visible from coastal area	Parking lot not visible from coastal area
25	SKYLINE	Very unattractive	Unattractive	Sensitively designed high / low	Very sensitively designed	Natural/ historic features
26	UTILITIES *****	>3	3	2	1	None

Notes: * Cliff special features: indentation, banding, folding, scree, irregular profile, etc.
** Coastal landscape features: peninsulas, rock ridges, irregular headlands, arches, windows, caves, waterfalls, deltas, lagoons, islands, stacks, estuaries, reefs, fauna, embayment, tombolo, etc.
*** Agriculture: where no agriculture can be seen and the natural vegetation cover parameter has scored a 5, then the 5 box should be ticked in this line. If the Natural Vegetation Cover box ticked was a 2, 3, 4 then tick the 3 box here.
**** Built environment: caravans will come under tourism, Grading 2: large intensive caravan site, Grading 3: light, but still intensive caravan sites, Grading 4: sensitively designed caravan sites.
***** Utilities: Power lines, pipelines, street lamps, groynes, seawalls, revetments, etc.

Table 2.5 *Litter survey*

Tick appropriate box
(Rating is based on lowest score litter category)

Category	Type	A	B	C	D
Sewage-related debris	General	0	1–5	6–14	15+
	Cotton buds	0–9	10–49	50–99	100+
Gross litter		0	1–5	6–14	15+
General litter		0–49	50–499	500–999	1000+
Harmful litter	Broken glass	0	1–5	6–24	25+
	Other	0	1–4	5–9	10+
Accumulations	Number	0	1–4	5–9	10+
Oil		Absent	Trace	Nuisance	Objectionable
Faeces		0	1–5	6–24	25+

Note: See Appendix 2.
Source: Based on EA/NALG (2000)

SECTION III EVALUATION OF RATINGS FOR BEACH USER PRIORITY CONCERNS

Table 3.1a *Evaluation of safety-related parameters in resort/urban bathing areas*

Parameter	Rating	Safety Measure
Presence of all 7 parameters	Rating A	– Safe bathing environment
Presence of safe bathing environment, lifeguards, zonation buoys and emergency vehicle access	Rating B	– Lifeguards – Bather/boating zonation buoys
Absence of either safe bathing environment, lifeguards and/or zonation buoys	Rating C	– Fixed safety equipment** – First aid post** – Beach safety warning notices*
Absence of safe bathing environment, lifeguards and zonation buoys	Rating D	– Emergency vehicle access

Notes: * Beach safety warning notices are notices providing information on safe code of conduct, presence of rip currents, telephone numbers and location of nearest health centre, latest records for water quality monitoring and other information.
** The presence of lifeguards negates the requirement for fixed safety equipment and first aid post.

Table 3.1b *Evaluation of safety-related parameters in Village-associated bathing areas (and rural/remote beaches with average bathing season occupancy rate > 40 per cent of beach carrying capacity).*

Parameter	Rating	Safety Measure
Presence of all 5 parameters*	Rating A	– Safe bathing environment – Bather/boating zonation buoys – Fixed safety equipment – Beach safety warning notices – Emergency vehicle access
Presence of safe bathing environment, zonation buoys, warning notices and emergency vehicle access	Rating B	
Absence of either, safe bathing environment, zonation buoys and warning notices, or fixed safety equipment*	Rating C	
An unsafe bathing environment	Rating D	

Note: *The presence of lifeguards negates the requirement for fixed safety equipment.

Table 3.2 *Evaluation of bathing water quality*

For resort, urban and village bathing waters (and rural/remote beaches with average bathing season occupancy rate > 40% of beach carrying capacity)			For remote and rural bathing waters with average bathing season occupancy rate < 40% of beach carrying capacity
EU water quality directive (2000/60/EC)		Barcelona Convention criteria for bathing waters	Visual observation
Rating	Classification	Classification	Classification
A	Blue quality	Passed	See Annex 1, Table 2.2
B	Green quality	–	
C	Red/orange quality	–	
D	Black quality	Failed	

Table 3.3a *Evaluation of facilities on resort beaches*

A Rating	B Rating	C Rating	D Rating
5 star accommodation*	4 star accommodation*	3 star accommodation*	2 star accommodation*
Clean toilet facilities on the beach	Clean toilets limited to beach-associated restaurant/cafe/ adjacent hotel grounds**	Poorly managed toilet facilities on the beach	Poorly managed toilets in beach-associated restaurant/cafe/ adjacent hotel grounds** OR No toilets
Clean beach-based shower facilities every 50m or less	Clean beach-based shower facilities every 51–100m OR Clean shower facilities limited to beach-adjacent restaurant/cafe/ adjacent hotel grounds**	Poorly managed shower facilities and/or shower facilities > every 100m	Shower facilities limited to hotel* OR No showers
Restaurant on beach or within beach-adjacent hotel grounds** AND Snack bar/cafe on beach	Restaurant on beach or within beach-adjacent hotel grounds** No snack bar/cafe on beach.	Limited to snack bar/cafe on beach or within beach-adjacent hotel grounds**	No restaurant /snack bar/cafe on beach or beach-adjacent hotel grounds** OR Restaurant/snack bar/cafe limited to hotel building
Up to 6 water-based sport-related facilities***	4–5	2–3	< 2
Regularly emptied litter bins and provision of receptacles for used cigarettes	Regularly emptied litter bins and no used cigarette receptacles	Poorly managed litter bins and receptacles OR Poorly managed litter bins and no receptacles	No litter bins
Provision of well-spaced (approx. 6m) mattress covered sun-loungers and umbrellas on beach	Provision of (approx. 4–6m) spaced nylon-net, plastic/wood sun-loungers and umbrellas on beach	Poorly spaced (too close or no order) sun beds (any type) and umbrellas Absence of either umbrellas or sun beds on the beach	Provision of sun-loungers and umbrellas restricted to beach-adjacent hotel* grounds or absent

Notes: * Includes hotels, accommodation/camping complexes; ** refers to hotel, accommodation/camping complex involved in beach management; *** Jet skis, para-sailing, wind surfing, pedaloes, canoes, speedboat towing activities (rings, banana boats, water skiing), boating, diving. Poorly managed facilities are facilities that are dirty, non-functioning or not easily accessible.

Table 3.3b *Evaluation of facilities on urban beaches*

A Rating	B Rating	C Rating	D Rating
Accommodation*# include 4 or 5 star facilities	The highest grade of accommodation is limited to 3 or 2 star facilities	The highest grade of accommodation is limited to 1 Star facilities	No accommodation *# is available
Clean toilets available on the beach	Clean toilets limited to restaurant/cafe in bathing area #	Poorly managed toilet facilities on the beach	Absence of or poorly managed toilet facilities in bathing area #
Clean beach-based shower facilities every 50–100m	Clean beach-based shower facilities > 100m apart	Poorly managed shower facilities	Shower facilities absent in bathing area #
Restaurant available on the beach	Snack bar available on the beach	Snack bar and/or restaurant not on beach but within bathing area	Absence of restaurant and snack bar within the bathing area
Up to 4 water based sport-related facilities**	3	2	< 2
Regularly emptied litter bins and provision of receptacles for used cigarettes	Regularly emptied litter bins and no used cigarette receptacles	Poorly managed litter bins	No litter bins
Provision of mattress covered sun-loungers and umbrellas on beach	Provision of nylon-net, plastic/wood sun-loungers and umbrellas on beach	Absence of either umbrellas or sun beds on the beach	Absence of umbrellas and sun beds on the beach

Notes: # Within walking distance of the beach. This has been shown to fall within a broad definition of 300–500m. * Includes hotels, accommodation complexes. ** Jet skis, para-sailing, wind surfing, pedaloes, speedboat towing activities (rings, banana boats, water skiing), boating, diving. This aspect is not considered if there is a deliberate policy against or legal restriction on water-based sport facilities. Poorly managed facilities are facilities that are dirty, non-functioning, or not easily accessible.

Table 3.3c *Evaluation of facilities on village-associated bathing areas*

A Rating	B Rating	C Rating	D Rating
Clean public shower facilities	Clean shower facilities limited to restaurants	Absence or poorly managed shower facilities	Total absence of facilities
Clean public toilet facilities	Clean restaurant-based toilet facilities	Poorly managed toilet facilities*	
Restaurant	Bar	–	
Adequate parking and good access**	Good access**	Poor access**	
Motel/B&B accommodation	Camping grounds	–	
Clean litter bins	Poorly managed litter bins	Insufficient litter bins	

Notes: * Facilities that are dirty, non-functioning, or not easily accessible. ** Facilities are easily visible, well signposted to beach access point and car park. Beach access should be well maintained to facilitate beach use by the elderly and less-able people.

Table 3.4 *Bathing area rating based on litter-related parameters*

Overall bathing area rating result for litter	

Note: See also Annex 1, Table 2.5.
Source: EA/NALG (2000)

Table 3.5 *Bathing area rating based on coastal scenic evaluation*

Coastal scenic classification	BARE equivalent for use in Bathing Area Classification Annex 1, Tables 4.1–4.3	Description
Class 1	A	Extremely attractive natural site with a very high landscape value, having a D value equal to or above 0.85
Class 2	B	Attractive natural site with high landscape value, having a D value between 0.65 and 0.85
Class 3	C	Mainly natural with little outstanding landscape features and a D value between 0.4 and 0.65, e.g. urban sites with exceptional scenic characteristics
Class 4	D	Mainly unattractive urban, with a low landscape value, and a D value between 0 and 0.4
Class 5	D	Very unattractive urban, intensive development with a low landscape value and a D value below 0

Note: See Annex 1, Table 2.4.

SECTION IV CLASSIFICATION SYSTEM

Table 4.1 *Bathing area classification system for resort bathing areas*

Site name:			Bathing area type:		
Parameter	Safety	Water quality	Facilities	Litter	Hinterland scenery
Parameter Rating					
Classification of bathing environment					
5 star	At least four parameter ratings awarded an 'A' rating for safety, water quality, facilities and either scenery or litter with the fifth parameter rating being not less than 'B'				
4 star	Where 'B' is the lowest score allocated to safety, water quality and facilities and where the lowest score for scenery and litter is not less than 'C'				
3 star	Where the lowest score awarded to safety, water quality, facilities and litter is 'C'				
2 star	Where 'C' is the lowest score awarded to safety, water quality and facilities and where scenery or litter awarded a 'D' score				
1 star	Where either safety, water quality or facilities parameter ratings awarded a 'D' score				

Table 4.2 *Bathing area classification system for urban and village bathing areas (and rural/remote beaches with average bathing season occupancy rate > 40 per cent of beach carrying capacity). For such beaches, rate facilities for Table 3.3c.*

Site name:			Bathing area type:		
Parameter	Safety	Water quality	Facilities	Litter	Hinterland scenery
Parameter Rating					
Classification of bathing environment					
5 star	At least four parameter ratings awarded an 'A' rating for safety, water quality, facilities and either scenery or litter with the fifth parameter rating being not less than 'B'				
4 star	Where 'B' is the lowest score allocated to safety, water quality and facilities and where the lowest score for scenery and litter is not less than 'C'				
3 star	Where the lowest score awarded to safety, water quality, facilities and litter awarded is 'C'				
2 star	Where 'C' is the lowest score awarded to safety, water quality and facilities and where litter awarded a 'D' score				
1 star	Where either, safety, water quality or facilities parameter ratings awarded a 'D' score				

Table 4.3 *Bathing area classification system for rural/remote bathing areas with average bathing season occupancy rate < 40 per cent of beach carrying capacity*

Site name:			Bathing area type:		
Parameter	Safety #	Water # quality*	Facilities	Litter	Hinterland scenery
Parameter Rating	Not applicable		Not applicable		
Classification of bathing environment					
5 star	'A' score rating awarded to water quality, scenery and litter				
4 star	'A' score rating awarded to water quality and litter and 'B' rating to scenery				
3 star	'B' is the lowest score rating awarded to water quality and litter and not less than 'C' class to scenery				
2 star	'C' score rating awarded to water quality, scenery and litter				
1 star	Where any parameter is awarded a 'D' score rating				

Notes: # Wherever possible strict adherence to national/international water quality monitoring and safety standards is highly recommended for all bathing areas. However, it is recognized that particularly in countries with extensive coastlines, water quality monitoring and provision of safety measures may not be feasible in all remote/rural bathing areas. A practical solution recommended by the BARE technique in deciding where such monitoring/provision of safety facilities becomes a justifiable requisite, would be to use an average bathing season occupancy rate of over 40 per cent of a beach's carrying capacity as a sign of sufficiently high numbers of bathers to justify adherence to strict water quality monitoring/safety requisites. Therefore, under such circumstances in rural or remote beaches, the water quality parameter is rated according to criteria set out in Annex 1, Table 3.2 (i.e. as for resort, urban and village beaches) while safety parameter is rated according to Annex 1, Table 3.1b (i.e. as for village beaches). Bathing area classification is then determined using Annex 1, Table 4.2 (as for urban and village bathing areas). * In the absence of such a justification, water quality rating is carried out through the visual observation method described in Annex 1, Tables 2.2 and 3.2.

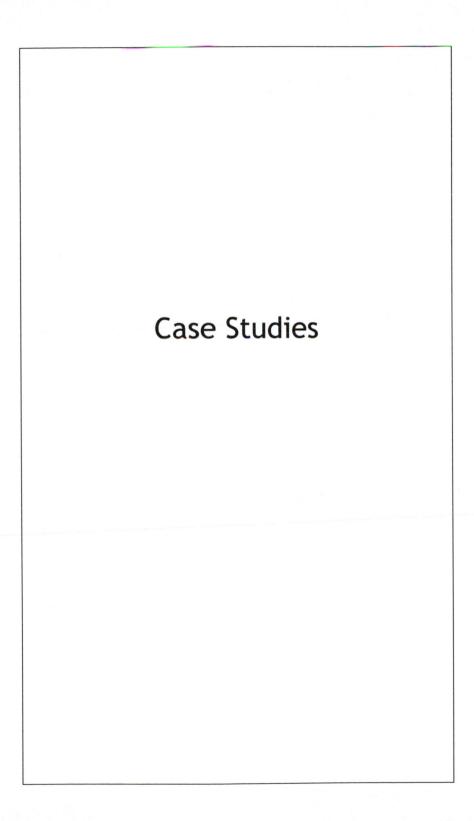

Case Studies

Case Studies

Beach Water Safety Management

Cliff Nelson

INTRODUCTION

'Nobody chooses to drown' – an interesting point for discussion! Of course, this statement is not exclusively true. However, the majority of people who find themselves in difficulty in the aquatic environment, which can ultimately result in death, do so unintentionally. The media all too often report accidental fatalities that occur from a seemingly harmless day out at the seaside. The impact of a drowning, in particular of a young person, is devastating and emotive.

Globally, the WHO estimates that approximately 382,000 people drown each year, with Africa alone contributing over 65,000 (WHO, 2004). WHO also recognizes that drowning is the third cause of accidental death, behind road accidents and falls. A number of water safety agencies monitor and publish water safety incidents: the Maritime and Coastguard Agency (MCA) records maritime fatalities (see Table CS1.1), the Royal Life Saving Society UK (RLSS UK) and Royal Society for the Prevention of Accidents (RoSPA) collate drowning statistics and report on annual incidents in the UK (RLSS UK/RoSPA, 2002). Figures CS1.1 and CS1.2 summarize the latest UK drowning statistics report showing that over the last decade, drowning figures have remained reasonably constant, with the odd anomalies, for example 1998 and 1999 (see Figure CS1.2). Year on year, approximately 80–150 people drown in the UK but only 20 per cent of deaths are coastal and a high differential exists across gender, with a significantly higher numbers of males drowning compared to females (see Figure CS1.1). The UK water safety agencies are working towards a standard format for recording data to provide an amalgamated and truer picture of drowning statistics (Water Safety Forum, no date). In contrast, in Australia over 5000 rescues are performed and on average there are 15 drownings per year (Short, 1997).

Table CS1.1 shows a breakdown of UK drownings and major and minor injuries against activity for 2007 (MCA, 2007). Although drowning statistics across the UK are relatively stable, the profile of activity is changing and the season is extending beyond the historical summer months. Extreme sports are shouldering the summer season and for particular sports such as surfing, the sport is conducted all year long. A new category of danger is 'tombstoning' which the MCA classes with 'coasteering' (see Table CS1.1 and Chapter 6). However, coasteering and tombstoning are quite different activities. Coasteering is an activity that was created by a company called Twr Y Felin Adventure, based in Pembrokeshire in Wales, UK and is defined by groups of people traversing across rocks, climbing and cliff jumping into water (Twr Y Felin, no date). The sport is generally controlled and run by a registered outdoor-type activity centre with trained instructors able to provide a robust risk assessment and implement resulting safety measures. Tombstoning, by contrast, is characterized by people, usually young men, taking daring and risky jumps from high natural or man-made structures into water. Tombstoning is an example of the changing nature of water 'sports' activity and the seeming need for people to experience an 'adrenalin rush' (Young, 2002). The National Beach Safety Council (NBSC) in the UK has identified 'tombstoning' as a key issue in their research programme (NBSC, 2008).

The UK has 11,232 miles of coastline and 494 identified bathing sites that are monitored by the Environment Agency (EA, 2008). A substantial beach lifeguard presence can be observed across the main tourist beaches in the UK, and without this operation, drowning figures would be significantly inflated. In addition, an unquantified number of rescues go unrecorded, being performed by other water users, in particular surfers. Therefore, it is difficult to obtain an accurate picture of drowning incidents in the UK. This case study is an adjunct to Chapter 6 and explores the framework surrounding beach safety management, purely in the context of drowning, who is responsible for safety on beaches and the importance being placed on risk assessments.

BRIEF HISTORY OF UK LIFESAVING

The first recorded lifesaving organization was the Maatschappji tot Redding van Drenkelingen, set up in The Netherlands in 1767, founded to restore life to those apparently drowned (Baker, 1980). The maritime industry was extremely buoyant in the UK during the early 19th century and concern was focused on deaths arising from shipwrecks and non-recreation-related drowning situations. This led to the formation of the National Institution for the Preservation of Life from Shipwrecks in 1824, later renamed the Royal National Lifeboat Institution (RNLI) in 1854. This organization continues to run a very effective lifeboat service today and in 2006, RNLI lifeboat crews launched 8377 times, rescuing 8015 people (RNLI, 2008).

The UK lifesaving movement, dedicated to swimming rescues, gained momentum towards the end of the 19th century with the establishment of RLSS UK in 1891. Today this is the governing body and leading provider

Table CS1.1 *MCA fatalities in the UK search and rescue records*
(1 January to 31 December 2007)

	Accidents	Total injuries	
		Major	Minor
Swimming	7	9	2
Diving	8	47	6
Cliff climbing	0	26	14
Motor boating	7	14	8
Falls and misadventure (non-boating)	30	2	9
Commercial fishing	9	45	7
Sailing	11	36	25
Beach activities	2	55	30
Angling	11	9	3
Canoeing and kayaking	6	9	8
Commercial	15	68	4
Personal water craft	1	3	10
Surfing	0	7	5
Water skiing and wake boarding	0	2	0
Rowing	0	6	2
Wind surfing and kite surfing	1	4	2
Coasteering/tombstoning	6	0	0
Canal boating	1	2	7
Coastal walking	7	44	17
Total accident maritime	**122**	**388**	**159**
Outside UK search and rescue	6		
Grand total accident maritime	128		

Source: RLSS/RoSPA

of training and education in lifesaving, lifeguarding, water safety and life support skills in the UK and Ireland. Each year its volunteers train approximately one million people in water safety, rescue techniques and life support, including 95 per cent of all pool and beach lifeguards. The Society has more than 13,000 members in 50 branches and over 1400

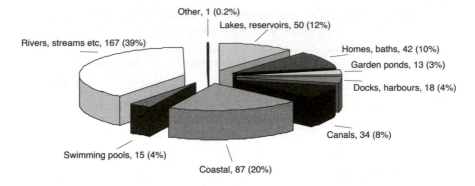

Source: RLSS/RoSPA

Figure CS1.1 *RLSS/RoSPA UK drowning statistics (2002)*

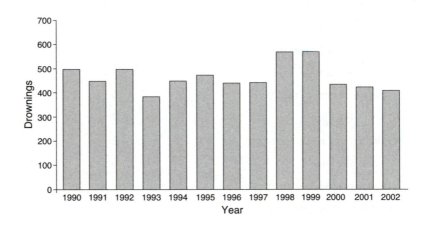

Source: RLSS/RPSPA

Figure CS1.2 *RLSS/RoSPA UK drowning statistics:*
Drowning trends (1990–2002)

lifesaving and lifeguarding clubs throughout the UK and Ireland (RLSS UK, 2008a).

Lifeguarding is often synonymous with Australia and Australian beaches. Surf bathing in Australia started to become popular in late 19th century, although there were restrictions on hours that bathing was allowed and costumes. The neck to knee costume was demanded and enforced to ensure decency at the beach (Baker, 1980). Through the development of surf clubs, the Surf Life Saving Association of Australia (SLS Australia,

2008) established in the early 1900s, has proudly saved 530,000 people and has over 130,000 affiliated members (SLS Australia, 2008). The Surf Life Saving Australia model was replicated in Great Britain, with the formation of the Surf Life Saving Association of Great Britain (SLSA GB) in 1955. There are over 60 lifesaving clubs affiliated to SLSA GB, who have contributed to over 20,000 rescues (SLSA GB, 2008).

International lifesaving dates back to 1878 in France, when the first World Congress was convened. With recognition that an international platform for exchange of ideas was needed, the Fédération Internationale de Sauvetage Aquatique (FIS) was formed, followed by World Life Saving (WLS). FIS and WLS were established to promote still water and surf lifesaving across the world (ILS, 2008). Both organizations merged to form the International Life Saving (ILS) Federation, formally constituted in 1994 (ILS, 2008). ILS is an international organization for tackling world water safety and sharing ideas, incorporating over 100 different bodies.

Who is responsible: Legal issues

It is beyond the scope of this case study to detail in full the legal framework that affects safety management of beaches. However, a number of key legal instruments are discussed. In the UK, there is no statutory requirement for beaches to be lifeguarded (RLSS UK/RoSPA, 2004). However, local authorities and beach operators are legally responsible for risk assessing their beaches to comply with the Management of Health and Safety at Work Regulations (Stationery Office, 1999). Where a risk assessment indicates the requirement for lifeguards, the local authorities or beach operator are legally obliged to make provision. In addition, the Occupiers Liability Act (1957) imposes upon the occupier a duty of care towards any visitors using the premises, which are either permitted or invited to be there (RLSS UK/RoSPA, 2004). Case law has defined premises as incorporating open land that includes beaches, as well as objects on that land, for example piers. The operator of a beach is not automatically exposed to liability under the act, especially if warning signs and/or safety provision is made. However, if the beach operator encourages visitors to the beach and in particular derives an income from visitors to the site, the duty of care is increased and the operator could be liable if adequate safety precautions are not provided.

BEACH SAFETY MANAGEMENT

Beach lifeguarding, as mentioned above, was a result of local communities realizing the need to provide safety cover at beaches and organizing themselves into voluntary patrols. This resulted in the development of lifesaving clubs. Increasing coastal tourism, especially around conurbations, has encouraged local authorities to consider beach safety more seriously. The last 20 years has seen the creation of a plethora of beach awards, starting with the prominent European Blue Flag by FEE in 1987 (see Chapter 8). The majority of these awards, including the Blue Flag, stipulate the provision of lifeguards or as a minimum, installation of public rescue equipment. Achievement of a beach award, in particular the Blue Flag, carries a significant amount of political kudos, motivating local authorities to ensure the criteria are met to qualify for the specific award. More recently, the introduction of the Management of Health and Safety at Work Regulations in 1999 has enforced local authorities to take an active approach to identifying beach hazards (HSE, 2008).

RISK ASSESSMENTS

Risk Assessments have become the 'norm' and commonplace in all aspects of life. There are a multitude of explanations describing risk assessment, for example the Health and Safety Executive (HSE, 2008) define a risk assessment as 'A simple careful examination of what, in your work, could cause harm to people, so that you can weigh up whether you have taken enough precautions or should do more to prevent harm'.

More generally the aim of conducting a risk assessment is to identify hazards associated with an activity, evaluate the risk and persons potentially (and equipment) affected and formulate control measures to either eliminate or reduce the risk to an acceptable level. A risk assessment requires a formal method of reporting the assessment of a hazard and the control measures put in place to mitigate the risks. However, generations have informally conducted risk assessments when carrying out any form of hazardous task or activity. For example, Captain Webb, who was the first person to successfully swim the English Channel in 1875, was sure to have conducted a risk assessment but it is unlikely that he would be familiar with the terms used today.

The risk assessment process

Box CS1.1 provides the Health and Safety Executive's five steps to carrying out a risk assessment (HSE, 2008). The science underpinning risk assessments has developed over the past 30 years, providing robust systems to minimize risk. Systems developed can be either quantitative or qualitative or a combination of both. Unfortunately, Captain Webb died when attempting to swim under Niagara Falls, which would question the effectiveness of his risk assessment.

Risk assessments are intrinsically subjective by their very nature, although systems have been designed to objectively assign numerical values to risks. Table CS1.2 details a sample risk assessment using a RLSS UK proforma, including a number of possible hazards, identified in column 1. Column 2 lists the persons at risk and column 3 details the

---

Box CS1.1 *Health and Safety Executive risk assessment model*

The five steps of the model are:

1 Identify the hazards.
2 Decide who might be harmed and how.
3 Evaluate the risks and decide on precaution.
4 Record your findings and implement them.
5 Review your assessment and update if necessary.

Source: HSE (2008)

---

type of injury that could arise from the hazard. Column 4 is a calculated risk. There are various systems for calculating risk, which represents the likelihood that the hazard is realized and the severity of the outcome if the hazard occurs. Mathematical models for calculating risk assign nominal values to likelihood and severity and form the risk value by multiplying the value for likelihood with the numerical value for severity. The nominal values provide a scale to gauge level of risk but this does not arithmetically mean a level 5 is equivalent to five times the risk rated as level 1.

The system used in the example in Table CS1.3 to calculate risk is designed by the Chartered Institute of Environmental Health (CIEH, 2002) and uses an alphanumeric scale, describing the likelihood as 'improbable', 'occasional' or 'frequent', and the 'severity' as 'minor', 'major' or 'fatal'. For each hazard, the probability of the event occurring is worked out and the consequence of the event is estimated, considering the impact and number of people potentially affected. Cross-tabulation results in an alphanumeric value, for example B2. In this example a medium risk rating is obtained that stipulates that action must be taken. It is the objective of the risk assessment process to reduce the risk to an acceptable level by introducing control measures where necessary. The control measures are set against cost–benefit outcomes so a balance is achieved. If the hazard cannot be totally eliminated, then a lower rating can be accepted on the basis of what the health and safety circles term 'reasonably practicable'.

The process does not finish here. Results must be recorded and monitored regularly. Risk assessments must be reviewed if the hazard changes or is removed completely or following an event, such as a personnel accident.

Beach risk assessments

The risk assessment process is now well developed and widely understood. However, while the principles of risk assessment (in any environment) are simple, they are not necessarily easy. Attempting to risk assess a 'beach' for public safety is an onerous task due to the coastal zone being one

Table CS1.2 *RLSS UK sample risk assessment 1*

Hazards	Persons harmed	Typical injuries	Risk level	Control measure	Revised risk level
Physical Rocks	Beach users	Muscle/skeletal Bleeding	Medium	Signage First aid facilities Telephone	Low
Weather	Beach users Swimmers Craft users	Hyperthermia Sunburn Heat stroke	Medium	Lifeguard First aid facilities	Low
Psychological Traumatic incident	Lifeguards	Post-traumatic stress	Medium	Counselling service	Low
Water hazards Waves Tides Rip currents	Lifeguards Swimmers Beach walkers	Death	High	Lifeguard Lifeguard training Educate users Signage Public rescue equipment	Low
Human Used syringes Alcohol Aggression	Lifeguards Beach users	Infection Assault	High	Lifeguard training Lifeguards First aid facilities Sharps box	Low
Watercraft Collision	Surfers Sailors Kite surfers Power boaters	Death Muscle/skeletal Bleeding	High	Beach zoning Lifeguards First aid facilities Cooperation sport bodies	Low
Chemical Fuel for lifeguards' boat Bleach	Lifeguards	Poisoning Burns	Medium	Operating procedures Storage facilities Training First aid facilities	Low

Source: RLSS

of the most dynamic environments on the planet. A number of leading lifesaving bodies have developed risk assessment programmes specifically for beaches, including the International Life Saving Federation of Europe (ILSE) and Australian Beach Safety and Management Programme (Short, 1997). The RLSS UK has responded to the challenge of beach risk

Table CS1.3 *RLSS UK sample risk assessment 2*

Risk	Minor A	Major B	Fatal C
Improbable 1	A1	B1	C1
Occasional 2	A2	B2	C2
Frequent 3	A3	B3	C3

Key
Priority levels:
☐ low risk: low priority, reduce risk or accept
▨ medium risk: must receive attention to remove/reduce risk
■ high risk: unacceptable, must receive immediate attention to remove or reduce risk or stop activity
Source: RLSS/RoSPA

assessments by developing a simple straightforward risk assessment model in conjunction with the CIEH. The hierarchy of control measures associated with the RLSS UK/CIEH risk assessment model is:

- provision of safety leaflets;
- public education;
- information signs;
- warning signs;
- prohibition signs;
- public rescue equipment;
- trained surveillance;
- first aid facility;
- lifeguards (with appropriate equipment);
- eliminate (with red flagging).

The RLSS UK/CIEH programme is in effect a checklist of all the hazard categories identified in the RLSS UK/RoSPA publication *Safety on Beaches* (RLSS UK/RoSPA, 2004) and listed in a format suitable for adaptation by individual operators.

Experience demonstrates that beach operators, who may have many years operational experience on the beach, appreciate additional guidance when it comes to putting practical knowledge down on paper. Significantly, the RLSS UK/CIEH risk assessment model is primarily a training programme that teaches beach operators to conduct their own risk assessments, certifying them via an assignment exercise. All those passing the beach RLSS UK/CIEH beach risk assessment programme receive a qualification and the appropriate paperwork to conduct the assessment.

BEACH SAFETY MANAGEMENT PLAN

The beach is a hazardous playground and inevitably people drown. A 'one-off' technical response to a water-based accident is 'reactive' and fails to identify causation factors leading to the accident or highlight weaknesses in the operator's safety management system (RLSS UK/RoSPA, 2004). Failure to recognize the weaknesses in the safety system can ultimately lead to further accidents and ineffective expenditure of resources. The beach risk assessment is the first step in developing a comprehensive beach safety management plan.

An unblemished safety record can often belie the lack of robust safety provision at a beach. The beach safety management plan (BSMP) is a comprehensive and proactive approach to establishing appropriate policies and organizational procedures to improve safety, including the beach risk assessment. The BSMP aims to give consideration to every link in the drowning chain, as detailed below (RLSS UK/RoSPA, 2004). Death by accidental drowning usually falls into one of four categories, which make up the drowning chain. The categories are detailed below along with remedial measures.

Uninformed or unrestricted access to the water

Beaches vary greatly in usage due to a wide range of factors, including proximity to urban areas and ease of access. A good example of contrast would be to compare Blackpool, a heavily visited tourist beach with a built infrastructure, to a remote beach in the north of Scotland, infrequently visited. In general, it is impractical to prevent access to a beach, unless privately owned and surrounded by a barrier restriction system. Most beaches are accessible to the general public.

The level of measures implemented to safeguard visitors from harm at a beach is determined by the risk assessment and will consider usage and type and nature of hazard. If the beach operator or local authority responsible for the beach has identified a real risk to the public, then the most basic level of safety provision is to erect warning signage. Research highlights the fact that barriers around water and parental supervision are the most effective prevention strategies to reduce drowning in young children (Asher et al, 1995).

Ignorance, disregard or misjudgement of danger

Of the four categories making up the drowning chain, the highest risk factor is ignorance, disregard or misjudgement of danger. The highest risk group is young males between teenage years and mid-twenties, fuelled by a lethal cocktail of bravado, peer pressure, alcohol and drugs (RLSS UK/RoSPA, 2002).

The counteractive measures are education and information. School-based water safety education has proved to create a considerable positive change in knowledge and attitude among very young pupils (Terzidis et al, 2007). Education tends to target pre-beach visits and numerous projects are run by leading lifesaving bodies to inform young people, especially school children, of the dangers of being near water.

Information is usually provided in situ, by beach signage, lifeguards or wardens. Education philosophy surrounding beach safety has commonly been top-down, making an assumption that the most effective communication is from parents to children. RLSS UK is trialling an alternative approach by promoting information material aimed at children, with the philosophy that the education message can also pass from child to parents. A good example of this is the Maritime and Coastguard Agency 'Information to keep in your pocket' water safety card, promoted by RLSS UK. This information leaflet is interactive, making it fun to learn and reduces the tendency to throw away, alleviating litter problems associated with leafleting.

Lack of supervision

Supervision covers a wide spectrum, including parents and lifeguards. The beach is often seen as a symbol of freedom and there is a tendency for parents, especially in the presence of lifeguards, to unwittingly reduce their observation of their children in what can be a treacherous environment. Where a beach operator or local authority can prove that a beach does not experience high visitor loads and where the risk assessment does not indicate the necessity to have a full beach lifeguard service, installation of public safety equipment is a remedial measure that can be taken. However, installation of such equipment can be expensive due to vandalism and theft in addition to the need to regularly monitor the presence and condition of the equipment. Finally, provision of lifeguards provides the highest level in the control measures hierarchy detailed above but obviously has high cost implications.

Inability of the victim to cope (or to be rescued) once in difficulty

The final link in the drowning chain is the inability of the victim to cope (or to be rescued) once in difficulty. The remedial measure to target this link in the drowning chain is to ensure that people acquire swimming and rescue survival skills. Lifesaving clubs provide training in rescue skills and swimming clubs obviously assist young people to learn to swim and increase their strength.

LANDSCAPE OF BEACH LIFEGUARDING AND KEY DEVELOPMENTS

UK local authorities have historically taken a strategic approach to managing their coastline and beaches and providing lifeguard cover on beaches that are heavily used. Voluntary lifesaving clubs usually work in partnership with the local authority and provide trained personnel to work for the authority and assist with voluntary patrols. The RNLI has been operating a beach lifeguard service for the past five years in partnership with local authorities. The RNLI has concentrated mainly on the southwest of England, covering the majority of Cornwall, Devon and Dorset and this year progressed to the east coast. The roll out programme for 2008 will see the RNLI enter Pembrokeshire in Wales (RNLI, 2008). The advantage of the RNLI operating a lifeguard service is to standardize provision of lifeguarding across the country.

THE FUTURE

The bathing season is being extended with an increasing interest in extreme sports, such as kite surfing, with enthusiasts enjoying the higher coastal energy provided outside of the summer season. In addition, cheaper and more technically advanced wetsuits are contributing to the increasing number of water sport users. With increased water use, lifeguarding has had to advance technically and a major contribution to lifeguarding has been the introduction of the personal watercraft (see Figure CS1.3), which are highly effective for water rescues.

Research is dispelling common myths surrounding drowning and identifying areas for further work. For example there are no data to support the 'old' safety message that eating before swimming significantly increases risk of drowning, but there are data highlighting young British Asian men as being a high-risk group. Combined initiatives by the lead water safety agencies to map factors contributing to drowning are providing a clearer picture and facilitating more appropriate targeting of resources in developing drowning prevention strategies and identifying vulnerable groups (ILS, 2008; ILSE, 2008) .

Figure CS1.3 *Lifeguard personal watercraft in operation*

ILS recognizes the need to create international standards and work towards reducing deaths from drowning across the globe, which present many unique political and cultural challenges. A study on Vietnamese-Americans demonstrated that decreasing drowning among this cultural group required changing the knowledge, attitude and safety practices in the Vietnamese language and targeting the dominant culture (Quan et al, 2006). The UK is heavily involved with ILS and advanced in lifesaving provision. The RLSS UK, RNLI and other lead lifesaving organizations have worked to standardize lifesaving procedures. Two key projects are to create a set of standard signage symbols (RNLI, 2005), in connection with the British Standards Institution, and to provide a standardized guidance document for evaluating the need for public rescue equipment (RNLI, 2007). Both projects are in print and are being considered by ILS for international implementation.

Managing Cars on Beaches: A Case Study from Ireland

J. A. G. Cooper and J. McKenna

INTRODUCTION

Much has been written on off-road driving and its effects on beaches and dunes (Godfrey and Godfrey, 1980; Buckley, 2004; Davenport and Davenport, 2006). Particular impacts on beach fauna (Schlacher and Thompson, 2007), turtle nesting (Hosier et al, 1981), bird nesting (Watson, 1992) and dune vegetation (Rickard et al, 1994) have been documented, as well as general noise and disturbance (McKenna et al, 2000). Rather less has been written on the means of control of such vehicles (for example Rosenberg, 1976 McConnell, 1977). The most extreme form of control is a blanket ban similar to that recently introduced in South Africa (Celliers et al, 2004), while other approaches include licensing and control of access.

Driving and parking of normal two-wheel drive cars on beaches has a long tradition on beaches in various parts of the world including the UK, Ireland, New Zealand and Denmark. This practice is based upon the compact nature of the sand, which allows cars to drive freely on most parts of the beach (see Figure CS2.1). It is also encouraged by the remoteness of many of the beaches (which requires them to be driven to in the first place). Many of the issues involved in the management of such vehicles are fundamentally different to those related to off-road vehicles. For one thing, they are often very numerous (thousands of cars may be parked on these beaches on occasional hot sunny days) and they coexist with other recreational activities, in many cases being undertaken by other car users. Once on the beach, the car becomes a focus around which visitor activity revolves. It serves as a store, shelter, windbreak and seat. Large numbers of cars interacting with pedestrians on the beach pose many safety-related problems for beach managers. There are also potentially negative environmental impacts on the beach fauna and on the exchange of sand between beach and dune.

Beaches are important economically as sites for visits both by local residents and home and international visitors. An analysis of the economic importance of Ireland's marine resources (Douglas Westwood Ltd, 2005)

Figure CS2.1 *Car parking on beaches in Ireland has a long history: Large numbers of cars on Portstewart Strand in (a) the 1930s and (b) 1960s*

shows that marine tourism (including beach visits) was worth €155 million to Ireland in 2004. As part of an initiative to stimulate rural economic activity through the development of coastal recreation and tourism, the local authority for Rossnowlagh beach in Ireland (Donegal County Council) embarked on a pilot project to improve beach management for the benefit of recreational users. Key to the success of the project was the goal of controlling traffic on the beach and this is the subject of this case study. The specific aims of this case study are: to describe the issues related to the use of vehicles on a rural recreational beach; outline the conflicting views of the management authority, local residents and beach users; and describe and assess the management approach adopted under these circumstances.

BEACH CHARACTER

The 2km-long beach at Rossnowlagh (see Figure CS2.2) is composed of well-sorted, fine sand. A narrow gravel ridge lies landwards of the sand beach along most of its length. The beach is backed by sand dunes along the central section and by cliffs to the north and south. The shoreline is experiencing slow but progressive retreat and about half the length of the beach is rock-armoured. The inter-tidal beach has a relatively impoverished fauna. The dunes are somewhat degraded and of marginal conservation value in a regional or national context.

The beach is a popular recreational site with a long tradition of unregulated beach parking and large resident and day-tripper populations in summer. It is also one of Ireland's main surfing beaches. In addition the beach serves as a thoroughfare for traffic as it links two public roads. These two aspects of vehicular access to the beach serve different purposes and attempts to control it were likely to meet with support from recreational

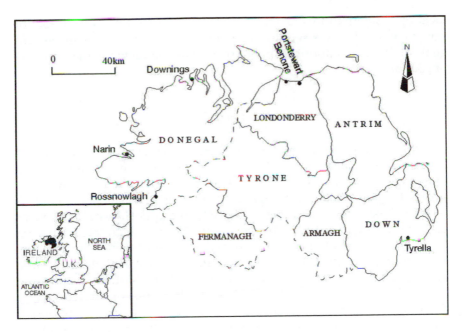

Figure CS2.2 *Map of the northern part of Ireland showing beaches with traditional car access*

visitors (because of enhanced safety) and opposition from locals (because of inconvenience).

Traffic congestion is often experienced on the beach and on surrounding roads as visitors approach and leave the beach. The presence of cars on the beach also adds to the risk of injury or accident on the beach, and motorized watercraft, surfing, kite and wind surfing all pose a risk in the water. Part of this problem is caused by the rising tide as cars rush to leave an ever-narrowing strip of sand. At high tide, water covers almost the entire beach right to the base of the dune or cliff.

The traffic congestion, overcrowding and danger that result from thousands of people and cars on the beach during the summer months led to a desire for improved services and management systems for the health and safety of the public and for the conservation of the natural environment. Control of traffic, and specifically, the creation of a car-free zone was also a prerequisite for maintenance of the Blue Flag beach award. Rossnowlagh first attained Blue Flag status in 1989 and has held it every year since with three exceptions, 1991, 1994 and 2000. The flag was awarded in 2000 but was withdrawn during the season due to a lack of traffic management and problems due to motorized watercraft.

Public opinion was divided regarding control of traffic on the beach and previous attempts by the local authority at control had met with strong local opposition and were abandoned. In order to achieve a system of traffic control that was socially acceptable and that met the management goals of the local authority, a pilot project was conducted in the summers of 2004 and 2005.

METHODS

Past top-down management failures dictated that in order to devise and implement a publicly acceptable car management system, it was necessary to engage with the public. This was done initially via a questionnaire survey to gauge the level of support for various management options. A residents' questionnaire and newsletter detailing a pilot beach management project was distributed to 6900 homes in the Rossnowlagh catchment area in June/July 2004. Of these, 1199 (over 17 per cent) were returned. The high return probably reflected the strength of interest, and the results (see Figure CS2.3) revealed local residents' perceptions of the most pressing issues. The survey was based on the local electoral area rather than simply dwellings adjacent to the beach in order to avoid a sample biased by vested local interests. This in itself was contentious, with some local residents questioning the relevance of opinions of beach users from adjacent towns but for whom Rossnowlagh was the nearest beach.

Visitor surveys were also carried out on the beach during August/September 2004 to determine where visitors come from, where they stay and what they look for when they visit the beach. Their general opinions of the beach and the services provided were also sought. Beach wardens who were deployed on the beach in the summer season also recorded the number and type of incidents to which they responded during the summer season.

On the basis of these pieces of information, coupled with discussions with local politicians, management goals and the beach management scheme were modified for the second season.

HOUSEHOLD SURVEY RESULTS

The preseason household survey showed that 93 per cent of respondents were in favour of improved toilet facilities, more car parks and activity zoning both in the water and on the beach. Aside from toilet facilities, the most important issues concern traffic management. Only 56 per cent of residents thought that car-free zones had worked well in the past, although 93 per cent thought zoning was a good idea, 83 per cent welcomed the idea of a one-way driving system at busy times and 67 per cent thought a fee should be charged for parking on the beach.

Public opinion of parking on the beach was divided: 49 per cent thought that parking on the beach should be prohibited, while 45.6 per cent agreed

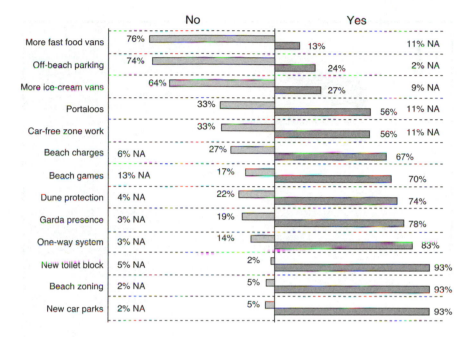

Note: NA = no answer

Figure CS2.3 *Results of the household survey conducted in May 2004 showing levels of support for various management options*

that parking on part of the beach was acceptable. Only 4.1 per cent thought cars should have access to the beach in its entirety. Charging for off-beach parking was also unpopular among 74 per cent of respondents.

2004 PILOT SCHEME

A pilot beach management scheme was trialled in the summer of 2004. A beach supervisor was appointed and four wardens employed for 15 weeks over the summer season in addition to lifeguards. The Blue Flag beach award and the pilot beach zoning scheme (see Figure CS2.4) were operational. The trial zoning scheme consisted of a car-free zone in the centre of the beach, which cut the route along the beach for vehicles (in an effort to reduce dangerous driving) and provided a safe area for pedestrians. This was fronted by the lifeguarded swimming zone and backed by an off-beach car park. A jet ski zone was established at the northern end of the beach. At the southern end of the beach the thoroughfare between two public roads remained open. Charging for access to the beach was not attempted because of uncertainties regarding the legal ability to charge.

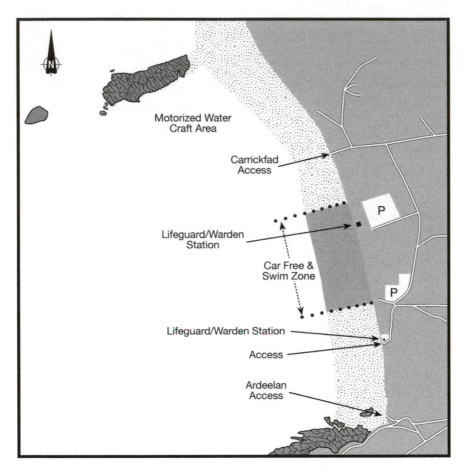

Figure CS2.4 *Beach and water zoning on Rossnowlagh in 2004*

POST-2004 SEASON ASSESSMENT

At the end of the summer season, observations of beach wardens were collated (see Figure CS2.5). The most common issue encountered on the beach was reckless driving. It appeared that some drivers regarded the beach as an area where the rules of the road no longer apply. Much of this unacceptable driving behaviour (ignoring speed limits and driving recklessly) was carried out to show off to passengers and onlookers. Although the beach wardens had no legal authority to stop and question drivers, the majority of drivers spoken to about their driving did immediately adhere to the advice given by the beach wardens. However, because the wardens were patrolling on foot or on bicycle, it was sometimes impossible to talk to drivers before they left the beach. When a Garda

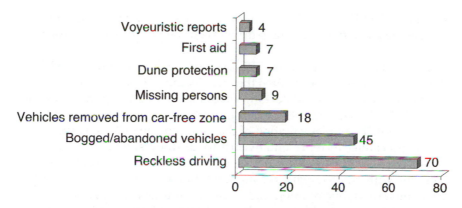

Figure CS2.5 *Issues encountered by beach wardens in summer 2004*

(Irish police) patrol car was present on the beach, drivers did not behave inappropriately.

Pushing vehicles that had become stuck in the sand was one of the most frequent warden chores; motorists often ignored signs warning of soft sand. The public was often unaware of the tide and despite wardens informing visitors of tide times, cars were frequently left unattended on the beach and were semi-submerged by the incoming tide. On the rising tide, wardens carried out searches for the owners of vehicles. If they could not be found an obliging four-wheel drive owner (if available) would tow cars up the beach.

Several car breakdowns were also experienced on the beach. Wardens helped members of the public by jump-starting or pushing vehicles and by phoning local garages for assistance.

On occasion, quad and four-wheel drive vehicles had to be removed from the dune area. Wardens succeeded in discouraging such behaviour by explaining the rationale behind dune protection.

Some deficiencies in the zoning scheme were also evident from warden observations:

- The car-free zone was not used to its full potential, mostly because many visitors were unaware of its existence as it was located some distance from the beach entrance. The middle of the zone was mainly used by the few visitors who parked in the off-beach car park.
- Swimmers underutilized the swim zone as it was located too far away from the busiest part of the beach and/or they were unaware of its existence.
- Motorists were often unaware of the reasons for marker buoys on the beach and on occasion attempted to drive over them assuming them to be soft. This caused damage to both cars and buoys.

- The line of buoys did not extend into the water at low spring tide, leaving a gap through which drivers could enter the car-free zone.

A survey of beach visitors during this season asked respondents to list up to three reasons why they visited the area. Of the 573 valid responses, only 8 per cent listed access and parking advantages, suggesting that vehicular access to the beach was not of major importance in selecting it for a visit.

Following the implementation of the pilot scheme in 2004, council staff met with local elected representatives to discuss the residents' questionnaire results together with a report on issues encountered by wardens in 2004, together with the council's recommendations for 2005. In an effort to accommodate public opinion and to improve beach management, these data were combined with feedback from beach wardens to plan to modify the approach for 2005.

ZONING PLAN FOR 2005

A revised zoning scheme and traffic management plan was devised for the summer of 2005 (see Figure CS2.6). In this scheme the vehicle access points to the southern part of the beach were closed, cutting the link between two roads that converged on the beach. No motorized vehicles were allowed on the southern end of the beach. Car access was permitted at the northern end free of charge. The car-free zone/swim zone was marked with a line of soft dense foam-filled buoys that extended to the low water mark.

Watercraft were permitted at the northern end of the beach at a zoned launch area. The watercraft launch zone was 200m to the north of the car-free buoys, thus providing a buffer zone to reduce the risk of jet skis and boats entering the swimming area.

The closure of the southern end of Rossnowlagh beach to motorists was envisaged to have a knock-on effect on traffic circulation in the area and signs were erected on the approach roads to inform motorists of the changes. Local people were informed of the planned changes via a newsletter and they were also advertised in the local newspapers.

This initial scheme for 2005 met with widespread opposition from residents. It was regarded as creating unnecessary inconvenience as an important local thoroughfare was blocked. A series of critical newspaper reports citing comments by a variety of local residents caused alarm among local politicians and the scheme had to be modified almost immediately. Rather than permit unimpeded access across the southern end of the beach as demanded by local residents, a compromise was reached that permitted one-way access between the two roads in the southern part of the beach for six weeks of the mid- to late summer season.

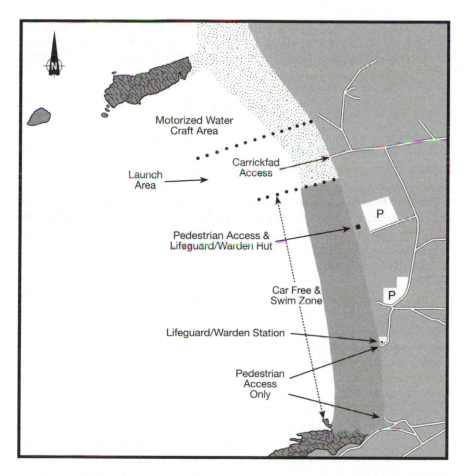

Figure CS2.6 *Zoning plan for 2005: Closure of southern access to cars*

POST-2005 SEASON ASSESSMENT

An assessment of the 2005 scheme was conducted at the end of the season. This noted a marked improvement in conditions on the beach during the period of the traffic management trial. There were far fewer incidents of reckless driving. Only two were noted during the trial period compared to 71 in an equivalent period of the previous year. There was still opposition to the traffic management trial from a small number of local residents but no complaints were received from beach users and visitors were supportive of the initiative.

The local authority subsequently decided to continue with the trial scheme and to implement seasonal traffic schemes. It was also agreed that alternative off-beach parking was needed to permit removal of cars from the beach, or beach charging should be allowed. The short-term goal was to keep the southern end of beach open for parking and driving, while the long-term environmental aim was to ban all beach parking and driving.

DISCUSSION

Beach management takes place in a particular socio-economic and cultural setting in which management goals are mediated by what is practically achievable under economic, social, environmental and political constraints. Management therefore does not always produce the ideal solution but often has to strike a balance. In many locations, local communities often have a particular affinity for a particular beach and traditions of behaviour that may be at odds with actions thought necessary to enhance visitor experience and economic activity (Villares et al, 2006). In such locations, in particular, coastal management might be defined as the 'art of the possible'.

In rural agricultural settings, local residents may feel a close affinity with, or sense of ownership of, a local beach. This is manifest at Rossnowlagh in the tradition of beach use as a vehicular thoroughfare. Tensions can easily arise with the demands of recreational users from further afield, and of beach managers to regulate traffic for the safety for beach users. There are several instances worldwide of injuries and deaths as a result of cars driving on beaches. In an effort to enhance the quality of beach visits and thereby promote economic activity at Rossnowlagh, it was recognized by the management authority that several steps were necessary to improve beach safety and visitor experience. Past experience had shown that top-down management schemes met with insurmountable opposition from local residents.

It was apparent at the outset that the strongly held views of a small number of local residents probably contrasted with the, albeit more weakly held, views of a much larger number of people from the surrounding area. Consequently the local authority sought to establish this and thereby gain a mandate from the wider community for more effective beach management. The results did indeed provide a mandate for change and although this was contested by a small number of residents, it was possible to implement a pilot scheme. By assessing visitor views, engaging with local politicians and recording practical problems, it was possible to adjust this scheme in subsequent years. However, despite an apparent popular mandate, attempts to create more major changes (closing a thoroughfare across the beach) met such strong local resistance that they could not be implemented directly.

The experience does show that while this form of public engagement can yield management gains, as suggested by advocates of participatory coastal management (for example Kearney et al, 2007), it is not without its problems (McKenna and Cooper, 2006). The approach demands a considerable investment of time and resources as well as particular dedication on the part of beach managers to overcome barriers to change. Even then some changes have to be approached incrementally if they are to gain popular support. Dalton (2006: 351) contends that:

> it is generally accepted that stakeholders, including resource users, scientists, conservationists, government and nongovernment organizations, and the general public, can contribute positively to management processes and may even benefit from such processes.

However, the means of involving such stakeholders have not been adequately investigated. This case study provides one example of a management authority faced with a previously insurmountable problem turning to a participatory approach in order to achieve management goals. Importantly in this case, the participation was instigated by a management authority with powers to implement changes and with a particular goal in mind. The spatial scale of the area in which participation was invited was crucial to the achievement of that goal in that it reduced the perceived power of a few local residents in asserting their preferences, by engaging a wider audience and thereby gaining a mandate for an alternative course of action more suited to the management objective.

Ameliorative Strategies at Balneário Piçarras Beach

*A. H. F. Klein, R. S. Araujo, M. Polette, R. M. Sperb, D. Freitas Neto,
F. C. Sprovieri, and F. T. Pinto*

INTRODUCTION

The main beach roles described in the literature are protection, aesthetics, landscape, recreation, leisure and tourism. Beaches can be defined as a space between the surf zone and foredune or man-made structures (e.g. pedestrian walks), made of components and complexes of different amplitudes, formed by the influence of natural processes (e.g. morphodynamic), as well as by human intervention (e.g. grading, using protection structures) and recreational activities (e.g. sport, driving, bathing) that permanently interact in a feedback process.

The beach landscape is the driving force behind beach use and urbanization, and all human interventions in coastal environments that must be considered in management. Shore scenery has an artistic appeal and may cause a positive impression on people's perception. It is important to question how coastal use and opportunities stem from perception, and how perception influences fulfilment of people's needs. Perception will generate potential use perspectives for each individual. From the landscape perspective, beach nourishment projects are the best solution to mitigate the erosion problem and create recreation space (Finkl and Walker, 2005).

Beaches are one of the major attractions for tourists in most parts of the world and for many developing countries tourism represents a source of economic benefits. However, several developed and developing nations have adopted tourism as a strategy to achieve economic development. This phenomenon, on a smaller scale, can be noticed in the state of Santa Catarina in Brazil (Reid et al, 2005). Santa Catarina is a summer tourist destination with an increasing number of tourists each year. The most popular destinations among visitors are the beaches. According to SANTUR (2007), over 3 million tourists enjoyed their summer holidays in the state in 2007, generating an income of over US$777 million. Some local economies are already tourism dependent and in most cases the tourism package is restricted to beach recreational usage.

In the past decade, beach nourishment has emerged as an appealing soft approach to deal with shoreline erosion problems (see for example Griggs, 1999; Dean, 2002; Finkl and Walker, 2005; Reid et al, 2005), and it became common practice to restore the tourism resource of sand beaches. In the state of Santa Catarina in 2000, there were nine projects in the process of design or execution (Reid et al, 2005, Klein et al, 2005), and the beach of Balneário Piçarras is an example of one of these. Beaches are considered a democratic space by the Brazilian constitution (7661/88) (Brasil, 1988), and consequently during summer, different types of stakeholders with different interests and degrees of organization and social activism meet (see, for example, Polette and Raucci, 2003). The challenge is how to manage the erosion hazards and risk, given the usage of beaches and the natural coastal process.

The aim of this case study is to present a beach nourishment programme in Piçarras beach, Santa Catarina, southeastern Brazil, that identifies both pro and contra positions regarding beach management.

ENVIRONMENTAL SETTINGS OF ITAPOCORÓI BAY

General characteristics of the study area

Piçarras beach lies in the city of Balneário Piçarras, in northern Santa Catarina state, and is considered an important tourism centre, especially during the summer. It is an 8km-long curved bay delimited in the north by the Itajuba headland, and the south by the Piçarras river inlet. At the south end of the bay (right side of the river) lies Alegre beach, a small and sheltered embayed 1km-long beach that belongs to the city of Penha, and comprises, together with Piçarras, the 'Itapocorói Embayment' (see Figure CS3.1). Piçarras beach is a headland bay beach in a micro-tidal (up to 1m) east swell environment (Klein and Menezes, 2001).

The sandy beach along Itapocorói Bay presents noticeable differences from south to north in subaerial sediment volume and width and shape of the profiles (Klein and Menezes, 2001; Araujo, 2008). In the northern area, with increase of wave exposure of the beach, morphology is more variable, while the southern portion presents a less mobile and less variable morphology. It is very wide, with a 3° slope, and reveals characteristics of a dissipative beach according to the model proposed by Klein and Menezes (2001). From the Piçarras river mouth north, the average width and volume of the subaerial portion increases. Piçarras presents characteristics of a semi-exposed to exposed reflective beach, with low wave energy, little or no surf zone, and steep slopes of between 5° and 7° (Araujo, 2008).

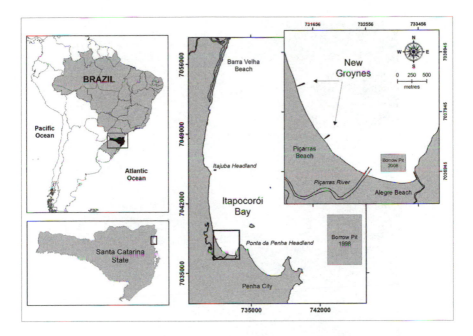

Notes: The two groynes are 115m long and designed to trap the planned northward sediment transport. Universal Transverse Mercator (UTM) coordinates used.

Figure CS3.1 *Location of Piçarras beach, Santa Catarina, southeastern Brazil and the borrow site that was dredged in 1998 as sediment source for the Piçarras nourishment project*

Coastline evolution

River inlet stability

For the last 70 years, Piçarras river inlet has had a very dynamic morphology, with migration behaviour and breaching and relocation of the sand barrier in an early period of tourist activity development. Figure CS3.2 summarizes the inlet migratory behaviour characteristics and shows the effect of anthropogenic activity on the system. During the 1930s, perceptible northerly inlet migration occurred. The river assumed a curved 'snake' format, with flood tidal deltas, revealing decrease of hydraulic competence. Migration occurred until hydraulic flow capacity reached critical levels, when high discharge resulted in barrier breaching, creating a straighter channel and higher velocity flows. In 1957, the inlet was naturally relocated to some 300m south of its 1930s position. Sand spit rupture caused formation of an extensive parallel lagoon adjacent to the coastline, and since then development of the ebb tidal delta has become more pronounced. Barrier rupture provided the transference of huge quantities of sediment to adjacent areas in a short period.

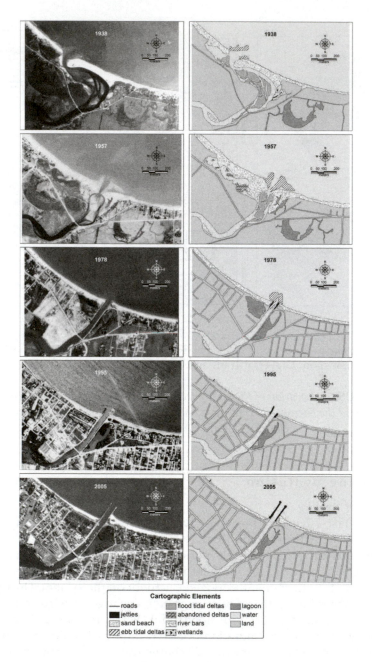

Cartographic Elements

—— roads	▨ flood tidal deltas	▨ lagoon
■ jetties	▨ abandoned deltas	☐ water
▨ sand beach	▨ river bars	☐ land
▨ ebb tidal deltas	☒ wetlands	

Souce: Aerial photographs from 1938, 1957 and 1978 were provided by the Secretaria do Patrimônio da União, Florianópolis, SC; 1995 by UNIVALI collection; and 2005 was obtained from Google Earth.

Figure CS3.2 *Morphological evolution of Piçarras river inlet and nearby coastal zone occupation*

The inlet and channel were fixed in the 1970s, interrupting this mechanism, when according to local inhabitants, the first indications of erosion problems adjacent to the river mouth occurred. Another important modification was the landfill in the lagoon in the left margin of the Piçarras river and construction of an avenue along the sand beach. These two factors increased occupation of the zone near the beach, seen in aerial photographs of 1978 and 1995 when Piçarras had an accelerated growth, with construction of many buildings and the opening of numerous streets and avenues.

Shoreline evolution

Figures CS3.3 and CS3.4 show, through aerial photographic interpretation, rates of coastline change for each 50m of the Piçarras and Alegre beaches. The methodology was based on previous works (Lélis and Calliari, 2004; Thieler et al, 2005; Vila-Concejo et al, 2006). Rates equal to or smaller than 4.5m are in the range of error (Araujo, 2008). Alegre beach had small variations through the years, especially in the 1950s and 1970s, with a median rate of seaward migration of around 7m. During the 1970s to 1990s, variation was slightly greater, with median rates of landward migration of around 20m. This region of the bay did not erode, as occurred with the north portion, from the left margin of the Piçarras river. This may be due to the sheltered condition of the beach and little or no longshore sediment transport to be trapped by the jetties.

Piçarras beach, in contrast, presented great variation in shoreline position, caused by local dynamics and human interference. Figure CS3.4 presents retreat rates during the last 38 years. From 1957 to 1978 the beach prograded in the northern sector with retreat in the southern, with a likely north-directed net sediment transport. The shore eroded from 1978 to 1995, with more variable rates than previously. This is coincident with strong rain events in the 1980s, with storm surges caused by El Niño events, and river mouth stabilization with accelerated occupation of the coast (Hoefel, 1998). The region from 600m to the north of the river had rates of retreat greater than adjacent areas. This erosive behaviour is known as an 'erosional hot spot' (EHS). The EHS was defined by Kraus and Galgano (2001) and Benedet et al (2007) as an area that erodes more than twice the average. It can be quantified by comparing the volume loss (m^3/m) or shoreline retreat rate (m/yr) of a specific segment with the average for the entire nourished area, and can be associated with longshore and/or cross-shore processes or a concentration of energy caused by refraction or diffraction of incoming waves, caused by obstacles such as islands, headlands or bathymetrical deformations (Benedet et al, 2007).

Observed rates of change in this area are not double adjacent area rates, but studies of the morphologic variation and beach profiles and erosive history of the region give reason to define this portion as a hot spot. The EHS is approximately where the Piçarras river inlet was located in the 1930s, before bar breaching at the southern position, where it is fixed

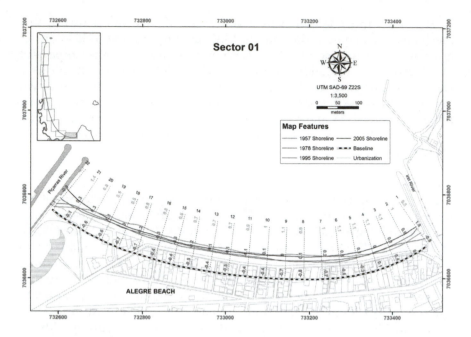

Notes: Positive rates represent accretion of the shoreline, and negative ones represent retreat.

Figure CS3.3 *Shore evolution rates (m/yr) at Alegre beach,*
Penha, Santa Catarian

today (see Figure CS3.2). The problem was partially solved in 1999 with the nourishment project, but as seen in the 2004 image, erosion still occurs, so the fill sediment did not remain. The fill was planned for a duration of approximately five years. It succeeded during this period but problems returned, in part because measures were not adopted for sediment retention, and nor was a maintenance plan for the beach fill elaborated.

The Balneário Piçarras beach is an example of the artificial process due to constant changes of economic and population dynamics, as well as land use imposed by the triad of the real estate market, tourism activities and civil construction. The process is not just felt in the interior where construction sites, tourism areas and real estate markets are present, but also the whole beach landscape. Today, the beach is totally changed as a result of the previous lack of management. The beach can now be considered between the development and consolidation stages proposed by Butler (1980).

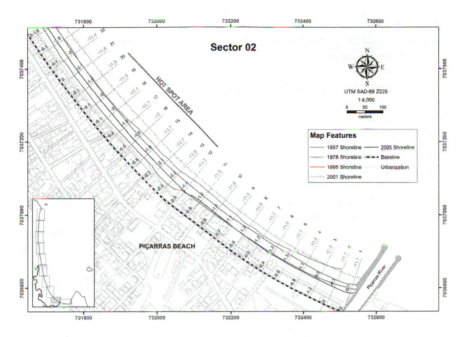

Notes: Positive rates represent accretion of the shoreline, and negative ones represent retreat.

Figure CS3.4 *Shore evolution rates (m/yr) at Piçarras beach, Piçarras, Santa Catarina*

AMELIORATIVE STRATEGIES AT BALNEÁRIO PIÇARRAS BEACH

This section presents a brief sequence of the erosion history and ameliorative actions at Balneário Piçarras beach and its socio-economic consequences based on previous works, such as INPH (1984, 1985a, 1985b, 1986, 1992), Hoefel and Klein (1997), Hoefel (1998), Abreu et al (2000), Reid et al (2005), Klein et al (2005) and Araujo (2008).

During the last three decades, Piçarras beach has experienced constant and progressive erosion due to natural causes, for example dynamic adjustment of the coastline to mean sea-level changes, wave climate and increased storm surge levels and flood events (Hoefel and Klein, 1997; Hoefel, 1998; Abreu et al, 2000). Those problems have been magnified by human activities related to bad occupation of the coastal zone and misuse of coastal structures (Reid et al, 2005; Klein et al, 2005). By 1941, construction of the road between the cities of Itajaí and Joinville, both in the coastal zone of Santa Catarina state, provided easy access to Balneário Piçarras, which at the time was a small and secondary choice for most tourists in the region, but has since became an important recreational centre (Hoefel, 1998). With the increase in economic activities and a tourism-based influx in the 1960s and 1970s, especially during summer, Balneário Piçarras and adjacent areas experienced accelerated growth in both population and number of buildings, most of the latter constructed right next to the beach (INPH, 1984).

Due to the need to improve the city's infrastructure, many engineering projects took place, including rectification of the Piçarras river mouth with two jetties in 1973, filling of three small lagoons close to the river mouth, and construction of the seaside avenue. Fast urbanization of the zone next to the shore occurred without planning permission, and increased pressure on the system. During the 1980s the most intensive El Niño events of the 20th century occurred along the Brazilian southern coast. Those events caused many environmental problems, strong rain regimes and floods that devastated portions of the region (INPH, 1984). Neves Filho (1992) also noticed an increase of storm surge height between the 1960s and 1980s.

An increase of high-energy storm surges with frequencies greater than beach recovery affected the backshore, while drainage of rainwater towards the beach contributed to sediment removal from the area by littoral drift (INPH, 1984; Hoefel and Klein, 1997). In 1980, gabions were installed on the beach to trap long-shore sediment transport, but the structures did not work and the beach remained in an erosional phase (Hoefel, 1998; see Figure CS3.5a). In 1995, a groyne almost 30m long and made of concrete was built in the EHS. This structure also did not work and downcoast erosion continued (see Figure CS3.5b). At the same time, a seawall was installed to protect the pedestrian walkway and side avenue (see Figure CS3.5c).

Natural processes and human-induced pressure caused an average loss of 40m of coastline width (around 140,000m^3 in volume), with the focus along a stretch 1.5km north of the Piçarras river mouth, a region partially protected from southeast waves (Hoefel, 1998; Abreu et al, 2000; Reid et al, 2005) (see Figures CS3.5c, CS3.5e and CS3.5f). The main city activities are based on tourism, so coastal degradation brought serious economic and environmental problems to the local administration and residents and tourists. Despite protection measures adopted over the years, problems became worse, especially after 1996. In February 1999, 880,000m^3 of sediment was placed along some 2200m of shoreline by a hopper dredger and floating pipelines. The borrow area was at the inner continental shelf, in 20m deep water and a distance of 15–20km offshore (see Figure CS3.1). The borrow area grain size was on average slightly coarser than native sediment (0.27mm versus 0.20mm). After nourishment, the upper layer of beach sediment had much shell and gravel, which is uncomfortable and can be unpleasant for beach users. Local citizens complained, especially those who played beach sports (for example volleyball and soccer). To

Source: Photographs from database of LOG-CTTMar-UNIVALI

Figure CS3.5 *Balneário Piçarras beach erosion process and ameliorative strategies: (a) the gabions; (b) concrete groyne; (c) the seawall; and the hot spot area next to profile 10, showing the continuity of the erosive problem in (d) October 1998, (e) May 1999 and (f) November 2007*

stop sediment removal by pluvial waters, especially during rainstorm events, parallel pluvial galleries were built to drain the water direct to the Piçarras river.

The total cost of the project according to the local government was about $3.2 million (almost $3.6/m^3 of sand). Half was paid by the local government with support of the federal government (Ministry of the Environment), and half by the local community in the form of extra taxes. The local community needed several years (six to seven) to pay for the project (or bank loan). The amount of payment per property was related to the size of property and to distance from the beach, with properties close to the beach paying a higher percentage.

It was not necessary to pay for dredge mobilization because the Belgium dredge system was nearby, working at the channel of Itajaí Harbour, some 15km south. This helped to substantially decrease the price of a cubic metre of sand. Projects of this nature have final costs directly related to the amount of sediment necessary, the distance from the borrow area to the site, mobilization/demobilization and equipment maintenance (dredge, pipes and so on).

SANTUR (2000) estimates that the number of tourists, in relation to the season before nourishment, increased significantly from 44,000 to 54,000. The value of ocean-front properties also increased significantly (Reid et al, 2005). The nourishment project triggered an influx of investment, and Balneário Piçarras has since enjoyed a continuous growth in development. For example, it moved up from 110th place in the social development index (state level) to 48th position. Today it is in 44th position (Piçarras, 2008).

Reid et al (2005) analyse the perception of realized impacts from a stakeholder's perspective and their results emphasize the perceived benefits of beach nourishment. They stress aspects related to economic benefits to the city, for instance, improvement of the infrastructure for leisure, increased tourism activities, increase in local trade, increase of real estate market values, increase in employment, improvement of beach aesthetics, incentive for residents and visitors to use the beach, a belief that development of the city will increase, and an expectation that the tourist profile will change with attraction of upmarket tourists. Results show that people were confident that return on the investment of the project would be 'guaranteed'.

Their analysis also reveals concern with public sector procedures and approaches to such projects. Respondents considered the collection of municipal taxes to finance the nourishment was fair when considering the city's potential benefits. This finding contrasts with research carried out directly with city residents, who objected to the taxes, and it illustrates the importance of applying scientific research methodologies, since it elucidates the logic that permeates the subject's perceptive dynamics, instead of interpreting opinions of the residents linearly.

Finally Reid et al's (2005) results reveal perceptions of the beach state and the situation of the municipality. There is strong evidence to suggest that the results are positive and that the project avoided storm damages to coastal residential infrastructure, businesses, hotels and so on. According SANTUR (2007), 70.24 per cent of tourists come to Balneário Piçarras for its natural landscape, including the beaches. Their results also demonstrate that, considering the beach state, there is no other option but to carry on with the nourishment.

Reid et al (2005) demonstrate that economic analysis of projects of this nature could generate a solid basis to justify support by the population for beach nourishment projects. Despite some predictable loss in sediment volume in the subaerial portion, considered normal in projects of this nature, the beach still has the same sedimentological conditions at work completion, but the system still remains erosional (see Figure CS3.6).

Figure CS3.6 shows the evolution of the beach nourishment programme from 1998 to 2007, revealing sediment loss along the project area, with more significant volume and width diminution to the south, especially around profile 05 (hot spot area), where about 93 per cent of the volume deposited was removed. In this region, the morphologic profile is similar to the profile observed prior to the project, and today the sea is advancing over houses and walls next to the shore. The rates diminish gradually to the north of the bay, with losses lower than 10 per cent in the final portion of the landfill near profile 20.

The city's local administration has a project to renourish the hot spot area and build two groynes on the beach. The plan is to use sediment from

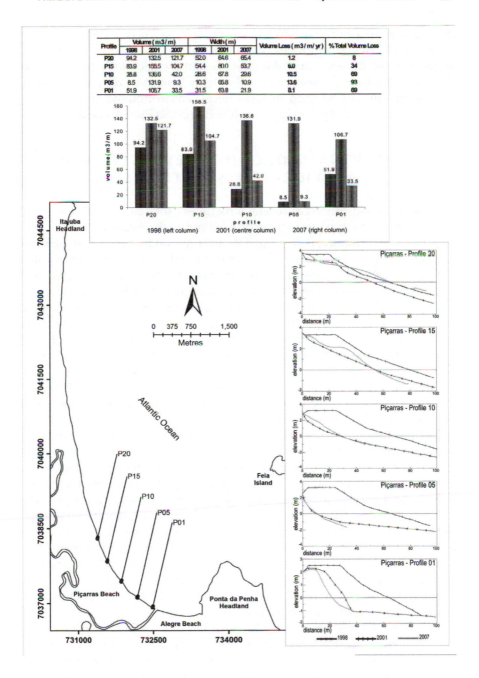

Profile	Volume (m3/m)			Width (m)			Volume Loss (m3/m/yr)	%Total Volume Loss
	1998	2001	2007	1998	2001	2007		
P20	94.2	132.5	121.7	52.0	64.6	65.4	1.2	8
P15	83.9	158.5	104.7	54.4	80.0	53.7	6.0	34
P10	28.8	136.6	42.0	28.6	67.8	29.6	10.5	69
P05	8.5	131.9	9.3	10.3	65.8	10.9	13.6	93
P01	51.9	106.7	33.5	31.5	63.8	21.9	8.1	69

Figure CS3.6 *Beach profile volume (m³/m) and width (m) variation along the nourished area at Balneário Piçarras beach, before the project (1998), after the project (2001) and in 2007* the shadow area nearshore in front of Alegre Beach (see Figure CS3.1). According to Hoefel and Klein (1997) this sediment is too fine (more than 10 per cent of silt and clay). An extra volume is necessary to reach the desired width because finer sizes will quickly be removed by suspension. This sediment can be used in low-energy environments, as at Alegre Beach, but not in higher-energy sites like Balneário Piçarras beach.

CONCEPTUAL MODEL OF PREVENTIVE AND AMELIORATIVE STRATEGIES

Traditional classifications of coastal structures ('soft' and 'hard') typically consider only the type or weight of material with minimal reference to structural performance. It is a plausible assumption that coastal structures were originally designed on the basis of empirical observations of naturally protective features in coastal environments and that engineering design tried to mimic nature where seawalls approximated rock cliffs and where artificial breakwaters acted as offshore coral reefs or islands (Klein et al, 2005). Klein et al (2005) proposed and developed a functional classification that organizes structures in terms of effect on: (1) wave reflection and/or dissipation, (2) sand trapping, and (3) sediment introduction (see Table CS3.1).

Along the Santa Catarina coastline, especially in the northern sector of Balneário Piçarras, sediment introduction (nourishment) is the most common type of coastal 'structure', followed by examples of wave reflection/dissipation and sand trapping (see Figure CS3.5). Sediment introduction is primarily used for coastal protection, for example to protect roads and houses against storm surge flooding and direct wave action. The construction of a beach recreation platform meets secondary use requirements at Balneário Piçarras beach. Beach nourishment projects in Santa Catarina have so far not evolved the beach restoration concept to the condition where it replicates natural environments as suggested by Nordstrom (2000). The paradigm of a system that approximates the original beach state prior to degradation by human-induced impacts should incorporate morphological and ecological functions by advanced engineering designs that are based on principles of form and function that mimic nature (Nordstrom, 2000; Klein et al, 2005).

Figure CS3.7 depicts a simplified conceptual model of preventive and mitigative actions modified by Klein et al (2005) from the original Nordstrom (2000) conception. These actions ideally should be performed before initiation of the main growth phase of the urbanization process, for example, before the construction of beachfront roads (Klein et al, 2005). That is not the case for Balneário Piçarras beach. According to this updated paradigm for creating accretion shorelines by repetitive episodes of beach nourishment that increase beach width, proper setbacks should be defined that use, for example, the rate of shoreline change as a dynamic

Table CS3.1 *Classification of coastal structures in terms of function*

Process/structural type	Function	Environmental similitude	Effect on sediment budget	Example
1. Wave reflection 1.1 Vertical seawall 1.2 Seawall with slope (revetment) 1.3 Breakwaters 1.4 T-groynes	Protection of roads, houses, sidewalks etc. against wave action, reflecting waves	Rock cliffs or rock platform	Negative as a result of turbulence wave and wave interaction and reflection at the base of structure	Pedestrian walks working as vertical seawall until the end of 1998 at Balneário Piçarras (Figure CS3.5c)
2. Sand trapping 2.1 Groynes, T-groynes 2.2 Breakwaters 2.3 Groundwater dewatering 2.4 Fences	Retain, trap sediments that are available for transport longshore or cross-shore on beach sub-environments	Headland, island, rock outcrop, vegetation, water table exchange and sediment deposition on beach face	Positive near the structure, but can be negative downcoast of structure	Gabions built in the 1980s at Balneário Piçarras (Figure CS3.5a) and concrete groyne built in 1994 at Balneário Piçarras (Figure CS3.5b)
3. Sediment introduction 3.1 Nourishment and renourishment 3.2 Bypassing 3.3 Backpassing 3.4 Overpassing	Add or maintain sediments within coastal cells	Sediment transport along and cross-shore	Null in the cell, negative in the borrow area, positive downcoast	Beach nourishment project in 1999 at Balneário Piçarras (Figure CS3.5e)

Source: Based on Klein et al (2005)

geo-indicator (Ferreira et al, 2006). Such procedures provide increased shore protection based on models that copy natural beneficial processes. Deliberate mitigative actions are, however, usually required along degraded beachfronts that are impacted by urban development. Degradation of natural coastal systems is especially profound where unsupervised or illegal (non-permitted) development takes place. Implementation of ameliorative measures is divided into two main categories: (1) simple protection using wave reflection/dissipation (for example seawalls and revetments) or sand trapping (groynes and dune vegetation) or sediment introduction (beach nourishment); and (2) beach and dune restoration (beach and dune introduction and renourishment).

Most developing countries tend to ignore mistakes made by developed countries and in so doing ignore advances in corporate knowledge (Klein et al, 2005). Duplication of mistakes that were made elsewhere can be avoided in Brazil and other developing countries by reference to advances in coastal environmental science and coastal engineering. Unfortunately, many corrective actions along degraded Brazilian beaches tend to focus exclusively on mitigation or ameliorative phases that provide immediate protection. A more effective approach would be to employ science-based restoration that is more durable and cost effective than to resort to political solutions that will fail due to lack of insight and appreciation of successful prior efforts elsewhere (Klein et al, 2005).

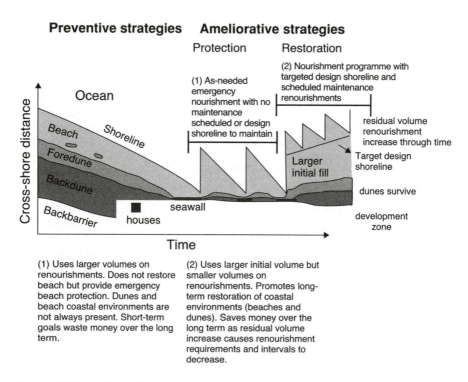

Source: Klein et al (2005)

Figure CS3.7 *Conceptual model of preventive and ameliorative actions according to the revised Nordstrom (2000) paradigm*

CONCLUSIONS

The beach nourishment project at Balneário Piçarras achieved the planned goals and can be considered both a good and bad case study in terms of coastal management because:

- Prior to project execution, the beach and properties along the coast were seriously damaged by erosional processes, and after the work, a well-developed sandy beach platform along the nourished area (about 40m width) was created.
- Nourishment took a long time to be implemented. First the local government implemented seawalls and groynes to contain the erosion process.
- The project needed a rationale and guidelines. Costs and objectives were shared and analysed with the local community for a better explanation and to obtain popular consent.
- Involvement of the government and local community was essential in order to reach the goal of reversing environmental degradation of the beach.
- Local government, with the support of the federal government (Environment Ministry) paid 50 per cent of the project and the local community paid 50 per cent as additional taxes, almost $2 million each for government and community.
- After eight years, there is no beach in the hot spot area because no renourishment project or maintenance plans were implemented. A renourishment project was not considered part of the design.

From Global to Local: Marine Policy and Legislation

David T. Tudor[1]

INTRODUCTION

The methods, scales and effectiveness of beach, coastal and ocean management differ enormously from one location to another. This case study illustrates current international large-scale ocean management policies and how, if at all, these policies filter down to the national, regional and local scales to ultimately influence beach management. It also considers future marine management policies at the international, national and local levels and discusses future proposed legislation in the UK and Europe, and focuses upon the national coastal management umbrella that is needed for any successful beach management.

To illustrate the numerous policy frameworks and statutory requirements, good examples of ocean management around the world are considered and the current case of UK marine management is highlighted as a useful case study. The past, current and future management in the UK serves as an effective example in managing and integrating policies and legislation relating to beach management.

This paper is split into four sections. First, the development of large-scale ocean policies is given. These include international conventions and laws as well as policies and legislation relating to the US and Europe. Following this, the UK context of present and future policies and legislation is considered – this ranges from non-statutory ICZM programmes and strategies to the potential for a marine act. Integration is often cited as the panacea for ineffective marine management and the third section of this case study highlights integration that exists at the large-scale regional and administrative levels in Australia, Canada and the UK; some of the reasons why integration proves so difficult are also covered. Finally, the applicability of land-based planning and management to the offshore area is appraised and the different complexities of the marine environment are highlighted.

THE RECENT DEVELOPMENT OF GLOBAL OCEAN POLICY AND LEGISLATION

There have been an increasing number of global, European and national policies and strategies published in recent years. This is a result of the need for action as pressure and impacts increase year on year, as illustrated by numerous agencies and reports (for example EEA, 1999; US Commission, 2004; DEFRA, 2005a), and perhaps also a reflection of the lobbying of politicians and publicity generated by environmental groups. There is no doubt that the marine environment is under increasing threat from development, sea-level rise, pollution, resource exploitation and unsustainable activities (Williams et al, 2005; UNEP, 2007). Some of the major international and national initiatives are laid out below.

The United Nations Convention on the Law of the Sea (UNCLOS) entered into force in 1994 and is the legal foundation upon which international ocean resource use and protection is built. The high seas are beyond the authority of any state and are, in the words of UNCLOS, 'the common heritage of mankind' (Slater, 2004). UNCLOS addresses fundamental aspects of ocean governance, including environmental control, scientific research, economic and commercial activities, delimitation of ocean space, and the settlement of disputes relating to ocean matters. Over 130 countries have ratified it (Pew, 2003).

The Convention on Biological Diversity is the international legal instrument devoted to biodiversity and ecological sustainability. It was signed by more than 150 governments at the UN Conference on Environment and Development in 1992 and entered into force the following year. The Earth Summit in 1992 brought to widespread prominence the concept of sustainable development, which was applied to the marine environment through Chapter 17 of Agenda 21; this chapter introduced the need for new approaches to the protection of the oceans, seas and coasts: 'managing the seas and oceans as an integrated whole, requiring states to develop domestic policy initiatives and to cooperate internationally and regionally for the purposes of sustainable use and environmental protection' (Foster et al, 2005: 391). Also at the global scale, the UN World Summit on Sustainable Development has the commitment to protect important marine resources and keep the oceans clean.

In the US, Congress passed the Coastal Zone Management Act (CZMA) in 1972. The Act, administered by the National Oceanic and Atmospheric Administration, provides for management of coastal resources. The CZMA outlines two national programmes: the National Coastal Zone Management Program and the National Estuarine Research Reserve System. The objectives of CZMA are to 'preserve, protect, develop, and where possible, to restore or enhance the resources of the nation's coastal zone' (NOAA, 2008).

Also in the US, the Oceans Act of 2000 charged the US Commission on Ocean Policy with carrying out the first comprehensive review of ocean-related issues and laws in more than 30 years (US Commission, 2004). The Commission presented over 200 recommendations with the aim of moving the country to a more coordinated and comprehensive ocean policy. In December 2004, in response to the Commission's findings and recommendations, the US president issued an executive order establishing a Committee on Ocean Policy as part of the Council on Environmental Quality and released the US Ocean Action Plan. Also in the US, the Pew Oceans Commission submitted recommendations for a coordinated and comprehensive national ocean policy (Pew, 2003).

At the European scale, the European Commission adopted in May 2002 the 'Recommendation Concerning the Implementation of Integrated Coastal Zone Management in Europe' (2002/413/EC). The ICZM Recommendation outlined the steps that the member states should take to develop national strategies for ICZM. The national strategies were due for completion in 2006. Successful beach management can be hampered by a lack of national ICZM plans or by plans providing insufficient consideration to beach management issues (see Chapter 4).

The Commission Communication of 7 June 2007, COM(2007)308, presented the conclusions of the Commission's review into implementation of the Recommendation and set out the main policy directions for further promotion on ICZM in Europe. The Communication stated that while the prevailing approach was still sectoral, the national strategies should provide a more strategic and integrated framework. The Communication goes on to assert that the EU ICZM Recommendation remains valid as a basis to continue to support these integration processes.

Also in Europe, in October 2005, the Commission adopted its Thematic Strategy on the Protection and the Conservation of the Marine Environment, including a proposed Marine Strategy Directive. The Thematic Strategy is designed to enhance and complement other EU policies and legislation concerning the terrestrial part of the coastal zone, supporting implementation of ICZM. The Marine Strategy and the EU ICZM Recommendation are to be also considered in the broader framework of the future EU Maritime Policy launched in June 2006 with the adoption of the Commission's Green Paper: *Towards a Future Maritime Policy for the Union: A European Vision for the Oceans and Seas* (EC, 2006). After considering responses from the Green Paper, in October 2007 the Commission published *An Integrated Maritime Policy for the European Union*, commonly known as the 'Blue Book' (EC, 2007). The Blue Book emphasizes the importance of integration in European policy development to ensure a coordinated approach to the delivery of the Maritime Policy.

THE UK PERSPECTIVE OF COASTAL AND MARINE POLICY: PRESENT AND FUTURE

The seas of the UK are three times the size of its land mass. As elsewhere in the world, UK marine and coastal waters are under increasing pressure from human activity and multiple competing uses, and there is concern over the fall in environmental quality and changes to marine life (DEFRA, 2005a; EA, 2005). The beach, coasts and seas around the UK are vitally important, both culturally and economically, to the nation (Peel and Lloyd, 2004; Tudor and Williams, 2006).

Management of the seas and oceans has been fragmented and sectoral; it has also often been based on policies aimed at short-term economic gain (DEFRA, 2002b; Slater, 2004). The sectoral nature of management regimes and consenting procedures has resulted in duplication in the regulation process. There are numerous government departments, devolved administrations and government agencies that have varying responsibilities for regulating activities and protecting the UK marine environment. It is felt by some that a single authority with overall responsibility for coastal management is more appropriate and that poor cooperation between government organizations hampers beach management (see Chapter 4).

At the Fifth North Sea Conference in 2002, the UK formally endorsed an ecosystem-based approach to the sustainable development of the marine resource. By 2010, the UK agreed to designate areas of sea for marine protection in a well-managed network (Peel and Lloyd, 2004; Slater, 2004). This agreement, along with the OSPAR (Ministerial Meeting of the Oslo and Paris Commissions) Convention for the Protection of the Marine Environment of the North East Atlantic, are instances where international agreements have influenced UK actions and policies.

As part of the EU, the UK is also committed to the policies of ICZM and Maritime Policy at the European level. The EU ICZM Recommendation lists eight principles illustrating characteristics of ICZM. Integration across sectors, the land–sea divide and levels of governance, as well as a participatory approach, are essential aspects of ICZM. Given the cross-border nature of many coastal processes, coordination and cooperation with neighbouring countries were stated as important parameters in the Recommendation. At the local scale, beach management faces similar problems because of artificial administrative coastal boundaries (see Chapter 4). The UK government and the devolved administrations decided that each nation should produce its own national strategy following the Recommendation, which may ultimately make up a UK ICZM strategy. The four countries that constitute the UK are England, Northern Ireland, Scotland and Wales and each has certain levels of devolved responsibilities from the UK government. Therefore, individual strategies for each nation were to be prepared. For example, in Wales, the Welsh Assembly government published a strategy for ICZM in March

2007; this was prepared in conjunction with key coastal stakeholders from an all-Wales network, the Wales Coastal and Maritime Partnership, with the aim of implementing the actions at a national level and refreshing the strategy in 2010. As well as the 'national' strategies, there are numerous other ICZM initiatives around the UK, many of which have their own local strategies and/or plans (for example North West Coastal Forum and the Pembrokeshire Coastal Forum).

The UK has seen a raft of initiatives, policies, reviews and consultations over the last decade relating to marine and coastal management. For example, SMPs provide a large-scale assessment of the risks associated with coastal processes and present a long-term policy framework to reduce these risks. UK government departments, devolved administrations and environmental groups have published many volumes on the current state of UK seas and the need for change. For example, the UK government, in association with the devolved administrations, has conducted reviews on nature conservation and fisheries management, as well as publishing a strategy on sustainable management of the seas (DEFRA, 2002b). To provide an evidence base, a report on the state of the seas was also published (DEFRA, 2005a). Specifically at the devolved level, there are initiatives such as the Welsh Assembly government's Environment Strategy and the Scottish Sustainable Marine Environment Initiative; in Northern Ireland, the Department of the Environment has published *An Integrated Coastal Zone Management Strategy for Northern Ireland 2006–2026* (DOENI, 2006). The WWF has been campaigning for many years for new marine legislation for the UK and even went as far as publishing its own draft marine bill to stimulate discussion and to raise awareness of the issue. Many other environmental groups have also been campaigning for changes in marine management.

All of these initiatives and reports have led to government consultations on a new marine bill for the UK. The process of drafting and implementing a marine bill has been complicated by the requirements of the four individual nations that make up the UK, but significant and encouraging progress has been made and it is hoped by many that a new marine act will be created. Currently, the proposed UK bill covers many areas of marine management, namely: a new integrated marine licensing system; fisheries management reorganization; new nature conservation management measures; a new organization to manage areas of the UK seas; coastal access provisions; and a new system of marine planning. In addition, in 2008 the Scottish government also published a consultation on a marine bill.

Marine planning, often termed marine spatial planning (MSP), aims for a more integrated approach to managing human activities in the seas and oceans. A new system of marine planning for UK waters has many advantages over the current system, although the implementation, development, design and integration (at the coast and between planning boundaries) need to be thoroughly and expertly considered if the system is to succeed. However, as illustrated in the previous section, management of the marine environment is a global issue and for effective management of the planet's seas and oceans, countries must cooperate, coordinate and ultimately integrate their procedures and plans.

INTEGRATION OF POLICY AND MANAGEMENT

The need for an integrated approach to the management of the marine environment is well documented (Cicin-Sain and Knecht, 1998; Slater, 2004; Foster et al, 2005); however, so far the true level of integration and the tangible results of this approach to management are questionable.

The complex nature of the marine environment, physically and legislatively, requires specific and appropriate management that differs considerably from the terrestrial environment – this issue comes to a head in the 'coastal' zone, where beaches are located. The different rights, uses, ownership, customs and institutions involved are extremely complicated. In fact, the regulatory and organizational structures of the marine and coastal environment have been portrayed as an administrative battleground (French, 1997).

The reasons for the lack of integration in marine and coastal policy are numerous around the world, but have a common basis whatever the location. Some of the common reasons for a lack of integration are:

- The complexity of responsibilities, particularly at the coast, acts as a barrier to agencies and organizations taking an integrated approach (Shipman and Stojanovic, 2007).
- A lack of clear policy regarding the marine environment leads to poor integration among countries, at the coast and between regional and local scales.
- There is self-interest among administrations, sectors and individuals who would find a non-integrated approach, or particularly the status quo, advantageous
- There is a lack of understanding that the oceans need specific clear policies and that their planning and management cannot simply be transferred from terrestrial policies or processes (although much can be learned from terrestrial regimes).

Integrated management has the aim of achieving sustainable development of the marine environment and its resources with the objective of integrating management of all activities through effective and collaborative processes. Integrated oceans management (IOM) is a tool for achieving sustainable use of marine resources and there are instances of where this approach has been implemented and which can serve as best practice exemplars for others to learn from.

Australia and Canada have taken a lead in IOM and have developed innovative approaches (Foster et al, 2005). Australia's Ocean Policy (AOP) utilizes a cross-sectoral ministerial board to focus on integration of protection and management. This board comprises federal government ministers responsible for environment, industry, fisheries, shipping, science and tourism. An important aspect of AOP is the use of regional marine plans to facilitate ecosystem-based management across sectors and jurisdictions.

Canada's Ocean Act of 1997 established a framework for cross-sectoral integrated management through an Oceans Management Strategy and by developing integrated management plans. The Eastern Scotian Shelf Integrated Management (ESSIM) Initiative is an example of the implementation of the integrated oceans management in Canada. The ESSIM Initiative consists of two main components: the cross-jurisdictional/cross-sectoral institutional arrangements and the development of an integrated plan for oceans management in the ESSIM area (Foster et al, 2005).

The UK has a number of similarities with both Australia and Canada. While the UK is a non-federal state, unlike Canada and Australia, the separate nations of the UK and the various levels of devolved powers they possess are analogous to the federal/commonwealth state systems of Australia and Canada. In Australia, commonwealth–federal–state integration is tackled through an Integrated Oceans Working Group, which consists of the various states and commonwealth governments working in collaboration to develop a national approach. This type of integration, in this case of sovereign states, is something that is being encouraged at a European level through the European 'Blue Book'.

Future marine management in the UK could follow the ESSIM Initiative model of using two scales, these being: large ocean management areas that extend from the coast to the 200 nautical mile limits of the Exclusive Economic Zone (EEZ), with boundaries based on ecological considerations and management units; and coastal management areas that are subdivisions of the large ocean management areas, where smaller-scale management and planning requirements are identified.

However, the UK has four nations, each with its own territorial waters to 12 nautical miles within which differing responsibilities coexist. The UK, as the sovereign state, also has jurisdiction out to its international boundary, with further exceptions in this area with regard to Scotland's devolved powers. This makes for a potentially difficult mix of duties. While the large-scale model and two-tier approach in Canada may be desirable based on ecological considerations, this does not preclude a fragmented geographical and statutory approach being unsuccessful. Marine management around the world faces integration and boundary issues, whether these are at the very local level (for example beaches and estuaries) or at the ocean scale, such as the Large Marine Ecosystems programme (Carleton Ray and McCormick-Ray, 2004). There are numerous policies and legislative and statutory requirements at various scales but in some cases they do not relate or interlink with one another and in other instances the integration is far more effective. For 'all-use' marine management to work effectively it is the coordination and integration of management that are essential and not where the geographical boundaries lie.

LINKING MARINE MANAGEMENT TO COASTAL AND TERRESTRIAL PLANNING AND MANAGEMENT

Governments have carved parts of the world's oceans into many zones, based on both international and domestic laws. These zones are often complex, with overlapping legal authorities and agency responsibilities. Internationally, the closer one gets to the shore, the more authority a coastal nation has. Similarly, for domestic purposes, the closer one gets to the shore, the more control an individual state/region has (US Commission, 2004). The legislative requirement of governments to manage areas is based on political boundaries. At the coast, statutory regulations often cease at low water mark or overlap with some marine regulations. It is this cessation of responsibility at low water, or at least the perception of it, that has partly allowed the lack of integration to foster and continue until now. Management of the coast is therefore often more complicated than large-scale oceans; the beach and the coast are more tangible to the public, are under greater pressure and therefore have many more competing demands, and it is here that beach management has its greatest challenge. According to Shipman and Stojanovic (2007: 376):

> In the case of the UK, one study estimated that 80 per cent of all decisions on the coast are taken at the local level (Local Government Association, 2002). Therefore, both the quality of coastal areas and the effectiveness of coastal management are still subject to what is referred to as the 'tyranny of small decisions' (Odum, 1982) rather than the grand and noble aspirations of ICZM.

As stated previously, there have been a number of policy initiatives over the last 20 years that have moved marine management forward at a rapid rate, but beach management lags behind. However, there is still much to do to improve the sectoral and sovereign self-interest that currently exists. The recent policy initiatives at the European and UK levels are laudable and the efforts of administrations, regulators and environmental groups should be commended. When considering integration of recent policies into the land-based system, it must be kept in mind that the two systems have very different natures and issues. The knowledge and methods used in land-based planning and management must be built upon and considered.

While land-based planning, such as the National Planning Framework (NPF) for Scotland, has moved forward and is now more strategic, it does not follow that this will work for the marine environment. The NPF and the Wales Spatial Plan encapsulate the ideas in the European Spatial Development Perspective and these high-level aspirations and tools are transferable to the marine environment, but the natural dynamics, actors and ownership are very different.

When terrestrial and marine planners consider integration at the coast there are numerous other plans and policies to consider: the river basin management plans of the Water Framework Directive, SMPs and the regional spatial strategies of England, to name but three. The importance of public buy-in and involvement in the management and decision-making process is paramount at the beach. In the UK, particularly in Wales, the much vaunted 'bottom-up' approach to terrestrial planning has been to the fore in recent years. There is every chance that this process can be replicated for marine planning at the coast with the potential for a new marine planning and management system in the UK, including Wales. It is essential, however, that focused guidelines regarding processes and objectives are created when dealing with such a wide range of stakeholders if any consultative process is to prove fruitful.

The legal basis of a marine (spatial) plan must be clearly set out and understood; a transparent process of consultation and implementation is essential at all levels, be it devolved, national, European or international, if it is to succeed and not be seen simply as an additional layer of legislation.

CONCLUSIONS

There have been an increasing number of global, European and national policies and strategies published in recent years. Many global policies influence the UK's national legislation and policy, such as those from the EU and OSPAR. Also, local or regional initiatives can influence the national and international agenda. At the UK scale, these international policies influence management but can lead to a fragmented and sectoral position. Whichever way policies are formulated – either top-down or bottom-up – is perhaps irrelevant; the essential factor is that the policies can deliver the requirements of the various interested parties and the environment as a whole, and deliver sustainable and responsible development. It is the effectiveness of integration of the disparate array of policies that will ultimately lead to successful marine and coastal management.

Management of the UK seas and coasts has become increasingly influenced by the devolution process in its constituent nations. Each nation has produced its own ICZM strategy and the possible marine acts introduced by UK and Scottish governments will probably bring different delivery and management regimes. With proposed European marine strategies and legislation on the horizon and the presence of other global initiatives, it is important for effective management of the seas, coasts and beaches that regions and nations cooperate and integrate their management and policies.

As exemplified by the Oceans Management Strategy and integrated management plans in Canada, much of the process of integrated marine management is improved by taking on others' best practice and 'learning-by-doing'. The approach in the UK can take much from other initiatives but also needs to begin its own system and this will evolve with time and as experience increases.

NOTE

1   This case study reflects the personal views of the author.

River Mouth Lagoon Science and Management

Deirdre E. Hart

INTRODUCTION

The river mouths of New Zealand's wave-dominated mixed sand and gravel coasts (Kirk, 1980) are characterized by a distinctive type of non-estuarine wetland-lagoon system locally known as hapua. Along the east coast of the South Island these lagoons, in conjunction with the coastal lakes called waituna, provide a corridor for migrating birds, ocean–river links for migrating fish and mahinga kai (traditional Māori food and resources) (Kirk and Lauder, 2000; Single and Hemmingsen, 2001).

Although common in New Zealand (Kirk and Lauder, 2000; Neale et al, 2007), non-estuarine coarse-sediment river mouth lagoons are rare internationally and predominantly found on paraglacial coasts in areas with low population densities and levels of coastal development (Zenkovich, 1967; Carter, 1984; Carter et al, 1989; Forbes et al, 1995; Cooper, 2001; Orford et al, 2002). Their behaviour is markedly different to that of sand coast lagoons due to the permeable nature of the barrier sediments, high degree of wave domination and absence of a tidal prism.

In contrast to estuarine systems, the management literature for these lagoons is small (Kirk, 1991; Kirk and Lauder, 2000) and derived from studies on a small number of examples. However, like estuaries, these lagoons are particularly sensitive to coastal and catchment development (Kirk, 1991; Jowett et al, 2005; Hart, 2007). Recent studies raise questions as to the success of current practices in managing the wide range of hapua that exist under increasing catchment development pressure (Hart, 1999; 2007; Neale et al, 2007). This investigation examines lagoon dynamics and change across a range of hapua in Canterbury, New Zealand, as the basis of an evaluation of the national and regional management framework.

HAPUA SYSTEMS

Lagoon occurrence

Hapua form where longshore drift builds a coarse-sediment barrier in front of a river, offsetting the outlet and producing a narrow shore-parallel extension of the coastal riverbed (see Figure CS5.1). They are non-estuarine, lacking a tidal prism and regular saltwater intrusion. Instead they experience a tidal backwater effect, where rising ocean levels limit lagoon drainage through the permeable barrier sediments, producing a small (up to 1m) increase in freshwater lagoon levels. Unlike estuarine entrances, tidal flows through hapua outlet channels are rare and limited to short periods after large floods or storms subside leaving an enlarged channel relative to lagoon discharge. Salt water is also introduced via wave overtopping during large storms, when barriers may be inundated by swash for an hour or more around high-tide. After such disturbances lagoons return to fresh water typically within a few hours to days (Hart, 1999; 2007).

Hapua are common in Canterbury (see Figure CS5.2) where rivers meet the high-energy wave-dominated Southern Ocean swell environment (Gorman et al, 2003). They do not occur in the sheltered sandy lee of Banks Peninsula, instead being associated with the exposed mixed sand and gravel beaches of the chronically-eroding to semi-stable open coast (see Figure CS5.1). Their rivers are characterized by a broad spectrum of catchment, discharge and channel types (see Figure CS5.3). These include large, braided, mountain-fed rivers with upper catchments in the Southern Alps such as the Waitaki, Rakaia and Rangitata, braided and meandering foothills rivers such as the Ashburton and Waipara, and the meandering streams of the Canterbury Plains and north Canterbury coastal ranges such as the Kowhai and Pareora (see Table CS5.1).

Lagoon gradients and dynamics

Common to all hapua is their dynamic nature, with each lagoon cycling though a number of states (see Figure CS5.4). These include progressive outlet offsetting via longshore drift and barrier scour, primary breaches where river floods induce barrier breaching opposite the main river channel and secondary breaches and channel truncations initiated downdrift of the main river channel by storms and/or river floods (Todd, 1983; Kirk, 1991; Hart, 1999; Single and Hemmingsen, 2001; Hart, 2007). The dominance of different behaviours at each site depends on the particular balance of fluvial and marine processes and antecedent barrier conditions operating on the lagoon system. This balance also determines the development and persistence of the lagoon environment over historical timescales.

Outlet offsetting, for example, is a common mode of behaviour in all hapua but more frequent and extreme offsets occur at low river discharges

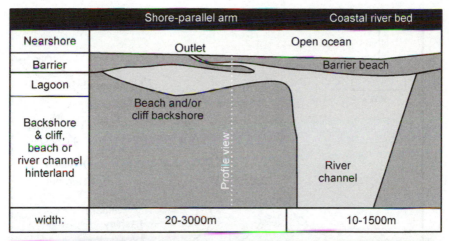

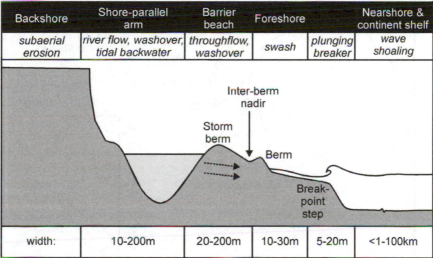

Notes: Morphological zones are shown with indicative widths, with profile process zones in italics. Note the distinctive mixed sand and gravel beach profile of the barrier enclosing the lagoon (bottom).

Figure CS5.1 *Planform (top) and profile (bottom) diagrams of hapua morphology based on surveys of the Ashburton river mouth lagoon*

(Todd, 1983; Kirk, 1991; Hart, 1999). Lagoons at the mouths of rivers with low base flows such as the Ashburton, Kowhai, Pareora and Opihi are thus more prone to sustained outlet offsets (see Table CS5.1). Extreme outlet offsets decrease the efficiency of flow from river to sea (see Figure CS5.4a), encouraging drainage through the permeable barrier sediments rather than the outlet proper and increasing the likelihood of lagoon closure.

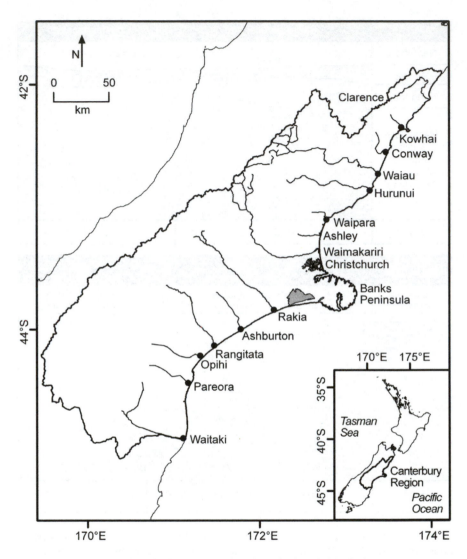

Note: River mouths classified as hapua are identified with black dots.

Figure CS5.2 *Location of rivers with hapua-type mouths and other major river systems draining to the coast in Canterbury on the East Coast of New Zealand*

Sustained closures raise significant management concerns, including long water residence times, poor water quality and lagoon expansion and flooding of adjacent low-lying areas. Closure also severs the link between river and sea, although this is less important for many migrating fish than the prolonged periods of low flow that lead to closure. This is because the warm outlet discharges associated with very low flows deter many fish from entering the lagoon environment even when the outlet is open.

Table CS5.1 *Channel form, catchment area and flow characteristics of Canterbury rivers with* hapua *lagoon mouths*

River	Dominant channel form	Catchment (km²)	Gauge site	Mean flow (m³s⁻¹)	Annual 7-day low flow (m³s⁻¹)	Mean annual flood (m³s⁻¹)	10-year flood (m³s⁻¹)	COV
Kowhai	Meandering	82	–	–	–	–	–	–
Conway	Meandering and braided	503	–	–	–	–	–	–
Waiau	Braided	2030	Marble Pt	98	32	1059	1413	0.9
Hurunui	Meandering and braided	2680	Mandamus	53	16.6	531	831	0.9
Waipara	Braided	741	White Gorge	3	0.11	129	249	–
Rakaia	Braided	2630	Fighting Hill	221	92	2514	3701	0.9
Ashburton	Braided	1816	SH1	11	3	108	–	0.8
Rangitata	Braided	1775	Klondyke	99	42	1085	2324	0.8
Opihi	Meandering and braided	2372	Rockwood	5.5	1.3	170	331	–
Pareora	Meandering	424	Huts	3.7	0.48	239	568	–
Waitaki	Braided	12,118	Kurow	373	–	–	–	0.8

Note: The flow regime for the Waitaki River is artificially controlled via a dam system. COV is the river flow coefficient of variation.

Source: Data from Hart (1999) and Environment Canterbury (ECAN, 2005; 2007)

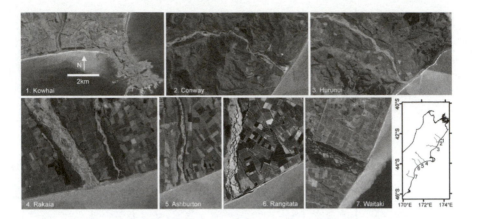

Note: *The scale shown in photograph 1 applies to all seven images.*

Source: *Aerial photographs from Google Earth*

Figure CS5.3 *Aerial photographs of example hapua lagoons in North Canterbury (top) and along the Canterbury Bight (bottom), with lagoon locations indicated in the insert*

Storm-induced secondary breaches and channel truncations also dominate hapua characterized by small discharges (see Table CS5.1), particularly during the low-flow summer season (Hart, 1999; 2007). During these events storm waves overtop the barrier beach for an hour or more around high tide, inundating the lagoon and increasing its water level and salinity. On the falling tide, hydraulic support on the seaward side of the barrier decreases and the head between lagoon and sea rapidly increases. Subsequent lagoon drainage through the barrier can lead to pipe failures, breaching an entirely new outlet or truncating an existing elongated channel (see Figure CS5.4b–c). Pre-storm outlet channels are abandoned and infilled as lagoon levels return to normal. These events can increase outlet efficiency if the new outlet is located closer to the main river channel, decreasing the likelihood of lagoon closure during low flows and maintaining a link for fish migration. However, if a new outlet is breached further from the river then outlet efficiency decreases, potentially increasing the length of the waterbody and likelihood of adjacent flooding and lagoon closure.

In contrast to these low-discharge behaviours, fluvial-induced breaches and truncations dominate the mouths of rivers with high base flows and flood discharges such as the Rakaia, Rangitata and Waiau (see Table CS5.1 and Figure CS5.4b–d). Such events have several impacts on lagoon functioning and development. They inject a slug of new bedload and convey lagoon and barrier sediments into the coastal environment. A large proportion of the coarse material is then reworked shoreward by waves to nourish the downdrift coast (Kirk, 1991; Kirk and Lauder, 2000). These are key events for fish passage and fishing recreation, particularly for hapua on rivers with low base flows, where fish passage may not occur except during floods. Field observation also indicates that flood events are important for eroding lagoon backshores, a behaviour that allows hapua to retreat landward and thus persist with coastal transgression and sea-level rise and distinguishes them from waituna, which infill or breach and disappear over geological time. They also cause the flooding of surrounding low-lying ecosystems, deliver fine sediments to these areas, and strip aquatic vegetation from the coastal river and lagoon beds. The lagoon and adjacent low-lying areas generally recover rapidly from flood events, with their ecosystems being adapted to such periodic disturbances. While such flood-induced breaches and channel truncations occur in all hapua under natural flow regimes, they are more frequent, and the increased outlet efficiency produced persists much longer at the mouths of rivers with large and variable discharges relative to the resistance of their enclosing barrier.

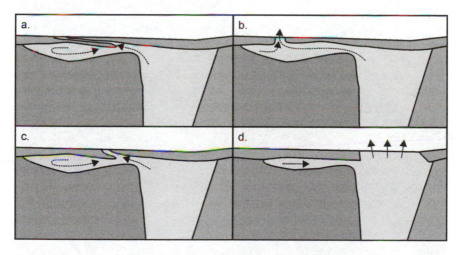

Note: For the Ashburton river mouth, large and small floods correspond to flows above and below 100m³s⁻¹ respectively, while storm-wave overtopping is associated with significant offshore wave heights of 1.5m or greater.

Figure CS5.4 *Example hapua behaviours based on surveys of the Ashburton river mouth. The lagoon is shown with (a) an initial elongated offset outlet channel, followed by change to (b) a secondary breach induced away from the main river channel by storm-wave overtopping and/or a small flood, (c) a short, truncated channel induced by storm-wave overtopping and/or a small river flood, or (d) a primary breach induced opposite the main river channel by a large flood*

THE CATCHMENT CONTEXT

Given the close links established between (a) the type and frequency of hapua behaviour and (b) the balance between river flow and wave conditions, these environments are potentially very sensitive to the effects of anthropogenic coastal and catchment development. In Canterbury this has comprised at least three phases and types of activity since European settlement. First, 170 years ago large wetlands extended across low-lying coastal areas linking several hapua with adjacent coastal swamps and lakes. Land drainage by early European colonizers progressively reduced these wetlands to the isolated fragments that comprise the river mouth lagoons and coastal lakes today (Johnston, 1961).

Second, over the last century small bach communities (see Figure CS5.5) have developed around the mouths of the Waitaki, Pareora, Opihi, Rangitata, Ashburton, Rakaia, Hurunui and Waipara Rivers, entrenching

Note: In New Zealand, the term bach refers to a small non-urban dwelling often used as a holiday home although, in the case of river mouths, many baches are permanently occupied, often by retired people.

Source: Photographs by Environment Canterbury and Bob Kirk

Figure CS5.5 *Aerial photographs of bach communities at the mouths of the Hurunui (left) and Waitaki (see arrow in right) rivers*

river mouth recreation in New Zealand outdoor culture. The greatest impacts of these communities on hapua have been to encourage regular river mouth monitoring and the sporadic practice of artificially opening lagoons closed for sustained periods during the low flow season.

Also over the last century, hydroelectricity-generation and irrigation infrastructure has been constructed in the upper catchments of a number of rivers in Canterbury, leading to altered flow regimes and sediment delivery to river mouth environments. This includes several large dams for electricity generation throughout the upper Waitaki catchment and smaller dams and diversion races for irrigation-water storage and/or electricity generation in the catchments of the Waiau, Rakaia, Rangitata and Opihi Rivers. Arguably the greatest changes have been those to the Waitaki and Rangitata Rivers. Waitaki River low flows have been artificially raised above pre-dam levels since 1935, while on the Rangitata River flows have been reduced since 1945, with up to $7m^3s^{-1}$ of water diverted for irrigation across the plains and into the Rakaia River. Given the close links identified above between hapua behaviour and river flow levels, it is almost certain that several of these developments have altered the dynamics and functioning of hapua downstream. However, there has been no peer-reviewed published research quantifying the effects of these works on the river mouth environments.

The third phase of hapua development stems from water resource-use changes over the last 50 years (Kirk, 1991; Hart, 1999). Early farming in the region was dominated by dry-land pasture grazing and agriculture suited to the semi-dry temperate climate: annual precipitation, which is dominated by rainfall, totals less than 400mm in coastal and plains areas of the region, less than 800mm in the inland foothills and up to 1600mm in the eastern Alps. This contrasts with the central Alps and humid west coast of the South Island where annual precipitation ranges from 1600–12,000mm (Sturman et al, 2001). Canterbury is also subject to strong interannual variation in precipitation and river flows, with drought common during prolonged El Niño conditions and greater rainfall under La Niña conditions.

Over the last two decades irrigated dairy farming and to a lesser extent viticulture and forestry have increasingly replaced dry-land practices in the province, transforming its land and rivers. Canterbury now contains approximately 350,000ha or 70 per cent of the total irrigated land and 60 per cent of the total allocated water nationally. Approximately 40 per cent of this area is irrigated from groundwater abstractions, the remainder coming from surface sources (Fenemor et al, 2006) including all but two of the rivers in Table CS5.1. Over 75 per cent of the area draining into the Canterbury Bight, including the Rakaia, Ashburton and Rangitata catchments, currently has more than 80–100 per cent of water available for abstraction allocated under resource consents. These water-use permits were issued on a first-come basis by the regional authority Environment Canterbury (ECAN), which calculates water available for abstraction as a proportion of the estimated groundwater recharge rate. Remaining catchments within the Canterbury Bight and North Canterbury have up to 80 per cent of the water available for abstraction allocated.

To date, few published studies have examined the effects of this water resource development on rivers and river mouths in Canterbury. At the broadest level, ECAN (2007) recognizes that the flow regimes of the region's rivers are significantly modified and that lowland stream health is vulnerable to interannual climate variation under this regime. Studies of the Ashburton lagoon indicate that river flow modification can cause lagoon water quality and ecological degradation and undermine hapua persistence in the face of coastal erosion. In correlation with increasing river-water abstractions, the area occupied by this hapua decreased by more than 50 per cent between 1950 and 2000, while low flow and closure states increased in frequency and severity. This has reduced anadromous fish passage and recreational opportunities reliant on high lagoon water quality and an open outlet (Hart, 1999; 2007).

Given the spectrum of hapua that exist in Canterbury more studies are needed on the effects of river flow changes on the hapua represented in Table CS5.1. The next section examines the scientific basis for determining and managing the impacts of development on hapua environments within the current New Zealand resource and environmental management framework.

HAPUA IN A NEW ZEALAND RESOURCE AND ENVIRONMENTAL MANAGEMENT CONTEXT

The scientific basis

The current scientific management framework for hapua is based on recognition of the close links between fluvial flows and lagoon state. Developed by Kirk (1991) using the Rakaia hapua as an example, it employs descriptive flow levels to predict whether a lagoon will be closed to the sea, have an open and migratory outlet channel, or have a new primary breach (see Table CS5.2). The occurrence of these states is linked to very low, moderate to mean and high river flow levels respectively. The model assumes that open outlet states are overwhelmingly dominant with closure being rare or, in the case of the Rakaia under the 1980s flow regime, unprecedented. Overall this model provides a useful theoretical basis for managing the coastal component of hapua environments in integration with the catchments that drain into these lagoons.

Despite its sound basis, problems have arisen with the application of Kirk's model (a) to the broad range of hapua environments with limited monitoring data and (b) under current management frameworks. The latter problem is discussed in the next section. The former problem arises, in part, from the model assumption that the flows that induce

Table CS5.2 *Links between river flow and lagoon state for hapua according to the Kirk (1991) model for water-resource planning, with Rakaia River discharge examples*

River flow level	Rakaia discharge $(m^3 s^{-1})$	Predicted frequency	Lagoon state
Very low	<45	Rare to never	Closed to sea
Moderate to mean	45–200	Very common	Outlet open and migratory and prone to elongation
High (flood)	>200	Common	New outlet breached though the barrier opposite the main river channel

lagoon closures and breaches are proportional to each river's regime. As indicated above, the sensitivity of a barrier to breaching or lagoon to closure is also the product of wave climate and sediment composition. All hapua in Canterbury occur in high wave-energy mixed sand and gravel environments. Thus barriers at the mouths of rivers with small discharges require floods of disproportionately greater return intervals to form primary breaches. Similarly, the frequency of very low flows leading to lagoon closure is much higher in these systems than for the larger Rakaia. Compounding this scientific problem is the monitoring reality that too few observations are available to determine thresholds for the majority of Canterbury's lagoons. In addition, the model does not take account of storm-induced hapua behaviour (see Figure CS5.4) and the important influence of antecedent barrier conditions (Hart, 2007).

The statutory management framework

The New Zealand Resource Management Act 1991 (RMA) was introduced as an overarching piece of environmental management legislation including guidelines for the use of coastal, catchment and atmospheric environments (see Figure CS5.6). It replaced environmental management guidelines in over 40 separate pre-existing acts. As outlined in Part 2(5), the Act's purpose is to promote the sustainable management of natural and physical resources, safeguarding the life-supporting capacity of air, water, soil and ecosystems by avoiding, remedying or mitigating any adverse effects of activities on the environment. It identifies the preservation and protection of the natural character and biodiversity of coastal environments, wetlands, lakes, rivers and their margins as a matter of national importance. The Act also mandated the introduction of the first New Zealand Coastal Policy Statement (NZCPS) and regional natural resource plans, and recommended the production of catchment plans.

Under this framework, effective management of hapua environments requires the assimilation of three types of regional plan, the national policy statement and the Act itself (see Figure CS5.6).

Introduced in 1994, the NZCPS detailed a new coastal management structure linking national RMA values and guidelines to regional planning and enforcement. The environmental management designations determined by the RMA and NZCPS are illustrated in Figure CS5.6 as they apply to hapua in Canterbury. The division of the lagoon system into catchment and coastal sub-environments relates to the separate resource plans they are managed under. Although the coastal part of the framework does not include catchments, ECAN is the principal manager of both hapua and their surrounding fluvial and marine environments under the RMA (see Figure CS5.6). Thus, the regional council has the potential to manage these sub-environments in an integrated manner. In practice, however, hapua are impacted more as a by-product of catchment water resource use than as a product of integrated management. This is because concerns associated with hapua, such as the maintenance of natural character, lagoon water quality and biodiversity values, are dwarfed by those associated with catchment water resource development.

On a daily basis the practice of regional resource management involves assessing the environmental effects of each new project with respect to the RMA purpose and principles. ECAN assesses applications for activities such as water resource use or artificial lagoon openings case by case, with natural character and ecosystem values weighed against the benefits of development and hazard mitigation. Recent water-use examples show that it is impossible under this regime to determine the environmental effects of each new project relative to catchment-wide cumulative effects to the level of certainty required by the Environment Court. This problem arises, in part, from the dearth of research conducted on the effects of river and catchment change on specific river mouth lagoon environments, as highlighted above. The application of a precautionary approach could address the current challenges of managing resource use between multiple coastal and catchment sub-environments, with respect to cumulative effects, given the current lack of lagoon-specific knowledge. Such an approach is written into the NZCPS (1994), but not into the RMA, so that it does not apply to catchments (Fenemor et al, 2006).

The broad links between river flows and lagoon state identified in Kirk's (1991) model are recognized as pertinent under the Canterbury coastal and catchment management framework. The need to keep flow thresholds above minimum levels to prevent lagoon closure, for example, is *mentioned* in the Natural Resources Regional Plan (ECAN, 2007), in several catchment water resource plans (for example Opihi, Ashburton and Hurunui) and in the Regional Coastal Plan. In the last of these, ECAN (2005) identifies river flow reductions leading to increased river mouth closure as a key management issue for the Canterbury Bight. This recognition, however, has not led to tangible changes in water resource-use practices or better

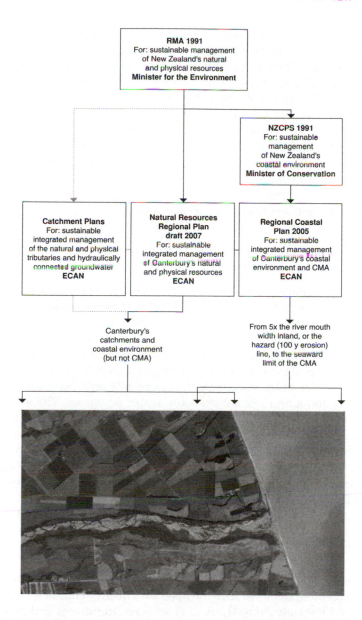

RMA 1991
For: sustainable management
of New Zealand's natural
and physical resources
Minister for the Environment

NZCPS 1991
For: sustainable
management
of New Zealand's
coastal environment
Minister of Conservation

Catchment Plans
For: sustainable
integrated management
of the natural and physical
tributaries and hydraulically
connected groundwater
ECAN

**Natural Resources
Regional Plan
draft 2007**
For: sustainable
integrated management
of Canterbury's natural
and physical resources
ECAN

**Regional Coastal
Plan 2005**
For: sustainable
integrated management
of Canterbury's coastal
environment and CMA
ECAN

Canterbury's
catchments and
coastal environment
(but not CMA)

From 5x the river mouth
width inland, or the
hazard (100 y erosion)
line, to the seaward
limit of the CMA

Note: Each box contains the statute or plan name, its purpose and the authority responsible for producing it. CMA indicates the coastal marine area, which covers the coastal strip from mean high water springs seaward to the 12 nautical mile (22km) limit of territorial seas.

Source: Aerial photograph from Google Earth

Figure CS5.6 *Management designations for the different sub-environments of hapua and their catchments according to the 1991 RMA, NZCPS and ECAN regional plans* environmental outcomes for hapua. Instead, concern over prolonged closures or mouth offsets has led to artificial barrier breaches. These are initiated regularly during the low flow season at the mouth of the Opihi River and have been performed sporadically at the mouths of the Ashburton, Waitaki and Waipara Rivers.

A further problem with current management practices relates to the case-by-case nature of effects assessment. Project-based assessments of environmental effects do not allow for consideration of the impacts of activities in relation to the entire wetland corridor system that hapua form in conjunction with waituna along the Canterbury coast. To date, there has been no analysis of the ecological merits of progressively altering the flow regimes feeding the majority of hapua environments.

Recommendations linking the science and current management reality

Based on this analysis of hapua functioning and management realities, consideration needs to be given to other management options. This could include, for example, a regime where minimum alteration is allowed in catchments draining into key lagoons while substantial alteration is allowed of those draining into other lagoons. Such a regime would allow management practices to reflect the physical, ecological and resource gradient realities of the spectrum of lagoons in Canterbury, and may not lead to any reduction in total available water resources. The application of alternative management practices for hapua systems could be achieved through a statutory lagoon plan. In the absence of such a focused statutory plan, prioritization of effective hapua management will remain inferior to water resource considerations. These problems are likely to increase if the forecast climate changes occur in Canterbury such as more severe and sustained El Niño type conditions.

CONCLUSION

This case study of mixed sand and gravel river mouth lagoon functioning and management demonstrates the need for effective coastal management to be based not only on analysis of coastal environments and associated human use values but also on practices that recognize the spatially and temporally variable and open nature of coastal systems. The product of high-energy fluvial and marine sub-environments, Canterbury's hapua include a broad spectrum of very sensitive and dynamic lagoons. Analysis of the current management framework reveals that it is grounded in sound purpose and principles. However, the current fluvial- and activity-focused practices are leading to progressive lagoon degradation. The development of a lagoon-focused statutory plan is recommended for improving the management of these important interface environments.

Protection Projects at Poetto and Cala Gonone Beaches (Sardinia, Italy)

Enzo Pranzini

INTRODUCTION

Beaches, either sandy, gravel or mixed, cover 53 per cent of the 7500km-long Italian coast (GNRAC, 2006). Most accreted during the last 2500 years as a consequence of the huge outflow of river sediments caused by soil erosion, this being the result of intense deforestation accompanying demographic and economic development of the Italian peninsula (Pranzini, 1994). In addition river deltas formed in this time, and study of their beach ridges and foredunes allows reconstruction of events involving the population living in each watershed, just as tree rings allow reconstruction of past climates. In this way, detection of rapid delta growth in Roman times and erosion in the Early Middle Ages may be documented, a consequence of social instability caused by the fall of the Roman Empire. A new expansion started around 1000 CE with intense episodes in the 14th, 17th and 18th centuries. These were periods of great economic and demographic growth; the last one, in particular, saw widespread forest cutting to produce coal for the industrial boom. Erosion phases were also recognized in this period; the most evident one (14th century) can be related to the Black Death, which halved the Italian population and induced a strong forestry expansion, since most cultivated land was abandoned (Pranzini, 2001). Therefore, the wide Italian beaches are the result of what is defined today as a policy of land theft, based on progressive reduction of naturally vegetated areas, inducing landslides, accelerated soil erosion and floods.

Italian beach erosion started in the mid-19th century as a consequence of marsh reclamation, reduction of cultivated areas, reforestation and slope stabilization. River sediment outflow was also reduced by dam construction and riverbed quarrying. Erosion started just when the population commenced migrating from inland areas to the coast. This migration was triggered by the eradication of malaria, the economic opportunities offered by reclaimed coastal land and development of the road and railway network; later, it was stimulated by the use of shores for recreational purposes. New towns called 'marinas' arose at that time, twins of settlements that could not in the past be situated on the sea for reasons of military and health safety. Most of these new settlements immediately had to tackle the problem of beach erosion.

Beach erosion gradually spread to ever wider coastal segments, so that today 42 per cent of Italian beaches are eroding, not considering segments protected by coastal structures and those that are stable or accreting thanks to their position updrift of harbours (GNRAC, 2006). In 1907, when erosion was affecting many coastal settlements, Italy passed a law making huge financial resources available for defence of coastal towns menaced by marine erosion. The main goal, if not the only one, was shoreline stabilization, without any attention to beach preservation, whose environmental and economic value had not been fully recognized.

Technical expertise came from harbour engineers who defended the coast with hard structures, mainly seawalls, detached breakwaters and groynes, forever modifying the Italian coastal landscape. In many cases, these hard structures did not solve the problem but shifted it to downdrift beaches, where more structures were built. An example is given by the Northern Adriatic coast, where erosion of small coastal segments, induced by the feeding effects of jetties protecting entrances of several river harbours, was countered by hard structures that replicated the problem downdrift; this approach produced tens of kilometres of armoured coastline. This solution was favoured in Italy by a wide availability of rock along the coast or a few kilometres inland, whereas the 'culture' of sand dredging was limited because of the scarcity of fluvial and lagoon harbours. In other countries, for example in Northern Europe, the logical answer to beach erosion was artificial nourishment, using the technologies (and frequently the sand) from harbour entrance maintenance.

Therefore, the Italian coast was covered with increasingly large and frequent breakwaters, and in some places more than 2km of hard structures protect each kilometre of coast, as at Marina di Massa. At Marina di Pisa, the 2km-long waterfront is protected by a seawall, ten detached breakwaters and some groynes, giving a total of 4.5 km of hard structures. The Italian coastal landscape was strongly modified and beach value reduced even when they were maintained or restored; what was defended was losing value because of the defence itself. Urban beaches were lost where buildings or roads prevented any 'guided' retreat; yet, outside of towns, tourist flow to the coast created conditions for which shoreline stabilization was required. After the Second World War, tourism industry growth further destroyed more natural environments, with holiday village development on dunes, the most sensitive part of the coastal zone. When beach erosion reached these areas, hard protection measures were applied, since it was no longer feasible to use dunes as buffers to moderate the process.

More recently, a soft shore protection strategy has been adopted in Italy, although very massive hard structures were sometimes realized under this term, albeit below sea level. However, the main soft shore protection strategy is based on artificial beach nourishment using sediment coming from inland quarries or offshore deposits, a technique recently supported by recommendations of the UN Intergovernment Panel on Climate Change (IPCC, 2001). An increasing ability to dredge at greater depths has driven the sediment search to the continental shelf edge and to sites far from the feeding areas. Approximately 20 million cubic metres of marine aggregates have been used for beach nourishment in the last ten years, mostly in Veneto, Latium and Emilia-Romagna (Pranzini, 2004). Although this is a huge volume, it is nothing compared to the 50 million cubic metres dredged each year along the US coast and to the 28 million cubic metres used in Europe every year (Hanson et al, 2002), which shows the importance of this technique in shore protection.

It is now possible to protect the coast with softer, more sustainable solutions, but the 'achaeostructures' built in the last century are still present along the Italian coast, and still produce negative effects. In many cases, their sudden conversion into softer defences is impossible, since they strongly induce profile deepening. Therefore, a gradual conversion is necessary, both to reduce maintenance costs and to return to a more natural coastal environment, able to sustain an increasing tourist demand. The motto 'Back to the beach' has been adopted for some projects currently being realized in Tuscany, aimed at a gradual return to more natural coastal morphologies (Aminti et al, 2003).

Transition often requires conversion of ripraps and seawalls into gravel beaches. Due to the permeability and porosity of coarse sediments, gravel beaches are more stable than sand beaches and can substitute for hard structures in coastal defence, with reduced costs and the possibility to utilize a beach for recreational activities (Cammelli et al, 2005). This possibility can be applied to urban coasts defended by seawalls, where the sea–land transition is now delegated to a strip of stones. This morphological waterfront recovery provides opportunities to seek new possibilities for the sea–land interface. Creation of a new beach where mounds of rocks are now present will be accompanied by an extensive land reclamation project. In this case, conversion of an old structure into gravel beaches will be an opportunity for land upgrading. In other cases, old structures are converted into new ones, as is happening at Follonica (Tuscany), where groynes are removed and detached breakwaters razed to –0.5m. Later, artificial nourishment will give the town a more natural beach.

Within this national framework, the two cases presented here show stakeholder's expectancies and the technical and legal problems related to the need for beaches for recreational use. Both beaches are in Sardinia (see Figure CS6.1), where 36 per cent of the 1117km of sandy coast are eroding, although at a moderate rate, and cover the case of an urban beach, intensively used by local people, and of a beach artificially created to answer the needs of the tourist industry.

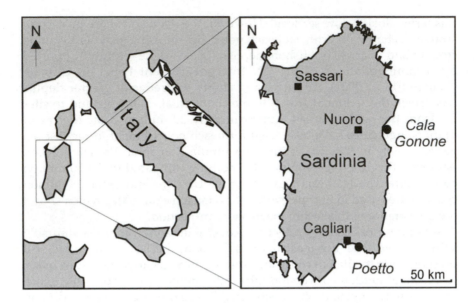

Figure CS6.1 *Location map of the two cases presented*

POETTO BEACH (CAGLIARI, SARDINIA)

Poetto, the urban beach of Cagliari (southern Sardinia), is located on a 7km-long barrier closing the Quartu lagoon and faces the wide Gulf of Cagliari (see Figure CS6.2). The beach comprises white quarz-feldspathic sand (quartz 87.3 per cent) mostly in the range 0.2–0.4mm, with some shell fragments (MSS, 1989). The lagoon is a Ramsar area and hosts a colony of several hundreds of flamingos. The coast extends from the municipality of Cagliari, in the west, to the municipality of Quartu, in the east.

The beach is intensively used as a summer bathing site, mostly by local people. It is also frequented in other seasons for open air activities, lunch breaks, dinners and cocktail parties in the many small facilities located on the beach. The town centre proximity and good availability of bus connections make it a valuable recreational urban area, accomplishing a very important social function in allowing beach use to all social classes. Site names along the barrier are named after the stop numbers of the tram that used to transport bathers to the coast after 1912. At that time, small wooden huts were present on the beach, which had then the look of a chaotic but charming 'shantytown', as can be seen from the many 'Poetto as it was' books published in recent years to celebrate this town symbol (see Figure CS6.3).

In spite of the attachment of the Cagliaritans to this site, the beach and nearshore were always considered as a cheap quarrying area by the construction industry. This activity increased significantly during the 1950s, due to sand demand for town reconstruction, which had

Figure CS6.2 *Poetto beach (Cagliari): Aerial view of the nourished sector from west to east*

Figure CS6.3 *The wooden huts at Poetto and the tram connecting the beach with the town centre (approximately 1950s)*

been widely destroyed during Second World War bombardments. The coastal authority realized that this exploitation was inducing beach erosion and issued an ordinance according to which sand mining was allowed only if the extracted sand volume would be replaced with ruins deriving from building demolition. This was a 'good practice' at that time, in an environment that even then was intensively used for recreational activities.

Nearshore dredging activities continued to be carried out, both authorized and unauthorized, during the 1960s and probably the 1970s. They are considered to be the main process responsible for the beach sediment deficit, estimated as 2 million cubic metres from 1943 to 1989, from which 75 per cent was located in the nearshore (MSS, 1989). A report entitled 'Volume Deficit', part of the restoration project (see below) updated the loss to the year 1997 with a value of 3 million cubic metres; it also gave some useful information, among which was the presence of a basement, buried in 1992 and now elevated to 55cm above the beach surface. During this period all huts were demolished and only a few small buildings restored to be used as bathing facilities, bars and restaurants. Public use of the beach was secured, but the flat barrier surface was easily swept by strong winds that transported sand onto the sea and lagoon. The wind-induced sand loss was 3000–7500m^3/km each year, according to data presented in documents supporting the project (MSS, 1989; Modimar, 1999, 2001).

Beach erosion and surface lowering made this beach prone to frequent flooding during moderate storms, with run-up reaching the coastal road under extreme events. Gravel and pebbles from old foundations and the ruins were exhumed more and more frequently, transforming Poetto beach from a very fine sandy shore into a mixed sand and gravel beach (see Figure CS6.4). Additional gravel came from some coarser layers or lenses comprising the barrier core when upper layers were eroded.

Several requests for financial support were made by the two munici-palities, the province and the region[1] to design and carry out a restoration project, but only in 1998 did the region succeed in getting IL30,000 million (approximately €15,494,000) within the 'Programma operativo di difesa ambientale, di risanamento del suolo e di salvaguardia delle coste in seguito a dissesti idrogeologici' of the Protezione Civile. The region designated the province as executing agency and as end payee of the funds. Two different projects were included in this budget: the construction of a new coastal road in order to close the present one that runs near the beach, and the realization of beach nourishment and an artificial dune.

The definitive beach restoration project was designed in 1997 by the province, based on research results obtained by Mediterranean Survey and Services (MSS, 1989) on behalf of the Ministry of the Environment, Regione Autonoma della Sardegna and Provincia di Cagliari; this executive project dates from June 1999.[2] The Sardinia Regional Authority requested an incidence evaluation[3] of Montelargius lagoon, the latter being part of a regional park and Site of Community Importance (SIC) (Habitat directive 92/43/CEE); this evaluation was performed in 1999. In October 2000, the European Commission asked for an environmental impact evaluation (EIA) but the Regione Sardegna subsequently decided that the project could be carried out without any environmental impact analysis.

Source: Photograph courtesy of Felice Di Gregorio

Figure CS6.4 *Cobbles and pebbles on the Poetto beach before the nourishment*

A first phase of the project planned a beach nourishment of 370,000m³ of fine sand (from 1.00–0.250mm) to be performed on the western side of the coast, the sector mostly hit by erosion. The required size of the borrow sediment was determined on the basis of native sediment characteristics, derived from the grain size distribution of several swash-zone samples (indicating 5.00–0.125mm to be acceptable). Considering the extreme environmental value of Poetto, a step-by-step execution was planned (two years of work with a filling of 185,000m³/yr), to be followed by properly designed monitoring. The project designer stated that fill material should come from inland quarries, and clearly warned that the use of offshore sediments could not grant good quality results due to the requirement of completing the work in a short time and to the impossibility of obtaining complete knowledge of grain size and mineralogy of source sediments. Therefore monitoring could not provide information to improve the project in such a time-compressed work period.

Shortly before the request for tenders for this project, the Cagliari municipality asked the province to clearly state in the request that the possibility of using offshore sediments should be evaluated by the winning party. Therefore, the tender established that the winning group should carry out, at its own expenses, search and characterization of offshore sediments; the choice between this material and sand from the inland quarries was delegated to a monitoring committee, to be officially entrusted by the province.

A group of companies proposing exclusive use of offshore sediments won the tender, but at the time did not provide the authorities with any samples. After contract signature, they performed seismic profiling and coring on a 'wide area' extending over the shelf in the Gulf of Cagliari, which allowed identification of sediments considered to be suitable for the beach nourishment below a blackish layer, mostly comprising shell fragments, averaging 1m in thickness. Grain size, mineralogical composition, colour and percentage of shell fragments were not the same as those of the native sand (for example the percentage of shell fragments in the borrow material was approximately 20 per cent, whereas in the native sediments this value was 1 per cent). However, the province, as contracting agency, accepted it, stating that by considering the use of offshore sediments in the tender they implicitly accepted the impossibility of respecting the sediment specification described in the same tender.

The group of companies that came second at the adjudication promoted an administrative suit against the winners, since marine sediments, used to justify the knockdown offer, did not fit the size range provided in the tender: a long and complex net of administrative resources developed, with uneven results. After a first debate, favourable to the applier, the winner proposed the use of land materials at the same price, but this solution was not acceptable being provided after the tender closure. The province ended up requesting the advice of a collegiate of legal experts on how to proceed; this led to the victory of the originally winners, who maintained the contract. From January to August 2001, additional geophysical surveys were performed by the winning party but this time on a 'smaller area' on the eastern side of the gulf, where several cores were taken. A potential sediment source was detected between 35 and 50m of water depth with a thickness of more than 2m, where medium-sized (1.00–0.25mm) quartz-feldspathic (41–66 per cent quartz) sand was present; gravel and pebble layers were also found. Approximately 22 per cent of carbonates (mostly shell fragments) and 1–7 per cent of fines were present (the latter to be lost by overflow during the dredging work). The blackish bioclastic layer appeared to be significantly reduced.

No authorization for dredging had yet been given by the Ministry of the Environment and therefore the legal availability of the sediment was still uncertain. After a technical meeting at the Ministry of the Environment in November 2001, the Province of Cagliari was finally authorized to promote dredging over a smaller area of 1000m by 400m at a depth of 1m, 3 nautical miles off the coast and at distance of over 750m from existing *Posidonia oceanica* prairie. No skimming was authorized to remove the upper blackish layer.

Authorization from the Ministry of the Environment determined that all nourishment activities needed to be performed within two months, which greatly reduced the effectiveness of activities by the monitoring committee. The Ministry, however, did not allow dredging in the area that had been first requested by the province (under the advice of the winning group), since it was too close to a *Posidonia oceanica* meadow, but instead gave authorization for dredging in a nearby area. It is worth stressing that cores taken in the 'smaller area' were far less numerous than those established in the ministerial decree, which defined which studies were required for authorizing offshore dredging (DM 26/01/1996). No cores at all were available regarding information on sediment characteristics in the second area, where the Ministry had authorized dredging to be performed.

After several delays due to legal disputes, dredging and nourishment activities started in March 2002. In order to be able to dredge 385,000m^3 of sand over a 400,000m^2 surface and at a depth of 1m, no sediment selection was possible, and in practice 'everything' was taken. Immediately most of the population in Cagliari expressed its disappointment with the sediment arriving on the beach: coarser, darker and full of shell fragments when compared with the original quartz sand that once formed the beach (see Figure CS6.5).

In spite of this and after some technical interruption, in May 2002 the nourishment project was executed and no one responsible for the project thought it wise to interrupt the work, because monitoring showed the presence of sediment that had characteristics within the project grain-size range. In April the upper layer of the beach was 'grided' (mechanically raked) to take out coarser clasts (over3cm).

Grain-size analysis performed by the University of Parma for the province on five samples collected from the beach in June 2002 showed that fines (up to 0.063mm) were less than 1 per cent, but coarse sediments (over 2mm) ranged from 0.2–36.4 per cent. The latter should have been present in quantities well above those from the fill material since sampling was carried out after beach 'griding'. Mineralogical analysis performed on the same samples gave a quartz/feldspar ratio within 55/45–65/35, whereas the tender had established it to be 85/15. As far as bio-clasts were concerned, a percentage between 43.4 and 67.1 was found, with a mean value of 54.6, which was far higher than what was present on the upper layer of the nearest core to the dredging site (21.9 per cent).

Frequent visitors to Poetto found that after renourishment, the beach was enriched with gravel, pebbles and stones, the swash zone became steeper (so much so that children and elderly people found it more difficult to enter the sea) and the water became less transparent because of suspended sediment (possibly produced by the abrasion of the shell fragments). In addition, after sea storms and heavy rains, wide ponds formed on the berm (see Figure CS6.6) more frequently than previously due to limited infiltration, supporting the development of algae that smelled while drying. The local press presented daily notes and letters from readers on this matter, which often appeared in the national press.

Based on the deleterious results from the Poetto renourishment, some stakeholders, including environmental organizations and, later, Regione Sardegna, started an action for damages, which is currently still

(a)

(b)

Figure CS6.5 *(a) Shell fragments and granules in the fill material; (b) the beach in the eastern side of the gulf, where the original material is still present*

Figure CS6.6 *Poetto beach: Ponds forming on the beach during intense rain or sea storms*

in progress. Regione Sardegna formed a consultant group to (1) analyse the administrative and technical procedures used during the setting and execution of the project, and (2) provide alternatives for restoring the pristine characteristics of the beach.

Results of the group for the first question (a) are summarized:

- The original design was careful about the environment and beach use, although sand available from the possible quarries was more yellow in colour than the original sand.
- A real project assessment for dredging and beach filling from the sea was never performed and work was based on the transposition of the previous project that had been based on quarried sand.
- The borrow material was practically unknown, since no cores were taken inside the authorized area.
- In-progress controls could have hardly halted the work since no alternative discharge area was available for unsuitable sediments, plus making the dredging ship stop activities could entail the payment of a very expensive penalty.
- No stakeholder participation was provided for during the design and approval phases of the project; expectations were of fine quartz sand like that present at Poetto, and which now remains rooted in common imagination.

As far as alternatives for the restoration project are concerned, removal of the fill material is not considered advisable for many reasons:

- The sand is not polluted and there is no risk for beach users, except for the difficulties of children and elderly people in entering into the sea (although this is a problem present on many beaches, it had not previously affected Poetto).
- It would be impossible to remove all nearshore sediments and the remaining material could move onshore under swell conditions.
- According to the law, the sand, due to its marine origin, would need to be relocated in a dump area at a high cost. A cost-effective possibility is relocation to another beach within 30km of Poetto, but other municipalities would hardly accept this 'rubbish'.

Three solutions were analysed:

- Ordinary and extraordinary maintenance works based on a first gravel extraction from the upper layer mobilizing approximately 10,000m³ of sediments. This implies an increase of water turbidity since more shell fragments will be exhumed as the swash zone will have lost most. Gravel will continuously accumulate on the step and on the storm berm crest; from here continuous cleaning is necessary during the summertime. Since the fill is gradually reducing in volume, due to both longshore transport and loss of shell fragments, additional nourishment could be done using better-sized sediments.
- Burial of the fill material under new sediments, which are available in Sardinia. The previously considered quarries can produce a yellow coloured medium-sized quartz sand, and from northern Sardinia fine grained sand even whiter that the original one. This hypothesis entails a beach expansion that could affect a long coastal sector since the beach now has a logarithmic spiral form that must shift offshore to prevent formation of a salient easily attacked by the erosion.
- Replacement of the upper marine sand layer with the sediment that is present below. Eleven 13m-long cores were taken on the berm in areas free from buildings in order to analyse barrier stratigraphy on the nourished sector. Most comprised white sand similar to that which was once present on the surface. It is therefore possible to dig a trench taking approximately 400,000m³ of this material to bury the fill material. Substitutions of sand unsuitable for beach nourishment were performed at Iesolo (Venice) where native golden-yellow sand now covers a trench filled with very fine dark sediments.

Very likely, no action will be initiated until the legal trial is closed and people are gradually getting used to the beach, which partially answers the requirements of coastal protection, the original goal of the project for the financing minister. Since any solution is technically, legally and politically difficult, the white fine sand will probably remain nothing but a recollection in the minds of elderly Cagliaritans.

CALA GONONE BEACH (DORGALI, SARDINIA)

Cala Gonone is a small village situated in the central part of the Golfo di Orosei (Eastern Sardinia) (see Figure CS6.1), where a tectonic dolomite-limestone coast is characterized by plunging cliffs (Sunamura, 1992) cut by a few creeks, and the area is unable to develop large beaches since sediment production is limited in permeable and soluble rocks. A discontinuous Quaternary basalt coverage dips into the sea with a mild slope, but even here beaches are not very frequent. The only beaches available for summer guests are placed in a small cove created by the harbour and at the cliff toe comprising poorly cemented Pleistocene deposits ('*gretz litées*' or '*éboulis ordonées*') (Özer and Ulzega, 1980), which is the only effective source of sediment for this coast (Mania and Pranzini, 1996). Finer sediments derive from some larger creeks that flow into the sea further to the south, but the high wave energy (wave height up to 8m; Cicala, 1998) does not allow deposition on the dry beach and are present only in the nearshore (Mania and Pranzini, 1996).

Until the 1960s, Cala Gonone had only a few houses located near a small harbour that supported the activity of some fishermen and those taking tourists to see the Grotta del Bue Marino – a cave accessible only by sea and famous as the last Mediterranean site where until a few years ago *Foca monaca* could be still found. The beauty of this site, with sea caves, rock arches and canyon, started to attract more and more tourists, and Cala Gonone has became one of the most visited coastal settlements of Sardinia (Arba et al, 2002). A few tourist resorts developed along the coast, and construction of several summer houses extended from the shore up the hills (see Figure CS6.7).

A shortage of beaches induced visitors to reach Cala Luna, an extremely beautiful and environmentally sensitive beach located at a canyon mouth where the river course is closed by a sand bar forming a small marsh (see Figure CS6.8). Along the coast an almost continuous notch marks sea-level position reached during the last interglacial period – (125,000 years BP at approximately 8m above sea level (asl) (Carobene, 1972); in addition, some small caves formed in the cliff added an extra appeal to the site. Since Cala Luna is reached only after four hours of walking along a path path, ferrymen extended their routes in order to include this site, and now during summer, hundreds of people crowd onto this beach and on the riverbank threatening the integrity of this ecosystem.

In order to strengthen the local tourism industry and simultaneously reduce human impact at Cala Luna, nourishment of the small beaches located near the village and the creation of new ones were considered necessary. In addition, landslides induced by toe erosion of an

Figure CS6.7 *Cala Gonone: (a) the urban development south of the harbour and (b) the Palmasera new tourist settlement*

unconsolidated cliff during intense storm events were threatening the road and tourist residences that had been built on the cliff top and these would also clearly benefit from nourishment works. On this coastal segment, two 30m-long groynes had been built in the 1980s to induce beach expansion,

Figure CS6.8 *Cala Luna: A sand bar closes the river mouth*
and creates a valuable marsh

and nourishment was performed in the early 1990s with 3000m³ of fine sediments taken from the dredging of the Bue Marino cave entrance. However, no long-lasting results were obtained.

In 1988, Regione Sardegna financed a project of coastal restoration (see Figure CS6.9). This was developed by Studio Volta (Studio Volta, 1988), based on geomorphological and sedimentological studies performed by the University of Florence (Mania and Pranzini, 1996) and on sea climate studies carried out by Cicala (1998). A three-dimensional physical model was set up at HR Wallingford's UK facilities, using anthracite to simulate the sediment dynamics (HR Wallingford, 1993). The unspoilt nature of the area, which was to become a national marine park, led to the decision to avoid large breakwaters to protect the beach, basing the project on artificial shoals that should work both as groynes and artificial islands. In order to make these look as close as possible to natural features, loose basaltic blocks were used for their construction in order to replicate similar morphologies that were present along the coast (boulders fallen from cliffs into the sea). To build these 'semi-natural' shoals, rounded boulders were collected in the countryside, giving great satisfaction to farmers and providing stones that looked more natural than those produced by quarries. Three groynes and three shoals were designed, the latter on the 2–3m isobath reaching mean sea level. In a high-energy environment such as this coast, they could not guarantee sand beach stability and therefore a gravel beach was preferred, to be created by a nourishment of 80,000m³.

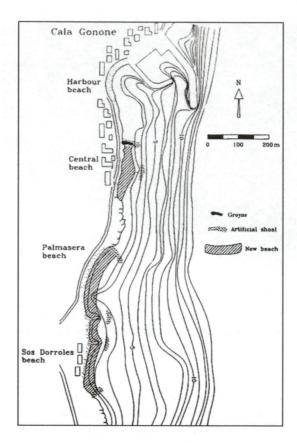

Figure CS6.9 *Cala Gonone beach restoration project*

Since no gravel is available in this part of Sardinia, it had to be produced by crushing hard rock from a white limestone quarry located 40km from Cala Gonone. Sediments from 40mm to 1mm in diameter were used for fill, with the addition of some sand from the dredging of a harbour entrance situated to the north. The coarsest fraction (40–20mm) was used to construct causeways necessary to build the shoals, and these were later covered by finer ones that constituted the real fill. In-progress checks ensured that fines (less than 0.063mm) were below 2 per cent in order not to induce water turbidity, which could have damaged the existing *Posidonia oceanica* meadow in the nearshore area.

Between autumn 1994 and spring 1995, after construction of the protection structures, approximately 23,000m³ of sediment were deposited on the beach: 10,000m³ on the Central Beach, 6000m³ on Palmasera Beach and 7000m³ at Sos Dorroles. Beach expansion was approximately 25m on the Central Beach (where no beach was present before the beginning of the works), and 10m on Palmasera and Sos Dorroles. During renourishment work, the fill was razed three times to approximately 30cm below sea level; and each time the berm was naturally rebuilt in a few days of moderate storm activity. Gravel, which originally was very angular (0.2 in the scale proposed by Krumbein, 1941), was reasonably rounded (0.4) one year later, which supported the tourist activity.

After the summer break, the company executing the work left the contract; and work resumed in the autumn of 1996 and finished in June 1997. A beach profiling carried out on May 1996 showed that almost all the fill had remained and grains had rounded to 0.5–0.6. The fill underwent a grain size separation, with the loss of the finest fraction, so that the beach ended up being formed mostly by grains in the range 1–8mm) (Pacini et al, 1997).

The new company that had won the tender for completing the project did not have the availability of the limestone quarry and proposed a pink granite beach fill. The material was extremely weathered and grains had been naturally separated during excavation, producing coarse sand (approximately 80 per cent within the range 1–8mm), which was accepted by the designer since previous studies had shown that this material is stable on the shore face. A fine tail was present in the grain-size distribution due to the presence of biotite lamellae. The remaining 57,000m^3 were discharged between autumn 1996 and spring 1997 and, due to the limited sharpness of the granules, the beach was fully enjoyed by users the following summer (see Figure CS6.10 and CS6.11).

In November 1997, a week of strong easterly winds produced a sea storm with a return period evaluated as 1 in 50 years, and damage of approximately €1 million was caused to the harbour breakwater. Beach profiling carried out on January 1998 proved that the beach remained stable on many sectors, where a berm crest at more than 3m asl was formed; wherever the beach was originally shorter, waves reached the wall supporting the coastal road and a flat profile formed. Some sediment moved to the harbour beach, since the northern groyne of the nourished sector was undersized. These results reflected the designer's decision to allow some overpassing in order to increase the dimensions of the harbour beach, in which no nourishment had been performed.

A further survey performed in 2002 to assess if the beach had remained stable, found that only a small amount of fine sand had moved to deeper water. Limestone gravel had been slightly rounded, reducing in size, whereas granite elements that continued being disaggregated were more pronounced and reduced in size. Roundness was found to be 0.6–0.7 for limestone and 0.4 for granite. Permeability and porosity of the borrow material was mainly responsible for the greater stability of the beach, both where the original beach expanded and where a new shore was constructed. Most beach visitors did not realize that the shoals present along the coast were artificial. A pink beach, present in other sites of northern Sardinia, where granite is the dominant rock, is a new attraction in this part of the coast. Sediment colour is the only aspect of the project that

(a)

(b)

Figure CS6.10 *Cala Gonone Central Beach (a) at the beginning of the nourishment and (b) at the end of the works*

is under discussion; some assess that it gives the beach an 'artificial' aspect, displacing it out of the natural local landscape context and differentiating it from all the natural beaches of the Gulf of Orosei that are characterized by calcareous sediments (Arba et al, 2002). Nevertheless the project was

(a)

(b)

Figure CS6.11 *Palmasera beach (a) before the nourishment and (b) after completion of works*

awarded the Mediterranean Prize for landscape, and comments of local stakeholders are positive, mostly because tourism is increasing in both 'number of visitors' and 'length of the tourist season'.

NOTES

1 In Italy, there are four administrative divisions: national (*stato*), regional (*regione*), provincial (*provincia*) and municipal (*comune*).
2 Italian law on public works defines three stages of planning: preliminary, definitive and executive.
3 Articles 6 and 7 of 92/43/EEC define Special Zones of Protection, where special measures of protection are set in order to avoid the habitat's degradation and where any other plan or project must be submitted to incidence evaluation.

A Proactive Programme for Managing Beaches and Dunes on a Developed Coast: A Case Study of Avalon, New Jersey, USA

Karl F. Nordstrom, Nancy L. Jackson and Harry A. de Butts

INTRODUCTION

Local governments can play a major role in management of coastal resources (Platt, 1994), but effects are highly variable and examples of bad and good management exist. Local governments may ignore the need to restrict shorefront development, reduce the likelihood of coastal hazards, protect natural coastal landscapes or build awareness about good practices (Gares, 1989; Good, 1994; Fischer et al, 1995), or they may render policies of higher levels of government ineffective because of lack of commitment (Burby and Dalton, 1993). Lack of emphasis on preservation of natural aspects of beaches and dunes is another problem (Healy and Zinn, 1985; Guilcher and Hallégouët, 1991).

Management of coastal resources at the local level does have many advantages. Local officials are familiar with local interests, are directly accountable to landowners and operate at the landform scale (Nordstrom, 2000). Regulations can be easier to enforce at the local level. Municipalities can go beyond minimum state/provincial requirements for reducing hazards and protecting resources (Beatley et al, 1994) and implement more stringent requirements for coastal construction (Yazdani and Ycaza, 1995). They can fund their own comprehensive beach management programmes, designate their own preservation areas and conduct their own restoration projects (Sanjaume, 1988; Breton and Esteban, 1995). Some municipalities have comprehensive programmes for maintaining dunes, strong ordinances regulating activities in them and a municipal budget for sand fences and programmes for planting vegetation (Godfrey, 1987; Mauriello and Halsey, 1987; Mauriello, 1989). Volunteer activities are best mobilized at the local level and can include beach cleaning (Breton and Esteban, 1995) and 'adopt a dune' programmes (Carlson and Godfrey, 1989).

Examples of good local approaches exist (City of Stirling, 1984; Best, 2003), but more case studies are needed to address the variability of potential scenarios and provide municipal managers with more alternatives. This case study identifies an approach to managing developed shorefront municipalities on barrier islands, with a focus on restoring and maintaining dunes. Avalon, New Jersey, is the study area because it has the most active, independent and creative beach and dune management programme in the state. Previous studies of ways that human actions changed landforms in Avalon include Jackson et al (2000) and Nordstrom et al (2002).

SITE CHARACTERISTICS

Avalon is on the north end of a sandy barrier island (see Figure CS7.1). The town was incorporated as a borough in 1892 and had an extensive infrastructure by 1910. There are approximately 30 businesses and 5600 residences, with 2000 residents living in 1000 homes all year round. Summer populations reach about 70,000 people during the day. Properties in Avalon are expensive. Old buildings are often eliminated to make room for larger residences. About 150 to 300 of the houses are rebuilt each year. Shorefront development consists primarily of single- and multi-family houses.

Net sediment transport is to the south. The storms that have had major effects on shoreline change are mid-latitude cyclones, but tropical storms occasionally cause damage. Shoreline types (see Figure CS7.1) include: (1) a sand-starved segment in the throat of Townsend Inlet, protected by a bulkhead/revetment; (2) a dynamic ocean-facing segment south of the inlet (called the 'improved beach' because it is an engineered structure

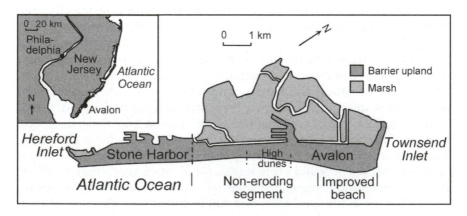

Figure CS7.1 *Study area, Avalon, New Jersey, showing segments where different natural processes and management practices have resulted in different dune characteristics*

Figure CS7.2 *The maritime forest in the high dunes area*

designed for shore protection); and (3) a non-eroding segment containing an undeveloped 1.5km-long section with remnant high dunes covered in maritime forest (see Figure CS7.2). The north end of the island has erosion problems caused by cycles of shoreline accretion and scour related to natural and dredging-induced alterations to the inlet ebb channel (Farrell and Sinton, 1983; Jackson et al, 2000).

Beach berm widths range from over 100m in the undeveloped segment to (at times) 0m on the improved beach. The developed ocean shore has protective foredunes built using sand fences or earth-moving equipment (see Figure CS7.3). Beaches in developed segments are raked to make the surface more desirable for recreation. Driving on the beach by private vehicles is not permitted, but municipal vehicles may use the beach between 15 September and 1 April, when there are no nesting birds and when tourist use is not intensive.

The municipal beach management plan (Avalon, 1998) concentrates on flood mitigation. Efforts to decrease hazards include increasing dune elevations, protecting the dune system from degrading human actions, replenishing beach sediment in nourishment operations, maintaining sediment budgets by backpassing, enacting and enforcing building codes, constructing seawalls and bulkheads at the north end of town, installing an outdoor flood warning system, flood-proofing infrastructure, and

Figure CS7.3 *The dune created in 1987 in the southern portion of the improved beach, showing the foredune crest on the right created by sand fences and the species diversity on the left resulting from protection by the high crest*

raising bulkheads on the landward side of the island. Dune revegetation with American beach grass (*Ammophila breviligulata*) is done at the scale of the entire municipality. Repair and replacement of damaged dune fences and emplacement of new fences are conducted as necessary.

RECENT HISTORY OF MANAGEMENT ACTIONS

A disastrous storm in March 1962 led to an aggressive programme for managing dunes. Actions included building dunes along the entire ocean front using sand fences and vegetation plantings and raising $165,000 to purchase undeveloped shorefront lots to retain a natural environment and reduce future property losses. The value, use and control of dunes were subsequently codified in regulations in 1967, 1968 and 1978. The programmes for dune building and purchase of properties were initially resisted by many landowners because of the costs and restrictions to access and views of the sea, but acceptance of dunes as shore protection has occurred over time through constant effort by the municipal authorities.

Avalon became a member of the National Flood Insurance Program as soon as it was available, providing an incentive to increase dune heights to protect against flooding. Insurance premiums are based on degree of risk, and municipal efforts to reduce vulnerability through dune building decreased premiums by 20 per cent over standard national rates (Avalon, 2007).

Artificial beach nourishment has been critical in maintaining dune integrity. The amount of fill placed in Avalon is nearly 5 million cubic metres, excluding sediment replaced by backpassing. The first large-scale project was in 1987 when 1,026,000m³ of fill were emplaced and the 2.5km-long improved beach was created. Dunes were built by bulldozers to 3.7m above mean low water according to guidelines by the Federal Emergency Management Agency (FEMA). The designation and maintenance of the improved beach as an engineering structure meant that FEMA could reimburse the municipality for sediment lost during subsequent storms at a 65/35 federal/non-federal cost share, where three-quarters of the non-federal share is paid by the state.

Maintenance of critically eroding sections of the improved beach by backpassing sediment was begun by the municipality in the early 1990s using three large pieces of surplus earth-moving equipment. Beach sand was transferred from the non-eroding segment at a rate of about 38,000m³ per year, which approximated the rate of loss. The cost was only about $0.75 per cubic metre in the late 1990s (Nordstrom et al, 2002). The municipality is not presently allowed to backpass sediment because the US Army Corps of Engineers declared that the operation would deliver sediment from a point source to the inter-tidal waters, which are under their jurisdiction. Backpassing is suspended until a Corps review of the effects of backpassing is complete. This interpretation of a regulation designed to limit discharges creates an interesting paradox in that most of the sediment involved would be sediment initially deposited by the Corps in a large (1,227,000m³) project conducted by them in 2002 and the backpassing would lessen the need for maintenance nourishment of erosional hot spots.

An evaluation of the potential impacts of a Category 3 hurricane indicated that the 1987 dune would be insufficient to protect people who could not evacuate the island, so the municipality increased the minimum dune elevation to 6.7m above mean low water using sand fences and vegetation plantings. The new foredunes are higher than in developed portions of other municipalities in New Jersey and higher than a natural dune would be this close to the water. The cross-shore zonation of vegetation in the improved beach segment (see Figure CS7.3) is typical of natural dunes, including an *Ammophila*-dominated crest and a woody shrub zone dominated by bayberry (*Myrica pennsylvanica*) farther landward. The environmental gradient is more compressed and farther seaward than it would be on a natural dune, but it provides a valuable image of nature in a location that would normally be dominated by human structures.

Public access to the beach is via pathways from the seaward ends of shore-perpendicular streets. Pathways across dunes in New Jersey are often low and subject to aeolian transport and overwash. The strategy in

Avalon is to keep pathways at the top elevation of the dune by applying gravel to the surface, preventing deflation and providing a more trafficable surface for wheelchairs, enhancing disabled access. Split rail fences (such as those shown in Figure CS7.2) are used to keep pedestrians off the dunes, in contrast to many municipalities that use sand-trapping fences. The split rail fences allow for free movement of fauna and do not cause a build up of sand that creates unnatural shore-perpendicular shapes. The high access paths reduce hazard potential and allow for the best public views of all of the cross-shore sub-environments within the dune (see Figure CS7.3).

The municipality raised the minimum height standard for new and reconstructed bulkheads on the bay/marsh side of the island and the lowest first floor of reconstructed houses. Houses must now be built 3.66m above mean low water, rather than the 3.35m identified in FEMA guidelines. Lower structures must be flood-proofed.

ADAPTIVE MANAGEMENT

The non-eroding segment and its undeveloped enclave has provided the municipality with many management options including: (1) evaluating the effects of suspending use of sand fences and beach raking; (2) providing a bird nesting area; and (3) providing locations for nature education programmes. The relationship between natural features and education is two way, in that preservation and restoration of natural areas are products of nature education efforts but the natural areas themselves serve as demonstration sites for the practicality of management actions and outreach programmes.

Most beaches in coastal towns in New Jersey are raked to remove beach wrack, resulting in elimination of the flora and fauna that would naturally colonize the beach. Dunes are often built with earth-moving equipment or sand fences and are relatively small linear dykes with little topographic diversity. Landforms and habitats on the backshore are rarely allowed to evolve by natural processes.

Experiments to evaluate results of suspending use of sand fences and raking are important in demonstrating the viability of dunes built by natural processes (Nordstrom, 2008). The undeveloped high dune area provided the opportunity to conduct this kind of experiment because it is not subject to intensive visitor use. The experiments were begun in 1991 at the request of personnel in the Wetlands Institute, a nearby research and education organization. The result of not raking or using fences is a foredune similar in volume to a dune built with fences but with a gentler seaward slope and fewer restrictions to cross-shore movement of sediment and biota.

Establishment of the bird nesting area was in response to the New Jersey State Division of Fish, Game and Wildlife requirement for municipalities to ensure that shore-nesting birds are not adversely affected by pedestrian and vehicle traffic, beach raking and beach nourishment. The undeveloped segment provided a place to accomplish this goal without restricting uses of the beach in developed areas where visitor demand is greater. Accordingly, Avalon was the first municipality to agree to a bird management plan/agreement with the state (New Jersey Division of Fish, Game and Wildlife, 1999). The undeveloped segment still has recreational value, but the type of recreation is alternative to other segments in that it is non-consumptive and nature-based, and it has great usefulness in the programme of outreach and public education.

OUTREACH AND PUBLIC EDUCATION

Municipal authorities in Avalon feel that education is crucial to acceptance of dunes. Stakeholders are encouraged to be active in the community, educate themselves about coastal protection and attend meetings of the Chamber of Commerce, Realtors Association and Land and Homeowners Association. Frequent meetings between representatives of the borough and landowners are held because the turnover in resident population is rapid. About 5 per cent of the population changes each year, and most new residents are unaware of the damaging effect of storms and the advantages of high dunes. Meetings are normally in August, when the population is largest. The meetings are open to the whole town and are announced by the press. Presentations are normally made by the director of public works and a construction official who talk about regulations concerning maintaining dunes and constructing houses to withstand storms. One of the most important take-home messages is the need to make the dunes high enough to prevent storm-wave overwash, which conflicts with resident desires for views of the beach. The basic message is 'If you see the ocean, the ocean sees you.' Another important item is finding ways to address erosion problems if state or federal funding is not available.

A municipal newsletter (*Borough of Avalon News*) and flood hazard information bulletins are regularly mailed to property owners and provided as handouts in the municipal building. Articles on the flood insurance programme and methods of reducing coastal hazards are regular features in the newsletter. Other information literature includes a description of the national flood insurance programme and a flyer containing information on nature walks in the dune, restrictions to accommodate beach-nesting birds, and other regulations on use of beaches. These items are normally located on the municipal webpage that also has links to webpages of the state, FEMA, the Wetlands Institute, the Avalon Museum and Historical Society, the Avalon public library and data on wind and wave conditions for Avalon.

Data on winds and waves are provided by the Coastal Monitoring Network established by Stevens Institute of Technology at a location offshore of the business district. Data include hourly summaries of wind speed and direction, atmospheric pressure, air and water temperature, significant wave height, wave period and water depth. A camera presents still photographs of wave conditions at five minute intervals. The data and photographs are readily accessible on the municipal website.

The historical museum traces the history of the dunes, beginning with photos from the 1890s. The photos reveal the contrast between the high forested dunes that previously characterized the landscape and the flatter treeless developed landscape of today. One interesting aspect of this comparison is that the understorey of the woodlands in the 19th century had fewer bushes and vines than the natural area today (see Figure CS7.2) due to the effects of cattle grazing. The photographs underscore both the profound impact of humans and the great differences that alternative human uses have on the landscape.

The grounds of the museum are landscaped using native coastal vegetation that contrasts markedly with the exotic species used by residents. Comments by visitors about the vegetation provide the opportunity to open a dialogue on the significance of natural landscaping on interior portions of the barrier island.

Dune planting is done using volunteer labour and treated as a public information programme as well as for shore protection. Participants invest in the process and become de facto wardens who watch over the dunes. The borough maintains a greenhouse that is used to grow vegetation for planting. The greenhouse is used by municipal workers, but it is also a component of the outreach programme. In the past, grade school children put sprigs in the greenhouse for growth in the winter and planted them in the spring. They no longer use the greenhouse for this purpose but they still plant vegetation. The greenhouse is used by the local garden club and is available for other user groups who wish to participate in restoration or demonstration programmes.

Dune stewardship is incorporated into primary education as part of the 4th grade curriculum. In-class lessons about the way plants grow and the significance of plants in the dunes are followed by a trip to the beach to plant *A. breviligulata* in late March or early April. The site to be planted is roughly three blocks long (275m) and planting by the students lasts about 90 minutes. The trips are attended by parents and siblings as well. The programme has existed for 20 years, and some of the parents participated in the plantings when they attended the school. This programme was suggested by a private citizen with an interest in dune stewardship and was successfully implemented because one of the teachers made it a permanent part of the curriculum. The cost of the vegetation is now supported by private individuals.

The Wetlands Institute is in Stone Harbor (see Figure CS7.1). Their mission is to promote appreciation and understanding of the vital role of coastal ecosystems. They have been working with Avalon to address issues of natural resource management since the institute was founded. The institute sponsors scheduled weekly guided tours of the dunes from mid-June until mid-September. The informal walks usually last between 90 and 120 minutes. Attendance ranges from 1 to 30 people. Usually the talk is about the natural setting and the impact of human modifications to the environment, including homes, dune fencing, beach-grass planting and shore protection structures. Visitor questions often refer to the development and care of the remaining maritime forest. Handouts include information about the Wetlands Institute programmes and schedule of events. The newly appointed outreach coordinator is now developing more programmes for Avalon school and community groups and the public. One programme being developed is called 'Life on a Sandy Beach', which will be geared towards elementary level students and taken into the classroom.

DISCUSSION AND CONCLUSIONS

Coastal construction is ongoing in Avalon, but it occurs through reconstruction rather than construction, and the buildings are rebuilt to higher standards of protection. At the same time, coastal landscape features are evolving more naturally and citizen awareness about the nature of coastal hazards and the value of natural features is maintained. The municipality has gone well beyond minimum state requirements for reducing coastal hazards and protecting resources. The reason is not so much that Avalon is quick to respond to policies imposed from higher levels but that the municipality already implemented policies that meet or exceed many of the standards imposed. Municipal officials are accountable to landowner needs in terms of safety, while not yielding to the desire for views of the sea.

The approach in Avalon is far-sighted relative to other municipalities in New Jersey. When their sand-fencing programme was revealing positive results in the late 1970s, only 27 of the 49 shorefront municipalities had coastal dunes at all (Nordstrom et al, 1978). The success of the dune management programme at Avalon is attributed to: (1) timing property-purchase and dune-building programmes to a period immediately after a damaging storm; (2) investing municipal economic resources in enhancing landforms as protection structures; (3) determining sediment budgets and maintaining control over local sediment supplies; (4) instituting a vigorous education programme; and (5) maintaining or augmenting biodiversity and accommodating natural processes.

Avalon is one of the wealthiest municipalities on the New Jersey shore, but it ranks in the lowest 1 per cent of overall property tax rates of the 566 municipalities in the state (Avalon, 2007). National support for projects in Avalon came about as a result of a long-term management plan and persistent actions by municipal managers to obtain state and national support. Many of the favourable programmes are due to the proactive stance taken by the municipal managers and interested citizens. These programmes, the willingness to experiment with new approaches, and the willingness to collaborate with interested people and organizations outside the borough brought new resources to the municipality, such as selection of Avalon by Stevens Institute to be part of the data-monitoring network.

Much can still be done to enhance coordination and cooperation among the entities that individually make Avalon an example of effective management. Dune walks could be improved by the development of a maritime forest, dune and beach guide that could also provide a publicity piece for programmes within the borough and the Wetlands Institute and be used for school groups that visit the area. Museum displays can focus on environmental history as well as cultural history, and signs at the beach can direct tourists to the museum for more information. The Avalon garden club now puts on flower shows for residents and tourists. They could also demonstrate the use of native vegetation on private shorefront lots to keep property owners from using exotic species and help establish a more natural image for the coast.

Initiatives such as these, which would be wishful thinking in most municipalities, can work in municipalities like Avalon, where management is effective, proactive and environmentally conscious. The influx of new residents with little or no prior experience of barrier island dynamics requires effective education programmes. The multifaceted approach of transferring information via governmental and non-governmental organizations and schools establishes and reinforces local knowledge. Many programmes in the municipality represent the initiatives of individual people. Continuation of these programmes depends on their willingness to devote time and the willingness of new people to carry on their efforts.

Analysis of Users' Perceptions at Praia Central, Balneário Camboriú (Santa Catarina, Brazil)

Marcus Polette

INTRODUCTION

Beaches, as democratic places, are shared by many different social actors holding a variety of interests, with their own organizational arrangements and various levels of socio-political engagement. According to Muehe (2000), the most important functions of beaches are protection, aesthetics, landscape, leisure and tourism. However, understanding the link between the societal longing and the growing coastland urbanization process, determined by the tourism industry, civil construction and the real estate market, remains a global challenge for beach managers. Therefore, it is imperative to propose innovative and creative environmental management initiatives following well-organized criteria oriented by guidelines and principles that not only suit current technocracy, but also fulfil expectations of these climate-change-vulnerable area users.

For managing an extensive and complex littoral, such as Brazil's coastal area, a meticulous analysis of an appropriate beach usage pattern becomes essential. Research on managerial criteria ought to have its starting point as the situation in Brazil, in order to produce more effective methodologies to support an ever-increasing participative coastal management process. In spite of the fact that planning and managing the beach environment depend on several aspects, there is a specific feature to which its utilization is conditioned: its carrying capacity. This indicator is fundamental once it demonstrates the relationship between recreational-use intensification and the quality of users' enjoyment; as the first aspect increases, the second may accordingly decrease (Silva, 2002).

Santa Catarina's centre-north littoral area, in south Brazil, expressively represents problematic and conflicting aspects regarding beaches. During the last four decades, there has been an urbanization process driven by civil construction, tourism and the real estate market that has left a legacy of problems and conflicts in shore areas, such as erosion, severe population density levels during the high season (summer), gaps in infrastructure, in addition to criteria for local environmental evaluation in which the population failed to take decisions regarding planned development. As a consequence of the absence of empowerment of several sectors of the local society, a small group of fortunate entrepreneurs became wealthy at society's expense through the privatization of benefits and socialization of damages among thousands of littoral users.

As in any coastal zone management process, changes in key population behaviour and beliefs must go through a long interest-mediation process depending on local government, private sector and beach users. To sum up, a process called coastal governance must happen. It is noteworthy that public policies, which began through plans, projects and programmes, unfortunately were not adopted by decision-makers. For instance, some coastal municipalities are growing socio-economically and are also facing a dilemma regarding their environmental quality. This fact brought to light an interesting issue about the process related to coastal development: the beach, which in the beginning attracted tourists and entrepreneurs, now presents problems regarding water pollution, inundations (see Figure CS8.1), shadowing by buildings and erosion processes reducing its shore area.

Figure CS8.1 *Inundations over Balneário Camboriú during summer of 2004*

The small municipality of Balneário Camboriú (46km²) (see Figure CS8.2 for location) fits this context since its development relies on a 6km-long beach area without minimum planning criteria. Nowadays, Balneário Camboriú possesses one of the most dynamic seasonal population flows of Brazil, which is responsible for local economic incomes obtained not only through tourism but also by the estate taxes paid by temporary residents.

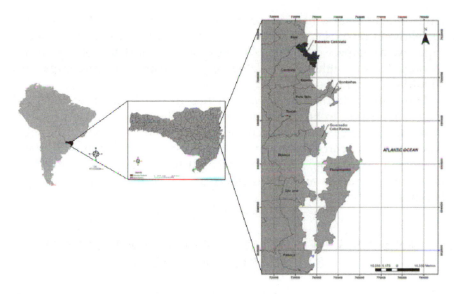

Figure CS8.2 *Balneário Camboriú municipality, Santa Catarina, south Brazil*

During winter the local population is over 100,000 habitants (IBGE, 2007) and during summer season it reaches over 1.6 million (SANTUR, 2008).

Aiming at immediately revitalizing the image of the city, sectors related to civil construction, together with the local administration, organized a project to increase the seashore area by about 120m in its entire 6km length. Through this landscape recovery, at least theoretically, local entrepreneurs and local administration aim at building a new image of the city based on beach enlargement, seashore walkway increase – including the implementation of cycling areas and promenade – in addition to a seashore avenue and the maintenance of seaside multi-family properties, some of them reaching 45 floors. The hypothesis of the project is that such a plan would increase the economic dynamics for tourism, civil construction and the real estate market.

It seems that increasing the seashore area is an acceptable alternative for both the present and future of the city, taking into account the absence of concrete solutions for existing problems. Nevertheless, it becomes necessary to comprehend local population demands and the relationship that exists between inhabitants and their living place.

By taking into account not only physical capacity but mainly social capacity during the decision-making process, Balneário Camboriú has the possibility of reaching a more democratic, equitable and inclusive development. Social capacity may be defined and understood as the perception that users of a determined tourism resource have about the higher or lower levels of congestion due to its intensive use (Pigram, 1983). Physical and social capacities are more significant to the beach environment than other indicators since this area is widely used for recreational purposes. The more restrictive characteristic of the social capacity, in comparison to others, makes it an appropriate tool to plan and manage this area, although the values of physical and ecological capacities should not be ignored.

The contribution of this research lies in understanding the local reality according to beach users' opinions. The research also proposes some adequate carrying capacity alternatives in the case of the local administrators' search for initiatives to achieve a new dynamics for land usage and occupation, taking into account the adequate comfort of the inhabitants, tourists and day-trippers at one of the liveliest Brazilian beaches.

ANALYSIS OF SOCIAL SUPPORT CAPACITY IN BALNEÁRIO CAMBORIÚ

The investigation carried out during 2005 regarding Balneário Camboriú beach users' opinions is the basis for the present social carrying capacity analysis. To accomplish this analysis, the following steps were taken: development and implementation of semi-structured interviews, which were tested through a trial application; evaluation and discussion on the questionnaires; application in all neighbourhoods of 260 questionnaires, of which 98 questionnaires were applied specifically on Balneário Camboriú seaside promenade.

To analyse the users' perspective, the present study focuses on understanding the beach users' profile. It also seeks to understand the relationship between the interviewed users and Praia Central in Balneário Camboriú regarding its water quality, shadowing caused by seashore buildings, beach comfort and enlargement of its shore area. From this, it was possible to examine strategies (see Figure CS8.3).

Profile of the interviewed users: Praia Central

Of the group of 260 citizens interviewed, 77 per cent used the beach, while 23 per cent did not. Considering only the users, 64 per cent went to the beach with their families, while 28 per cent went together with friends and 8 per cent went alone. These results showed the predominant family use of Praia Central in Balneário Camboriú.

Analysis of how often users go to the beach indicated that 28 per cent used it during the weekends, 17 per cent once a week, 15 per cent used it daily and 40 per cent used it sporadically. Regarding the importance of the beach area for these users, 29 per cent considered it as an important leisure area, 18 per cent stated that it was an ideal place for walking, 15 per cent considered it useful for personal aesthetic purposes (sunbathing), while

Figure CS8.3 *Balneário Camboriú is considered the most densely occupied resort in south Brazil during summer*

14 per cent considered it useful because of the sports played there and 24 per cent gave other diverse answers.

It was also possible to gather information on infrastructure considered relevant by users interviewed. Sanitation was judged to be a fundamental aspect by 55 per cent, 26 per cent believed beach cleanliness was important and 19 per cent valued other aspects. Beach users were also asked about how deep in the water they usually go, using the waistline as a reference. The number of people who swim or go deeper than this waistline was around 64 per cent, while 29 per cent went up to the stomach line and only 7 per cent remained at shallower depths.

Users' concern about water quality in Praia Central

Considering all the citizens interviewed, a surprisingly high percentage of 66 per cent did not check signs verifying water quality, while 34 per cent checked water quality before bathing. Moreover, regarding water quality perception by the interviewed citizens, 64 per cent considered the water to be of 'bad' quality, 29 per cent judged it to be 'regular' and only 7 per cent considered it as 'good'. According to previously assembled data, the local administration emerges as the main body responsible for improvements in Praia Central's water quality in Balneário Camboriú. According to the interviewed citizens, 54 per cent had never had health problems caused by bathing at Praia Central, whereas 46 per cent had. Considering the users who had their health affected, 61 per cent reported suffering from mycosis.

Users' concerns about shadowing in Praia Central

Among the most significant problems regarding Praia Central is shadowing caused by seashore buildings, as a result of lack of planning (see Figure CS8.4). Most people interviewed (89 per cent) considered the shadowing 'unlikeable', while 6 per cent considered it 'good' and 5 per cent considered it 'regular'. When asked about the responsibility for shadowing, 34 per cent judged the city hall, represented by the present administration, as responsible; 19 per cent considered the civil construction industry to be responsible, 12 per cent attributed responsibility to the previous administration and 35 per cent cited other causes. Noteworthy is the fact that only 23 per cent of interviewed citizens considered beach nourishment as the most appropriate solution for the shadowing process.

Users' concern about comfort in Praia Central

When asked about the concept of carrying capacity, 72 per cent stated that they were not familiar with this concept, while 28 per cent believed they knew its definition. When beach users were invited to select among four alternatives in a picture regarding agglomeration density, 14 per cent preferred to have 25m^2 of beach area for each user, 37 per cent considered

Figure CS8.4 *Among the most significant problems regarding Praia Central in Balneário Camboriú is shadowing caused by seashore buildings, responsible for the desire for beach enlargement*

$10m^2$ satisfactory, 35 per cent believed that $5m^2$ was sufficient and 14 per cent were comfortable with no more than $3m^2$.

Users' concern about nourishment to increase the shore area in Praia Central

Regarding beach nourishment aimed at increasing the shore area, 46 per cent of interviewed users were not in favour, while 42 per cent were favourable to the approach. Some 12 per cent did not have an opinion about the subject. Analysing which actors would benefit by such beach nourishment, 30 per cent considered tourists to be the most benefited group, whereas 26 per cent stated that commerce would have significant gains. Furthermore, 20 per cent believed that it would be beneficial to everybody and 24 per cent reckoned that not only local inhabitants but also other diverse actors would take advantage of the beach nourishment.

Respondents were also asked about possible consequences of beach nourishment and most of them, reaching a total of 69 per cent, had no knowledge of possible consequences, while only 31 per cent affirmed they knew of them. It is remarkable that 69 per cent of the respondents declared that they did not know what possible relationships exist between enlarging the shore area and improvements made in the beach quality and public health. Also, 32 per cent confirmed that they knew of such relationships and 7 per cent had no knowledge of any impacts such as improvement in seawater and sand quality.

Almost all respondents (98%) considered that a nourishment project should be subject to his/her consultation and just 2 per cent considered that it was unnecessary to consult his/her opinion. When asked about suitable facilities to be implemented alongside beach enlargement, 11 per cent considered public toilets as important facilities while 9 per cent opted for cycling areas. Likewise, 8 per cent proposed showers, 8 per cent asked for more sports facilities, 5 per cent suggested increasing street widths, 5 per cent recommended lifeguards and 49 per cent raised other aspects. It is worthy of mention that when asked about willingness to finance the project, 76 per cent stated that they would not finance it, while 24 per cent expressed a willingness to help finance the project.

CONCLUSIONS

Today, Balneário Camboriú is going through a unique period in its history. The small littoral town is rapidly becoming a densely populated coastal metropolis. The economy is becoming diversified and migration is increasing. In addition to these phenomena, urban development and seasonal tourism during the summer promote the real estate business and, consequently, its beach occupation. More than ever, decision-makers ought to understand inhabitants' and tourists' perceptions of what is acceptable in order to promote a promising future for the city. It is noteworthy that adequate management must take into account several technical, legal, institutional and administrative factors based on beach system resilience.

The present analysis produces questions such as: how is it possible to manage a beach following the ideal environmental quality patterns proposed by its population if inhabitants are not willing to pay for the necessary infrastructure? Still, it is noteworthy that the present situation is a result of the process of privatization – driven especially by tourism, civil construction and the real estate sector – in addition to socialization of damages. Notwithstanding, there is an urgent need for a continuous and dynamic process that would integrate local administration, civil society, the private sector and scientific society.

Managing interests from specific sectors and the general public in order to prepare and implement an integrated plan to protect and develop the beach area through coastal governance seems to be the only way to avoid technocratic decision making, such as the present beach nourishment process. If this kind of decision becomes inevitable, it is imperative that the project be supported not only by entrepreneurs interested in a strong local real estate market, but also by all actors involved.

It is inconceivable that decision-makers still consider the coastal environment and, more specifically, the seashore as unlimited usage areas. Beaches in tropical zones may be considered inductive urbanization spaces that are rapidly exploited, developed and strengthened, but which could collapse quickly if mismanaged. Revitalizing the area is generally taken to be the only solution. It is essential not to consider revitalization as one continuous normal cycle.

The Oregon Coast Experience: Good Management but 'Bad Apples' (A Personal Assessment)

Paul D. Komar

INTRODUCTION

Coastal management programmes in the US were established mainly during the 1960s and 1970s, each coastal state having developed its individual programme with monetary support from the federal government. Like many states, Oregon formulated a series of goals and guidelines that covered the management of both the ocean beaches and estuaries, but then delegated the responsibility for its implementation to the coastal cities and counties. While to a degree that delegation resulted in the non-uniformity of the management strategies, such as approaches used to establish setback lines, and even the spirit to enforce those regulations, by and large Oregon can be viewed as having an enlightened programme for managing its coast.

Important to the management of the state's beaches, in 1967 the Statutory Vegetation Line (SVL) was defined, in essence being the demarcation separating the area of the active sand beach from the vegetated foredunes or the base of sea cliffs that back many of the beaches. Although the SVL does not necessarily correspond with the seaward edge of private property ownership, it represents an easement whereby the state has control over the sand beach based on its long-term recreational use, and beginning early in the state's history when the beach had been a dedicated highway, used prior to the completion of the coastal Highway 101. Although challenged all the way to the US Supreme Court, Oregon's 'Beach Bill' establishing the SVL and its jurisdiction over the beaches has been repeatedly upheld.

While the implementation of the management programme placed most of the day-to-day decisions on the coastal cities and counties, the state retains some control through the presence of the SVL and more broadly by permitting 'cut-and-fill' activities. For example, both may be relevant to permits for the construction of seawalls and riprap revetments to protect coastal developments from erosion. The result has been that in a number of cases, while the local authority approved a permit for construction, the state agencies (State Parks and the Department of Land Conservation and Development) exerted their authority and declined the permit. This decision has often been based on the regulation that shorefront developments constructed since 1976, when the management programme was implemented, are not automatically eligible for protection by hard structures and that they instead should rely on having used adequate setback distances established as part of their original development plan.

While some counties and cities have established setback lines for their jurisdictions, when it comes to a specific property considerable reliance is placed on analyses and opinions of a consulting geologist or engineer, registered by the state and hired by the developer. With a degree of optimism when the state's management guidelines were formulated, they included this reliance on site inspections to provide developers with sound guidance concerning the natural hazards, to avoid building on landslides, or where the development was in foredunes or atop sea cliffs, to establish a sufficient setback to maintain the construction safe from erosion. With this idealism we expected that coastal geologists and engineers, having been registered by state agencies, would work toward avoiding problems associated with the known hazards. We failed to anticipate that there would be 'bad apples' within those groups, individuals who turned out to be 'ethically challenged', ready to provide the developer with whatever he wanted to maximize his profits in developing the site. This case study examines two developments that illustrate this problem, probably the worst that have occurred in spite of Oregon's overall record in having successfully managed its coast.

CONDO CONSTRUCTION ON THE JUMP-OFF JOE LANDSLIDE

The most obvious coastal hazard on the Oregon coast is an active landslide, the Jump-Off Joe landslide in Newport being the most infamous example (Sayre and Komar, 1988; 1989; Komar, 1997). While the erosion and instability of this site had been recognized back in the 19th century, it having been the chief location for Newport's ocean recreation, it became forcefully evident in 1942 when an abrupt expansion of the landslide extended inland (see Figure CS9.1), carrying more than a dozen homes to their destruction.

In spite of the obvious instability of this site, in 1982 it was proposed to construct condominiums directly on the down-dropped block of the landslide, even though there was active wave erosion of its toe, resulting in the progressive subsidence and slow seaward movement of the slide. The site was graded in preparation for construction, but the development required a massive riprap revetment to halt the erosion and continued movement of the slide. However, the state rejected the application, partly

Note: The remnant terrace on the left edge of the photo was the site of condominium construction in 1982.

Source: Lincoln County Historical Society, Newport, Oregon

Figure CS9.1 *The 1942 landslide photographed in 1961, with two houses remaining on the slump block, inhabited until 1966*

on technical grounds: while the developer's consulting geologist had identified the wave-cut escarpment as being the seaward limit of the landslide, other experts demonstrated that it extended further seaward and that the constructed revetment would be atop the slide, its added weight exacerbating the instability.

Not having acquired permission to construct the revetment, the site of condominium construction shifted to the adjacent bluff, thereby avoiding the need for the state's approval since no protection structure was proposed. This site consisted of the small remnant terrace between two massive landslides, that to its south which had failed in 1942 (see Figure CS9.1), and an equally large slide to its north that had developed during the 19th century. The developer's geologist concluded that this site could be made stable by the installation of drainage pipes and downplayed the wave erosion of the bluff, even though in a study several years earlier for Lincoln County, he had concluded that this stretch of cliff had the highest rate of erosion in the county. The developer received the approval of the city of Newport, which was anxious to place the property on its tax roles. But as seen in Figure CS9.2, before the condominiums could be completed and inhabited, movement of this remnant terrace began, cracking the foundation and stressing the building as a whole, causing its windows to pop. The structure eventually had to be destroyed by the city. The developer, contractor, a lumber company and an insurance company that had insured the project were bankrupt (Sayre and Komar, 1988; 1989; Komar, 1997).

Figure CS9.2 *The initial stages in the destruction of condominiums built in the Jump-Off Joe area of Newport*

The consulting geologist moved on to other projects. Only after additional problems of a similar nature, did the Board of Geologist Examiners undertake an investigation (Sayre and Komar, 1989). Their decision was to rescind his certification, but only temporarily, allowing him to regain it if he took a course in ethics. He decided otherwise and took up another occupation.

THE CAPES DEVELOPMENT AND EL NIÑO EROSION

The development of condominiums at The Capes came during the mid-1990s, located on the northern Oregon coast (see Figure CS9.3), within a stretch of beach between headlands that is referred to as the Netarts Littoral Cell. The site compounded nearly all of the potential hazards faced on the Oregon coast — its condominiums are located on a high bluff (see Figure CS9.4), most of which consists of loose Holocene dune sand,

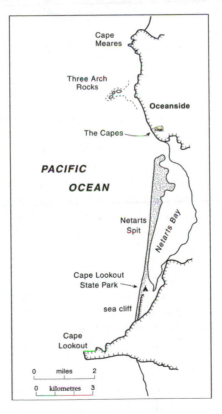

Figure CS9.3 *The Netarts Littoral Cell, the stretch of sand beach between Cape Meares and Cape Lookout, with the site of The Capes being an example of 'hot spot' El Niño erosion*

Figure CS9.4 *The front line of condominiums of The Capes development,
lining the edge of an old landslide*

beneath which is a layer of mud that is highly susceptible to movement.
The morphology of the bluff clearly demonstrated that it had experienced
large-scale landsliding in the not-too-distant past.

The developer had contracted three reports on the hazards of the site,
the first two undertaken by engineering firms, the third by a registered
consulting geologist. The engineering reports characterized the site as
being extremely hazardous and concluded that setback distances for
development would have to be considerable, in the order of 75m. In
contrast, the geologist concluded that the site was safe, that it had not even
experienced landsliding in the past, and that the recent formation of a
vegetated foredune in front of the high bluff attested to its not having been
subject to wave attack for a number of years. He recommended a setback
distance only in the order of 10m for the line of bluff-top condominiums
that were individually valued at about $500,000, the total in the stretch of
cliff amounting to some $10 million. The developer decided to go ahead
with construction, following the recommendations of the geologist.

The bad judgement in having developed this site soon became evident
during the El Niño winter of 1997–1998 when high storm waves and
elevated tides cut back the bluff, threatening the loss of the front line of
condominiums. Erosion along the Oregon coast during major El Niños is
characterized by 'hot spot' sites of maximum impacts due to the approach
of storm waves from the southwest, temporarily shifting the beach sand

Figure CS9.5 *The toe (foreground) of the landslide and its slip face in front of The Capes condominiums (1999)*

within the littoral cells to the north (Komar, 1998). In the case of the Netarts Littoral Cell (see Figure CS9.3), the hot spot erosion occurred at Cape Lookout State Park due to its being immediately north of a headland and at The Capes when the bay's inlet shifted to the north. The migration of the inlet rapidly cut away the foredune the consultant had thought would protect the bluff from the waves, and then began to erode into the bluff itself, forming a near-vertical escarpment that exposed the mud layer at its base. This led to a reactivation of the landslide that had been recognized by the consulting engineers (see Figure CS9.5), but supposedly not by the geologist. The erosion and landsliding continued through the winter of 1998–1999, noted for its series of extreme storms (Allan and Komar, 2002).

The slip face at the back of the slide was located immediately in front of the condos, so several had to be evacuated. A permit was applied for by the developer to construct a revetment along the base of the slide on a huge scale to protect it from wave attack and to provide the mass in hope of stabilizing the slide. This would have been doubtful, considering that the bulk of the slide consisted of loose sand that would have continued to slump (see Figure CS9.5). The proposed revetment was estimated to involve the importation of some 800 truckloads of rock, with the developer promising to remove it later when 'no longer needed'. The permit application was forwarded all the way to the governor's office, where it was rejected. In the end, The Capes development survived that episode of erosion, and soon thereafter a wall of gunite was constructed on the near-vertical slip face in front the condominiums (its construction did not require state approval). This thin wall is of doubtful stability, so it is likely to be only a matter of time before the erosion and landsliding return, probably awaiting the next major El Niño.

This episode of development and threat of loss, like so many others, landed in court but the case was settled by payment of an undisclosed amount to the owners of the condominiums. In the meantime the consulting geologist had died, having been quite elderly. Other than the blame having been directed by the defence lawyers toward the 'dead guy', there were no reactions that might have improved the level of competence and ethics of consultants involved in coastal hazard assessments.

REFLECTIONS

With my background in geology it is personally upsetting to see that the 'bad apples' consulting on the Oregon coast have come from that profession. I hasten to add that they represent a very small percentage, with the majority of consultants endeavouring to undertake honest assessments of the hazards faced by developments. Furthermore, much of the blame needs to be placed on a few greedy developers, The Capes illustrating that some are willing to hire as many consultants as needed, until they have the 'right answer'. Word soon gets out who those consultants are, and unfortunately they become the most financially successful.

The problem within Oregon's coastal management programme has been the inability or unwillingness to deal with those few 'bad apples'. One limitation has been that the coastal jurisdictions generally do not have a geologist or engineer on their staff to assess the veracity of the consultant's report. Even though their management personnel may recognize that the potential hazards of the site are being misrepresented, time and again I have been told they simply had to accept the report, since it was the product of a registered 'expert'. Even in cases when the management staff recommended that the plan for development be rejected, they are often overruled by politicians who have the final say. The commonly stated reason is to avoid being sued by the developer, or simply to let it be the state that rejects the permit.

A major problem for many years had been the Board of Geologist Examiners, a committee composed of registered geologists. It is not surprising they were more intent on protecting their members, seemingly no matter how incompetent or unethical. I had a personal experience in that regard when testifying at a county hearing in opposition to the construction of a seawall, having been asked by State Parks to become involved as the site was adjacent to a park and there had been no erosion warranting the construction of a seawall. Having testified, the consulting geologist turned me in to the Board with a complaint that I was practising geology without being registered. The Board's decision was to fine me $1000, but I brought this to the attention of my university's attorney, who passed it on to the State's Attorney General (who I was then advising on another legal problem on the coast). Soon thereafter my fine was withdrawn, and I haven't had subsequent problems with the Board. Of interest, the geologist I had opposed in that case of the unneeded seawall was hired a few years later by The Capes developer.

I am pleased to report that matters have improved. Several years ago the Board similarly fined a professor of geology at the University of Oregon for his opposition to and testimony against the development of a gravel pit. Unlike my case, the pros and cons involving this gravel pit became a newsworthy item, so the Board's action against that professor was widely reported, and in turn caught the attention of his representative in the state legislature. In short, a new law was passed, so one would not have to face the Board's wrath when testifying in opposition to the 'bad apples' among their members. At the same time, I cannot point to any clear examples of 'bad apples' presently involved in consulting on the Oregon coast, and my impression is that with recent changes in the Board's membership, it now recognizes that they have an important role in policing their members. Hopefully, the problems experienced in the past are history, even though the pressures for unhindered development remain, so the temptation still exists.

A Holistic Approach to Beach Management at Çıralı, Turkey: A Model of Conservation, Integrated Management and Sustainable Development

Ayşen Ergin

INTRODUCTION

Tourism is essential to the economic well-being of the Turkish nation, as long as no despoliation of the natural and cultural resource base occurs. With the exception of ecotourism, tourists have rarely been explicitly confronted with an explanation of the detrimental environmental consequences of their actions and/or given an opportunity to provide part of any solution. Socio-economic development in coastal regions is in many respects more rapid than elsewhere, which is partially due to the high potential for tourism activities in these regions. Due to its favourable climatic conditions and naturally beautiful coastal areas richly decorated with historical treasures, the Mediterranean basin is one of the leading coastal tourism areas in the world. The UN World Tourism Organization (UNWTO, 2007) states that over 30 per cent of the total tourism activities in the world takes place in the Mediterranean basin. Tourism in Turkey, especially along its Mediterranean coast, has developed rapidly since the early 1980s. In fact Turkey has the third fastest growth rate (over 9 per cent) compared to a total growth rate of 7 per cent. The share of tourism receipts for Turkey in export income alone was 19.8 per cent and was 4.2 per cent of gross national product (CBMCT, 2007).

Turkish coastal tourism shows a dominantly upward trend, which places pressure on natural resources, as well as threatening the region's biodiversity especially on the Mediterranean coast (Broderick, 1997). For example, once found all over the Mediterranean basin, the 100-million-year-old species of loggerhead turtles (*Caretta caretta*) is now at risk from ever-growing threats, mainly marine pollution, together with loss of beach nesting habitats due to infrastructure and tourism development. Today, only a small population nest in Cyprus, Greece, Israel, Italy, Libya, Syria, Tunisia and Turkey. In fact, Çıralı beach in Turkey is one of the last refuges and a major nesting site on Turkey's Mediterranean coastline, crucial for the survival of *Caretta caretta*. A 1998 survey by the WWF on the Turkish Mediterranean coast showed that 40 per cent of the 2500km coastline was severely affected by rapid tourism developments and almost half of the beach areas used as nesting areas by *Caretta caretta* (classified as endangered under the World Conservation Union's Red List) had been destroyed by uncontrolled tourism development activities (Oruç et al, 2003).

Çıralı beach epitomizes Strange's (2005: 401) dictum that 'Beaches are economic as well as natural resources. As economic resources they provide services to people and property and have an economic value. They also generate impacts on the economy and tax base.' In view of this, Çıralı beach is discussed as a unique example of beach management, where beach management is much more than analysis of beach processes, economics and anthropogenic activities. It involves a holistic approach of all local stakeholders to a much wider platform where public awareness necessitates management following a 'bottom-up' approach.

ÇIRALI

Location

Throughout history Çıralı has been home to numerous civilizations, as well as the subject of many legends, and is outstanding for its natural attributes. It is located 70km west of Antalya within Antalya's Kemer township district. Extending to the beach from Ulupınar village, Çıralı can be reached by a 7km road leading east of the Antalya-Kaş highway. The gulf is surrounded by the Tahtalı range of the Toros Mountains in the north, Yazır village in the south, Musa Mountain in the west and the Mediterranean on the east. Northwest of the villages, 3.2km inland from the shore occurs natural permanently burning gas fires known as Yanartaş (Chimeira). The southern extremity of the Çıralı shoreline ends at the Olympos stream, which runs through the ancient city of Olympos. The northern end is bounded by Karaburun, a rocky cape. Ulupınar, a major river, meets the sea on the southern Çıralı shore (see Figures CS10.1, CS10.2 and CS10.3).

History

Historical sources report that there was once a temple to the blacksmith god Hephaistos at the Olympos site. It was believed that Hephaistos' furnaces were located beneath volcanoes; therefore temples in his name were erected at sites of constantly burning flames, such as those at Yanartaş. When Prometheus stole fire from Olympos to bring to man, Zeus ordered Hephaistos to create Pandora to obtain revenge on Prometheus, as of all the gods on Olympos, Hephaistos alone possessed this creative power.

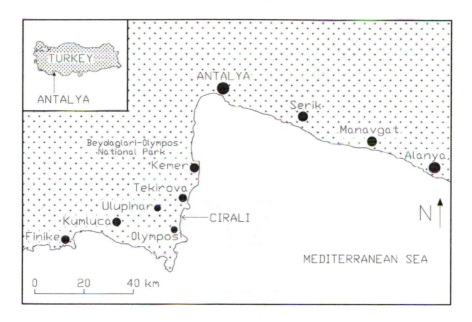

Figure CS10.1 *Antalya region*

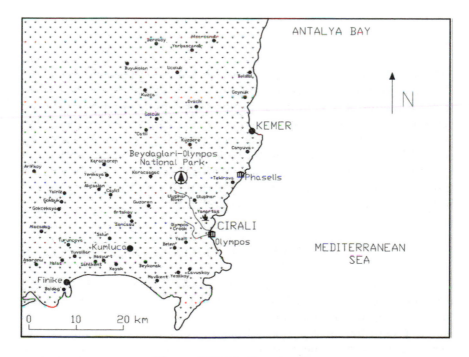

Figure CS10.2 *Kemer region*

Figure CS10.3 *Çıralı beach*

This is the legend as related in Homer's Iliad about Lycia's undying flame ('Burning Rock' or Yanartaş) of the Çıralı region. However, this legendary flame is the result of natural gas produced at points of contact between serpentine and limestone, the two rock type's characteristic of the region (www.cirali.org). Çıralı's historical and natural riches are protected by several legal statutes. The coastal valley sheltering the ancient city of Olympos has been designated as an *archaeological* SPA. The beach and immediate inland zone extending for 3km to the north of Olympos has been declared a 1st and 2nd degree *natural* SPA.

THE SITUATION

Çıralı is a coastal community that remained untouched for a long period due to its isolated location. Surrounded by the high hills and mountains of the Olympos National Park, Çıralı's spectacular 3.2km beach is, as stated, one of the most important nesting grounds for the loggerhead turtle (*Caretta caretta*). The presence of this turtle is an indicator of the high quality of the beach and coastal waters. The town, which previously had depended upon agriculture, moved towards tourism in the late 1980s. As in neighbouring Mediterranean coastline towns, Çıralı was drawn to tourism because younger generations saw it as an easier way of making money. Consequently, construction of tourism facilities threatened loggerhead nesting sites. Pesticides from agricultural activities had already polluted soil and water resources, and the growing number of restaurants around the village's main spring posed an even greater environmental threat. Moreover, illegal construction was on the rise due to lack of implementation of existing land development regulations.

SWOT analysis for Çıralı

SWOT analyses are widely used and simple planning techniques, particularly appropriate to the formative project stage in building up planning strategies and effective in conveying information to a variety of stakeholders (planners, politicians, the public) due to its visual, 'easy on the eye' format (see Figure CS10.4).

The SWOT analysis clearly shows the need for beach protection and management of land resources. In the light of these outcomes, a project was developed for Çıralı that can be divided into two components: protection of biodiversity and management of land resources.

Protecting biodiversity: Marine turtle conservation
The coastal conservation priority for the Turkish south coast is beaches used for nesting by the loggerhead turtle (*Caretta caretta*) or the green turtle (*Chelonia mydas*). Therefore, successful nesting of loggerhead turtles was a prime goal of Çıralı beach management. It is estimated that about a quarter of the Mediterranean coastline consists of sand beaches, of which only 20 per cent are of significance for turtle nesting (Yerli and Demirayak, 1996). Çıralı beach, along with Belek, is the one of the major nesting sites along Turkey's Mediterranean coastline. Therefore in the Çıralı Project marine turtles were considered as the flagship species. Success in their conservation meant a positive impact not only for them, but also for thousands of other marine and coastal species that are less charismatic.

Survival of this threatened species involves being careful not to disturb the turtles, their nests and young turtles. Every year, during a reproduction cycle from May through September, it is thought that turtles swim thousands of kilometres to return for nesting at their birth places. At Çıralı, field surveys and conservation efforts on *Caretta caretta* nesting and newly hatched turtle survival commenced in 1994 as part of a beach management plan. WWF and the Turkish Society for the Protection of Nature (Doğal Hayatı Koruma Derneği – DHKD) commenced a three year (1994–1997) project geared to marine turtle conservation called 'Assessment of Major Nesting Sites of *Caretta caretta* on Turkey's Mediterranean Coastline at a Selected Site: Çıralı'.

STRENGTHS	WEAKNESSES
Aesthetics (superb scenery)	Cobble not sand beach
Environmental management	Poor vertical integration
Willingness of locals to protect area	Existing beach driving in front of restaurants
Very good climate	No boat traffic lanes to beach
Geographical position (Mediterranean)	Insufficient safety facilities
Turtles breeding site (Caretta caretta)	Not enough financial support and personnel for
NGO activity e.g. improved education wareness	protection of turtles.
'Conservation Zoning Physical Development	Turtle rules are still disobeyed by tourists in spite
Plan' and the Çıralı Coastal Management Plan	of being informed about these by the authorities
Frequent water quality measurements	Mismatch between protected area aspirations and
SPA and national park	practice, e.g. lack of enforcement of statutes and
Daily waste collection system	regulations
Established ecotourism and responsible tourism	Lack of strategy for the implementation of land-
Unique natural phenomena, e.g. permanent	use plans
flames at Olympus mountain	Lights/noise from restaurants
Abundant fresh water	Uncontrolled urbanization that puts pressure on
Dune system	the beach especially at the turtle area
Spectacular cultural heritage	
Archaeological SPA, e.g. Olympus	
Low-rise buildings	
Organic agriculture	
Reputation and model project	
International networking Websites: Sea turtles,	
University of Akdeniz www.akdeniz.edu.tr/	
Ulupinar Co-operative info@ulupinarkoop.org	

Controlled development	Pollution of underground water and fresh water
Improved political cooperation with Kemer	Tourism exposure
Better waste management	Political change
Low-key tourism	Chrome mining in the north
Improved legislation	Hotel/golf interests
LA21 strategy increasing opportunities for public	Population pressure – migration to coastal zone
participation	Dune destruction
Biodiversity hot spots – emphasis on turtle	Climate change making high season too hot/sea-
conservation/ information/ education centre	level rise
Controlled beach access	Illegal beach sand extraction
Bigger organic agricultural input	Damage to cultural heritage
Further opportunities regarding international	Noise pollution
research collaboration	Illegal building
More promotion of ecotourism	Fish farming along the river
	Increase in solid waste
	Damage to ecosystem
	Loss of aesthetic value
	Loss of agricultural land
	Cultural dilution/ alteration

OPPORTUNITIES	THREATS

Figure CS10.4 *SWOT analysis for Çıralı*

From 1997–2000, these surveys and conservation efforts were carried out by DHKD and WWF under a LIFE project called 'Coastal Management and Tourism in Turkey: Çıralı and Belek', funded by the EU. The Çıralı component of the project received the United Nations Centre for Human Settlements (UNCHS – now UN-Habitat) 'Best Practice Award' in 2000 in partnership with the Municipality of Dubai. Of 770 projects submitted for the award from 110 countries, a total of ten best practices were identified. Selection was based on three criteria: a tangible impact on human living conditions; partnership between two or more stakeholders; and sustainability, in terms of lasting changes in policies, management practices, attitudes and behaviour. The award, presented to the beneficiary, WWF and DHKD, in Dubai in November 2000, was a clear indication of the quality and success of the beach management activities implemented in Çıralı during the LIFE project (www.wwf.org.tr).

Field surveys on marine turtle nesting in Çıralı after 1994 were carried out between June and October. After laying their eggs and the turtles returning to the sea, the site is marked by specially designed cages, placed to protect eggs from predators (dogs and even humans) until hatching time for each nest along the 3.2km shoreline. Surveys were carried out in the morning between 6 and 10am and at night between 10pm and 1am. Locations of observed nesting places were recorded by a 50 × 50m grid system established for the beach. Since 2001, marine turtle surveys and conservation efforts have been coordinated by WWF-Turkey and by members of the Ulupınar-Çıralı Cooperative, which was established in 2001. Volunteers for the field surveys and constant monitoring have been supplied since 1998 by the British Trust for Conservation Volunteers (BTCV).

Marine turtle conservation efforts were enhanced by festivals, courses and seminars conducted for villagers and local government authorities in order to raise awareness. Visitors were informed by means of the special protective cages around turtle nests and sign boards in strategic beach locations that gave information about the project scope and marine turtle conservation issues, especially during the nesting season, which coincides with the high tourism season. A bilingual information brochure, in Turkish and English, was also distributed. The local community participated in many beach cleaning days during the turtle nesting season. Successful nesting beach management practices, such as screening restaurant lights, avoiding usage of lights after 11pm, placing sun chairs and beach umbrellas behind a 35m line from the sea and closing the beach to vehicles were introduced and followed by locals and tourists.

The efforts in Çıralı have produced very good results: increased turtle track numbers in the Olympos beach section have been recorded, for example as a result of vehicle restriction. Entrance to the beach at night, fires, light and noise pollution on the beach are now under control and marine turtle nests are well marked. As a result of pressure on the sand dunes, dune vegetation and marine turtle nests have been protected, and the number of turtle hatchlings has increased. Field surveys carried out since 1994 show an increasing trend in nest numbers since the start of conservation activities. Nest numbers on Çıralı beach since 1994 are shown in Figure CS10.5 (Ulupınar-Çıralı Cooperative Field Study Reports, 2003–2004; Oruç et al, 2003; Kuzutürk and Kütle, 2005). These conservation and population studies will continue in the future, since Çıralı, due to its natural characteristics, is considered as the alternative to already destroyed marine turtle nesting beaches in the Antalya region.

In 2001, the Ulupınar-Çıralı Cooperative (an NGO) was established during that LIFE project to ensure sustainable development and conservation of biodiversity and natural resources in tourist areas, Belek and Çıralı being targeted. In Çıralı, which was a smaller-scale tourist destination, the Cooperative aimed to promote socially sound development through integrated planning, nature protection and traditional and alternative economic activities, which involved local stakeholders in the project by raising awareness of the problem and enlisting their support. Since establishment, the Cooperative has twice received financial support from the Global Environment Facility's Small Grants Programme. The Cooperative's first project supported by the Programme was a 'Sustainable Development Model for Local People Living in a Protected Area'. The project was implemented from 2001–2003 and covered training of locals and Cooperative members on the adoption of a local development model based on organic agriculture (soil structure, problems faced in conventional agriculture, organic agriculture as a concept and conditions necessary for organic agriculture). During the project, members of the Cooperative increased to 35 and the number of organically produced certified products rose to 18. The project also served to develop the capacity of women by

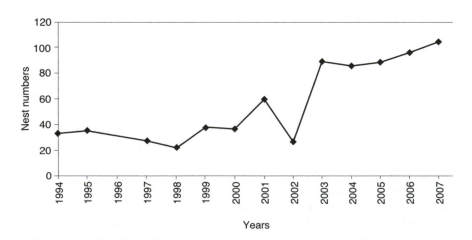

Figure CS10.5 *Turtle nest numbers on Çıralı beach, 1994–2007*

allowing them to express themselves and therefore become more relevant actors in sustainable management of the area. The Cooperative's second Small Grant Programme project was for two years and called 'Participatory Implementation of Eco-agriculture and Eco-Tourism in Ulupinar-Çıralı', which is now being implemented in the area. The project aims to promote organic agriculture and agro-ecological tourism (Kuzutürk and Kütle, 2005).

The Cooperative has taken an active role in raising awareness on sustainable tourism, agriculture and protection of the coast, all springing from management of the marine turtle initiative, as well as preparing local stakeholders for supporting and contributing to the project. The Ulupınar-Çıralı Cooperative will be involved in awareness raising, communication and dissemination activities, as well as efforts aimed to encourage community mobilization and local stakeholders' consultation and cooperation, and assist in similar activities at the national level. The Cooperative is still responsible for day-to-day project implementation in the area, diagnosing and solving bottlenecks among local stakeholders together with active lobbying at the national level.

Managing land resources: Land-use and management plans

Land-use and management plans   On 24 June 1998, WWF and DHKD were commissioned to prepare the Çıralı Physical Plan by the Turkish Ministry of Tourism. This was the first example of such a task being requested of a Turkish NGO. Prevention of illegal development and finding a solution to the infrastructure problems of Çıralı was one of the main objectives of this physical land-use plan, together with guidelines and recommendations for the wise use of land resources. For the project, WWF and DHKD, with the help of a team of experts and consultants, compiled results from several disciplines (such as city planning, socio-economics, biology, law, public administration, marine turtle biology, ecotourism, organic agriculture and environmental engineering). A 'Local Coordination Committee' formed by the local governor of Kemer, with representatives of WWF-Turkey, the director of the South Antalya Tourism and Infrastructure Development Association, the director of Infrastructure Exploitation and Tourism Corporate, a representative of the Antalya Preservation Council for Cultural and Natural Heritage, the village head of Ulupınar, a representative of the Elderly Committee of the village, a representative of the Cooperative and representatives of each working group in the village (for example innkeepers, fishermen and so on), was established to achieve stakeholder participation in the project. Meetings were held regularly with the Committee and local governmental institutions to take into account their interests. Land-use plans were prepared by a private design office and on 20 April 2000, a 'Report for Çıralı Physical Plan' and related map sections (1/25000 and 1/5000) were sent to the Directorate of Investments of the Ministry of Tourism.

In July 2000, land-use plans revised by the Ministry of Tourism (1/5000) were sent to the Antalya Preservation Council for Cultural and Natural Heritage, and received approval with minor changes and were sent back to the Ministry of Tourism. On 2 January 2001, plans approved by the Ministry of Tourism were sent to the Ministry of Public Works and Settlement. After review, the Ministry of Public Works and Resettlement sent the revised plans to the Ministry of Agriculture and Rural Affairs plus the Antalya Provisional Directorate of Public Works on 18 August 2000. On 27 March 2002, inter-ministerial coordination was completed by receiving views from the relevant authorities.

Finally on 6 July 2002, after a period of 16 months, the plans were evaluated in light of the Act for the Conservation Protection of Agricultural Lands in meetings organized by the Ministry of Culture and Tourism. In these meetings, the attendance of relevant organizations, project consultants and local people was sought, plus regular field meetings were carried out in order that relevant parties could exchange ideas and become actively involved in the project. For the first time, locals had the opportunity to communicate with representatives of governmental institutions during these meetings. Following the meetings, in October 2007, the Çıralı land-use plans, rectified by the Ministry of Culture and Tourism were publicly exhibited in Çıralı. Final approval of the Çıralı land-use plans by the Ministry Culture and Tourism was completed in March 2008.

Enforcing existing laws   At the beginning of the project in 1998, Çıralı's coastal borders were defined by the Ministry of Public Works and Resettlement in order to apply existing laws more effectively. As a result, existing laws have been enforced, particularly the Coastal Law (under which the coast belongs to the public and no construction is allowed), defining the distance of constructions from the coastline. During the next stage, with support from locals, numerous kiosks and restaurants too close to the shore and in violation of the Coastal Law were moved to the permitted distance, since light from kiosks and restaurants could disorient marine turtle hatchlings, thereby preventing them from reaching the sea. Çıralı management plans defined in principle zones of strict conservation, low-impact activities and regular use, and were concerned with natural sources (beach/land/agriculture) to be utilized in a sustainable manner. Delineation zoning was produced in map format. More importantly, the plans defined the roles of all stakeholders and put special emphasis on ecotourism and organic agriculture, in view of preliminary studies that had identified viable alternatives to conventional agriculture and unplanned tourism.

Although the Çıralı land-use plan was finally approved by the national government in March 2008, implementation is still difficult as conflict has arisen with respect to landownership issues. Land that has been farmed for several centuries by single families frequently has no legal deeds pertaining to ownership. In direct contrast are delineated map boundary lines that frequently show these lands as belonging to the Ministry of Environment and Forestry. Until resolution of this issue is acheived, it will be a barrier for conservation (Directorate of Investment, Development and Planning, Ministry of Culture and Tourism, www.kultur.gov.tr).

Organic agriculture in Çıralı   The Çıralı land-use management project gave special priority to organic agriculture with a view to creating diverse, sustainable and environment-friendly economic opportunities for locals people in order to produce a steady income throughout the year. Furthermore, it stops conversion of agricultural fields into tourism uses. Within the framework of the project (UNDP, 2003), DHKD promoted continuation of agricultural activities by active involvement of the Ulupınar-Çıralı Cooperative members. In view of this approach, local farmers were trained on soil structure, problems of conventional agriculture, and concepts and implementation of organic agriculture. In addition, the shift to organic farming is expected to help restore soil and groundwater quality.

The first production of organic agriculture commenced in June 2000, and is ongoing. Recent actions to promote the Çıralı brand include monthly mailings of organic products to subscribers from all over Turkey. Currently, among the major activities of the Ulupınar-Çıralı Cooperative is the training of women and young people in the production and marketing of organic food, the preparation of an organic agriculture handbook, brand-making for Çıralı's products, and production and marketing of traditional goods (UNDP, 2003).

Ecotourism for Çıralı   The choice of ecotourism was another source of income for Çıralı. Ecotourism has a low impact on nature and benefits the local community, in contrast to large-scale tourism where economic resources circulate mostly among resorts, tour operators and tourists. WWF and DHKD conducted several activities in Çıralı to generate awareness of and support for conservation and to create economic opportunities for the community, thus enhancing quality of life. Courses on ecotourism were organized particularly to train the younger inhabitants of Çıralı. With local help, trekking paths were identified and a guidebook was prepared on ecotourism covering information on flora, fauna and geomorphologic history walks. All these activities have raised the interest of young inhabitants in ecotourism. Today, young people, girls in particular, see this as an opportunity to be involved in the community's economic activities. This gender component is noteworthy as one of the most important outcomes of the project since, prior to the project, women in Çıralı did not have an important role in the community's decision-making mechanisms, and the project provided them with a role in the management of the area. Judging by these outcomes it can be stated that Çıralı is on the way to becoming a well-managed ecotourism destination.

FUTURE SCENARIOS

A novel coastal scenic evaluation technique was applied to Çıralı using fuzzy logic methodologies, with values obtained from a checklist that itemized 26 human and physical parameters rated on a five-point attribute scale (Ergin et al, 2004; 2006b). The methodology enabled calculation of an evaluation index (D) that categorized the scenery of coastal sites, and evaluated and statistically best described attribute values in terms of weighted areas. Results showed that Çıralı beach on a five-class scale was Class 1 – the top grade (Gezer, 2004; Uçar, 2004).

Short-term and long-term scenarios for Çıralı were hypothetically generated using the technique. With regard to beach management, this technique is suitable for evaluating future potential changes in view of preservation, conservation and sustainable development of the coastal areas, especially, with regard to anthropogenic influences (for example the built environment, litter, sewage and so on) by simulating alternative beach management plans (Gezer, 2004).

With respect to the threats identified in Table CS10.1, in the short term (about five years), assuming that the legal conservation status of Çıralı is not be changed, it is likely that only parameters such as litter, pollution, urbanization and yacht traffic will result from increased tourist pressure, the effect being that Çıralı beach would drop to a Class 3 category (Ergin et al, 2006b). For longer-term scenarios and if legal conservation and protection statutes are removed, the beach would drop to a Class 5 (poor) category, as a result of hotel construction, 'concretization', marina, noise disturbance and more pollution and litter, which would probably ensure the end of existing turtle sites (Ergin et al, 2006b). The above scenarios are unlikely to take place because of extremely high local public awareness of conservation, rooted in the diligent work of the local NGO, Ulupınar-Çıralı Cooperative and WWF-Turkey through beach management associated with the turtle project. This has been assessed through public perception studies involving interviews with local people that clearly show people's behaviour, appreciation and favourable approach to environmental issues (Gezer, 2004; Uçar, 2004).Two examples of quotes from interviews carried out at the village are:

> If huge hotels were built here, Çıralı would lose its atmosphere. Also Çıralı would not be as clean as today. Look at the situation in Kemer. Hotels placed barriers everywhere, stopping access to the beaches. Swimming is a problem there. (Local taxi driver)

> They have built hotels at the most beautiful sites of our country. They should build them on the mountains. They are killing the sea. They filled at least 3000m^2 of sea in Kemer. European tourists are not coming to Kemer now, although they made the rooms cheaper and cheaper. Now, they are trying to attract Russian tourists at low prices. (Local farmer)

Lessons learned from the Çıralı project

Turkey, an important Mediterranean country for biodiversity, still hosts many relatively pristine areas threatened by tourism development. The Çıralı model of sustainable tourism is to be replicated in similar small-scale tourism areas. Replication of the Çıralı scenario would give nature a breathing space along developed coasts. Enforcement of the Coastal Law and of SPA law (Law on Protection Status) at Çıralı could be utilized as a model for lobbying central authorities in Ankara for national-level enforcement. Lessons learned from the Çıralı project will be an important reference for similar projects:

- In successful sectoral land-use and management plan integration, socio-economic, conservation, legislation and land planning are the essential components.
- Keys to successful nature conservation are the participation of local people, therefore the relationship between local communities and nature conservation has to be clearly understood and improved through their involvement.
- Sustainable tourism development should be considered along with other economic development options. Ecotourism benefiting the local community can be a tourism option.
- Effective tools are required to enable the community to participate, influence, manage and benefit from the activities.

CONCLUSIONS

The most important outcome of the project was involvement of the local community as guardians of their natural heritage, especially the beach. The beach management turtle project epitomized the old adage that 'out of little acorns, mighty oak trees grow'. Acheivements include:

- The community actively participated and implemented activities to protect the loggerhead turtle. This subsequently led to a larger project involving a cooperative for agricultural products and ecotourism development. The community has a sense of ownership and responsibility for the entire project and its need for long-term sustainability, and have been trained in the necessary skills to carry on activities in a society with strong ownership and pride in their cultural and natural heritage.
- The land-use plan has met with endorsement from the local community, local government institutions and relevant ministries, and local people have actively taken up organic agriculture and ecotourism activities, which ensure better-managed cultural and natural resources. WWF-Turkey worked in strict collaboration with the relevant local people

and organizations at all levels. The concerns and demands of the community were always paramount.

- Diversified economic activities (tourism, organic agriculture, non-timber forest products) for environmentally and social sound development have all been successfully promoted.
- Ecotourism has been taken up enthusiastically by the community, and the town has become a famous 'nature-friendly tourism destination' and a sustainable tourism business (high occupancy rate, good prices and longer season) is booming. Çıralı, owing to its high quality tourism services, is able to compete with neighbouring mass tourism areas.
- Organic agriculture is well adapted and the Çıralı brand is becoming a household name for high quality organic products.
- Improved protection of the marine turtle habitat, demonstrated by an increase in the number of nests, implies a positive effect on the marine and coastal biodiversity of Çıralı.
- Quality of life has improve, for example through access to sanitation services, improved infrastructure, solid waste collection, chemical-free soil and educational activities that heighten local residents' awareness of the value of nature.
- Currently WWF-Turkey is aiming to create a professional team committed to solving problems and to making plans for the future of Çıralı that will serve as a model for environmental protection along the entire Mediterranean coast.

In conclusion, the Çıralı project represents a sound model for sustainable tourism in the Mediterranean that is much more than the standard beach management approach. This multifaceted model occurred as a result of a beach management programme geared to turtles.

New Directions in Beach Management in the Barcelona Metropolitan Area Coastal Systems (Catalonia, Spain)

Silvia Banchini, Lorenzo Chelleri, Antonio José Trujillo Martínez and Françoise Breton Renard

INTRODUCTION

Coastal areas are among the most threatened ecosystems in the world, hosting an increasingly larger proportion of productive activities when compared with inland regions. Exploitation of these territories is causing great environmental challenges. In general terms, as we can learn from past decades, the choice to exploit coastal resources results in a reduction of a number of environmental goods and services, with a consequent risk of increasing natural hazards (for example floods, beach erosion, decreasing water quality and loss of biodiversity). Short-term economic benefits from lowland areas and exploitation of beaches have generated substantial long-term costs, with a consequent loss of ecosystem goods and services providing life support (POST, 2007).

Resilience can be defined as the capacity of an ecosystem to tolerate disturbance without collapsing into a less qualitative state that is controlled by a different set of processes. Therefore a threshold exists in ecosystem dynamics and functions over which the ecosystem would not survive due to impacts and changed conditions (Chopra, 2005).

In coastal areas, the beach environment is strictly connected with the sea, the climate and the nearby inland ecosystem dynamics. Human impacts due to nearby land utilization usually disturb most of the environmental connections between these systems. Therefore in most cases, the extreme beach erosion processes or destructive sea floods are examples of the collapse of the beach ecosystem. This is often because riverine sediment has been intensively reduced by dams. Moreover, dune ecosystem dynamics, which help the beach to be a resilient ecosystem against storms and seasonal changes, have been destroyed and cannot undertake this protective function.

Demographic trends show that coastal populations are rapidly increasing. Nearly 40 per cent of the world's population lives within 100km of the coast, and Europe has lost more coastal wetlands between 1990 and 2000 than in previous decades (Hassan et al, 2005). In several coastal regions, for example of Spain, France and Italy, the coverage of built-up areas in the first kilometre of coastal strip now exceeds 45 per cent, and during 1990–2000, trends in the European coastal zone showed that the growth rate of artificial surfaces was a third faster than inland (EEA, 2006).

As in most Mediterranean urban beaches, the Barcelona metropolitan coastal areas have been overexploited due to planning of national and regional infrastructures and the high artificial development of the metropolis. The coast of Regional Metropolitan Barcelona (RMB) represents only 1.3 per cent of the Catalan territory (see Figure CS11.1). It is a narrow strip of land configured by the presence of near steep hill ranges and the coastline. Two and a half million people, around 35 per cent of all Catalan citizens, live in the RMB according to the last population register of 2007, and the high density of population (5261 inhabitants/km^2 versus the 148 inhabitants/km^2 of the Catalonia hinterland) has strong impacts on the socio-economic reality of these coastal areas (IDESCAT, 2008).

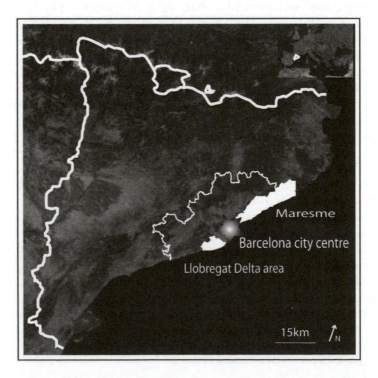

Figure CS11.1 *Location map of Maresme and Llobregat Delta study areas*

In this case study two examples are analysed: the Maresme beach system to the north of Barcelona and the Llobregat Delta to the south. The two sites are both part of the continuous Barcelona coastal system delimited in the north by the Tordera River and by the Llobregat to the south, with the presence of a high number of short seasonal streams. In the Llobregat area, development of the Barcelona harbour and airport, mixed with industrial land use, has strongly impacted the delta system and beaches. The Maresme coastal area has suffered strong human pressure caused by construction in the 19th century of a railroad running directly on the beaches and dunes, with subsequent construction of the national road N-II along the shoreline. A dense and continuous urbanization process took place along these infrastructures, which acted as a concrete transversal barrier to coastal processes producing consequent degradation of beaches and of the coastal landscapes.

In both examples, the environment and ecosystems have been highly degraded and show difficulty in maintaining their resilience capacity to react to these impacts. But in the Llobregat Delta, the infrastructure presence helps boost the economy of the whole region. Barcelona Airport allows protection to part of the beach ecosystems, which partly compensates for the loss. Additionally, in the 1990s some municipalities put in place interesting beach management schemes to 'renaturalize the beaches' and to regenerate the dunes and habitats (Breton and Esteban, 1995). Maintenance of environmental functions depends on a number of physical and ecological processes (Breton, 1996). Analysis of ecosystems status, active adaptive local management actions and policies to coastal system changes is undertaken in this case study, the aim of which is to a call for new coastal management practices oriented toward resilience of coastal systems.

The Maresme beaches

The Maresme region runs through a narrow strip of land between la Serralada Litoral mountain range and the sea, from Barcelona to the famous Costa Brava. The 398.9 km^2 are divided into 30 municipalities, 16 located on the coast and 14 inland, which makes it difficult to develop a single agenda for integral management of common services and economic activities. There are 134 watersheds that cross Maresme, which remain dry for most of the year except during the equinoctial rainy season when occasionally violent flash floods are produced. The coast itself has a length of 47km, composed mainly of coarse sand. Originally it was a continuous stretch of beach, but due to the construction of five marinas and ports along the shoreline (Arenys, Balís, Mataró, Premiá and Masnou) it has been divided into six different sectors. Erosion is very pronounced at the south side of the marinas because of the interruption of longshore sediment transport (see Figure CS11.2). Over the last 14 years, the beaches have lost between 10m and 15m, losing 5–10 per cent of their sand in storm seasons. The erosion is caused by a set of different factors:

- building of port facilities, both commercial, sporting and fishing that stops the coastal sediment stream;
- presence of infrastructure (national road N-II, regional railways and promenades), and also breakwaters that render the coastline more artificial;
- channelling and damming of streams and rivers, especially the Tordera, which is the main sediment source for nourishing beaches; urban development in the higher parts of the catchment and drainage works regulated by the highland municipalities reduce sediment contribution and increase runoff water speed and flood effects, which causes erosive impacts on beaches managed by the coastal municipalities;
- extraction of sand and gravel from the streams and the Tordera Delta by building companies, which is a loss of sediment and also changes riverbed morphology;
- urbanization of the coast, especially the front line, which has destroyed many ecosystems together with their functions; dunes have been cut in many places to construct buildings or promenades, and *Posidonia* beds, which naturally protect the beach from erosion by acting as a buffer to absorb wave energy, have been eliminated because of trawling practices, water quality and construction of coastal infrastructures.

Therefore, Maresme's coastal condition depends on the roles that infrastructure, the processes of soil occupation and urban planning have played, defining its current functional structure: metropolitan residence, intensive agriculture, industry and leisure services (Busquets, 2003).

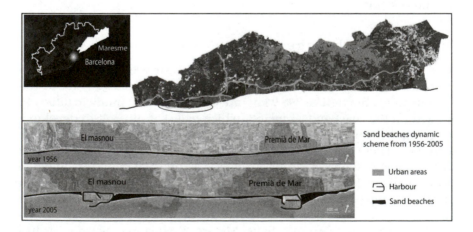

Source: Based on GIS database of Generalitat de Catalunya

Figure CS11.2 *Example of the erosion trend of the marinas due to the interruption in the sediment transport in the Maresme region from 1956–2005*

Initially, transport infrastructure encouraged growth of urban centres along the coastal corridor. In the 1950s two more factors impacted on urban growth in coastal municipalities: in-migration flows and the first coastal tourist boom in Catalonia (Nuell, 2001; Martí, 2001).

During the 1980s the Spanish Ministry of Environment promoted beach nourishment in the municipalities of Cabrera de Mar, Vilassar de Mar and Premiá de Mar, using 1 million cubic metres of sand extracted from the sea bottom, at a total cost of €6 million. This had a high impact on the *Posidonia* beds and other benthic communities.

Recently, new planning regulations have been launched for coastal areas. In 2005, due to the impacts of the high level of coastline urbanization, the Regional Government of Catalonia (Generalitat) promoted the General Plan of the Urban Coastal System (PDUSC), an instrument of urban planning that works at the inter-municipality level and attempts to preserve the remaining pieces of natural coast. The Plan catalogues as 'protected areas' those plots that were classified by urban local plans (Plan de Ordenación Urbana Municipal) as having 'no building rights', and also those 'with building rights' but that do not permit building within 500m of the sea and impose restrictions between 500m and 2km. This planning figure has protected more than 38,000ha of coastal land in Maresme, playing a key role in the creation of natural sea–mountain corridors and patches for agricultural production (Nel·lo, 2005). Since 2004, the government of Catalonia has been issuing a call to the Catalan coastal municipalities for projects related to the PDUSC regulation, offering them 50 per cent of funding, up to €180,000 maximum. Until now, participation of municipal governments has been very low, generally due to the common difficulty of how to make protected areas socially and economically profitable.

Recently, in 2007, the county council achieved a common agreement among 30 municipalities by approving the Maresme Strategic Plan 2015, as a result of a participatory and negotiated process between urban planners, citizens, entrepreneurs and political institutions at different levels – regional government of Generalitat of Catalonia, Barcelona Metropolitan Area and the 30 municipalities of the county. It required a process of negotiation among all municipalities to sign a common document focused on management and development of comprehensive projects for the whole county. Integrated beach management is part of the proposed goal. It is a first step; however, guidelines have still not been developed on how to arrive at this goal.

The Llobregat Delta beaches

The Llobregat Delta is located southwest of RMB and exerts a strong environmental influence on the dynamics of the southern beaches. In its natural morphological condition there are no natural barriers to sediment flow along the delta shore. Development of the Barcelona harbour has created a tremendous change in these natural conditions, as it acts as a barrier to sediment flow exchange from the north. Erosion is very active at the south of the harbour, due to a dyke that affects the delta mouth, which had to be artificially protected with the building of an artificial beach that needs constant nourishment. Erosion processes are also affecting the delta's north coast into the El Prat municipality. Additionally, groynes of the Port Ginesta Marina, located to the south of the delta, are retaining sediment and these acumulate in the area of Castelldefels (Barcelona Regional Team, 2005).

Originally the delta area was connected with a vast and continuous extension of marsh, perpendicular lagoons and coastal dune systems. Historically, it was a large flooded area that then became lagoons. Continuous transformation imposed by human activities began with intensifying agricultural land use of the low-lying areas, with drainage channel construction. Industrial and logistical activities developed in the 1950s near the river mouth, which was still vulnerable to seasonal floods (see Figure CS11.3). These industrial uses and contaminated river-water discharge transformed the beaches into a very degraded environment. However, the airport has impeded high and intensive urban development along the coastal area, so that long stretches of beach exist, unspoiled by construction. Therefore wetlands, dunes and natural ecosystems still offered considerable potential for regeneration in the 1990s (Breton and Saurí, 1997). Moreover the Kentish plover (*Charadrius alexandrinus*) breeding population area confers international importance on the site,

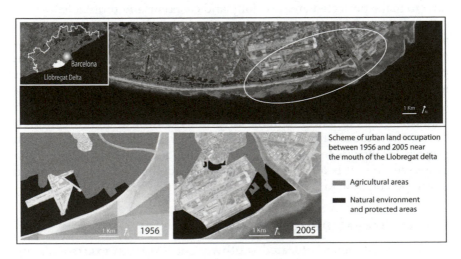

Source: Based on GIS database of Generalitat de Catalunya

Figure CS11.3 *Main land-use changes near the mouth of the Llobregat Delta from 1956–2005*

which is 3704m long and has 300,000m^2 of protected beach ecosystems which allow for natural preservation of this environment.

In recent times, river-water pollution has diminished with the building of one of Europe's biggest sewage treatment plants, situated near the old mouth of the River Llobregat, which has been diverted to the south. €240 million were spent in 2002 on its construction. Coastal water quality improved dramatically once the sewage treatment plant started operating in 2003. More than €60 million were spent in 2006 to clean up the nitrogen and phosphorus presence in the treated water so as to be able to use this water for agriculture and for wetland and lagoon recharge. These actions also prevented saltwater intrusions in the delta (AMB, 2008).

This water treatment plant is part of the most recent and meaningful territorial strategy developed in the delta, the Llobregat Delta Infrastructure Plan (LDIP) launched in April 1994 by the main stakeholders acting in the delta – the central state (airport and harbour), the regional state and the municipality of El Prat, among others. This agreement included the main strategic actions of: Barcelona harbour expansion (started in 2002 to be completed in 2009); construction of a third Barcelona airport runway (approved in 1999 and completed in 2004); and an improvement of the highway and rail infrastructure networks connecting Barcelona with other regions (DPTOP, 2008).

With these huge infrastructural developments, the delta area has been converted into a logistic platform and the LDIP is expected to have other cumulative impacts on the delta's environment. One of the visible actions of the LDIP is the protection of the coastline and wetlands of the north delta, with the airport being involved in the privatization of land and investment in the planning of a huge coastal park.

Another expected impact is related to the new harbour expansion that will produce a change in sediment transportation along the delta's coast (see Figure CS11.4). Normally, sediment transportation varies between 200,000 m^3 and 300,000m^3 per year, decreasing in the northern zone of the delta.

The recent diversion of the Llobregat river mouth and the harbour expansion were backed by a corrective measure (Declaration of Environmental Impact of the Directive Plan of the Port of Barcelona) that saw the realignment of the coast through the creation of a new artificial beach, which was finished in 2005. This beach is highly vulnerable to erosion, therefore the 3.5 million cubic metres of sand will need to be maintained by periodical renourishment (see Figure CS11.4a). In the delta centre, the coastal sediment balance is negative (see Figure CS11.4b), but in the south (between Gavà and Castelldefels municipalities) the balance gradually becomes positive. This area where sediment accretion occurs will be used to refill the northern part (see Figure CS11.4c).

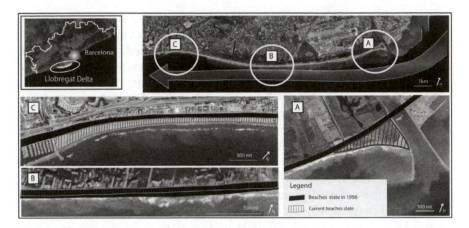

Figure CS11.4 *Current sediment balance dynamic of sand beaches
in the Llobregat Delta*

SOME REFLECTIONS ON NEW PLANNING DIRECTIONS AND BEACH MANAGEMENT

In both areas, even though their situations are diverse, over the last ten
years new strategic tools have emerged: the Maresme Strategic Plan 2015
and the Delta Llobregat Plan. Both have very different settings but are
based on agreement among stakeholders to allow for new governance
models. Both represent the first step toward a common protocol for beach
management more oriented to a resilience model, even though impacts
are still important.

In order to establish this common protocol, Maresme should coordinate
and monitor issues related to environmental values (level of disturbances,
degree of erosion of the beaches, frequency of flooding, legal tools of
protection, agricultural areas, woodlands, wetlands), urban structure
(degree of urbanization, beach services, location of restaurants, hotels,
parking, emergency services, public transport, rental services, cleaning
services) and users (frequency, profiles, demands, activities). The continued
and rapid pace of urbanization and related impacts on the environment
require networks and institutions able to improve their capacity for long-
term observation, monitoring and better information and decision making
based on new systems of governance (Cisnero, 2006). Erosion needs to be
understood together with the urbanization model and both need to be
integrated into regional and local plans and controlled by an integrated
management protocol aiming to improve resilience of the system and
make it reversible.

In the Llobregat Delta, one of the first beach management programmes
was designed by the local council of El Prat de Llobregat. The aim of this

programme was sustainable use of the coastal areas for preservation of botanical and zoological values, coupled with light wood paths to allow better access to the beach. This initiative included selective beach cleaning that encouraged community participation, carried out by volunteers, and a programme of environmental education that was implemented in 1989 (Breton et al, 2000). Similarly, El Prat council had to reach agreement with higher administrative levels to negotiate the various infrastructure derived from the Delta Plan in order to ensure good quality bathing water and a sustainable plan of beach and ecosystem protection.

The local council action, which was presented as a 'David versus Goliath fight', has opened a new way of collaboration among institutions in order to solve socio-environmental problems. This experience can be seen as an adaptive approach to obtain a better quality of life (recuperation of degraded beach ecosystems) through new social ways of using beaches and ecosystem services. It is a first step towards good planning practices that take into account increasing the resilience of socio-ecosystems.

CONCLUSIONS

These two examples are indicative of new ways of action by local, regional and national institutions trying to solve conflictive situations arising from past actions. They are both good examples of ICZM implementation on the Catalan coast. It is also very important for local administration initiatives – such as those in the cases presented above – to be supported by higher policy bodies and legislation, such as the PDUSC of the Catalan government. But regional governments should now go a step further, promoting not only protection but also recuperation of ecosystem functions. This should be followed by a joint effort by local, regional and central administration, to move towards a resilience concept.

For this objective, it is essential to build the necessary tools to understand and value ecosystem services. Land and ecosystem accounting, developed by the European Environment Agency and its European Topic Centre on Land Use and Spatial Information, is a method that has significant potential to match these objectives and goals, following the Millenium Ecosystem Assessment concepts. However, further research is needed at local and regional scales to give scientific support to these conceptual developments and methods. Valuation of ecosystem services should bring a new understanding of the value of natural capital, where most goods and services are not fully replaceable by human technology and investments. Planning for socio-ecosystem resilience should look at long-term costs and benefits, making transparent the high cost of any hidden externalities of human land and ecosystem uses.

Beach Consequences of an Industrial Heritage

M. R. Phillips

INTRODUCTION

Europe's coast is under increasing threat from erosion. A fifth of the enlarged EU's coastline is already severely affected, with coastlines retreating by between 0.5 and 2m per year and by 15m in a few dramatic cases (Europa, 2007a). A worldwide tendency to coastal erosion (Cipriani et al, 2004) has been locally aggravated by some of the very strategies implemented to reverse the pattern (Gillie, 1997; Weerakkody, 1997). Of the 875km of European coastlines that have started to erode within the past 20 years, 63 per cent are located less than 30km from coastal areas altered by recent engineering works (Europa, 2007b). Natural beach changes usually involve erosive and sedimentary processes that are mainly a response to changes in incident wave regime and tidal range (Anfuso et al, 2000). Since 1100 AD there has been evidence of shoreline volatility on the eastern flank of Swansea Bay (Bullen, 1993) (see Figure CS12.1). Historically, the development of South Wales, industrial docks have to some degree affected the equilibrium of the coastline, and the Institute of Oceanographic Sciences (IOS, 1980) concludes that human intervention, including port developments and seawall construction, has been the main erosion mechanism along South Wales beaches. Cipriani et al (1999; 2004) report similar findings on downdrift beaches at other European locations.

At the end of the Second World War changes in ship design meant that many were too large to negotiate the locks of South Wales' ports. Coupled with limitations posed by the large tidal range, which meant access was limited to a narrow window of entry during the tidal cycle, it signalled the end of many previously commercially viable trading routes. The construction of the Port Talbot Tidal Harbour (see Figure CS12.1; OS ref: SS750880) was a commercial venture between British Steel (now Corus) and the British Transport Docks Board (now Associated British Ports). The need for large cargoes of imported iron ore and coal for economic steel production necessitated construction of a sheltered deepwater harbour. During the capital dredging of the harbour, 11.2×10^6 tonnes of gravel,

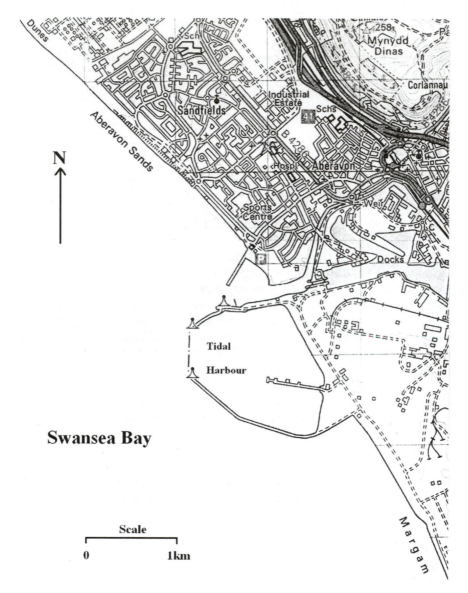

Figure CS12.1 *Tidal harbour*

sand and silt were removed, which incidentally was similar to the volumes removed during maintenance dredging between 1960 and 1976 (Bullen, 1993). Current navigation dredging of the harbour entrance removes sand from the littoral system to a spoil area in Swansea Bay and there is a weak recirculation to the shore. The deepwater harbour dominates the area (SBCEG, 1999) and there is an extensive industrial hinterland, mostly occupied by Corus and related industries. It has impacted on natural processes and affected the adjacent coastline to the north and south (see Figure CS12.1), including the beaches at Aberavon, Margam and Kenfig. This case study therefore assesses beach consequences and the management implications of this industrial heritage.

PHYSICAL BACKGROUND

Aberavon Sands

Aberavon (OS ref: SS735904) is a recreation beach (see Figure CS12.2) with a long seawall/revetment and long promenade (approximately 2.5km). It has a high degree of exposure with a spring tidal range of 8.4m, and coal waste is often found on the beach, brought ashore by wave action (SBCEG, 1999). At low water there is a wide sandy beach on which a number of water-related activities take place, such as sea bathing, wind and wave surfing, jet skiing and angling (MCS, 2008). There is a RNLI station and a surf lifesaving club. However, the promenade seawall developed many internal voids and in January 1991, as a result of these cavities, a section collapsed in a not very severe storm (Bullen, 1993). The seawall location has resulted in two conflicting problems: (1) the north-western half was constructed landwards of the natural high water line and dry sand is blown against and over the wall; and (2) the south-eastern part has been constructed seawards of the natural high water line and toe erosion is occurring due to wave reflection and turbulence.

Comparative beach data from local authority records in 1958 and 1975, together with 1991 aerial survey information, show falls in beach level. Between 1958 and 1975, this was 0.8m while between 1975 and 1991, maximum erosion was 0.3m (Bullen, 1993). Furthermore, the tidal harbour interferes with accepted northerly net longshore transport (SBCEG, 1999), which therefore reduces sediment supply to the beach.

Margam Sands

At Margam Sands (OS ref: SS768855), the Corus frontage, southeast of the tidal harbour (see Figure CS12.1), has experienced erosion over many years and a once extensive dune line has been replaced by a 3km length of slag (waste from steelmaking processes) and rock armour revetment (SBCEG, 1999). Comparative beach data from profiles established by the Institute of Oceanographic Sciences in 1975 (IOS, 1980) and an aerial survey in 1991 show recession in the backbeach/dune line of between 20m and 40m. This was a pattern along the full frontage of this coastal section. Furthermore, a maximum fall in beach level of 1.1m was measured and parallels were

Figure CS12.2 *Aberavon beach*

drawn to similar losses between 1830 and 1870, where the coastline was seen to recede due to disruption caused by construction of Port Talbot docks. Bullen (1993) concludes there was significant sediment loss and determines that in the 16-year period between 1975 and 1991, 950,000m³ of material was lost from backbeach recession and eroding foreshore, equivalent to an average fall in beach level of 0.7m over the whole area.

Kenfig Sands

Kenfig Sands (OS ref: SS782815) front a national nature reserve and are located southeast of Margam Sands and separated by the River Kenfig. Analysis of data from 1975 (IOS, 1980) and the 1991 aerial survey indicate that the backbeach had eroded while the lower beach had either accreted or remained constant. The maximum recorded fall of beach level was 0.7m and Bullen (1993) once again estimates a 16-year loss of approximately 600,000 m³, equivalent to an average reduction in beach level of 0.43m. This is approximately 40 per cent less than Margam Sands and may be explained by the diminishing influence of the tidal harbour. There is no built environment within 1km of the shoreline and the hinterland is comprised mainly of dunes with important conservation interests (SBCEG, 1999). The spring tidal range is 8.6m and due to the high-energy but shore-normal wave climate, the sandy foreshore is subjected to a weak southerly drift. Coastal defence is mainly provided by the Margam and Kenfig dune systems (SBCEG, 1999).

BEACH MANAGEMENT

Aberavon

The tidal harbour interferes with accepted northerly net longshore transport (SBCEG, 1999), thereby reducing sediment supply to the beach. If a line joining the extremities of the breakwaters (see Figure CS12.1) is projected onto the shoreline, beach consequences differ to the north and south of this location. To the southeast, there is northward sediment movement with little replenishment. This causes beach levels to fall, resulting in exposure of sheet piles at the seawall toe and in the past this has been managed by placing rock armour against the seawall (see Figure CS12.3). To the northwest, beach levels increase as sediment supply is restored and the area is subject to wind blown sand (SBCEG, 1999). The Coastal Protection Authority (CPA) periodically removes this (see Figure CS12.4) and redeposits it on the southeast beach section (see Figure CS12.1).

Figure CS12.3 *Rock armour fronting promenade seawall*

Margam Sands

The Corus frontage, southeast of the tidal harbour (see Figure CS12.1) is experiencing ongoing erosion and slag has been used for coastal defence, which protects the steelworks and infrastructure such as access roads (see Figure CS12.5). However, the slag tip revetments themselves were susceptible to erosion and consequently are further reinforced at certain locations with stone armour revetments (see Figure CS12.6). This coastal sector was highlighted as a priority area for erosion monitoring by SBCEG (1999) and they recommend implementation of recording and/or protection strategies.

Figure CS12.4 *Sand redistribution on foreshore*

Source: SBCEG (1999)

Figure CS12.5 *Coastal defence at Corus*

Source: SBCEG (1999)

Figure CS12.6 *Slag and rock armour revetment*

Kenfig Sands

Kenfig Sands are generally in a good condition but there are areas where patches of angular stone exist on the beach and this indicates sand loss. The current situation, however, mirrors the findings of Bullen (1993) and may well be cyclical. Coastal defence along this section is primarily provided by the dune system, although erosion is ongoing, evidenced by vertical faces in the dune line. However, because human assets are located considerable distances inland, there is no active intervention.

DISCUSSION

Post-war development trends have been to separate residential areas from employment centres, recreational facilities and retail outlets (Fuller, 1999). Development is increasing in tandem with growing economic prosperity but growth in coastal areas affects sustainability since issues become more complex (Cummins, 2004). The factors that influence sustainability in coastal management span social, economic, institutional, biophysical and legal conditions (Christie, 2005). Therefore there is a need to evaluate resource demands of coastal communities and assess socio-economic influences.

Aberavon and surrounding areas, as well as other Welsh cities and towns, originally expanded in response to successful coal and steel industries. Many of these urban centres are being regenerated using their waterfronts as the development focus and the process is well advanced at many locations. Along with the attraction of new industries, the redevelopment rationale includes taking advantage of potential increases in tourism income. It is only with the recent decline of the coal and steel industries that Aberavon's high redevelopment potential has been realized. It is close to industrial and commercial activities while the beach has no recommendation from the Marine Conservation Society or Blue Flag award. Therefore Aberavon will benefit from regeneration and subsequent improvement (MCS, 2008). This is currently ongoing with residential and commercial development, which due to location has little conservation impact (Phillips et al, 2007a; Williams et al, 2008). New executive residential development is screened from the tidal harbour and orientation is northwest so that properties have a coastal view. Coupled with an extensive buffer zone between the promenade and the older housing stock that once accommodated an industrial workforce, Aberavon is becoming a desirable executive location (Phillips et al, 2007b). Other Welsh regeneration examples have shown that run-down areas can be transformed into vibrant centres of entertainment, providing attractions for new tourism markets. They are also attracting new commercial development and 'high-tech' industries, which in turn, have reinforced their status as desirable residential areas. This is the rationale behind the local authority's redevelopment strategy for Aberavon.

An assessment of Aberavon's scenery following the methodology of Ergin et al (2004) identifies many low-scoring parameters and an overall low classification representative of poor scenic quality. However, it scores well on three of the highest-weighted human parameters, 'Disturbance Factor', 'Litter' and 'Sewage'. This is good for an urban beach and shows the value of the beach's buffer zone and local authority beach cleaning measures. The beach scores poorly on other human parameters such as 'Skyline', 'Built Environment' and 'Utilities'. These are a direct consequence of urbanization and, in particular, the predominant steelworks that seriously blights the beach panorama (see Figures CS12.2 and CS12.3). The beach also scores poorly on many physical parameters, including 'Water Colour', 'Landscape Features' and 'Vegetation Cover', indicating that the industrial environment has further influenced scenic quality. Consequently, industrial heritage has transformed Aberavon to a point where it retains little to none of its original landscape. However, current improvements to the built environment have a positive impact on its overall assessment.

The Aberavon coastline has low ecological value (Phillips et al, 2007a), while beaches suitable for development are generally urban, situated near large cities or towns that are already highly developed (Williams et al, 2008). This often leads to further beach development pressures to increase economic growth. It appears there is likely to be more benefit from developing these areas rather than introducing conservation measures, and nearby beaches such as Kenfig Sands can be managed for conservation. This helps achieve a sustainable balance of development and conservation. Kenfig Sands and dune system have a diversity of habitats/species of European importance and its large slacks support fen plants. Although it is a national nature reserve, there are no coastal defence interventions despite ongoing erosion. However, as argued by Schroeder (2000), erosion does not represent a problem for unmodified areas and often provides a net benefit, while it represents a serious recurring problem for human development. This is once again highlighted by coastal defence interventions either side of the tidal harbour.

The tidal harbour is a substantial structure that is here to stay, irrespective of the consequences of reduced steel production and poor economic outlook. According to SBCEG (1999) it receives over 12 million tonnes per annum of iron ore and other raw materials for steel production. Interestingly, the harbour is used only for importing material and no ships carry cargo when they leave. If the Corus steelworks (see Figure CS12.7) are closed it will follow the pattern of previous industrial decline in the area, where the old docks (see Figure CS12.1) have been run down

Source: Lobb (2008)

Figure CS12.7 *Steelworks viewed from Kenfig dunes*

BEACH MANAGEMENT

and derelict for over 20 years. However, there will be future uncertainty regarding maintenance of the slag and rock armour revetments.

CONCLUSIONS

Industrial developments at Port Talbot have historically caused local beach and dune system loss. The tidal harbour, necessary for maintaining economic steel production, has impacted on the adjacent coastline, up and down drift. Coastal defence measures to combat beach erosion impact on human infrastructure and include rock armour revetments to protect concrete and blast furnace slag seawalls at Aberavon and Margam respectively. However, at Kenfig where human assets are located considerable distances inland, there is no active intervention. This confirms erosion is not considered a problem for unmodified coastlines. Regeneration at Aberavon is continuing and utilizes its coastal location to good effect. However, the recent economic decline threatens its continued success and if steel production stops, a significant rethink of beach management strategies along the whole coastal sector will be needed.

References

Aagaard, T. and Greenwood, B. (1995) 'Suspended sediment transport and morphological response on a dissipative beach', *Continental Shelf Research*, vol 15, no 9, pp1061–1086

AB (Adjuntament de Barcelona) (2005) 'Temporadoa de plages', AB, www.bcn. cat/platges and www.bcn.es/platges/pdf/ca/balanc_temporada_2007.pdf

ABP (Associated British Ports) (1997) *A Guide to the Environmental Risk Assessment Package*, ABP Research Report No R717, Southampton, ABP

Abreu, J. G. N., Klein, A. H. F., Diehl, F. L., Santos, M. I. F. and Alves Jr, L. A. (2000) 'Alimentação artificial de praias no litoral centro-norte do Estado de Santa Catarina: Os casos de estudo das praias de Piçarras, Praia Alegre e Gravatá', in *Simpósio Brasileiro de Praias Arenosas*, pp426–427, Itajaí, SC, Livro de Resumos

Abu Zed, A. I. (2006) 'Hydrodynamic factors affecting sedimentation regimes in Damietta harbour, Nile Delta coast, Egypt', *Sedimentology of Egypt*, vol 14, pp15–28

ACA (Agéncia Catalana de l'Aigua) (2002) 'Tossa de mar: Resultas de la temporada de bany de l'estiu de 2002', Barcelona, ACA

AENOR (Asociación Española de Normalización y Certificación) (2003) 'PNE 150104. Sistemas de gestión ambiental. Guia para la implantación de sistemas de gestión ambiental conforme a la norma UNE-EN-ISO 14001 en playas', Barcelona, AENOR

Aeron-Thomas, M. (2002) 'Integrated coastal zone management in Sri Lanka', Policy Review Paper 4, Improving Policy–Livelihood Relationships in South-Asia, London, DFID

Ahmed, M., Umall, G. M., Chong, C. K., Rull, M. F. and Garcia, M. C. (2006) 'Valuing recreational and conservation benefits of coral reefs: The case of Bolinao, Philippines', *Ocean and Coastal Management*, vol 50, pp103–118

Allan, J. C. and Komar, P. D. (2002) 'Extreme storms on the Pacific Northwest coast during the 1997–98 El Niño and 1998–99 La Niña', *Journal of Coastal Research*, vol 18, no 1, pp175–193

AMB (Barcelona Metropolitan Area Administration) (2008) 'Depuradora del Baix Llobregat', www.amb.es/web/emma/aigua/sanejament/depuradores/depuradora_llobregat

Aminti, P. L., Cipriani, L. E. and Pranzini, E. (2003) '"Back to the beach": Converting seawalls into gravel beaches', in Goudas, G., Katsiaris, G., May, V. and Karambas, T. (eds) *Soft Shore Protection, Coastal Systems and Continental Margins*, vol 7, pp261–274, Dordrecht, Kluwer Academic Publishers

Anfuso, G., Gracia, F. J., Andres, J., Sanchez, F., Del Rio, L. and Lopez-Aguago, F. (2000) 'Depth of disturbance in mesotidal beaches during a single tidal cycle', *Journal of Coastal Research*, vol 16, no 2, pp446–457

Anon (1994) *Creative Management Techniques*, Open Business School, B882, Group 4: Mapping and Structure – the KJ Method, Milton Keynes, Open University

Araujo, R. S. (2008) 'Caracterização dos processos erosivos observados na enseada do Itapocorói, Santa Catarina, Brasil', unpublished MSc dissertation, Programa Acadêmico de Mestrado em Ciência e Tecnologia Ambiental, Itajaí, SC

Arba, P., Arisci, A., De Waele, J., Di Gregorio, F., Ferrara, C., Follesa, R., Piras, G. and Pranzini, E. (2002) 'Environmental impact of artificial nourishment of beaches of Cala Gonone (Central-East Sardinia)', in EUROCOAST (ed) *Littoral 2002, 6th International Symposium, Porto, Portogallo*, pp465–468, EUROCOAST

Ariza, E., Jiminez, J. A. and Sardá, R. (2008a) 'A critical assessment of beach management on the Catalan coast', *Ocean and Shoreline Management*, vol 51, pp141–160

Ariza, E., Sardá, R., Jiménez, J. A., Mora, J. and Ávila, C. (2008b) 'Beyond performance assessment measurements for beach management: Application to Spanish Mediterranean beaches', *Coastal Management*, vol 36, pp47–66

Ash, J. R., Nunn, R. and Lawton, P. A. J. (1995) 'Shoreline management plans: A case study for the north Norfolk coast', in Institution of Civil Engineers (ed) *Proceedings of Conference on Coastal Management '95 – Putting Policy into Practice*, pp20–30, Institution of Civil Engineers, Bournemouth, Thomas Telford

Asher, K. N., Rivara, F. P., Felix, D., Vance, L. and Dunne, R. (1995) 'Water safety training as a potential means of reducing risk of young children's drowning', *Injury Prevention*, vol 1, pp228–233

Austin, M. J., Scott, T. M., Brown, J. A. and MacMahan, J. H. (2009) 'Macrotidal rip current experiment: Circulation and dynamics', *Journal of Coastal Research*, special issue 56, pp24–28

Avalon (1998) 'Flood mitigation plan', unpublished report, Avalon, NJ, Department of Public Works

Avalon (2007) 'Federal officials declare Avalon's flood plan amazing', *Borough of Avalon News*, Spring/Summer, pp1–2

Avis, A. M. (1995) 'Recreational use of three urban beaches in South Africa and effects on dune vegetation', in Salmon, A. H. P. M., Berends, H. and Bonazountas, M. (eds) *Coastal Management and Habitat Conservation*, pp467–485, Leiden, EUCC'95, Leiden

Baker, R. D. (1980) *Lifeguarding Simplified*, London, Thomas Yoseloff

Balance, A., Ryan, P. G. and Turpic, J. K. (2000) 'How much is a clean beach worth? The impact of litter on beach users in the Cape Peninsula, South Africa', *South Africa Journal of Science*, vol 96, no 5, pp210–213

Balas, C. E., Balas, L. and Williams, A. T. (2004) 'Risk assessment of revetments by Monte Carlo simulation', *Proceedings of the Institution of Civil Engineering, London – Maritime Engineering*, Issue MA2, pp61–70

Balas, L. and Tunaboylu, S. (2007) '3D modelling of density induced coastal currents', in Ozhan, E. (ed) *Proceedings of the 8th International Conference on the Mediterranean Coastal Environment, MedCoast 07*, pp1253–1262, Ankara, Turkey, METU

Ball, I. (2003) 'The management of vessel-related waste at recreational boating facilities', unpublished thesis, Cardiff, Cardiff University

Barcelona Regional Team (2005) 'Pla estratègic litoral de la regió metropolitana de Barcelona: Diagnosi i propostes', Technical study, www.mcrit.com/plalitoral/

Bartoletti, E., Cipriani, L. E., Dreoni, A. M., Montelatici, M. and Pranzini, E. (1995) 'Beach first response to stabilisation works: A case study at the Cecina River

Mouth, Italy', in Ozhan, E. (ed) *MedCoast '95*, pp1173–1188, Ankara, Turkey, METU

Barwise, P. (1996) 'Strategic management and implementation: Mastering management', *Financial Times*, London, part 15, pp1–5

Bascom, W. (1964) *Waves and Beaches*, Garden City, NY, Anchor Books

BBC (1993) 'The Cruel Sea', BBC2, Public Eye Series on Coastal Erosion, London, British Broadcasting Corporation

Beachmed (2009) 'POSIDuNE: Interaction of sand and *Posidonia Oceanica* with the environment of Natural Dunes', Beachmed website, www.beachmed.it/Beachmede/SousProjets/POSIDUNE/tabid/99/Default.aspx, accessed 29 April 2009

Beatley, T., Brower, D. J. and Schwab, A. K. (1994) *An Introduction to Coastal Zone Management*, Washington, DC, Island Press

Beech, N. W. and Nunn, R. (1996) 'Shoreline management plans: The next generation', in Taussik, J. and Mitchell, J. (eds) *Partnership in Coastal Zone Management*, pp345–352, Cardigan, Samara Publishing

Benedet, L., Finkl, C. W. and Hartog, W. M. (2007) 'Processes controlling development of erosional hot spots on a beach nourishment project', *Journal of Coastal Research*, vol 23, no 1, pp33–48

Bennett, M., Dearden, P. and Rollins, R. (2003) 'The sustainability of dive tourism in Phuket, Thailand', in Landsdown, H., Dearden, P. and Neilsen, W. (eds) *Communities in South East Asia: Challenges and Responses*, pp97–106, Centre for Asia Pacific Initiatives, Victoria, University of Victoria

Best, P. N. (2003) 'Shoreline management areas: A tool for shoreline ecosystem management', *Puget Sound Notes*, vol 47, pp8–11

Bird, E. C. F. (1996) *Beach Management*, Chichester, John Wiley and Sons

Blakemore, F. B. and Williams, A. T. (2008) 'British tourists' valuation of Turkish beaches using contingent valuation and travel cost methods', *Journal of Coastal Research*, vol 24, no 6, pp1469–1480

Blakemore, F. B., Williams, A. T., Coman, C., Micallef, A. and Unal, O. (2002) 'A comparison of tourist evaluations of beaches: Malta, Romania and Turkey', *Journal of World Leisure*, vol 44, no 2, pp29–41

Blanksby, B. A., Wearne, F. K., Elliot, B. C. and Blitvitch, J. D. (1997) 'Water safety training as a potential means of reducing risk of young children's drowning', *Injury Prevention*, vol 1, pp228–233

Bluck, B. (1967) 'Beach sedimentation of gravels: Examples from South Wales', *Journal of Sedimentary Research*, vol 37, pp128–156

BMIF (British Marine Industry Federation) (1999) *Marine Industry Statistics Report: An Annual Survey*, Surrey, BMIF

Bodge, K. R. (1992) 'Representing equilibrium beach profiles with an exponential expression', *Journal of Coastal Research*, vol 8, pp47–55

Boruff, B. J., Enrich, C. and Cutter, S. L. (2008) 'Erosion hazard vulnerability of US coastal counties', *Journal of Coastal Research*, vol 24, no 1A, pp79–86

Brasil (1988) 'Lei n° 7661 de 16 de maio de 1988. Lei Nacional de Gerenciamento Costeiro', Brasília, Government of Brazil

Breakwell, G. M. (1990) *Interviewing*, London, British Psychological Society and Routledge

Breton, F. (1996) 'El litoral: Bases per al planejament i la gestió integrada d'un espai dinàmic i vulnerable', in Sureda Obradors, V. (ed) *El Sistema Litoral: Un equilibri sostenible?*, pp45–100, Barcelona, Quaderns d'Ecologia Aplicada no 13

Breton, F. (ed) (1998) 'Metodologia d'ordenació i gestió dels espais lliures en les zones litorals', Support to Social Science Emerging Groups, UAB CIRIT 1995–1997, Department of Geography, Barcelona, UAB

Breton, F. and Esteban, P. (1995) 'The management and recuperation of beaches in Catalonia', in Healy, M. G. and Doody, P. (eds) *Directions in European Coastal Management*, pp511–517, Cardigan, Samara Publishing

Breton, F. and Saurí, D. (1997) 'Toward a redefinition of resources and hazards in coastal management: Examples from the lowland areas of Catalonia, Spain', *Coastal Management*, vol 25, pp363–385

Breton, F., Clapés, J., Marquès, A. and Priestley, G. K. (1996) 'The recreational use of beaches and consequences for the development of new trends in management: The case of the beaches of the Metropolitan Region of Barcelona (Catalonia, Spain), *Ocean and Coastal Management*, vol 32, pp153–180

Breton, F., Esteban, P. and Miralles, E. (2000) 'Rehabilitation of natural beaches by local administration in Catalonia: New trends in sustainable coastal management', *Journal of Coastal Conservation*, vol 6, pp97–106

Broderick, A. C. (1997) 'The reproductive ecology of marine turtles, *Chelonia mydas* and *Caretta caretta* nesting at Algadi, Northern Cyprus, Eastern Mediterranean', unpublished PhD dissertation, Glasgow, University of Glasgow

Bryan, K. (1940) 'Gully gravure, a method of slope retreat', *Journal of Geomorphology*, vol 3, pp89–107

Buanes, A., Jentoft, S., Maurstad, A., Soreng, S. U. and Karlson, G. R. (2005) 'Stakeholder participation in Norwegian coastal zone planning', *Ocean and Coastal Management*, vol 48, pp658–669

Buceta, J. L. (2002) 'Evaluar la calidad de las playas', *Ingeniería Civil*, vol 128, pp145–154

Buckley, R. (2004) 'Environmental impacts of motorized off-highway vehicles', in Buckley, R. (ed) *Environmental Impacts of Ecotourism*, pp83–98, Wallingford, CABI Publishing

Bullen (1993) 'Coastline response study', *Worms Head to Penarth Head: Final Report*, vol 1, Mold, Bullen and Partners

Burby, R. J. and Dalton, L. C. (1993) 'State planning mandates and coastal management', in *Coastal Zone 93*, pp1069–1083, New York, American Society of Civil Engineers

Busquets, J. (2003) *Les Formes Urbanes del Litoral Català*, Barcelona, Diputació de Barcelona

Butcher, J. (2003) *The Moralisation of Tourism: Sun, Sand and Saving the World?*, Routledge Contemporary Geographies of Leisure, Tourism and Mobility, London, Routledge

Butler, R. W. (1980) 'The concept of a tourist area cycle of evolution: Implications for management of resources', *Canadian Geographer*, vol XXIV, no 1, pp5–12

Buttigieg, M., Vassallo, M. and Schembri, J. A. (1997) 'Basic geomorphological studies of shore platforms in the Maltese islands', in Ozhan, E. (ed) *MedCoast '97*, pp79–88, Ankara, Turkey, METU

Cafaro, P. (2001) 'Thoreau, Leopold, and Carson: Toward an environmental virtue ethics', *Environmental Ethics*, vol 23, no 1, pp3–17

Cammelli, C., Jackson, N. I., Nordstrom, K. F. and Pranzini, E. (2005) 'Assessment of a gravel nourishment project fronting a seawall at Marina di Pisa, Italy', *Journal of Coastal Research*, vol SI39, pp770–775

Campillo-Besses, X., Priestley, G. K. and Romagose, F. (2004) 'Using EMAS and LA21 as tools towards sustainability: The case of a Catalan coastal resort', in Bramwell, B. (ed) *Coastal Mass Tourism: Diversification in Sustainable Development in Southern Europe*, pp220–248, Clevedon, Channel View Publications

Cannell, C. F. and Kahn, R. F. (1968) 'Interviewing', in Lindzey, G. and Aronsen, E. (eds) *The Handbook of Social Psychology*, vol 2, Reading, Addison-Wesley

Capobianco, M., Larson, M., Kraus, N. C. and Nicholls, R. J. (1997) 'Depth of closure: Towards a reconciliation of theory, practice and evidence', *Coastal Dynamics 1997*, New York, ASCE, pp506–514

Carleton Ray, G. and McCormick-Ray, J. (2004) *Coastal-Marine Conservation: Science and Policy*, Oxford, Blackwell

Carlson, L. H. and Godfrey, P. J. (1989) 'Human impact management in a coastal recreation and natural area', *Biological Conservation*, vol 49, pp141–156

Carobene, L. (1972) 'Osservanzioni sui solchi di battente attuali ed antichi nel golfo de Orosei i Sardegna', *Bollettino della Società Geologica Italiano*, vol 91, pp583–601.

Carter, R. W. G. (1984) 'Stream outlets through mixed sand and gravel coastal barriers: Examples from southeast Ireland', *Zeitschrift fur Geomorphologie*, vol 28, pp427–442

Carter, R. W. G., Forbes, D. L., Jennings, S. C., Orford, J. D, Shaw, J. and Taylor, R. B. (1989) 'Barrier and lagoon coast evolution under differing relative sea-level regimes: Examples from Ireland and Nova Scotia', *Marine Geology*, vol 88, pp221–242

Cassar, L. F. (1996) 'Coastal dunes: Form and process', unpublished MSc dissertation, Tal Qroqq, University of Malta

CBMCT (Central Bank, Ministry of Culture and Tourism) (2007) 'Tourism receipts', Istanbul, CBMCT

CEC (Council of the European Communities) (1976) 'Bathing Waters Directive, 1976. Council Directive of 8 December 1975 concerning the quality of bathing water (76/160/EEC)', *Official Journal of the European Communities*, 19 (L31)-1-7

CEC (2006) EC 2006/7/EC European Parliament and the European Council 2006. Directive 2006/7/EC of the European Parliament and of the Council of 15 February 2006, concerning the management of bathing water quality and repealing Directive 76/160/EEC. *Official Journal of the European Communities*, L64 of 4.3.2006

CEES (Coastal & Environmental Engineering Solutions Inc.) (2006) 'Beach management project: Best practices guidelines for 50 beaches along the coastline of Barbados', draft report submitted to the Government of Barbados, St Michael, Barbados, Coastal & Environmental Engineering Solutions Inc.

Celliers, L., Moffett, T., James, N. C. and Mann, B. Q. (2004) 'A strategic assessment of recreational use areas for off-road vehicles in the coastal zone of KwaZulu-Natal, South Africa', *Ocean and Coastal Management*, vol 47, pp123–140

Cendrero, A. and Fischer, D. (1997) 'A procedure for assessing the environment quality of coastal areas for planning and management', *Journal of Coastal Research*, vol 13, no 3, pp732–744

Chaverri, R. (1989) 'Coastal management: The Costa Rica experience', in Magoon, O. T. (ed) *Coastal Zone '87, Proceedings of the 5th Symposium on Coastal and Ocean Management*, Vol 5, pp1112–1124, Seattle, American Society of Civil Engineers

Chiotoroiu, B., Stoica, E. and Williams, A. T. (2006) 'Beach systems and management', in Constantin, B., Plesea, D., Visean, M. and Tigu, G. (eds) *Proceedings of the 2006 International Conference on Commerce*, pp400–406, Bucharest, Faculty of Commerce, Academy of Economic Studies

Chopra, K. R. (ed) (2005) *Ecosystems and Human Well-being: Policy Responses: Findings of the Responses Working Group of the Millennium Ecosystem Assessment*, Millennium Ecosystem Assessment Series 3, Working Group of the Millennium Ecosystem Assessment, Washington, DC, Island Press

Christie, P. (2005) 'Is integrated coastal management sustainable?', *Ocean and Coastal Management*, vol 48, no 3–6, pp208–232

Cicala, A. (1998) 'Studio delle condizioni meteomarine nel Golfo di Orosei', in *Progetto di Ricostruzione delle Spiagge di Cala Gonone*, unpublished report, Dorgali Municipality

Cicin-Sain, B. and Knecht, R. W. (1998) *Integrated Coastal and Ocean Management: Concepts and Practices*, Washington, DC, Island Press

CIEH (Chartered Institute of Environmental Health) (2002) *Risk Assessment Principles and Practice*, London, CIEH

Cipriani, L. E., Pelliccia, F. and Pranzini, E. (1999) 'Beach nourishment with nearshore sediments in a highly protected coast', in Ozhan, E. (ed) *Land-Ocean Interactions: Managing Coastal Ecosystems*, vol 3, pp1579–1590, Proceedings of the MedCoast-EMECS Joint Conference, MedCoast, Ankara, Turkey, METU

Cipriani, L. E., Wetzel, L., Aminti, D. L. and Pranzini, E. (2004) 'Converting seawalls into gravel beaches', in Micallef, A. and Vassallo, A. (eds) *Management of Coastal Recreational Resources: Beaches, Yacht Marinas and Coastal Ecotourism*, pp3–12, Valletta, Malta, ICoD

CIRIA (Construction Industry Research and Information Centre) (1996) *Beach Management Manual*, Report 153, edited by Simm, J. D., London, CIRIA

Cisnero, J. (2006) *Maresme 2015. Strategical Plan Maresme 2015*, Barcelona, Consejo Comarcal del Maresme

City of Stirling (1984) *Coastal Report: A Report on Coastal Management and Development in the Coastal Reserve for the City of Stirling Municipality in Western Australia*, Perth, Imperial Printing Company

Clark, J. R. (1996) *Coastal Zone Management Handbook*, Boca Raton, FL, Lewis Publishers

Claridge, G. (1987) 'Assessing development proposals', in UNESCO (ed) *UNESCO Coral Reef Management Handbook*, pp131–137, Paris, UNESCO

Coelho, C., Scott, M., Istemil, A. and Williams, A. T. (2003) 'Environmental impacts of coastal developments and activities: Coastal user conflicts', in Ozhan, E. (ed) *Proceedings of the 6th International Conference on the Mediterranean Environment*, *MedCoast '03*, pp 121–132, MedCoast, Ankara, Turkey, METU

Cooper, J. A. G. (2001) 'Geomorphological variability among microtidal estuaries from the wave-dominated South African coast', *Geomorphology*, vol 40, pp99–122

Cooper, N. J. and Pethick, J. S. (2005) 'Sediment budget approach to addressing the erosional problems in St Quen's Bay, Jersey, Channel Isles', *Journal of Coastal Research*, vol 21, no 1, pp112–122

Cooper, N. J. and Pontee, N. I. (2006) 'Appraisal and evolution of the littoral "sediment cell" concept in applied coastal management: Experiences from England and Wales', *Ocean and Coastal Management*, vol 49, pp498–510

Cooper, N. J., King, D. M. and Hooke, J. M. (1996) 'Collaborative research studies at Elmer Beach, West Sussex, UK', in Taussik, J. and Mitchell, J. (eds) *Partnership in Coastal Zone Management*, pp369–376, Cardigan, Samara Publishing

Cornwall Council (2009) *Strategic Beach Management Plan*, Cornwall Council, Truro

Crossett, K., Culliton, T. J., Wiley, P. and Goodspeed, T. R. (2004) *Population Trends Along the Coastal United States, 1980–2008*, Silver Spring, MD, National Oceanographic and Atmospheric Administration

Crowell, M., Edelman, S., Coulton, K. and McAfee, S. (2007) 'How many people live in coastal areas', *Journal of Coastal Research*, vol 23, no 5, ppiii–vi

Cummins, V. (2004) 'National considerations for implementing best practice in ICZM in Ireland', in Green, D. (ed) *Littoral 2004 – Delivering Sustainable Coasts: Connecting Science and Policy*, pp242–247, Cambridge, Cambridge Publications

Cutter, S. L., Nordstrom, K. F. and Kucma, G. A. (1979) 'Social and environmental factors influencing beach site selection', in West, N. (ed) *Proceedings of the 5th Annual Conference: Resource Allocation Issues in the Coastal Environment*, pp183–194, Arlington, VA, The Coastal Society

Dalton, T. (2006) 'Exploring participants' views of participatory coastal and marine resource management processes', *Coastal Management*, vol 34, pp351–367

Davenport, J. and Davenport, J. L. (2006) 'The impact of tourism and personal leisure transport on coastal environments: A review', *Estuarine, Coastal and Shelf Science*, vol 67, pp280–292

Davies, P., Curr, R. C. H., Williams, A. T., Hallégouet, J. B., Bodéré, J. C. and Koh, A. (1995a) 'Dune management strategies: A semi quantitative assessment of the interrelationship between coastal dune vulnerability and protection measures', in Salman, A. P. H. M., Berends, H. and Bonazountas, M. (eds) *Coastal Management and Habitat Conservation*, pp313–331, Leiden, EUCC

Davies, P., Williams, A. T. and Curr, R. C. H. (1995b) 'Decision making in dune management: Theory and practice', *Journal of Coastal Conservation*, vol 1, no 1, pp87–96

Davos, A. (2000) 'Sustainable cooperation as a challenge for new coastal paradigm', *Journal of Coastal Conservation*, vol 5, pp171–180

Dean, R. G. (1977) 'Equilibrium beach profiles: US Atlantic and Gulf coasts', Ocean Engineering Report No 12, Department of Civil Engineering, Newark, University of Delaware

Dean, R. G. (2002) *Beach Nourishment: Theory and Practice*, New Jersey, World Scientific

de Araujo, M. C. B. and Costa, M. F. (2005) 'Municipal services on tourist beaches: Costs and benefits of solid waste collection', *Journal of Coastal Research*, vol 22, no 5, pp1070–1075

DEFRA (Department for Environmental, Food and Rural Affairs) (2002a) *Futurecoast CD*, Swindon, Halcrow Group

DEFRA (2002b) *Safeguarding our Seas: A Strategy for the Conservation and Sustainable Development of our Marine Environment*, London, DEFRA

DEFRA (2004) *Foresight, Future Flooding*, Executive summary, London, DEFRA

DEFRA (2005a) *Charting Progress: An Integrated Assessment of the State of UK Seas*, London, DEFRA

DEFRA (2005b) *Making Space for Water*, London, HMT, ODPM, DT, DEFRA

DEFRA (2006) *Shoreline Management Guidance*, vol 1 'Aims and objectives', vol 2 'Procedures', London, DEFRA

de Groot, R. S. (1992) *Functions of Nature. Evaluation of Nature in Environmental Planning, Management and Decision Making*, Groningen, Wolters-Noordhoff

De Vaus, D. A. (1986) *Surveys in Social Research*, London, Allen & Unwin

Dharmaratne, G. S. and Braithwaite, A. E. (1994) *Economic Valuation of the Coastline*, Barbados, National Conservation Commission

Dixon, T. (1995) 'Temporal trend assessments of the sources, quantities and types of litter occurring on the shores of the United Kingdom: Introduction and methods with results from paired observations 8–11 years apart on 63 sampling units in mainland Scotland and the Western Isles', *Marine Litter Research Programme, Stage 7*, Wigan, The Tidy Britain Group

DoE (Department of the Environment) (1995) *A Guide to Risk Assessment and Risk Management for Environmental Protection*, London, HMSO

DoE (1996) *Coastal Zone Management: Towards Best Practice*, London, Department of the Environment, Transport and the Regions

DOENI (Department of the Environment Northern Ireland) (2006) *An Integrated Coastal Zone Management Strategy for Northern Ireland, 2006–2026*, Belfast, DOENI

Doody, J. P. (1995) *Sand Dune Inventory of Europe*, Joint Nature Conservancy Council, Peterborough, UK

Doody, J. P. (ed) (2008) *Sand Dune Inventory of Europe*, 2nd Edition, National Coastal Consultants and EUCC–The Coastal Union, in association with the IGU Coastal Commission

Douglas Westwood Ltd (2005) *Marine Industries Global Market Analysis*, Marine Foresight Series No.1, Dublin, Marine Institute

DPTOP (Department of Territorial Policy and Public Works, Regional Government of Generalitat of Catalonia) (2008) 'Pla director urbanístic del sistema costaner (PDUSC)', www10.gencat.net/ptop

EA (Environment Agency) (2005) *The State of the Marine Environment*, Bristol, Environment Agency

EA (2008) 'Bathing water quality', www.environment-agency.gov.uk/yourenv/eff/1190084/water/213925/bathing/?lang=_e

EA/NALG (Environment Agency and the National Aquatic Litter Group UK (2000) *Assessment of Aesthetic Quality of Coastal and Bathing Beaches. Monitoring Protocol and Classification Scheme*, London, EA/NALG

Earll, R., Williams, A. T. and Tudor, D. T. (2000) 'Pilot project to establish methodologies and guidelines to identify marine litter from shipping', Maritime and Coastguard Agency Research Project 470, Kempley, Coastal Management for Sustainability Ltd

EC (European Commission) (2001) 'Strategic Environmental Directive 2001/42', Brussels, European Commission

EC (2006) *Towards a Future Maritime Policy for the Union: A European Vision for the Oceans and Seas*, Green Paper, COM(2006) 275 final, 7 June, European Commission, Brussels, available at http://ec.europa.eu/maritimeaffairs/policy_en.html, accessed 29 April 2009

EC (2007) *An Integrated Maritime Policy for the European Union ('The Blue Book')*, Communication from the Commission to the European Parliament, the Council, the European Economic and Social Committee and the Committee of the Regions, COM(2007) 575 final, 10 October, European Commission,

Brussels, available at http://ec.europa.eu/maritimeaffairs/subpage_en.html, accessed 29 April 2009

ECAN (Environment Canterbury) (2005) 'Regional Coastal Environment Plan for the Canterbury Region', Environment Canterbury Report, R04/13/1, Christchurch, ECAN

ECAN (2007) 'Proposed Natural Resources Regional Plan', Environment Canterbury Report, R04/15, Christchurch, ECAN

Edge, B. L., Cruz-Castro, O. and Magoon, O. T. (2002) 'Recycled glass for beach nourishment', in Allsop, N. W. H. (ed) Solving Coastal Conundrums, 28th International Conference on Coastal Engineering, paper 278, pp3630–3041, London, Thomas Telford

Edge, B. L., Magoon, O. T. and Cruz-Castro, O. (2002) 'Recycled glass for beach nourishment', in Allsop, N. W. H. (ed) Proceedings of the 28th International Conference on Coastal Engineering, paper 279, Cardiff, UK, Thomas Telford

Edwards, S. (ed) (1987) An Introduction to Coastal Zone Economics: Concepts, Methods and Case Studies, New York, Taylor and Francis

Edwards, S. (1994) 'Managing coastal recreation in environmentally sensitive areas', in Soares de Carralho, G. and Velos Gomes, F. (eds) Littoral '94, pp953–964, Lisbon, Instituto de Hidraulica e Recursos Hídricos, Universidade do Porto

EEA (European Environment Agency) (1999) 'State and pressures of the marine and coastal Mediterranean environment', Copenhagen, EEA

EEA (2001) 'Reporting on environmental measures. Are we being effective?', Environmental Issues Report No 25, Copenhagen, EEA

EEA (2006) 'The changing faces of Europe's coastal areas', EEA Report no 6, edited by Breton, F. and Meiner, A., Luxembourg, Office for Official Publications of the European Communities, http://reports.eea.europa.eu/eea_report_2006_6/en/eea_report_6_2006.pdf

Eke, F. (1997) 'Coastal legislation and implementation in Turkey: Prospects for co-operation', in Ozhan, E. (ed) MedCoast '97, pp665–678, Ankara, Turkey, METU

Elms, D. G. (1992) 'Risk assessment', in Blockley, D. (ed) Engineering Safety, pp28–46, MacGraw-Hill International Series in Civil Engineering, London, MacGraw-Hill

El Sayed, W. R., Ali, M. A., Iskander, M. M. and Fanos, A. M. (2007) 'Evolution of the Rosetta promontory on the Nile delta coast during the period from 1500–2005, Egypt', in Ozhan, E. (ed) Proceedings of the 8th International Conference on the Mediterranean Coastal Environment, MedCoast '07, pp1003–1015, Ankara, Turkey, METU

Epaedia (2008) 'European Environment Agency', www.eea.europa.eu/themes and www.eea.europa.eu/multimedia

Ergin, A. and Balas, C. E. (2002) 'Reliability-based risk assessment of rubble mound breakwaters under tsunami attack', Journal of Coastal Research, vol SI36, pp266–272

Ergin, A. and Balas, C. E. (2006) 'Damage risk assessment of breakwaters under tsunami attack', Natural Hazards, vol 39, pp231–243

Ergin, A., Karaesmen, E., Micallef, A. and Williams, A. T. (2004) 'A new methodology for evaluating coastal scenery: Fuzzy logic systems', Area, vol 36, no 4, pp367–386

Ergin, A., Karaesmen, E. and Gezer, E. (2006a) 'Simulation models for CZM: A pilot study for Çıralı', in Micallef, A. and Vassella, A. (eds) *International Conference on the Management of Coastal Recreational Resources, Beaches, Yachting and Coastal Ecotourism*, pp57–68, Valletta, Euro-Centre of Insular Coastal Dynamics, University of Malta

Ergin, A., Williams, A. T. and Micallef, A. (2006b) 'Coastal scenery appreciation and evaluation', *Journal of Coastal Research*, vol 22, no 4, pp958–964

ETC/WTB/STB (English Tourist Council/Welsh Tourist Board/Scottish Tourist Board) (2004) *UK Tourism Survey*, London, ETC/WTB/STB

Europa (2007a) 'Coastal zone policy', Europa, http://ec.europa.eu/environment/iczm/home.htm

Europa (2007b) 'European Commission puts spotlight on coastal erosion', Europa, http://ec.europa.eu/fisheries/press_corner/press_releases/archives/com04/com04_21_en.htm

Farrell, S. C. and Sinton, J. W. (1983) 'Post-storm management and planning in Avalon, New Jersey', in *Coastal Zone 83*, pp662–681, New York, American Society of Civil Engineers

FEE (Foundation for Environmental Education) (2008) 'Blue Flag Campaign', Foundation for Environmental Education, www.blueflag.org/Criteria/Beaches

FEE (2009) 'About Blue Flag', Foundation for Environmental Education website, www.fee-international.org/en/Menu/Programmes/Blue+Flag, accessed 29 April 2009

Fenemor, A., Davie, T. and Markham, S. (2006) 'Hydrological information in water law and policy: New Zealand's devolved approach to water management', in Wouters, P. and Wallace, J. (eds) *Hydrology and Water Law: Bridging the Gap*, pp297–336, London, IWA Publishing

Ferreira, O., Garcia. T., Matias, A., Taborda, R. and Dias, J. M. A. (2006) 'An integrated method for the determination of set-back lines for coastal erosion hazards on sandy shores', *Continental Shelf Research*, vol 26, pp1030–1044

Figueras, M. J., Borrego, J. J., Pike, E. B., Robertson, W. and Ashbolt, N. (2000) 'Sanitary inspection and microbiological water quality', in Bartram, J. and Rees, G. (eds) *Monitoring Bathing Waters: A Practical Guide to the Design and Implementation of Assessments and Monitoring Programmes*, pp113–167, London and New York, WHO

Fink, A. (1995) *How to Sample in Surveys: The Survey Kit*, vol 6, London, Sage

Finkl, C. W. and Kruempfel, C. (2005) 'Threats, obstacles and barriers to coastal environmental conservation: Societal perceptions and managerial positionalities that defeat sustainable development', in Veloso-Gomez, F., Taveira Pinto, F., da Neves, L., Sena, A. and Fereira, O. (ed) *Proceedings of the 1st International Conference on Coastal Conservation and Management in the Atlantic and Mediterranean Seas*, pp3–28, Porto, Portugal, University of Porto

Finkl, C. W. and Walker, H. J. (2005) 'Beach nourishment', in Schwartz, M. (ed) *Encyclopaedia of Coastal Science*, pp147–161, Dordrecht, Springer

Finkl, C. W., Bededet, L. and Campbell, T. J. (2006) 'Beach nourishment in the United States: Status and trends in the 20th century', *Shore and Beach*, vol 74, no 2, pp8–16

Fischer, D. L., Rivas, V. and Cendrero, A. (1995) 'Local government planning for coastal protection: A case study of Cantabrian municipalities, Spain', *Journal of Coastal Research*, vol 11, pp858–874

Forbes, D. L., Orford, J. D., Carter, R. W. G., Shaw, J. and Jennings, S. C. (1995) 'Morphodynamic evolution, self-organisation and instability of coarse-clastic barriers on paraglacial coasts', *Marine Geology*, vol 126, pp63–85

Foster, E., Haward, M. and Coffen-Smout, S. (2005) 'Implementing integrated oceans management: Australia's south east regional marine plan (SERMP) and Canada's eastern Scotian shelf integrated management (ESSIM) initiative', *Marine Policy*, vol 29, pp391–405

Fox, R. J., Crask, M. R. and Kim, J. (1988) 'Mail survey response rate: A meta-analysis of selected techniques for inducing responses', *Public Opinion Quarterly*, vol 52, pp467–491

Frankfort-Nachmias, C. and Nachmias, D. (1992) *Research Methods in the Social Sciences*, London, Edward Arnold

French, P. (1997) *Coastal and Estuarine Management*, London, Routledge

Fuller, R. A. (1999) 'A new urban environment: Is it achievable?', *Environmental Scientist*, vol 8, no 50, p11

Futrell, D. (1994) 'Ten reasons why surveys fail', *Quality Progress*, April, pp65–69

Galgano, F. A. (1998) 'Geomorphic analysis of modes of shoreline behaviour and the influence of tidal inlets on coastal configuration', unpublished PhD thesis, Geography Department, College Park, University of Maryland

Gallop, S. L., Bryan, K. R. and Coco, G. (2009) 'Video observation of rip currents on an embayed beach', *Journal of Coastal Research*, special issue 56, pp49–53

Gares, P. A. (1989) 'Geographers and public policy making: Lessons learned from the failure of the New Jersey Dune Management Plan,' *Professional Geographer*, vol 41, pp20–29

Garrity, S. D. and Levings, S. C. (1993) 'Marine debris along the Caribbean coast of Panama', *Marine Pollution Bulletin*, vol 26, no 6, pp317–324

Geelen, L. H. W., Cousin, E. F. H. and Schoon, C. E. (1985) 'Regeneration of dune slacks in the Amsterdam Waterwork Dunes', in Healey, M. G. and Doody, J. P. (eds) *Directions in European Coastal Management*, pp525–532, Cardigan, Samara Publishing

Getz, D. (1987) 'Capacity to absorb tourism: Concepts and implications for strategic planning', *Annals of Tourism Research*, vol 10, no 2, pp239–261

Gezer, E. (2004) 'Coastal scenic evaluation: A pilot study for Çıralı' unpublished MSc thesis, Ankara, Middle East Technical University

Gillie, R. D. (1997) 'Causes of coastal erosion in Pacific Island nations', *Journal of Coastal Research*, Special Issue, vol 24, pp173–204

Glavovic, B. C. (2004) 'ICM as a transformational practice of consensus building: A South African perspective', *Journal of Coastal Research*, vol SI39, pp1706–1710

GNRAC (Gruppo Nazionale per la Ricerca sull'Ambiente Costiero) (2006) 'Lo stato dei litorali italiani', *Studi Costieri*, vol 10, pp5–7

Godfrey, P. J. (1987) 'A successful local program for preserving and maintaining dunes on a developed barrier island', in Platt, R. H., Pelczarski, S. G. and Burbank, B. K. R. (eds) *Cities on the Beach*, pp163–169, University of Chicago Department of Geography Research Paper 224, Chicago, University of Chicago

Godfrey, P. J. and Godfrey, M. M. (1980) 'Ecological effects of off-road vehicles on Cape Cod', *Oceanus*, vol 23, pp56–67

Goggin, M. L., Bowman, A., Lester, J. P. and O'Toole, L. J. (1990) *Implementation Theory and Practice: Towards a Third Generation*, Glenvie, Scott Foresman and Co

Goldberg, E. D. (1994) *Coastal Zone Space: A Prelude to Conflict*, UNESCO Environment and Development Series, Paris, UNESCO

Good, J. W. (1994) 'Shore protection policy and practices in Oregon: An evaluation of implementation success', *Coastal Management*, vol 22, pp325–352

Goodman, S. L., Daniel, H. M., Seabrooke, W. and Jaffry, S. A. (1996) 'Using public surveys to estimate the total economic value of natural coastal resources', in Taussik, J. and Mitchell, J. (eds) *Partnership in Coastal Zone Management*, pp103–109, Cardigan, Samara Publishing

Gorman, R. M., Bryan, K. R. and Laing, A. (2003) 'Wave hindcast for the New Zealand region: Nearshore validation and coastal wave climate', *New Zealand Journal of Marine and Freshwater Research*, vol 37, pp567–588

Gregoire, T. G. and Valentine, H. Y. (2008) *Sampling Strategies for the Natural Environment*, London, Chapman-Hall CRC

Grenfell, R. D. and Ross, K. N. (1992) 'How dangerous is that visit to the beach? A pilot study of beach injuries', *Australian Family Physician*, vol 21, no 8, pp1145–1148

Griffin, T. and de Lacey, T. (2002) 'Green globe: Sustainability accreditation for tourism', in Harris, R., Griffin, T. and Williams, P. (eds) *Sustainable Tourism: A Global Perspective*, Chapter 7, Oxford, Butterworth-Heinemann, pp58–88

Griggs, G. B. (1999) 'The protection of California's coast: Past, present and future', *Shore and Beach*, vol 67, no 1, pp18–28

The Guardian (2007) 'Giant lobster attacks diver in Dorset', *The Guardian*, 10 July 2007, p7

Guerra, R., Bruzzi, L. and Darzia, G. (2004) 'Dredged material for beach nourishment along the Adriatic coast', in Micallef, A. and Vassallo, A. (eds) *Proceedings, First International Conference on the Management of Coastal Recreational Resources: Beaches, Yacht Marinas and Ecotourism, Malta*, pp49–58, Valletta, Malta, Euro-Mediterranean Centre on Insular Coastal Dynamics (ICoD)

Guilcher, A. and Hallégouët, B. (1991) 'Coastal dunes in Brittany and their management', *Journal of Coastal Research*, vol 7, pp517–533

Hallemeier, R. J. (1981) 'A profile zonation for seasonal sand beaches from wave climate', *Coastal Engineering*, vol 4, pp253–277

Hanson, H., Brampton, A., Capobianco, M., Dette, H. H., Hamm, L., Laustrup, C., Luchuga, A. and Spanhoff, R. (2002) 'Beach nourishment projects, practices and objectives: A European overview', *Coastal Engineering*, vol 47, pp81–111

Harlow, D. A. and Cooper, N. J. (1995) 'Bournemouth beach monitoring: The first twenty years', in Institution of Civil Engineers (ed) *Proceedings of Conference on Coastal Management '95: Putting Policy into Practice*, pp123–135, Institution of Civil Engineers, Bournemouth, Thomas Telford

Hart, D. E. (1999) 'Dynamics of mixed sand and gravel river mouth lagoons: Hapua', unpublished Master's dissertation, Christchurch, University of Canterbury

Hart, D. E. (2007) 'River-mouth lagoon dynamics on mixed sand and gravel barrier coasts', *Journal of Coastal Research*, Special Issue, vol 50, pp927–931

Hartman, D. (2006) 'Drowning and beach safety management along the Israeli Mediterranean beaches of Israel', *Journal of Coastal Research*, vol 22, pp1505–1514

Harvey, I. (1995) *Prevention of Skin Cancer: A Review of Available Strategies*, Bristol, University of Bristol

Haslett, S. K. (2000) *Coastal Systems*, London and New York, Routledge

Hassan, R., Scholes, R. and Ash, N. (eds) (2005) *Ecosystems and Human Well-being: Current State and Trends: Findings of the Condition and Trends Working Group*, Millennium Ecosystem Assessment Series 1, Working Group of the Millennium Ecosystem Assessment, Washington, DC, Island Press

HVRI (Hazards and Vulnerability Research Institute) (2004) 'The spatial hazard events and losses database for the United States', Version 6.2, Columbia, SC, University of South Carolina, www.sheldus.org.

HCEC (House of Commons Environment Committee) (1990) *Fourth Report: Pollution of Beaches*, vol 1, London, HMSO

Health Education Service (1990) 'Recommended standards for bathing beaches', A Committee Report on Policies for the Review and Approval of Plans and Specifications for Public Bathing Beaches, Albany, Board of State Public Health and Environmental Managers

Healy, R. G. and Zinn, J. A. (1985) 'Environment and development conflicts in coastal zone management,' *Journal of the American Planning Association*, vol 51, pp299–311

Heinz Center (2000) *The Hidden Costs of Coastal Hazards*, Washington, DC, Island Press

Hewitt, K. (1997) *Regions of Risk: A Geographical Introduction to Disasters*, Edinburgh, Longman

Hodgson, A. M. (1992) 'Hexagons for systems thinking', *European Journal of Operational Research*, vol 59, pp220–230

Hoefel, F. (1998) 'Diagnóstico da erosão costeira na praia de Piçarras', unpublished MSc dissertation, Universidade Federal do Rio de Janeiro, COPPE, Programa de Engenharia Oceânica, Rio de Janeiro

Hoefel, F. and Klein, A. H. F. (1997) 'Potencialidades da enseada de Itapocoroi e imediações como areas fontes de sedimento para engordamento artificial da praia de Piçarras, SC', in *VI Congresso da ABEQUA, Curitiba, PR*, pp396–400, Curitiba, ABEQUA

Holmes, C. W. and Beverstock, P. (1996) 'The Beach Management Plan for Lancing and Shoreham', in Taussik, J. and Mitchell, J. (eds) *Partnership in Coastal Zone Management*, pp361–369, Cardigan, Samara Publishing

Hosier, P. E., Kochhar, M. and Thayer, V. (1981) 'Off-road vehicle and pedestrian track effects on the sea-approach of hatchling loggerhead turtles', *Environmental Conservation*, vol 8, pp158–161

House, C. and Phillips, M. R. (2007) 'Islands of theory in a sea of practice: Implementation theory and coastal management', in Ozhan, E. (ed) *Proceedings of 8th International Conference on the Mediterranean Coastal Environment, MedCoast '07*, pp105–116, Ankara, Turkey, METU

Houston, J. R. (1996) 'International tourism and US beaches', *Shore and Beach*, vol 63, pp3–4

Houston, J. R. (2002) 'The economic value of beaches: A 2002 update', *Shore and Beach*, vol 70, no 1, pp3–10

HR Wallingford (1993) 'Verifca su modello fisico del progetto di ricostruzione delle spiagge "Palmasera" e "Sos Dorroles" di Cala Gonone, Golfo di Orosei', unpublished report, Dorgali Municipality

HR Wallingford (2000) 'St. George's Bay (Malta) Beach re-nourishment: Wave and sediment transport modelling', Report EX 4239 prepared for the Euro-Mediterranean Centre on Insular Coastal Dynamics, Valletta

HSE (Health and Safety Executive) (2008) 'Five steps to risk assessment', www.hse.gov.uk/pubns/indg163.pdf

Hutchison, J. and Leafe, R. N. (1995) 'Shoreline management: A view of the way ahead', in Institution of Civil Engineers (ed) *Proceedings of Conference on Coastal Management '95 – Putting Policy into Practice*, pp209–218, Institution of Civil Engineers, Bournemouth, Thomas Telford

IBGE (Institutio Brasileiro de Geografia e Estatística) (2007) *Censo Demográfico*, Rio de Janeiro, IBGE, www.ibge.gov.br

IDESCAT (Catalan Institute of Statistics) (2008) 'Institut d'Estadística de Catalunya', www.idescat.cat/

ILS (International Life Saving Federation) (2008) 'Drowning', www.ilsf.org

ILSE (International Life Saving Federation Europe) (2008) 'Home page', www.ilseurope.org

INPH (Instituto de Pesquisas Hidroviárias) (1984) 'Relatório de Viagem, Inspeções às Erosões da Praia de Piçarras, Relatório 251/84, Piçarras 500/01', Rio de Janeiro, INPH

INPH (1985a) 'Estudo de Proteção da Praia de Piçarras – SC, Levantamento Topohidrográfico e Perfis da Praia de Piçarras. Relatório 189/85, Piçarras 720/01', Rio de Janeiro, INPH

INPH (1985b) 'Estudo de Proteção da Praia de Piçarras – SC, Medições Hidráulicas e de Vento. Relatório 192/85, Piçarras 160/01', Rio de Janeiro, INPH

INPH (1986) 'Projeto de Proteção às Benfeitorias da Praia de Piçarras – SC. Relatório 05/86, Piçarras 930/01', Rio de Janeiro, INPH

INPH (1992) 'Projeto Básico para Recuperação das Praias de Piçarras e Penha – SC. Relatório 14/92, Piçarras 900/01', Rio de Janeiro, INPH

IOS (Institute of Oceanographic Science) (1980) 'Offshore sediment movement and its relation to observed tidal current and wave data', Report No 93, Southampton, Institute of Oceanographic Sciences

IPCC (Intergovernmental Panel on Climate Change) (2001) *Synthesis Report: A Contribution of Working Groups I, II and III to the Third Assessment Report of the IPCC*, edited by Watson, R. T. and the Core Writing Team, Cambridge and New York, Cambridge University Press

Jackson, D. W. T. and Cooper, J. A. G. (2009) 'Geological control on beach form: accommodation space and contemporary dynamics', *Journal of Coastal Research*, special issue 56, pp69–72

Jackson, N. L., Nordstrom, K. F., Bruno, M. S. and Spalding, V. L. (2000) 'Classification of spatial and temporal changes to a developed barrier island, Seven Mile Beach, New Jersey, USA', in Slaymaker, O. (ed) *Geomorphology, Human Activity and Global Environmental Change*, pp269–283, Chichester, John Wiley & Sons

James, R. J. (2000). 'The first step for environmental management of Australian beaches: establishing an effective policy framework', *Coastal Management*, vol 28, pp149–160

Jernelov, A. (1990) 'Recovery of damaged ecosystems', UNEP Technical Annex to the Report on the State of the Environment, UNEP Regional Seas Reports and Studies No 114/1, Nairobi, UNEP

Jensen, J. V. (1978) 'A heuristic for the analysis of the nature and problem', *Journal of Creative Behaviour*, vol 12, pp168–180

Johnson, G. and Scholes, K. (1988) *Exploring Cooperative Strategy*, Hemel Hempstead, Prentice Hall

Johnston, W. B. (1961) 'Locating the vegetation of early Canterbury: A map and the sources', *Transactions of the Royal Society of New Zealand (Botany)*, vol 1, no 2, pp5–15

Jones, A. L. and Phillips, M. R. (2008) 'Tourism development in the coastal zone: Managing natural and cultural change', in Krishnamurthy, R. R., Glavovic, B. C., Kanne, A., Green, D. R., Ramanathan, A. L., Han, Z., Tinti, S. and Agardy, T. (eds) *Integrated Coastal Zone Management: The Global Challenge*, pp375–389, Singapore, Research Publishing Services

Jowett, I. G., Richardson, J. and Bonnett, M. L. (2005) 'Relationship between flow regime and fish abundances in a gravel-bed river', *New Zealand Journal of Fish Biology*, vol 66, pp1419–1436

Jurado, E., Dantas, A. G. and Pereira da Silva, C. (2009) 'Coastal zone management: Tools for establishing a set of indicators to assess beach carrying capacity (Costa del Sol-Spain)', *Journal of Coastal Research*, special issue 56, pp1125–1129

Kahn, J. and Gowdy, J. (2000) 'Coping with complex and dynamic systems: An approach to an trans-disciplinary understanding of coastal zone developed partnerships', *Journal of Coastal Conservation*, vol 5, pp163–170

Kaluwin, C. and Smith, A. (1997) 'Coastal vulnerability and integrated coastal zone management in the Pacific island region', *Journal of Coastal Research*, vol SI14, pp95–115

Kamphius, J. W. (1980) 'Basic near-shore processes in coastal engineering', A. J. Bowen (convenor), short-course lecture notes, ACROSES, National Research Council, Ottawa, 4.1–4.45

Kates, R. W. (1962) 'Hazard and choice perception in flood plane management', Department of Geography Research Paper 78, Chicago, University of Chicago

Kay, D., Wyer, M., McDonald, A. and Woods, N. (1990) 'The application of water quality standards to United Kingdom bathing waters', *Journal of the Institute of Water and Environmental Management*, vol 4, no 5, pp436–441

Kay, R. and Alder, J. (1999) *Coastal Planning and Management*, Abingdon, Oxon, E. & F. N. Spon

Kearney, J., Berkes, F., Charles, A., Pinkerton E. and Wiber, M. (2007) 'The role of participatory governance and community-based management in integrated coastal and ocean management in Canada', *Coastal Management*, vol 35, pp79–104

Kenyon, J. C., Brainard, R. E., Hoeke, R. H., Parrish, F. A and Wilkinson, C. B. (2006) 'Towed diver surveys, a method for mesoscale spatial assessment of benthic reef habitat', *Coastal Management*, vol 34, pp339–349

Ketchum, B. H. (1972) *The Waters Edge*, Woodhole, MA, MIT Press

Kidder, L. H. and Judd, C. M. (1986) *Research Methods in Social Relations*, 5th edition, Holt, New York, Reinhart and Winston

King, P. (1999) *The Fiscal Impact of Beaches in California*, Public Research Institute, San Francisco, University of California

Kirk, R. M. (1980) 'Mixed sand and gravel beaches: Morphology, processes and sediments', *Progress in Physical Geography*, vol 4, pp189–210

Kirk, R. M. (1991) 'River-beach interaction on mixed sand and gravel coasts: A geomorphic model for water resource planning', *Applied Geography*, vol 11, pp267–287

Kirk, R. M. and Lauder, G. A. (2000) *Significant Coastal Lagoon Systems in the South Island, New Zealand: Coastal Processes and Lagoon Mouth Closure*, Wellington, Department of Conservation

Klein, A. H. F. and Menezes, J. T. (2001) 'Beach morphodynamics and profile sequence for a headland bay coast', *Journal of Coastal Research*, vol 17, no 4, pp812–835

Klein, A. H. F., Diehl, F. L. and Benedet, L. (2005) 'The paradigm between beach protection and beach restoration: Case studies in Santa Catarina State, Southeastern Brazil', *ICCCM'05, Book of Abstracts*, Algarve, Tavira

Klein, Y. L., Osleeb, J. P. and Viola, M. R. (2004) 'Tourism generated earnings in the coastal zone: A regional analysis', *Journal of Coastal Research*, vol 20, no 4, pp1080–1088

Komar, P. D. (1976) *Beach Processes and Sedimentation*, New Jersey, Prentice-Hall

Komar, P. D. (1997) *The Pacific Northwest: Living on the Shores of Oregon and Washington*, Durham, NC, Duke University Press

Komar, P. D. (1998) 'The 1997–98 El Niño and erosion of the Oregon coast', *Shore and Beach*, vol 66, pp33–41

Kraus, N. C. and Galgano, F. A. (2001) 'Beach erosional hot spot: Types, causes, and solutions', Coastal Hydraulics Laboratory (CHL), Coastal and Hydraulics Engineering Technical Note (CHETN), US Army Corps of Engineers (USACE), (CHLCHETN-II-44, September), Vicksburg, Virginia, USACE, http://cirp.wes.army.milVcirp/cirpcetns.html

Kraus, N. C., Larson, M. and Wise, R. A. (1999) 'Depth of closure in beach fill design', in FSBPA (ed) *Proceedings of 1999 National Conference on Beach Preservation Technology*, Tallahasse, FL, FSBPA

Krumbein, W. C. (1941) 'Measurement and geologic significance of shape and roundness of sedimentary particles', *Journal of Sedimentary Research.*, vol 11, pp64–72

Kullenberg, G. (2001) 'Contributions of marine and coastal area research and observations towards sustainable development of large coastal cities', *Ocean and Coastal Management*, vol SI44, pp283–294

Kuzutürk, E. and Kütle, B. (2005) 'Çıralı Deniz Kaplumbağası Yuvalama Kumsalı, Tekirova, Beycik, Maden ve Boncuk Koyları Alan Çalışması Raporu', Çıralı, Ulupinar-Çıralı Cooperative

Larson, M. (1991) 'Equilibrium profile of a beach with varying grain size', in *Proceedings of Coastal Sediments 1991*, pp861–874, New York, ASCE Press

Lazarow, N. (2009) 'Using observed market expenditure to estimate the value of recreational surfing to the Gold Coast, Australia', *Journal of Coastal Research*, special issue 56, pp1130–1134

Leatherman, S. P. (1991) 'Modelling shore response to sea level rise on sedimentary coasts', *Progress in Physical Geography*, vol 14, pp447–464

Leatherman, S. P. (1997) 'Beach rating: A methodological approach', *Journal of Coastal Research*, vol 13, no 1, pp253–258

Leatherman, S. P. (1998) *America's Best Beaches*, Coastal Laboratory, International Hurricane Research Centre, Miami, Florida International University

Leatherman, S. P. (2001) 'Socio and economic costs of sea level rise', in Douglas, B.C., Kearney, M.S. and Leatherman, S. P. (eds) *Sea Level Rise: History and Consequences*, pp181–223, San Diego, CA, Academic Press

Lechua, A. and Spanhoff, R. (2002) 'Beach nourishment projects, practices, and objectives: A European overview', *Coastal Engineering*, vol 47, pp81–111

Lélis, R. J. F. and Calliari, L. J. (2004) 'Historical shoreline changes near lagoonal and river stabilized inlets in Rio Grande do Sul state, southern Brazil', *Journal of Coastal Research*, Special Issue, vol 39 (Proceedings of the 8th International Coastal Symposium), pp301–305

Li, M., Fernando, P. T., Pan, S., O'Connor, B. A. and Chen, D. (2007) 'Development of a quasi-3D numerical model for sediment transport prediction in the coastal region', *Journal of Hydro-environment Research*, vol 1, nos 2 & 4, pp143–156

Llewellyn, P. J. and Shackley, S. E (1996) 'The effects of mechanical beach cleaning', *British Wildlife*, vol 7, no 3, pp147–155

Lobb, M. (2008) 'Margam steelworks, conveyors and stacks', www.geograph.org. uk/photo/980405

Local Government Association (2002) 'On the edge: The coastal strategy', A report prepared by the Local Government Association Special Interest Group on Coastal Issues, London, LGA

Lockhart, D. G. and Ashton, S. E. (1991) 'Tourism in Malta', *Scottish Geographical Magazine*, vol 107, no 1, pp22–32

MAFF (Ministry for Agriculture, Fisheries and Food) (1995) 'Shoreline management plans: A guide for coastal defence authorities', London, MAFF

MAFF (2000) 'A review for shoreline management plans, 1996–1999', London, MAFF

MAFF/Welsh Office (1993) 'Strategy for flood and coastal defence in England and Wales', MAFF publications PB1471, London, MAFF

Makowski, C. and Rusenko, K. (2007) 'Recycled glass cullet as an alternative beach fill material: Results of biological and chemical analysis', *Journal of Coastal Research*, vol 2393, pp545–552

Malhotra, N. K. and Birks, D. F. (1999) *Marketing Research*, European edition, London, Prentice Hall

Mania, R. and Pranzini, E. (1996) 'Sedimentological study of the nearshore of Cala Gonone (Eastern Sardinia, Italy) oriented to the beach improvement', *Bollettino della Società Geologica Italiano*, vol 115, pp95–104

Mannoni, S. and Pranzini, E. (2004) 'From agriculture to tourism: A cause of beach erosion', in Micallef, A. and Vassallo, A. (eds) *Proceedings of the First International Conference on the Management of Coastal Recreational Resources: Beaches, Yacht Marinas and Coastal Ecotourism*, pp79–85, Euro-Mediterranean Centre on Insular Coastal Dynamics, Valletta, University of Malta

Marin, V. (2006) 'La gestione integrata del Litorale: Elaborazione ed applicazione di un metodo di valutazione degli aspetti ambientalle e socio-economici per la gestione della spiagge della riviera del Beigua', unpublished PhD thesis, Genova, Italy, University of Genova

Marin, V., Dursi, R., Ivaldi, R., Palmisani, F. and Fabiano, M. (2004) 'Users' perception analysis in Ligurian beaches, Italy', in Micallef, A. and Vassallo, A. (eds) *1st International Conference on the Management of Coastal Recreational Resources: Beaches, Yacht Marinas and Coastal Ecotourism*, pp141–149, Euro-Mediterranean Centre of Coastal Dynamics, Valletta, University of Malta

Marin, V., Ivalsi, R., Palmisani, F. and Fabiano, M. (2007) 'Application of participatory method for beach management', in Ozhan, E. (ed) *Proceedings of 8th International Conference on the Mediterranean Coastal Environment, MedCoast '07*, pp283–294, Ankara, Turkey, METU

Marlowe, H. (1999) 'Assessing the economic benefits of America's coastal regions', in *Trends and Future Challenges for US National Ocean and Coastal Policy: Proceedings of a Workshop*, pp27–29, Washington, DC, US Government Printer

Marson, A. (1994) 'Planning the coastal zone: A case study of special programmes in Italy', in Soares de Carralho, G. and Velos Gomes, F. (eds) *Littoral '94*, pp743–752, Instituto de Hidraulica e Recursos Hídricos, Porto, University of Porto

Martí, C. (2001) 'La transformació del paisatge litoral del centre de la Costa Brava en els darrers cinquanta anys. Palamós, Calonge i Castell-Platja d'Aro', Memòria de recerca del doctorat de Medi Ambient de la UdG, Girona, Italy, University of Girona

Masselink, G. and Hughes, M. G. (2008) *Introduction to Coastal Processes*, London, Hodder Arnold

Mastronuzzi, G., Palmentola, G. and Sanso, P. (1992) 'Morphological types of rocky coasts on south-eastern Apulia, Italy', in Sterr, H., Hofstide, J. and Plag, P. (eds) *Interdiciplinary Discussions of Coastal Research and Coastal Management Issues and Problems*, pp784–792, Frankfurt, Peter Lang

Mauriello, M. N. (1989) 'Dune maintenance and enhancement: A New Jersey example', in *Coastal Zone '89*, pp1023–1037, New York, American Society of Civil Engineers

Mauriello, M. N. and Halsey, S. D. (1987) 'Dune building on a developed coast', in *Coastal Zone '87*, pp1313–1327, New York, American Society of Civil Engineers

Mazmanian, D. and Sabatier, P. (1978) 'Policy evaluation and legislative reformulation: The California Coastal Commissions', San Franscico, Amererican Political Sciences Association

MCA (Maritime and Coastguard Agency) (2007) *Fatalities in the UK Search and Rescue Records*, London, MCA

McConnell, K. (1977) 'Congestion and willingness to pay: A study of beach use', *Land Economics*, vol 53, pp185–195

McCool, S. and Lime, D. W. (2003) 'Tourism carrying capacity: Tempting fantasy or useful reality', *Journal of Sustainable Tourism*, vol 9, no 5, pp372–388

McCue, J. W. (1995) 'A coherent approach for establishing coastal zone management units: A case study on the east coast of Qatar', in Institution of Civil Engineers (ed) *Proceedings of Conference on Coastal Management '95 – Putting Policy into Practice*, pp1–14, Institution of Civil Engineers, Bournemouth, Thomas Telford

McIntyre, A. D. (1990) 'Sewage in the sea', Annex XII of 'State of the Marine Environment', GESAMP Reports and Studies No 39, IMO/FAO/UNESCO/WHO/IAEAA/UN/UNEP

McKenna, J. and Cooper, J. A. G. (2006) 'Sacred cows in coastal management: The need for a cheap and transitory model', *Area*, vol 38, pp421–431

McKenna, J., Power, J., Macleod, M. and Cooper, J. A. G. (2000) *Rural Beach Management: A Good Practice Guide*, Lifford, Donegal County Council

MCS (Maritime and Conservation Society) (2008) 'Good beach guide', MCS, www.goodbeachguide.co.uk/details.php?beach=Aberavon

Micallef, A. (1996) 'Socio-economic aspects of beach management: A pilot study of the Maltese islands', in Ozhan, E. (ed) *Proceedings of the International Workshop on ICZM in the Mediterranean and Black Seas: Immediate Needs for Research, Education, Training and Implementation*, pp111–124, Ankara, Turkey, METU

Micallef, A. (2002) 'Bathing area management in the Maltese Islands', unpublished PhD thesis, Swansea, University of Wales

Micallef, A. and Cassar, M. (eds) (2001) 'An environmental impact statement on the proposed beach nourishment project at Bajja ta' San George, San Giljan, Malta: A technical report and non-technical summary', St Julians, Malta Ministry for Tourism

Micallef, A. and Williams, A. T. (2002) 'Theoretical strategy considerations for beach management', *Ocean and Shoreline Management*, vol 45, no 4–5, pp261–275

Micallef, A. and Williams, A. T. (2003a) 'Application of function analysis to bathing areas in the Maltese islands', *Journal of Coastal Conservation*, vol 9, no 2, pp147–158

Micallef, A. and Williams, A. T. (2003b) 'Application of a novel bathing area evaluation (BARE) system: A pilot study of selected areas of the Dalmatian coast', Report commissioned by the WWF/MedPO, Rome, Italy

Micallef, A. and Williams, A. T. (2004) 'A novel beach registration/rating scheme: A case study of the Maltese islands', *Ocean and Shoreline Management*, vol 47, no 5–6, pp225–242

Micallef, A. and Williams A. T. (2005) 'Report to the Priority Actions Programme/ Regional Activity Centre of the Mediterranean Action Plan (United Nations Environment Programme) on the evaluation of bathing area management in the Mediterranean'

Micallef, A., Morgan, R. and Williams, A. T. (1999) 'User preferences and priorities on Maltese beaches: Findings and potential importance for tourism', in Randazzo, G. (ed) *Coastal Environmental Management*, EUCC-Italy/EUCC

Mifsud, C. R., Stevens, D. T. and Baldacchino, A. E. (2002–2003) *Strategic Action Plan for the Conservation of Maltese Coastal and Marine Biodiversity*, SAP-BIO Project, RAC/SPA, Mediterranean Action Plan, Valletta, Malta Environment and Planning Authority

Mills, K., Kennish, M. J. and Moore, K. A. (2008) 'Research and monitoring components of the National Estuarine Research Reserve System', in Kennish, M. J. (ed) *Research and Monitoring of NEERS Aquatic Ecosystems*, Special Issue no 55 of *Journal of Coastal Research*, Royal Palm Beach, FL

Ministry of Works, Transportation and the Environment (1993) *Recovering the Coast*, Spain, State Coast Office

Mintzberg, H. (1994) 'Crafting strategy', Readings 1, B822 Creative Management, Open University Business School, Milton Keynes, Open University

Mintzberg, H. and Waters, J. A. (1989) 'Of strategies, deliberate and emergent', in Asch, D. and Bowman, C. (eds) *Readings in Strategic Management*, pp37–56, London, Macmillan in association with the Open University

Mitchell, J. K. (1988) 'Confronting natural disasters: An international decade for natural hazard reduction', *Environment*, vol 30, no 2, pp25–29

Modimar (1999) 'Studio della deflazione eolica', unpublished report, Provincia di Cagliari

Modimar (2001) 'Aggiornamento dell studio della deflazione eolica', unpublished report, Provincia di Cagliari

Montoya, F. J. (1990) 'Management and protection of the coast: The Spanish Act of 1988', in Quelennec, R., Ercolani, E. and Michon, G. (eds) *Littoral '90*, pp602–606, Luminy, Marseilles, Association EuroCoast, BRGM

MOR (Monitorul Oficial al României) (1996) *Martie, nr. 48, (Hotărâre nr. 107 pentru aprobarea normelor privind utilizarea turistică a plajei litoralului Mării Negre)*, MOR

MOR (2004) *Martie, nr. 242 (Ordinul 455 privind autorizarea, clasificarea, avizarea șicontrolul activităților de turism în zona costieră)*, MOR

Moreno, L. J. (2005) 'Headland-Bay beach', in Schwartz, M. L. (ed) *Encyclopaedia of Coastal Science*, pp508–511, Dordrecht, Springer

Morgan, R. and Micallef, A. (1999) 'The use and management of rocky shore platforms in relation to coastal tourism in Malta', in Ozhan, E. (ed) *Proceedings of the Joint Conference on Land–Ocean Interactions: Managing Coastal Ecosystems, MedCoast-EMECS '99*, pp895–906, MedCoast Secretariat, Ankara, Turkey, METU

Morgan, R. and Williams, A. T. (1995) 'Socio-demographic parameters and user priorities at Gower Beaches, UK', in Healy, M. G. and Doody, J. P. (eds) *Directions in European Coastal Management*, pp83–90, Cardigan, EUCC and Samara Publishing

Morgan, R., Jones, T. C. and Williams, A. T. (1993) 'Opinions and perceptions of UK Heritage Coast beach users: Some management implications from the Glamorgan Heritage Coast', *Journal of Coastal Research*, vol 9, no 4, pp1083–1093

Morgan, R., Bursalioglu, B., Hapoglu-Balas, L., Jones, T. C., Ozhan, E. and Williams, A. T. (1995) 'Beach user opinions and beach ratings: A pilot study on the Turkish Aegean Coast', in Ozhan, E. (ed) *MedCoast '95*, pp373–383, MedCoast Secretariat, Ankara, Turkey, METU

Morgan, R., Gatell, E., Junyant, R., Micallef, A., Ozhan, E. and Williams, A. T. (1996) 'Pilot studies of Mediterranean beach user perceptions', in Ozhan, E. (ed) *ICZM in the Mediterranean and Black Sea: Immediate Needs for Research*, pp99–110, Ankara, Turkey, METU

Morgan, R., Gatell, E., Junyent, R., Micallef, A., Ozhan, E. and Williams, A. T. (2000) 'An improved beach user climate index', *Journal of Coastal Conservation*, vol 6, no 1, pp41–50

Moser, C. and Kalton, G. (1983) *Survey Methods in Social Investigation*, London, Heinemann

Motyka, J. M. and Brampton, A. H. (1993) 'A coastal management mapping of littoral cells', HR Wallingford Report SR328, Oxon, HR Wallingford Ltd

MSS (Mediterranean Survey and Services) (1989) 'Studio dell'erosione dell'arenile del Poetto di Cagliari', unpublished report for the Provincia di Cagliari, Comune di Cagliari and Ministero della Marina Mercantile, financed by the CEE

Muehe, D. (2000) *Orla: Definição de Limites e Tipologias sob o Ponto de Vista Morfodinâmico e Evolutivo*, LGFCS, Depto de Geografia, Rio de Janeiro, UFRJ

NBSC (National Beach Safety Council) (2008) 'Beach safety', www.nationalbeachsafety.org.uk/

Neale, D. M., Pindur, N. B., Reedy, M. C. and Watson, B. (2007) *The West Coast Marine and Coastal Environment: An Initial Report for the West Coast Marine Protection Forum*, Hokitika, West Coast Marine Protection Forum

NELC (North East Lincolnshire Council) (2007) *North East Lincolnshire Council's Benchmarking Exercise*, Grimsby, NELC

Nel·lo, O. (2005) 'El Pla director del Sistema Costaner: Una aposta de futur', in *Generalitat de Catalunya Pla Director del Sistema Costaner-PDUSC*, Barcelona, Generalitat de Catalunya

Nelson, C. and Botterill, D. (2002) 'Evaluating the contribution of beach quality awards to the local tourism industry in Wales: The Green Coast Award', *Ocean and Coastal Management*, vol 45, pp157–170

Nelson, C. and Williams, A. T. (1997) 'Bathing water quality and health implications', in Rajar, R. and Brebbia, C. A. (eds) *Water Pollution: IV. Modelling, Measuring and Prediction*, pp175–183, Southampton, Computational Mechanics Publications

Nelson, C., Williams, A. T., Rees, G., Botterill, D. and Richards, A. (1999) 'Beach health risk assessment and pollution perception', in Trudgill, S. T., Walling, D. and Webb, B. (eds) *RGS IBG Water Quality Processes and Policy*, pp65–72, London, John Wiley & Sons

Nelson, C., Morgan, R., Williams, A. T. and Woods, J. (2000) 'Beach awards and management in Wales, UK', *Ocean and Coastal Management*, vol 43, no 1, pp87–98

Nelson, C., Williams, A. T. and Botterill, D. (2003) 'Conceptual modelling of beach management: South Wales case studies', in Ozhan, E. (ed) *Proceedings of the 6th International Conference on the Mediterranean Environment*, pp1321–1332, MedCoast, Ankara, Turkey, METU

Nepal, S. K. (2000) 'Tourism in protected areas', *Annals of Tourism Research*, vol 27, no 3, pp661–681

Neves Filho, S. C. (1992) 'Variações da maré meteorológica no litoral sudeste do Brasil', unpublished MSc dissertation, Programa de Engenharia Oceânica, COPPE, Rio de Janeiro, Universidade Federal do Rio de Janeiro

New Jersey Division of Fish, Game and Wildlife (1999) 'Avalon Beach Nesting Bird Management Plan/Agreement', unpublished Draft, Trenton, NJ, New Jersey Department of Environmental Protection

Nir, Y. (2004) 'Israel Mediterranean coasts: Faults and mistakes in beach management or the seven pillars of unwisdom', in Micallef, A. and Vassallo, A. (eds) *The First International Conference on the Management of Coastal Recreational Resources: Beaches, Yacht Marinas and Ecotourism*, pp87–89, Euro-Mediterranean Centre on Insular Coastal Dynamics, Valletta, University of Malta

NOAA (National Oceanic and Atmospheric Adminstration) (2008) 'Coastal Zone Management Act', http://coastalmanagement.noaa.gov/czm/czm_act.html

Nordstrom, K. F. (2000) *Beaches and Dunes of Developed Coasts*, Cambridge, Cambridge University Press

Nordstrom, K. F. (2008) *Beach and Dune Restoration*, Cambridge, Cambridge University Press

Nordstrom, K. F., Psuty, N. P. and Fisher, S. F. (1978) 'Empirical models of dune formation as the basis for dune district zoning', in *Coastal Zone '78*, pp1489–1507, New York, American Society of Civil Engineers

Nordstrom, K. F., Jackson, N. L., Bruno, M. S. and de Butts, H. A. (2002) 'Municipal initiatives for managing dunes in coastal residential areas: A case study of Avalon, New Jersey, USA', *Geomorphology*, vol 47, pp137–152

Nordstrom, K. F., Jackson, N. L. and Pranzini, E. (2004) 'Beach sediment alteration by natural processes and human actions: Elba Island, Italy', *Annals of the Association of American Geographers*, vol 94, pp794–806

Nuell, H. (2001) 'Evolució dels usos del sòl a la Costa Brava, 1957–1993', Memòria de recerca del doctorat de Medi Ambient de la UdG, Girona, University of Girona

OCRM (Office of Coastal Resource Management) (2004) 'The EC 1999 ICZM: A strategy for Europe', EC, Brussels, USA 1872 CZN Act, Office of Coastal Resource Management, http://coastalmanagement.noaa.gov/about/welcome.html

Odum, E. (1982) 'Environmental degradation and the tyranny of small decisions', *BioScience*, vol 32, no 9, pp728–729

Olsen, S. B., Tobey, J. and Kerr, M. A. (1997) 'Common framework for learning from ICM experience', *Ocean and Coastal Management*, vol 37, no 2, pp155–174

Olsen, S. B., Lowry, K. and Tobey, J. (1998) 'A manual for assessing progress in coastal management', Coastal Resources Centre, Report No 2211, Narragansett, RI, University of Rhode Island

Orford, J. (1977) 'A proposed model for storm beach sedimentation', *Earth Surface Processes and Landforms*, vol 2, pp381–400

Orford, J. D., Forbes, D. L. and Jennings, S. C. (2002) 'Organisational controls, typologies and time scales of paraglacial gravel-dominated coastal systems', *Geomorphology*, vol 48, pp51–85

Oruç, A., Türkozan, O. and ve Durmuş, H. (2003) 'Deniz Kaplumbağalarının İzinde, Deniz Kaplumbağası Yuvalama Kumsalları Değerlendirme Raporu', Istanbul, WWF-Turkey

Ozer, A. and Ulzega, A. (1980) 'Su la repartition des éboulis ordonnés en Sardaigne', *Builetyn Peryglacjalny*, vol 28, pp259–265

Ozhan, E. (1996) 'Coastal zone management in Turkey', *Ocean and Coastal Management*, vol 30, nos 2–3, pp153–176

Ozhan, E. (2005) *Coastal Area Management in Turkey*, Split, Croatia, PAPRAC

Ozhan, E., Uras, A. and Aktas, E. (1993) 'Turkish legislation pertinent to coastal zone management issues', in Ozhan, E. (ed) *MedCoast '93*, pp333–346, MedCoast Secretariat, Ankara, Turkey, METU

Ozhan, E., Trumbic, I., Sjaricic, Z. and Prem, M. (2005) *Coastal Area Management in Turkey*, Split, PAPRAC

Pacini, M., Pranzini E. and Sirito G. (1997) 'Beach nourishment with angular gravel at Cala Gonone (Eastern Sardinia, Italy)', in Ozhan, E. (ed) *MedCoast '97*, pp1043–1058, Ankara, Turkey, METU

Parkin, J. (2000) *Engineering Judgement and Risk*, London, Thomas Telford

Payne, S. L. (1951) *The Art of Asking Questions*, Princeton, NJ, Princeton University Press

Peel, D. and Lloyd, M. G. (2004) 'The social reconstruction of the marine environment: Towards marine spatial planning?', *TPR*, vol 75, no 3, pp359–378

Pendleton, L., Martin, N. and Webster, D. G. (2001) 'Perceptions of environmental quality: A survey study of beach use and perceptions in Los Angeles county', *Marine Pollution Bulletin*, vol 42, no 11, pp1155–1160

Pereira da Silva, C. (2002) 'Beach carrying capacity – assessment: How important is it?', *Journal of Coastal Research*, vol SI36, pp190–197

Pereira da Silva, C. (2003) 'Definição da capacidade de carga de praias. O troço litoral S.Torpes Ilha do Pessegueiro', unpublished PhD thesis, Lisbon, Universidade Nova de Lisboa

Peterlin, M., Dursi, R. and Koss, B. C. (2005) 'Public perception of environmental pressures within the Slovenian coastal zone', *Ocean and Coastal Management*, vol 48, pp189–204

Pew (2003) 'A report to the nation: Recommendations for a new ocean policy', Arlington, VA, Pew Oceans Commission

Philipp, R., Pond, K. and Rees, G. (1995) 'A study of litter and medical waste on the UK coastline', *Health and Hygiene*, vol 16, pp3–8

Phillips, M. R. (2007) 'Beach response to a total exclusion barrage: Cardiff Bay, South Wales, UK', *Journal of Coastal Research*, vol 23, no 3, pp794–805

Phillips, M. R. and Williams, A. T. (2007) 'Depth of closure and shoreline indicators: Empirical formulae for beach management', *Journal of Coastal Research*, vol 23, no 2, pp487–500

Phillips, M. R., Abraham, E. J., Williams, A. T. and House, C. H. (2007a) 'Sustainability and function analysis as a management tool: The South Wales (UK) coastline', *Journal of Coastal Conservation and Management*, vol 11, pp159–170

Phillips, M. R., Duck, R. W. and Williams, A. T. (2007b) 'Beach consequences of an industrial heritage: Future opportunities for Scotland and Wales?', in Ozhan, E. (ed) *Proceedings of the Eighth International Conference on the Mediterranean Coastal Environment, MedCoast '07*, vol 1, pp305–316, Ankara, Turkey, METU

Piçarras (2008) 'Home page', www.balneariopicarras.com.br/

Pigram, J. (1983) *Outdoor Recreation and Resources Management*, New York, St Martins Press

Pike, E. B. (1994) 'Health effects of sea bathing (WM1 9021). Phase III. Final report to the Department of the Environment', WRc Report DoE 3412 (P), Medmenham, WRc plc

Pike, E. B. (1997) 'Quality at the beach-head', *Current Quality – a Newsletter on Recreational Water Issues*, Robens Institute, Guildford, Robens Centre for Public and Environmental Health

Piqueras, V. Y. (2005) 'Gestión del uso público según el sistema de calidad turístico Español', paper at VIII Jornadas Españolas de Ingeniería de Costas e Puertos conference, 17–18 May, Sitges, Spain

Planning Services Division (1990) 'Malta Structure Plan', Report of Survey (1), Valletta, Ministry for the Development of Infrastructure

Platt, R. H. (1994) 'Evolution of coastal hazards policies in the United States', *Coastal Management*, vol 22, pp265–284

Platt, R. H. (1995) 'Private land, public uses', *Issues in Science and Technology*, vol 12, no 2, pp85–89

Polette, M. and Raucci, G. D. (2003) 'Methodological proposal for carrying capacity analysis in sandy beaches: A case study at the Central Beach of Balneário Camboriú (Santa Catarina, Brazil)', *Journal of Coastal Research*, Special Issue, vol 35, pp94–106

Pond, K. and Rees, G. (2000) 'Coastwatch UK: A public participation survey', *Journal of Coastal Conservation*, vol 6, no 1, pp61–66

Pond, K., Cavalieri, M. and van Maale, B. (2000) 'Management frameworks', in Bartram, J. and Rees, G. (eds) *Monitoring Bathing Waters: A Practical Guide to the Design and Implementation of Assessments and Monitoring Programmes*, pp69–82, London and New York, WHO

Pos, J. D., Young, S. W. and West, M. S. (1995) 'Lizard Point to Land's End Shoreline Management Plan', in Institution of Civil Engineers (ed) *Proceedings of Conference on Coastal Management 95 – Putting Policy into Practice*, pp163–177, Institution of Civil Engineers, Bournemouth, Thomas Telford

POST (Parliamentary Office of Science and Technology) (2007) 'Ecosystem services', *Postnote*, vol 281, pp1–4, www.parliament.uk/post

Potts, J. S. (1999) 'The information needs and resource requirements of coastal defence groups in England and Wales', unpublished PhD thesis, Cardiff, University of Wales

Powell, K. A. and Brampton, A. H. (1995) 'Regional process modelling for shoreline management: Example studies from southern England', in Institution of Civil Engineers (ed) *Proceedings of Conference on Coastal Management 95 – Putting Policy into Practice*, pp65–77, Institution of Civil Engineers, Bournemouth, Thomas Telford

Pranzini, E. (1994) 'Bilancio sedimentario ed evoluzione storica delle spiagge', *Il Quaternario*, vol 7, pp197–202

Pranzini, E. (2001) 'Updrift river mouth migration on cuspate deltas: Two examples from the coast of Tuscany (Italy)', *Geomorphology*, vol 1–2, pp125–132

Pranzini, E. (2004) *La Forma delle Coste. Geomorfologia Costiera, Impatto Antropico e Difesa dei Litorali*, Bologna, Zanichelli

Purnell, R. G. (1995) 'Shoreline management plans: National objectives and implementation', in Institution of Civil Engineers (ed) *Proceedings of Conference on Coastal Management 95 – Putting Policy into Practice*, pp110–122, Institution of Civil Engineers, Bournemouth, Thomas Telford

Quan, L., Crispin, B., Bennett, E. and Gomez, A. (2006) 'Beliefs and practices to prevent drowning among Vietnamese-American adolescents and parents', *Injury Prevention*, vol 12, pp427–429

Quinn, R. (1980) *Strategies for Change*, Homewood, IL, Irwin

Radic, M., Micallef, A., Williams, A.T. and Ergin, A. (2006) 'Application of the Bathing Area Registration and Evaluation (BARE) system: Experience from Istria County on the northern Croatian coastline', in Micallef, A. and Vassallo, A. (eds) *Proceedings of the Second International Conference on the Management of Coastal Recreational Resources: Beaches, Yacht Marinas and Ecotourism, Malta*, pp179–190, Euro-Mediterranean Centre on Insular Coastal Dynamics, Valletta, University of Malta

Rees, G. (1997) 'Lies, damned lies and beach awards', *Current Issues*, vol 1, pp1–2, Guildford, Robens Institute, University of Surrey

Rees, G. and Pond, K. (1995) 'Marine litter monitoring programmes: A review of methods with special reference to national surveys', *Marine Pollution Bulletin*, vol 30, no 2, pp103–108

Reid, J., Santana, G. G., Klein, A. H. F. and Diehl, F. L. (2005) 'Perceived and realized social and economic impacts of sand nourishment at Piçarras beach, Santa Catarina', *Shore and Beach*, vol 73, no 4, pp14–18

Rickard, C. A, McLachlan, A. and Kerley, G. I. H. (1994) 'The effects of vehicular and pedestrian traffic on dune vegetation in South Africa', *Ocean and Coastal Management*, vol 23, pp225–247

RLSS UK (Royal Life Saving Society UK) (2008a) 'Life savers', www.lifesavers.org.uk

RLSS UK (2008b) *Risk Assessment Principles and Practice for Beaches*, Training programme, Broom, RLSS UK

RLSS UK/RoSPA (Royal Society for the Prevention of Accidents) (2002) *Drowning Statistics 2002*, database, RLSS UK/RoSPA

RLSS UK/RoSPA (2004) *Safety on Beaches: Operational Guidelines*, RLSS UK, RoSPA and Birmingham University

RNLI (Royal National Lifeboat Institution) (2005) *A Guide to Coastal Signs and Symbols*, Poole, RNLI

RNLI (2007) *A Guide to Coastal Public Rescue Equipment*, Poole, RNLI

RNLI (2008) 'Lifeboats', www.rnli.org.uk

Robson, S. (1995) *Real World Research: A Resource for Social Scientists and Practitioner-Researcher*, Oxford, Blackwell

Rosenberg, G. A. (1976) 'Regulation of off-road vehicles', *Boston College Environmental Affairs Law Review*, vol 175, pp199–200

Runcie, R. and Fairgrieve, I. (1995) 'A case study for the Mablethorpe to Skegness first phase beach nourishment', in Institution of Civil Engineers (ed) *Proceedings of Conference on Coastal Management '95 – Putting Policy into Practice*, pp34–42, Institution of Civil Engineers, Bournemouth, Thomas Telford

Saarinen, T. F. (1966) 'Perception of drought hazard on the Great Plains', Department of Geography Research Paper 209, Chicago, University of Chicago Press

Sanjaume, E. (1988) 'The dunes of Saler, Valencia, Spain,' *Journal of Coastal Research*, Special Issue, vol 3, pp63–69

Santos, I. R., Friedrich, A. C., Wallner-Kersanach, M. and Fillmann, G. (2005) 'Influence of socio-economic characteristics of beach users on litter generation', *Ocean and Coastal Management*, vol 48, pp742–752

SANTUR (Santa Catarina Turismo) (2000) 'Pesquisa mercadológica – estudo da demanda turística – temporada 2000 (sinopse comparativa de 1998, 1999 e 2000)', Florianópolis, Secretaria do Estado de Desenvolvimento Econômico

SANTUR (2007) 'Estatísticas da demanda turística 2007', www.sol.sc.gov.br/index. php?option=com_content&view=article&id=57&Itemid=74

SANTUR (2008) 'Pesquisa mercadológica estudo da demanda turísta, Município de Balneário Camboriú', Florianópolis, SANTUR, www.santur.sc.gov.br/ index.php?option=com_docman&task=cat_view&gid=45&Itemid=215

Sardá, R., Avila, C. and Mora, J. (2005) 'A methodological approach to be used in integrated coastal zone management processes: The case of the Catalan Coast (Catalonia, Spain)', *Estuarine and Coastal Shelf Science*, vol 62, pp427–439

Satumanatpan, S. and Juntarshote, K. (2008) 'Performance assessment on coastal management of the Bangpakong River mouth, using a pressure-state-response framework', paper presented at the Sustainable Coasts and a Better Life, 4th Coastal Zone Asia Pacific Conference CZAP 2008, 19–22 October, Qingdao, China, www.czapa.org

Sauer, C. O. (1963) 'Morphology of landscape', in Leighly, J. (ed) *Land and Life*, pp315–350, Berkley, CA, University of California Press

Saveriades, A. (2000) 'Establishing the social tourism carrying capacity for the tourist resorts of the east coast of Cyprus', *Tourism Management*, vol 21, pp147–156

Sayre, W. O. and Komar, P. D. (1988) 'The Jump-Off Joe landslide at Newport, Oregon: History of erosion, development and destruction', *Shore and Beach*, vol 56, pp15–22

Sayre, W. O. and Komar, P. D. (1989) 'The construction of homes on four active coastal landslides in Newport, Oregon: Unbelievable but true!', in *Coastal Zone '89*, pp3286–3296, New York, American Society of Civil Engineers

SBCEG (Swansea Bay Coastal Engineering Group) (1999) 'Swansea Bay Shoreline Management Plan', Sub-Cell 8b: Worms Head to Lavernock Point, Rossett, Shoreline Management Partnership and HR Wallingford

Schembri, P. J. and Lanfranco, E. (1994) 'A survey of the sandy beaches of the Maltese Islands', Management Systems Unit Ltd, Msida, Malta University Services

Schlacher, T. A. and Thompson, L. M. C. (2007) 'Exposure of fauna to off-road vehicle (ORV) traffic on sandy beaches', *Coastal Management*, vol 35, pp567–583

Schroeder, W. W. (2000) 'Disturbances: Their role in shaping coastal environments', in Rodriguez, G. R., Brebbia, C. A. and Perez-Martell, E. (eds) *Environmental Coastal Regions III*, pp431–440, Southampton, WIT Press

Schuman, H. and Presser, S. (1981) *Questions and Answers in Attitude Surveys*, Orlando, FL, Academic Press

Shipman, B. and Stojanovic, T. (2007) 'Facts, fictions, and failures of integrated coastal zone management in Europe', *Coastal Management*, vol 35, pp375–398

Shore Protection Manual (1981) *Shore Protection Manual*, US Army Corps of Engineers, 3 volumes, Washington, DC, Government Printer

Shore Protection Manual (1984) *Shore Protection Manual*, 2 volumes, Washington, DC, US Government Printer

Short, A. D. (1991) 'Macro-meso tidal beach morphodynamics: An overview', *Journal of Coastal Research*, vol 7, pp417–436

Short, A. D. (1993) *Beaches of the New South Wales Coast, Sydney*, Sydney, University Printing Services

Short, A. D. (1997) 'Beaches of the New South Wales coast: A guide to their nature, characteristics', *Surf and Safety*. Sydney, University of Sydney

Short, A. D. (1999) *Handbook of Beach and Shoreface Morphodynamics*, Chichester, John Wiley & Sons

Shuolin Huang (personal communication) Vice President, Ocean University, Shanghai, China, 20 October 2008

Silva, C. P. (2002) 'Gestão litoral. Integração de estudos de percepção da paisagem e imagens digitais na definição da capacidade de carga de praias. O troço litoral S. Torpes Ilha do Pessegueiro', unpublished PhD disseration, Lisbon, Universidade Nova de Lisboa

Simm, J. D. (ed) (1996) *Beach Management Manual*, CIRIA Report 153, London, CIRIA

Simm, J. D., Beech, N. W. and John, S. (1995) 'A manual for beach management', in Institution of Civil Engineers (ed) *Proceedings of Conference on Coastal Management 95 – Putting Policy into Practice*, pp143–162, Institution of Civil Engineers, Bournemouth, Thomas Telford

Single, M. B. and Hemmingsen, M. A. (2001) 'Mixed sand and gravel barrier beaches of South Canterbury, New Zealand', in Packham, J., Randall, R., Barnes, R. and Neal, A. (eds) *Ecology and Geomorphology of Coastal Shingle*, pp261–276, Otley, Smith Settle

Skoloff, B. (2007) 'Florida to sprinkle glass on beaches', Discovery Channel, 27 August 2007

Slater, A. (2004) 'Marine spatial planning: Implications for the marine environment through examination of the Darwin Mounds and the James 'Toxic' Fleet cases', *Environmental Law and Management*, vol 16, no 6, pp287–295

SLS Australia (Surf Life Saving Australia) (2008) 'Surf life saving', www.slsa.com.au

SLSA GB (Surf Life Saving Association of GB) (2008) 'Heroes of the surf', www.surflifesaving.org.uk

Small, C. and Nichols, R. J. (2003) 'A global analysis of human settlement in coastal zones', *Journal of Coastal Research*, vol 19, no 3, pp584–600

Smith, K. (2004) *Environmental Hazards, Assessing Risk and Reducing Disaster*, London, Routledge

Smith, T. F. and Lazarow, N. S. (2004) 'Social learning and the adaptive management framework', *Journal of Coastal Research*, vol SI39, pp952–954

Soltau, C. and Theron, A. K. (2006) *Final Report: Development Setback Lines for the Northern Beaches, Richards Bay, and Evaluation of the Mhlathuze Beaches*, CSIR Report NRE/ECO/ER/2006/0048/C, Council for Scientific and Industrial Research, Stellenbosch, South Africa

Soltau, C. and Theron, A. K. (2006). *Final Report: Development Setback Lines for the Northern Beaches, Richards Bay, and Evaluation of the uMhlathuze Beaches*, CSIR Report NRE/ECO/ER/2006/0048/C, Stellenbosch, South Africa, Council for Scientific and Industrial Research (CSIR),

Spurgeon, J. and Brooke, J. (1995) 'Use of the contingent valuation method to quantify some aspects of the environmental effects of coastal defence schemes', in Institution of Civil Engineers (ed) *Proceedings of Conference on Coastal Management 95 – Putting Policy into Practice*, pp190–204, Institution of Civil Engineers, Bournemouth, Thomas Telford

Stationery Office (1999) *Limited as the Management of Health and Safety at Work Regulations*, London, Stationery Office

Stive, M. J. F., De Vriend, H. J., Nicholls, R. J. and Capobianco, M. (1992) 'Shore nourishment and the active zone: A timescale dependent view', in *Proceedings of the 23rd Coastal Engineering Conference*, pp2464–2473, New York, ASCE Press

Strange, W. B. (2005) 'Economic value of beaches', in Schwartz, M. L. (ed) *Encyclopedia of Coastal Science*, pp400–401, Dordrecht, Springer

Studio Volta (1988) 'Progetto di ricostruzione delle spiagge di Cala Gonne', unpublished report, Dorgali Municipality

Sturman, A., Owens, I. and Fitzharris, B. (2001) 'Precipitation processes and water storage', in Sturman, A. and Sproken-Smith, R. (eds) *The Physical Environment: A New Zealand Perspective*, pp152–174, Melbourne, Oxford University Press

Subordinate Courts of the Republic of Singapore (2006) 'SGDC 51: District Court Suit No. 731 of 2005 between Adam Bin Sit (Plaintiff) and Sentosa Development Cooperation (Defendants)', 13 March 2006

Sunamura, T. (1992) *Geomorphology of Rocky Coasts*, Chichester, John Wiley & Sons

Svarstad, H., Kjerule, L. P., Rothman, D., Siepel, H and Watzo, F. (2008) 'Discursive biases of the environmental research framework DPSIR', *Land Use Policy*, vol 25, pp116–125

Szlichicinski, K. P. (1979) 'Telling people how things work', *Applied Ergonomics*, vol 10, no 1, pp2–8

Tanner, W. F. (1976) 'The "a-b-c..." model', in *Proceedings of the 15th Coastal Engineering Conference*, pp1113–1132, Honolulu, American Society of Civil Engineers

Terzidis, A., Koutroumpa, A., Skalkidis, L., Matzavakis, I., Malliori, M., Frangakis, C. E., DiScala, C. and Petridou, E. T. (2007) 'Water safety: Age-specific changes in knowledge and attitudes following a school-based intervention', *Injury Prevention*, vol 13, pp120–124

Thieler, E. R., Himmelstoss, E. A., Zichichi, J. L. and Miller, T. L. (2005) 'Digital Shoreline Analysis System (DSAS) version 3.0: An ArcGIS extension for calculating shoreline change', US Geological Survey Open-File Report 1304, Woods Hole, MA, US Geological Survey

Tian-Jian Hsu, Elgar, S. and Guza, R. T. (2006) 'Wave-induced sediment transport and onshore sandbar migration', *Coastal Engineering*, vol 53, no 10, pp817–824

Todd, D. J. (1983) 'Effect of low flows on river mouth closure in the Opihi River', unpublished Master's dissertation, Christchurch, New Zealand University of Canterbury

Trenhaile, A. S. (1987) *The Geomorphology of Rock Coasts*, Oxford, Oxford University Press

Tudor, D. T. and Williams, A. T. (2006) 'A rationale for beach selection by the public on the coast of Wales, UK', *Area*, vol 38, no 2, pp153–164

Twr Y Felin (no date) 'Pure adventure', www.tyf.com/?c=act-coastering

Uçar, B. (2004) 'Coastal scenic evaluation by application of fuzzy logic mathematics', unpublished MSc dissertation, Ankara, Middle East Technical University

Ugolini, A., Ungherese, G., Somigli, S., Galanti, G., Borghini, F., Baroni, D. and Focardi, S. (2006) 'Human trampling, sandy beaches and sandhoppers', in Micallef, A. and Vassallo, A. (eds) *Proceedings of the Second International Conference on the Management of Coastal Recreational Resources: Beaches, Yacht Marinas and Coastal Ecotourism, Malta*, pp199–205, Euro-Mediterranean Centre on Insular Coastal Dynamics (ICoD), Valletta, University of Malta

Ugolini A., Ungherese, G., Borghini, F., Baroni, P., Bruni, P. and Focardi, S. (2007) 'Talitrid amphipods as bio-indicators of sandy beaches, contamination and human disturbance', in Ozhan, E. (ed) *Proceedings of the 8th Conference, MedCoast '07*, pp819–828, Ankara, Turkey, METU

Ulupınar-Çıralı Cooperative (Ulupınar Çevre Koruma, Geliştirme ve İşletme Kooperatifi) (2003–2004) 'Çıralı Deniz Kalumbağası Yuvalama Kumsalı Alan Çalışması Raporları', Antalya, Ulupınar-Çıralı Cooperative

UNDP (United Nations Development Programme) (2003) 'Global Environment Fund, Support Programme; Ulupinar-Çıralı Organic Agriculture and Eco-Tourism Development Plan and Implementations', Çıralı, UNDP

UNEP (United Nations Environmental Programme) (1995) *Guidelines for Integrated Management of Coastal and Marine Areas – with special reference to the Mediterranean Basin*, UNEP Regional Seas Reports and Studies No 161, Split, PAP/RAC (MAP-UNEP)

UNEP (1996) *The State of the Marine and Coastal Environment in the Mediterranean Region*, Mediterranean Action Plan Technical Report Series No 100, Athens, MAP

UNEP (2005) *Marine Litter: An Overview*, Nairobi, UNEP

UNEP (2007) *Global Marine Assessments: A Survey of Global and Regional Assessments and Related Activities of the Marine Environment*, Nairobi, UNEP/UNESCO-IOC/UNEP-WCMC

UNWTO (UN World Tourism Organization) (2007) *Tourism Highlights*, www.unwto.org

USCB (United States Census Bureau) (2002) *State and County Quick Facts*, Washington, DC, USCB

US Commission (2004) 'An ocean blueprint for the 21st century', Final Report, Washington, DC, US Commission on Ocean Policy

US National Research Council (1990) *Managing Coastal Erosion*, Committee on Coastal Erosion Zone Management, Washington, DC, National Academy Press

Vallejo, S. M. A. (1991) 'The development and management of coastal and marine areas', in Smith, H. D. and Vellega, A. (eds) *The Development of Integrated Sea Life Planning*, London, Routledge, pp17–34

Valle-Levinson, A. and Swanson, R. L. (1991) 'Wind induced scattering of medically-related and sewage-related floatables', *Marine Technology Society Journal*, vol 25, no 2, pp49–56

van der Maarel, E. (1979) 'Environmental management of coastal dunes in the Netherlands', in Jefferies, R. L. and Davy, A. J. (eds) *Ecological Processes in Coastal Environments*, pp543–570, Oxford, Blackwell

van der Meulen, F. (2005) 'ICZM some ten years after Rio: Where do we stand and which way to go?', in Ozhan, E. (ed) *Proceedings of the Seventh International Conference on the Mediterranean Coastal Environment*, MedCoast '05, vol 1, pp1–8, Ankara, Turkey, METU

Van der Salm, J. and Unal, O. (2001) 'Towards a common Mediterranean framework for potential beach nourishment projects', in Ozhan, E. (ed) *Proceedings of 5th International Conference, MedCoast '01*, pp1333–1346, Ankara, Turkey, METU

van der Weide, J., van der Meulen, F., Sarf, F., Gengic, S. and Gabunia, M. (1999) 'Assessing the value of two coastal wetlands in Turkey', in Ozhan, E. (ed) *MedCoast '99 – EMECS '99 Joint Conference on Land–Ocean Interactions: Managing Coastal Ecosystems*, pp1009–1020, MedCoast Secreteriat, Ankara, Turkey, METU

van Grundy, A. B. (1988) *Techniques of Structured Problem Solving*, New York, Van Nostrand Reinhold Co

van Maele, B., Pond, K., Williams, A. T. and Dubsky, K. (2000) 'Public participation and consultation', in Bartram, J. and Rees, G. (eds) *Monitoring Bathing Waters: A Practical Guide to the Design and Implementation of Assessments and Monitoring Programmes*, pp85–99, London and New York, WHO

van Vuren, S., Kok, M. and Jorisson, R. E. (2004) 'Coastal defense and societal activities: Compatible or conflicting interests?', *Journal of Coastal Research*, vol 20, no 2, pp550–561

Venturelli, R. C. and Galli, A. (2008) 'Integrated indicators in environmental planning: Methodological considerations and applications', *Ecological Indicators*, vol 6, pp228–237

Vila-Concejo, A., Matias, A., Pacheco, A., Ferreira, Ó. and Dias, J. M. A. (2006) 'Quantification of inlet-related hazards in barrier island systems: An example from the Ria Formosa (Portugal)', *Continental Shelf Research*, vol 26, pp1045–1060

Villares, M. and Roca, E. (2007) 'Analysis of beach users' perception in tourist coastal areas: A case study in the Costa Brava, Spain', in Ozhan, E. (ed) *Proceedings of the 8th International Conference on the Mediterranean Coastal Environment, MedCoast '07*, pp295–304, Ankara, Turkey, METU

Villares, M., Junyent, R., Gea, T. and Gatell, E. (1997) The aesthetic and environmental perception applied to the regeneration of the Mediterannean beaches of Degur de Calafell, Calafell, Coma-Ruga, El Francas and Sant Salvador (Catalonia, Spain)', in Ozhan, E. (ed) *Proceedings of the Third International Conference on the Mediterranean Coastal Environment (MEDCOAST '97)*, pp621–633, Ankara, Turkey, METU,

Villares, M., Roca, E., Serra, J. and Montori, C. (2006) 'Social perception as a tool for beach planning: A case study on the Catalan coast', *Journal of Coastal Research*, vol SI48, pp118–123

Vogt, G. (1979) 'Adverse effects of recreation on sand dunes: A problem for coastal zone management', *Journal of Coastal Zone Management*, vol 6, pp37–68

Wang, P. and Davis, R. A. (1999) 'Depth of closure and the equilibrium beach profile: A case study from Sand Key, West-Central Florida', *Shore and Beach*, vol 67, nos 2 & 3, pp33–42

Water Safety Forum (no date) 'Home page', www.nationalwatersafety.org.uk

Watson, J. (1992) 'Dune breeding birds and off-road vehicles', *Naturalist*, vol 36, pp8–12

Weerakkody, U. (1997) 'Potential impact of accelerated sea-level rise on beaches of Sri Lanka', *Journal of Coastal Research*, Special Issue, vol 24, pp225–242

White, G. F. and Haas, J. E. (1975) *Assessment of Research on Natural Hazards*, Cambridge, MA, MIT Press

White, J. J. (2009) Recording gravel transport at a barrier beach, *Journal of Coastal Research*, special issue 56, pp5–9

WHO (World Health Organization) (1998) *Guidelines for Safe Recreational Water Environments: Coastal and Fresh Waters*, Geneva, WHO

WHO (World Health Organization) (2000) *Monitoring Bathing Waters*, edited by Bartrum, J. and Rees, G., London/New York, WHO

WHO (World Health Organization) (2004) *World Health Report: Changing History*, Geneva, WHO

Willemyns, M., Gallois, C., Callan, V. J. and Pittman, J. (1997) 'Accent accommodation in the job interview: Impact of interviewer accent and gender', *Journal of Language and Social Psychology*, vol 16, no 1, pp3–22

Williams, A. T. and Caldwell, N. E. (1988) 'Particle size and shape in pebble beach sedimentation', *Marine Geology*, vol 82, pp199–215

Williams, A. T. and Davies, P. (1999) 'Beach management guidelines: Dimensional analysis', in Randazzo, G. (ed) *Coastal Environmental Management*, EUCC-Italy/EUCC (electronic publishing)

Williams, A. T. and Ergin, A. (2004) 'Heritage Coasts in Wales, UK', in Micallef, A. and Vassallo, A. (eds) *Proceedings of the First International Conference on the Management of Coastal Recreational Resources: Beaches, Yacht Marinas and Ecotourism, Malta*, pp219–227, Euro-Mediterranean Centre on Insular Coastal Dynamics, Valletta, University of Malta

Williams, A. T. and Morgan, R. (1995) 'Beach awards and rating systems', *Shore and Beach*, vol 63, pp29–33

Williams, A. T. and Tudor, D. T. (2006) 'The question of dogs on beaches', *Shore and Beach*, vol 74, no 4, pp1–5

Williams, A. T. and Williams. M. J. (1991) 'The perceived effectiveness of coastal warning signs', in Cambers, G. (ed) *Coastlines of the Caribbean*, pp70–84, New York, American Society of Civil Engineers

Williams, A. T., Jones, T. C., Davies, P. and Curr, R. C. H. (1992) 'Psychological profile of the beach/dune user in South Wales, UK', *Shore and Beach*, vol 60, no 2, pp26–30

Williams, A. T., Leatherman, S. P. and Simmons, S. L. (1993a) 'Beach aesthetic values: The south west peninsula, UK', in Sterr, H., Hofstide, J. and Plag, P. (eds) *Interdisciplinary Discussions of Coastal Research and Coastal Management Issues and Problems*, pp240–250, Frankfurt, Peter Lang

Williams, A. T., Gardner, W., Jones, T. C., Morgan, R. and Ozhan, E. (1993b) 'A psychological approach to attitudes and perceptions of beach users: Implications for coastal zone management', in Ozhan. E. (ed) *MedCoast '93*, pp218–228, Ankara, Turkey, METU

Williams, A. T., Davies, P., Ergin, A. and Balas, C. E. (2000) 'Environmental risk assessment for Colhuw beach in the Glamorgan Heritage Coast, Wales, UK: What price conservation?', *Journal of Coastal Conservation*, vol 6, no 2, pp125–134

Williams, A. T., Alveirinho-Dias, J., Garcia Novo, F., Garcia-Mora, M. R., Curr, R. H. and Pereira, A. (2001) 'Integrated coastal dune management: Checklists', *Continental Shelf Research*, vol 21, pp1937–1960

Williams, A. T., Davies, P. and Ergin, A. (2002a) 'Coastal erosion at the Glamorgan Heritage Coast, UK', in McKee Smith, J. (ed) *Proceedings of the 28th International Conference, 'Coastal Engineering, 2002'*, pp3539–3551, Cardiff, World Scientific

Williams, A. T., Micallef, A. and Ergin, A. (2002b) 'A theoretical framework for beach management guidelines', in Ozhan, E. (ed) *Beach Management in the*

Mediterranean and the Black Sea, pp191–200, MedCoast, Ankara, Middle East Technical University

Williams, A. T., Tudor, D. T. and Gregory, M. R. (2005) 'Marine debris: Onshore, offshore, seafloor', in Schwartz, M. (ed) *Encyclopaedia of Coastal Science*, pp623–628, London, Springer

Williams, A T., Sellars, V. and Phillips, M. R. (2007) 'An assessment of UK Heritage Coasts in South Wales: J. A. Steers revisited', *Journal of Coastal Research*, vol SI50, pp453–458

Williams, A. T., Phillips, M. R. and Banfield, K. (2008) 'Coastal erosion management, Swansea Bay, Wales, UK: The application of function analysis and strategic environmental assessment', in Krishnamurthy, R. R., Glavovic, B. C., Kanne, A., Green, D. R., Ramanathan, A. L., Han, Z., Tinti, S. and Agardy, T. (eds) *Integrated Coastal Zone Management: Current Global Scenario*, pp305–325, Singapore, RPS Publishing

Wilson, M. and Liu, S. (2008) 'Non-market value of ecosystem services provided by coastal and nearshore and marine systems', in Patterson, M. and Glavovicic, B. (eds) *Ecological Economics of the Oceans and Coasts*, pp119–139, Cheltenham, Edward Elgar

Winter, S. (1990) 'Integrating implementation research', in Palumbo, D. J. and Calista, D. (eds) *Implementation and the Policy Process: Opening up the Black Box*, New York, Greenwood Press

Work, P. A. and Dean, R. G. (1991) 'Effect of varying sediment size on equilibrium beach profiles', in *Proceedings of Coastal Sediments 1991*, pp891–904, New York, ASCE Press

Yalciner A. C. and Synolakis, C. E. (2007) 'Tsunamis and their impacts on marine structures, submitted to guidelines on seismic-induced liquefaction around marine structures', LIMAS Special Issue in *ASCE Journal of Waterway, Port, Coastal and Ocean Engineering*, vol 133, no 1, pp55–82

Yalciner, A. C., Dogan, P., Sukru, E., Gegar, S., Presateya, G. S., Hidayat, R. and McAdoo, B. (2005) 'December 26, 2004 Indian Ocean Tsunami field survey (Jan. 21–31, 2005), north of Sumatra island', UNESCO, http://ioc.unesco.org/iosurveys/Indonesia/yalciner/yalciner.htm

Yazdani, N., and Ycaza, I. D. (1995) 'Multi-agency integrated code for coastal construction', *Journal of Coastal Research*, vol 11, pp899–903

Yeemin, T. (personal communication) Biology Dept., Ramkhamhaeng University, Bangkok, Thailand, 21 October 2008

Yepes, V., Sánchez, I. and Cardona, A. (2004) 'Criterios de diseño de aparcamientos y accesos a las playas', *Equipamiento y Servicios Municipales*, vol 112, pp40–44

Yerli, S. and Demirayak, F. (1996) 'Marine turtles in Turkey: A survey of nesting site status', CMS Rep. No. 96/4, Istanbul, DHKD

Young, C., Barugh, A., Morgan, R. and Williams, A. T. (1996) 'Beach user perceptions and priorities at the Pembrokeshire Coast National Park, Wales, UK', in Taussik, J. and Mitchell, J. (eds) *Partnership in Coastal Zone Management*, pp111–118, Cardigan, UK, Samara Publishing

Young, C. C. (2002) 'Extreme sports', *Injuries and Medical Coverage*, vol 1, pp306–311

Zenkovich, V. P. (1967) *Processes of Coastal Development*, London, Oliver and Boyd

Zukin, C. (1998) 'The shore – looking up (Save the beach passes)', *The Star-Ledger/Eagleton Poll*, http://slerp.rutgers.edu/retrieve.php?id=119-3

Beach Questionnaires

| TABLE A1.1 BEACH QUESTIONNAIRE | Beach .... |
| | Date .... |

- THIS QUESTIONNAIRE ASKS ABOUT THE WAY YOU **VALUE THE BEACH ENVIRONMENT**.
- PLEASE THINK CAREFULLY ABOUT THE ANSWERS YOU GIVE.
- **IMPORTANT – THE QUESTIONNAIRE IS ANONYMOUS AND CONFIDENTIAL, AND WILL BE USED FOR RESEARCH PURPOSES ONLY. Please do complete the questions on employment and earnings.**
- **ONE PERSON** should complete the whole questionnaire.

1) Age .... 2) Sex (male/female) ....
3) How many adults are in the group? ....

4) What are the ages of children in your group?

5) What is your home town and country? ....
....

6) On average, how often do you go to the beach when on holiday?

every day	
most days	
2–3 days per week	
about once a week	
only rarely	

7) How long do you usually stay at the beach?

Less than one hour	
1–4 hours	
4–8 hours	
more than 8 hours	

8) Which beach do you most frequently visit in [insert country]?
....

9) What is the purpose of your visit here today? Please tick as many boxes as necessary.

Enjoy views and fresh air		Swimming	
Nature and wildlife		For children's play	
Walking		Water sports	

Other reason (please specify) ....

10) What **three** things do you most dislike on a beach?

Washed up litter and man-made debris	
Poor water quality	
Washed up sewage debris	
Excessive seaweed (algae)	
Bad smells from industry	
Dog waste/excrement	
Noise from industry or vehicles	
Lack of sand	
Difficult access	
Poor facilities	

11) Are you concerned about coastal erosion? *Yes/No/Don't know*

12) Could you give an example of a daytime holiday activity that you enjoy **more** than going to the beach ....
How much do you usually spend on this?
....

13) Could you give an example of a daytime holiday activity that you enjoy **less** than going to the beach ....
How much do you usually spend on this?
....

14) Considering question 11, would you like to see the beach improved?
Yes/No/Don't know
If "Yes", in what way? ....
....

15) Would you be willing to pay to use the beach if this meant that the beach would be better maintained or improved?   *Yes/No/Don't know*
If "Yes", how would you prefer to pay (*tick one box*)

By a local tax	
A box to put contributions into	
Paying a fixed price per visit	
A car parking charge	
By doing voluntary work	
Other means	

16) What would you consider a reasonable charge per person for this beach?
....
Should children be free of charge?   *Yes/No/Don't know*

17) How did you travel to the beach today?

On foot	
By car/motorcycle	
By bicycle	
By taxi	
By train	
By bus	

18) How long did it take you to get to the beach? ....

19) Do you enjoy the travelling time to the beach or do you consider it a waste of time?   *Enjoy/Waste of time*

20) How do you rate the visual appearance of **this beach** (please tick one box only)?

excellent	
good	
fair	
poor	
very bad	

21) Are you aware of specially protected areas of the coast? ....

22) What is your occupation? ....

23) What are your average earnings? ....
This is needed for our research

24) If you are not local, how many days in total will you stay at this resort? ....

25) How many times per week (or per year) do you visit the beach?

26) If you are not local, are you on a package holiday or coach tour?   Yes/No

27) How much will your holiday cost:

   ■ **in total**
   ....

   ■ **for travel** (estimate percentage if on a package holiday/tour)
   ....

   ■ **for accommodation** (estimate percentage if on a package holiday/tour)
   ....

■ **for breakfast/breakfast and one meal/three meals** (state which and estimate percentage if on a package holiday/coach tour) ....
....

28) How much does your enjoyment of the beach contribute to the overall enjoyment of your holiday?
(estimate percentage) ....%

29) How long did it take you to travel to this resort from your home:

■ in total ....

■ in a car/train/by foot/other...................................

■ waiting at a bus stop/other ....

■ other time (please state event)
....

THANK YOU FOR COMPLETING THIS QUESTIONNAIRE

Enquiries:

Name and address of questioner

TABLE A1.2 BEACH USER QUESTIONNAIRE

We would appreciate your views regarding beach quality. Your opinions may help to improve the coastal environment. You may miss any questions you are not comfortable with. It will only take a few minutes.

Part 1 – Personal Details

Q1 *Age:* ....…............   **Q2** *Sex:* Male [   ]   Female [   ]
Q3 *Occupation:*..
Q4 *Are you here :*
      On Holiday [   ]   Just for the day (travelled over 10m) [   ]   Live locally [   ]
Q5 *If you are on holiday, where are you staying?*   Hotel [   ]   B&B [   ]
Camping [   ]   Caravan [   ]   Self Catering [   ]
With Friends/Relatives [   ]   Youth Hostel [   ]

Q6 *What is your home town?:* ....

Part 2 – Beach Quality

- How would you describe the condition of this 100 metre stretch of beach with regards to litter pollution? (50 metres either side of where you are)
                  Tick **one box** only
  (A) Very Good   [   ]
  (B) Good   [   ]
  (C) Fair   [   ]
  (D) Poor   [   ]

- How many items of the following would need be present for you to consider this 100m stretch of beach to be described as poor?

  General litter (e.g. crisp packet, drinks can): ....
  Gross litter (>50cm, e.g. barrel, shopping trolley): ....
  Sewage related debris (e.g. condom, sanitary towel, cotton bud stick): ....

- Have you noticed any accumulations / piles of litter on this stretch of beach?
  Yes [   ]   No [   ]

- Which of these types of faeces do you find offensive on a beach?
  Horse [   ]   Human [   ]   Dog [   ]   Sheep [   ]

- Do you enter the sea? No [   ]   Yes, but only to paddle [   ]   Yes, swim [   ]

- Please rank what you consider the most offensive forms of beach/sea pollution. 1 being the most offensive followed by 2, then 3 etc.
            *Place a **different** number in **each** box*   **Example**

Discoloured Water	[ ]	**[5]**
Sewage-related Debris	[ ]	**[7]**
Beach Litter	[ ]	**[6]**

Unusual Smell	[ ]				**[1]**
Foam/Scum	[ ]				**[2]**
Floating Debris	[ ]				**[3]**
Oil (on the beach)	[ ]				**[etc]**
Oil (in the sea)	[ ]				**[etc]**
Any other? (please state)	[ ]	....			**[etc]**

- Please rank what you consider to be the best form of presentation to grade a beach, with regards to litter/debris. **1** being the **best**, followed by 2, 3,4, 5, 6.

Example

a)	Very Good	Good	Fair	Poor	[ ]	**[2]**
b)	A	B	C	D	[ ]	**[4]**
c)	Grade 1	Grade 2	Grade 3	Grade 4	[ ]	**[1]**
d)	★★★★	★★★	★★	★	[ ]	**[3]**
e)	Very Clean	Clean	Dirty	Very Dirty	[ ]	**[etc]**
f)	Absent	Trace	Unacceptable	Objectionable	[ ]	**[etc]**

Part 3 - Beach Management

- In the summer season (May–September) do you think dogs should be allowed on:
  a) Resort Beaches?   Yes [ ]   No [ ]   Unsure [ ]
  b) Rural Beaches?   Yes [ ]   No [ ]   Unsure [ ]
- Please rank the *most important reasons for selecting a beach* to visit. 1 being the **most important** followed by 2, then 3 etc.

Place a <u>different</u> number in <u>each</u> box

Views and Landscape	[ ]	Accessibility	[ ]
Toilet facilities	[ ]	Car Parking	[ ]
Clean seawater	[ ]	Safety	[ ]
Clean sand	[ ]	Refreshment kiosk	[ ]
Distance to travel to beach	[ ]	Beach Award Flag	[ ]
Any other? (please state)	[ ]	....	

THANK YOU FOR YOUR TIME AND EFFORT IN COMPLETING THIS QUESTIONNAIRE

<u>**Enquiries:**</u>

<u>**Name and address of questioner**</u>

TABLE A1.3 BEACH USER QUESTIONNAIRE

To be completed by interviewer. Beach:	Date:	Time:

We would appreciate your views regarding beach quality. Your opinions may help to improve the coastal environment. You may miss any questions you are not comfortable with. It will only take a few minutes.

Part 1 – Personal Details

Q1 *Age:* .... **Q2** *Sex:* Male [ ] Female [ ] **Q3** *Religion:*...............................

Q4 *Occupation:*..

Q5 *Are you here on:* Holiday [ ]   Just for the day (travelled over 10m) [ ]
Live locally [ ]

Q6 *If you are on holiday, where are you staying?*   Hotel/B&B [ ]   Camping [ ]
Caravan [ ]   Self Catering [ ]   With Friends/Relatives [ ]

Q7 *What is your home town?* ....

Part 2 – General Beach Quality

- Please put in order what you consider the most offensive forms of beach/sea pollution on a scale of 1 to 8. **1** being the **most offensive** followed by 2, then 3 etc., **8** being **least offensive**.
               *Place a **different** number in **each** box*
    Discoloured Water   [ ]
    Sewage Related Debris   [ ]
    Beach Litter   [ ]
    Unusual Smell   [ ]
    Foam/Scum   [ ]
    Floating Debris   [ ]
    Oil (on the beach)   [ ]
    Oil (in the sea)   [ ]

- How would you describe the state of this beach with regards to litter pollution?
                    Tick **one box** only
    (A) Very Good   [ ]
    (B) Good   [ ]
    (C) Fair   [ ]
    (D) Poor   [ ]

- Do you think dogs should be allowed on:
    a) Resort Beaches?   Yes [ ]   No [ ]   Unsure [ ]
    b) Rural Beaches?   Yes [ ]   No [ ]   Unsure [ ]

- Please put in order the most important reasons for selecting a beach to visit on a scale of 1 to 10. **1** being the **most important** followed by 2, then 3 etc., **10** being **least important**.

*Place a **different** number in **each** box*

Views and Landscape	[ ]	Accessibility	[ ]
Toilet Facilities	[ ]	Car Parking	[ ]
Clean sea water	[ ]	Safety	[ ]
Clean sand	[ ]	Refreshment kiosk	[ ]
Distance to travel to beach	[ ]	Beach Award Flag	[ ]

Part 3 – Flags – Beach Awards I

- Are you aware of the existence of beach rating and award schemes, sometimes represented in the form of a flag? (Note: not lifesaving safety flags)
  Yes [ ]   No [ ]

- *If yes to the above, can you name any?*...

- *What does a flag at a beach represent?* **(Note: not lifesaving safety flags)**......

- *Does this beach have a flag?*   Yes [ ]   No [ ]   Unsure[ ]

If so, do you know what kind? **(Note: not lifesaving safety flags)** ....

Part 4 – Litter Pollution (using a series of photographs)

Please name the litter item shown in the photographs:
Note: Photos have not been given in this example, but include items such as plastic bags, condom, pill box etc,
Number 5?...
Number 20?...
Number 27?...

- Please circle on the scale how offensive each of the following litter items shown in the photographs is to you.

	Not offensive							Very offensive
Photo 1	1	2	3	4	5	6	7	8	9
Photo 2	1	2	3	4	5	6	7	8	9
Photo 3	1	2	3	4	5	6	7	8	9
Photo 4	1	2	3	4	5	6	7	8	9
Photo 5	1	2	3	4	5	6	7	8	9

| Photo 6 | 1 | 2 | 3 | 4 | 5 | 6 | 7 | 8 | 9 |
| Photo 7 | 1 | 2 | 3 | 4 | 5 | 6 | 7 | 8 | 9 |

Photo 8	1	2	3	4	5	6	7	8	9
Photo 9	1	2	3	4	5	6	7	8	9
Photo 10	1	2	3	4	5	6	7	8	9
Photo 11	1	2	3	4	5	6	7	8	9
Photo 12	1	2	3	4	5	6	7	8	9
Photo 13	1	2	3	4	5	6	7	8	9
Photo 14	1	2	3	4	5	6	7	8	9

Photo 15	1	2	3	4	5	6	7	8	9
Photo 16	1	2	3	4	5	6	7	8	9
Photo 17	1	2	3	4	5	6	7	8	9
Photo 18	1	2	3	4	5	6	7	8	9
Photo 19	1	2	3	4	5	6	7	8	9
Photo 20	1	2	3	4	5	6	7	8	9
Photo 21	1	2	3	4	5	6	7	8	9

Photo 22	1	2	3	4	5	6	7	8	9
Photo 23	1	2	3	4	5	6	7	8	9
Photo 24	1	2	3	4	5	6	7	8	9
Photo 25	1	2	3	4	5	6	7	8	9
Photo 26	1	2	3	4	5	6	7	8	9
Photo 27	1	2	3	4	5	6	7	8	9
Photo 28	1	2	3	4	5	6	7	8	9

Are there any items of beach litter, which you have not been shown, that you find particularly offensive? ....

Part 5 – Flags – Beach Awards II

- Have you heard of the following?:
  Good Beach Guide   Yes [ ]   No [ ]   Unsure [ ]
  EEC Blue Flag   Yes [ ]   No [ ]   Unsure [ ]
  ENCAMS Flag   Yes [ ]   No [ ]   Unsure [ ]

- *Please tick which attributes apply to each of the awards below?*

	EEC BLUE FLAG	ENCAMS AWARD	GOOD BEACH GUIDE
Clean beach			
Clean bathing water			
Safety			
Sandy beach			
Provision of toilets			
Boating facilities			
Popular beach			

Comments

Are there any comments you would like to make about the coastal environment?

....

....

THANK YOU FOR YOUR TIME AND EFFORT IN COMPLETING THIS QUESTIONNAIRE

Enquiries:

Name and address of questioner

Assessment of Aesthetic Quality of Coastal and Bathing Beaches: Monitoring Protocol and Classification Scheme

Environment Agency and the National Aquatic Litter Group

INTRODUCTION

This document details the method to be used to assess the aesthetic quality of coastal and bathing beaches that are used for recreational purposes. This scheme is designed to be used by Agency staff in either surveys to assess the aesthetic state of the coastal environment or in local operational monitoring programmes. The scheme has been developed in collaboration with the NALG and will be used by other members of the NALG when conducting their own surveys.

The parameters chosen for the assessment are sewage-related litter and debris, potentially harmful litter items, gross litter, general litter, accumulations of litter, oil pollution and the occurrence of faeces of non-human origin. These parameters are assessed over a standard sampling unit on the beach.

This section provides guidance on completing the field survey form and the methodology for classifying the site according to a four-grade classification scheme.

FIELD METHODOLOGY

Before beginning the assessment the following general information about the site should be recorded:

- Region
- Name of sampler
- Site name (for example Beach)
- Location of site
- National grid reference
- Site reference code (Regional)

- Date of survey
- Time of survey
- State of tide
- Weather conditions
- Beach cleaning regime (if known)
- Description (salient features)

A detailed sketch map (or photograph) of the site should be produced in advance of the survey and held for future reference in the appropriate sampling point description manual. This should detail the exact location of the survey area, recording salient points (permanent structures) to aid in locating the site and ensuring consistent assessments by samplers. A record should also be made of the type of beach and its substrata.

Sampling unit

The standard sampling unit consists of a 100m-wide transect of the beach with assessments made over an area comprising the following zone.

Sampling zone
The area of usable beach behind the highest high water strandline, up to, for example, a seawall or the edge of the dune line (to assess primarily, wind blown accumulations of litter). The section along the highest high water strandline, the area between this line and the current high water strandline (up to a maximum depth of 50m).

The zone that comprises the sampling unit is shown in Figure A2.1.

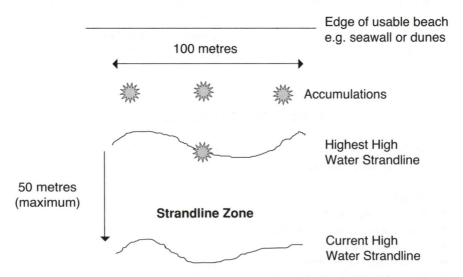

Figure A2.1 *Assessment zone comprising the sampling unit*

The sampler should assess the area behind the high water strandline, then walk along the high water strandline and back between the two strandlines, recording the number of items in each category. This is also illustrated in Figure 1.

NB: Sampling must be undertaken after high tide. Note the state of the tide at the time of sampling.

Assessment of litter categories

Sewage-related debris
Sewage litter items should include:

- feminine hygiene products (sanitary towels, tampons and applicators),
- contraceptives,
- toilet paper,
- fatty deposits,
- identifiable faeces of human origin.

These items are termed as *general* sewage-related debris.

Cotton bud sticks should be counted as a separate item. The grade is determined by the worst case. Any other general comments should be recorded in the appropriate box on the survey form.

Examples of sewage-related debris are depicted in Figure A2.2.

This category includes items that are considered dangerous to either humans or animals using the beach. These are:

- sharp broken glass (counted as a separate category),
- medical waste (for example used syringes),
- sharps (metal wastes, barbed wire etc.),

Figure A2.2 *Potentially harmful litter*

- soiled disposable nappies,
- containers marked as containing toxic products,
- other dangerous products such as flares, ammunition and explosives,
- dead domestic animals.

Any other general comments should be recorded in the appropriate box on the survey form. In this case, note the type of potentially harmful litter found. For example, what hazardous material may be in a container or specific details about other dangerous products such as ammunition.

Examples of potentially harmful litter are shown in Figure A2.3 and A2.4.

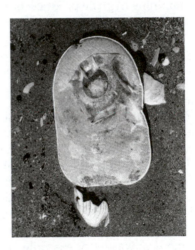

Figure A2.3 *A used syringe*   **Figure A2.4** *A colostomy bag*

NB: Health and safety warning. This is a visual survey. On no account should the sampler handle material found during the survey. This applies to all categories of litter. This of course particularly applies to the potentially harmful litter category. If the sampler suspects that an item poses a significant risk to the public, for example, suspected live ammunition is found, the emergency services should be contacted immediately.

Gross litter
Gross litter comprises items that have at least one dimension greater than 50cm. These include such items as:

- shopping trolleys,
- pieces of furniture,
- large plastic or metal containers,

- road cones,
- bicycles, prams,
- tyres,
- large items of processed wood, for example pallets.

Driftwood should not be included.

General litter
General litter includes all other items less than 50cm in dimension such as:

- drink cans,
- food packaging,
- cigarette packets,
- any other items.

Items with a maximum diameter of less than 1cm should **not** be counted.

Oil and other oil-like substances
Oil should be assessed as to its general presence or absence, and whether it is objectionable. This should cover all oil waste (mineral or vegetable), either from fresh oil spills or the presence of weathered oil deposits and tarry wastes. The assessment will necessarily be subjective.

The following guidelines should be used to help in the categorization of oil pollution:

Grade A: No oil present at all within the survey area. Beach considered pristine in this respect.

Grade B: Traces of oil found but in a weathered state i.e. obviously old residues. Traces found but only on other litter items such as plastic containers.

Grade C: Quantities of oil present that are a nuisance and interfere with proper use of the beach. For example, oil is found in places that are immediately noticeable, can be smelled or seen, which would prevent for example a person sitting on parts of the beach.

Grade D: Objectionable quantities of oil that prevents normal use of the entire beach at which the survey area is located.

Faeces (non-human)
The numbers of animal faeces (dogs) should be counted in the survey zone. Faeces from animals such as sheep or horses should not be counted. These are not considered to be a general nuisance or hazard. However, their presence should be recorded in the comments box.

Accumulations

Accumulations of litter can occur behind the highest high water strandline, either as a result of being blown by the wind or dumped by users of the beach, and in the high water strandline, often in seaweed. The numbers of significant accumulations of litter are recorded. An accumulation is defined as a discrete aggregation of litter clearly visible when approaching the survey area.

An example of an accumulation of litter is shown in Figure A2.5.

Figure A2.5 *Accumulation*

Other items

In addition to the seven commonly occurring categories of beach litter defined above, there will be occasions when other items will be found during a survey. While these are not included in the formal classification of the beach they should be recorded on the survey form in the space provided. Examples of such items are, coal and other types of industrial waste, and naturally occurring deposits such as foam (which when decaying may be offensive and look and smell rather like oil).

Note: If during the survey there is any doubt as to which category an item should be allocated, default to the worst case. For example, if an item of general litter *could* be deemed harmful, but the surveyor is unsure, then **default to the harmful category**.

CLASSIFICATION SCHEME

General principles

The classification scheme is based on four Grades A–D, describing the aesthetic quality as Very Good, Good, Fair and Poor. The overall grade is the **worst grade** of the individual grades for each parameter.

Table of grades for each parameter

Table A2.1 shows how to assign a grade to each parameter. Litter items are graded on the total numbers counted in each category. Accumulations are graded according to the number of occurrences. Oil is assessed on an estimate of its presence or absence in the survey zone.

Table A2.1 *Litter categories*

Category	Type	A	B	C	D
1 Sewage-related	General	0	1–5	6–14	15+
Debris	Cotton Buds	0–9	10–49	50–99	100+
2 Gross Litter		0	1–5	6–14	15+
3 General Litter		0–49	50–499	500–999	1000+
4 Harmful Litter	Broken Glass	0	1–5	6–24	25+
	Other	0	1–4	5–9	10+
5 Accumulations	Number	0	1–4	5–9	10+
6 Oil		Absent	Trace	Nuisance	Objectionable
7 Faeces		0	1–5	6–24	25+

Grading scheme

The final grading is simply the worst grade for any of the above parameters. For example, a beach is graded 'A' for all parameters except General Litter, which was 'B'. The overall grade assigned to the beach is therefore 'B'. Table A2.2 describes the grades.

Table A2.2 *Grading scheme*

GRADE	DESCRIPTION
A	Very Good
B	Good
C	Fair
D	Poor

Table A2.3 *Survey form for the assessment of aesthetic quality of coastal and bathing beaches*

Overall Grade

Site						
National Grid Reference		Site Code			State of Tide	
Date		Time	Weather Conditions			

Category	Number of Items		Total	Number and Grade			Grade
Sewage-related Debris	General			0 1–5 6–14 15+	= = = =	A B C D	
	Cotton Buds			0–9 10–49 50–99 100+	= = = =	A B C D	
Gross Litter				0 1–5 6–14 15+	= = = =	A B C D	
General Litter				0–49 50–499 500–999 1000+	= = = =	A B C D	
Potentially Harmful Litter	Broken Glass			0 1–5 6–24 25+	= = = =	A B C D	
	Other			0 1–4 5–9 10+	= = = =	A B C D	
Accumulations				0 1–4 5–9 10+	= = = =	A B C D	
Faeces				0 1–5 6–24 25+	= = = =	A B C D	
Oil				None Trace Nuisance Objectionable	= = = =	A B C D	
Other Items							

General Comments

Sewage-related Debris	
Gross Litter	
General Litter	
Potentially Harmful Litter	
Accumulations	
Faeces	
Oil	

Source: Keep Scotland Beautiful

List of Contributors

Rafael Sangoi Araujo graduated in Oceanography (2005) and subsequently the Master's degree in Environmental Science and Technology (2008), from the Universidade do Vale do Itajaí, SC, Brazil. He is a Lecturer and Researcher at the Universidade do Vale do Itajaí/CTTMar and currently holds a PhD scholarship granted by the National Counsel of Technological and Scientific Development, CNPq/Brazil at Universidade Federal do Rio Grande do Sul, RS, Brazil. His main research field is related to coastal processes and beach morphodynamics.

Silvia Banchini is an architect and urban planner; the co-director of the Master's course, 'Intelligent Coast: nuevas estrategias turísticas, nuevas estructuras territoriales', of the Universitat Politècnica de Catalunya (UPC) (www.intelligentcoast.es), and is also a researcher of the Doctoral Programme on 'Knowledge and Information Society' of the Universitat Oberta de Catalunya (UOC). She is a private consultant on coastal urban planning projects. Her research area is mainly on the relation between tourism phenomenon and development of qualitative urban models.

Lorenzo Chelleri, holds a Master's degree in Urban Planning and Policies from the Istituto Universitario di Archittetura di Venezia (IUAV) and the Universitat Autònoma de Barcelona (UAB). He is a member of the Research Group on Coastal Resources and Landscape INTERFASE of UAB. He is currently working on a PhD degree on adaptive landscape planning in coastal areas, taking into account climate change impacts and resilience of coastal socio-ecosystems.

Andrew Cooper is Professor of Coastal Studies and Head of the Coastal Research Group at the University of Ulster. His research centres on coastal processes at historical timescales and on coastal management, and he has published extensively in both areas. He has been involved in several coastal management projects in South Africa and Europe, and is course director for the online MSc in Coastal Zone Management at the University of Ulster.

Harry A. de Butts recently retired as Director of Public Works and Utilities and Emergency Manager for the Borough of Avalon, where he still currently serves in an advisory capacity to the Mayor on beach and emergency management issues. His specific interest is in coastal processes that affect the viability of dunes and beaches as measures of shore protection and recreation for the residents and visitors to the Borough of Avalon.

Ayşen Ergin is a Professor of Coastal Engineering in the Middle East Technical University, Ankara, Turkey, responsible for teaching courses in coastal hydraulics, coastal structures, port engineering, physical and mathematical modelling, port simulation models and marinas. She has supervised over 70 masters'/doctoral students and been involved in a large number of consulting activities in coastal engineering works focusing particularly on the Turkish coastline. She has been responsible for more than 60 applied research and consulting activities, sponsored by the Ministry of Public Works, Ministry of Transportation and national and international private firms.

Deirdre Hart, University of Canterbury, Christchurch, New Zealand, specializes in researching and teaching about coastal environments. Her approach to understanding the functioning of coastal systems is multidisciplinary, drawing on principles from geomorphology, ecology, hydrodynamics, and environmental and hazard management. Current research interests include high-energy mixed sand and gravel lagoons in NZ and projects on Pacific reef island beaches, toxic algal blooms off Korea, and coastal management issues internationally. She is the 2008/2009 New Zealand Zonta Scientist.

Nancy Jackson is a Professor in the Department of Chemistry and Environmental Science at New Jersey Institute of Technology. She is trained as a geographer with a speciality in coastal geomorphology. Her research interests include beach and dune processes and geomorphic-biotic interactions on estuarine shorelines.

Antonio Henrique da Fontoura Klein, graduated in Oceanography from the Universidade Federal do Rio Grande, RS, Brazil (1990), and has a Master's degree in Geoscience from Universidade Federal do Rio Grande do Sul, RS, Brazil (1996) and PhD in Marine Science, Marine Geology, from the Universidade do Algarve, Portugal (2004). He is a Professor and Researcher at the Universidade do Vale do Itajaí/CTTMar, Brazil, and currently works as a Level 2, CNPq Researcher. His main research interests relate to Brown water oceanography.

Paul Komar grew up in Michigan, and his first awareness of coastal problems came during outings to the shore of Lake Michigan where he saw homes tumbled into the surf. This interest led to a PhD from the Scripps Institution of Oceanography in La Jolla, California. As a Full Professor at Oregon State University, USA, the Oregon coast has served as his laboratory for studying coastal processes for the past 40 years. He is author of, *The Northwest Coast: Living with the Shores of Oregon and*

Washington, published in 1997 by Duke University Press, and also the classic textbook *Beach Processes and Sedimentation*, published by Prentice-Hall (1998).

Antonio José Trujillo Martínez, is a geographer and holds a Master's degree in GIS from the Universitat Autònoma de Barcelona (UAB). He is a researcher and GIS technician for the Research Group on Coastal Resources and Landscape INTERFASE of the UAB, specializing in spatial analysis and indicators. He has worked as a consultant to the government of Catalonia to test coastal sustainability indicators as part of the European Union Expert Group on ICZM, DG-Environment of the European Commission.

John McKenna is a member of the Coastal Research Group at the University of Ulster where his research focuses on coastal process and coastal management. He has been involved in a number of European and national research projects, including the EU Demonstration Programme in ICZM. He is lead author of *Rural Beach Management: A Good Practice Guide*.

Cliff Nelson has an academic background in coastal research. While working in academia he investigated health implications from bathing in seawater, exploring the relationship between water-borne pathogens and illness rates from immersion. This time included a number of coastal research post-doctoral programmes in Australia and Portugal, working on projects ranging from water quality to beach geomorphology. As a Coastal Manager for a local authority in South Wales, UK, he developed skills that aided his route into his current role as Coastal Programme Manager for the Royal Life Saving Society. UK. He sits on a number of national and international committees developing water safety programmes aimed at reducing drowning rates.

Dominicio Freitas Neto graduated in Oceanography at the Universidade do Vale do Itajaí, SC, Brazil (2008), and is currently a Master's student in Geoscience at the Universidade Federal do Rio Grande do Sul, RS, Brazil. He has worked mainly on morphodynamic and coastal evolution, focusing on coastal erosion, sea-level rise, storm surges and setback lines.

Karl F. Nordstrom is a Professor of Marine and Coastal Sciences at Rutgers University. His research efforts are devoted to determining the spatial aspects of coastal sedimentary processes and landform changes in three overlapping areas: aeolian processes and coastal dunes; wave and current processes and beach change in fetch-limited beach environments; and evolution of landforms of human-altered coasts.

Michael Phillips has a BSc in Civil Engineering, an MSc in Environmental Conservation Management and a PhD in Coastal Processes and Geomorphology. He is the Head of School of the Built and Natural Environment Department at Swansea Metropolitan University and has published more than 60 research papers. Research interests include coastal processes and morphological responses to climate change and sea-level rise. He has been an invited speaker and presenter at many major international conferences and is a member of the Climate Change Working Group of the Global Forum on Oceans, Coasts and Islands, and vice-chairman of the Royal Geographical Society's Coastal and Marine Working Group.

Francisco Taveira Pinto, Graduated in 1989 (Civil Engineering), PhD 2002 (Coastal Engineering), Faculty of Engineering, University of Porto (FEUP), Porto, Portugal. He is an Associated Professor with Habilitation (2007, FEUP); Hydraulics and Water Resources Institute (IHRH) Board Member; International Secretary of the European Union for Coastal Conservation (EUCC–The Coastal Union); Secretary of the Maritime Hydraulics Section of the International Association of Hydraulics Research (IAHR); and Director of the Hydraulics, Water Resources and Environment Division of FEUP. His main research field is coastal engineering (physical modelling). He has organized several national and international conferences and short courses; published around 100 publications (national and international congresses and journals) and has edited several conference proceedings.

Marcus Polette graduated in Geography (1987) and Oceanography (1989) from the Universidade Federal do Rio Grande (FURG), Brazil. He holds a Master's degree in Ecology and Natural Resources (1993) from the Universidade Federal de São Carlos (UFSCa), Brazil, and a PhD (Integrated Coastal Zone Management; 1997) from the Universidade Federal de São Carlos (UFSCar), Brazil. He did post-doctoral research in Political Sciences (2005) at the Universidade Federal de Santa Catarina (UFSC), Brazil. He is a Professor and Researcher at the Universidade do Vale do Itajaí/CTTMa, Brazil, and currently works as a Level 2, CNPq Researcher. His main research area relates to integrated coastal zone management.

Enzo Pranzini is a Full Professor of Physical Geography at the University of Florence, Italy. His research field comprises coastal morphology and sedimentology, with particular reference to beaches, harbours and shore protection structures. His work in support of public administration, planning and the design of coastal reclamation works has resulted in several innovative projects being carried out on the Italian coastline. He is editor of the Italian scientific journal *Studi costieri*.

Françoise Breton Renard has a PhD in Social Ethnology from the College de France and MA in Geography from the Universitat Autònoma de

Barcelona (UAB). She is an expert on integrated coastal management issues. She is the Lead Researcher of the Research Group on Coastal Resources and Landscape INTERFASE of UAB and Scientific Director of the Europea Topic Centre on Land Use and Spatial Information of the European Environment Agency (ETC-LUSI/EEA). Since 2002, she has been chair of the Working Group on Indicators and Data set up by the European Union Expert Group on ICZM of the DG-Environment of the European Commission.

Rafael Medeiros Sperb, graduated in Oceanography from the Universidade Federal do Rio Grande, RS, Brazil (1989), and gained a Master's degree in Environmental Science and Technology from IHE, Delft, Holland (1996), and PhD in Production Engineering and Applied Intelligence from the Universidade Federal de Santa Catarina, Brazil (2002). He is a Professor and Researcher at the Universidade do Vale do Itajaí/CTTMar and currently coordinates the Applied Computing Lab. His main research interests relate to geo-information, interoperability, information systems, and risk analyses.

Felipe Caetano Sprovieri, graduated in Oceanography from the Universidade do Vale do Itajaí, SC, Brazil (2008). Currently, he is studying on the Master's Program in Ocean Engineering at the Universidade Federal do Rio Grande, RS, Brazil.

David Tudor has many years of experience working in the marine science and environmental management sector. He worked for the UK Environment Agency for a number of years before joining The Crown Estate as the Marine Policy Manager in 2008. He completed his PhD in 2001 and has worked for universities, environmental pressure groups, and government agencies in both the UK and overseas and is the author of numerous journal articles covering many aspects of marine and coastal management. He has been a guest lecturer at a number of universities. He is the former Chair of the Wales Coastal Maritime Partnership and chaired many of the Working Groups set up by the Partnership, including those on Integrated Coastal Zone Management Progress Indicators and the UK Marine Bill.

Index

Note: bold page numbers refer to figures.